GCSE Spanish for OCR

Teacher's Book

Abigail Hardwick

with answers and additional material by:

Isabel Alonso de Sudea

Vincent Everett

María Isabel Isern Vivancos

Shirley Buckley

Emma Díaz Fernández

OCR RECOGNISING ACHIEVEMENT · OXFORD UNIVERSITY PRESS

— Official Publisher Partnership —

Great Clarendon Street, Oxford OX2 6DP

Oxford University Press is a department of the University of Oxford.

It furthers the University's objective of excellence in research, scholarship, and education by publishing worldwide in
Oxford   New York
Auckland   Cape Town   Dar es Salaam   Hong Kong   Karachi
Kuala Lumpur   Madrid   Melbourne   Mexico City   Nairobi
New Delhi   Shanghai   Taipei   Toronto

With offices in
Argentina Austria Brazil Chile Czech Republic France Greece Guatemala
Hungary Italy Japan South Korea Poland Portugal Singapore Switzerland
Thailand Turkey Ukraine Vietnam

Oxford is a registered trade mark of Oxford University Press
in the UK and in certain other countries

British Library Cataloguing in Publication Data

Data available

ISBN 978 019 918073 8

10 9 8 7 6 5 4 3 2 1

Printed in Great Britain by Ashford Colour Press Ltd

Paper used in the production of this book is a natural, recyclable product made from wood grown in sustainable forests. The manufacturing process conforms to the environmental regulations of the country of origin.

Acknowledgements
Spanish GCSE Copymasters Assesment Sheets (photos):
1.16 INTERFOTO Pressebildagentur/Alamy, 1.17 Horacio Villalobos/epa/Corbis, 1.18 Frantzesco Kangaris/epa/Corbis, 6.1 Danny Lehman/Corbis, 6.2 Keith Dannemiller/Corbis, 13.1 purchased from www.bigstock.com.

Illustrations by Clive Goodyer, Tim Kahane, Theresa Tibbetts, Ian West.

Cover image: Photodisc/Getty

The authors and publisher would like to thank the following people for their help and advice: Amy Hodson, Joanne Askew, Janine Drake, Timothy Guildford, Leonora King, Ainara Solana, Jaime Veiga-Perez.
Audio recordings studio production: Colette Thomson and Andrew Garrett (Footstep Productions). Activity and Assessment sheets by Shirley Buckley and Emma Díaz Fernández.

Contents

Symbols used in this Teacher's Book:

 a pairwork activity

 a groupwork activity

 a listening activity – audio on accompanying CD

 a speaking activity

 a reading activity

 a writing activity

 reference to a Languages Ladder grade

X–X

PLTS an activity that has been selected as an example of particular Personal Learning and Thinking Skills

Summary of Unit Contents					
Unit, contexts	**Topics**	**Skills**	**Grammar**	**Cross-curricular links**	**Scenario**
1A Mi vida: *Life at home; family, friends and relationships*	Talk about yourself and your family and friends Describe your daily routine Household chores	**Speaking** Improving your pronunciation Starting a conversation Using fillers **Writing** Extending your sentences Checking your work	Question words Present tense (regular and irregular) Immediate future (*ir a …*) Possessive adjectives	PHSE	• Interview the family member of a contestant on *Télon Abierto* • Write a horoscope
1B Nuestro entorno: *Local area, facilities and getting around*	Describe where you live and compare it with other places Ask for information about a place Plan a day out Use public transport in Spain Describe a journey	**Listening** Identifying opinions Anticipating **Reading** Finding the right information Identifying details Deciphering sentences	Personal pronouns *tú* and *usted* Preterite and imperfect Comparative and superlative	Geography, Leisure and tourism, Citizenship	• Act out a sketch about a tourist who asks for advice about transport but ends up totally confused • Write an email to a Spanish friend who is coming to visit
2A Une vida sana y activa: *Sports, outdoor pursuits and healthy lifestyle*	Sports and sports injuries Sporting heroes Healthy living Discuss outdoor activities Survival skills	**Speaking** Using intensifiers Stressing words **Writing** Using descriptions and linking words Adding 'colour'	Impersonal verbs Reflexive constructions Preterite irregular forms Use of *desde hace* Perfect tense Adverbs	PE, PHSE	• Create a television advert about healthy living • Write a diary entry about an activity centre
2B Comer y beber: *Food and drink*	Prepare a meal Food and drink in different cultures Favourite food Table manners Eating healthily Order in a restaurant	**Listening** Listening for clues Deducing opinion from tone **Speaking** Using tone to express interest Agreeing/disagreeing Complaining politely	Comparatives Numbers Expressions followed by infinitive Pronouns with a preposition Present continuous	Food technology, PHSE/Citizenship	• Interview the chef and customers in a restaurant • Write the webpage of a 3-star restaurant for the Michelin Guide
3A Las fiestas: *Socialising, special occasions and festivals*	Make arrangements to go out with friends Plan a party Go shopping Compare festivals in different countries	**Listening** Listening for gist Listening for detail and key phrase **Reading** Skimming for gist Working out meanings of words	Pronouns Continuous form of the imperfect	PHSE Citizenship	• Organise an evening activity for your group and your exchange. • Write an email to a Spanish friend who will be here during a special time of year.
3B Cine y televisión: *TV, films and music*	Express views about books, films and music Talk about famous performers Compare your tastes now and in the past	**Reading** Dictionary skills Recognising suffixes and prefixes **Writing** Using synonyms Avoiding repetition	Preterite and imperfect Comparatives and superlatives Negatives Verbs with prepositions	Music, Cinema	• Prepare a film review to be spoken aloud in Spanish. • Write an account of the *Festival de Benicássim*.
4A Mis vacaciones: *Holidays and exchanges*	Compare different climates Choose and book a holiday destination Plan an exchange Talk about past holiday experiences	**Listening** Listening for questions and tenses Understanding through context **Reading** Working out unfamiliar words Using grammar	Ordinal numbers Formal and informal *Ser* and *Estar* Reflexive and non-reflexive verbs Expressions of time	Geography, PHSE	• Prepare a presentation about a proposal for an end-of-year school trip for your Spanish class. • Write a letter to parents with an overview of the trip you have planned.

4B Nuestro mundo: *Environmental issues and life in other countries*	Talk about threats and dangers to the environment Conservation and recycling Eco-tourism Comparing lives in different countries	**Listening** Listening strategies Taking effective notes Checking your answers **Reading** Reading with questions in mind Finding specific details	Positive and negative instructions Subjunctive mood Indirect questions Time clauses	Geography, Citizenship	• Explain to the rest of the class an aspect of Spanish or Latin America life. • Do some research about a local environmental group.
5A Mis estudios y mi trabajo: *School life in the UK and Spanish speaking countries*	Exchange information and opinions about school life Describe and compare school and school subjects in different countries Talk about money and part-time jobs	**Listening** Making accurate guesses Reducing the possibilities in multiple choice questions **Speaking** Pronouncing words that look English	The definite and indefinite articles Quantifiers and intensifiers Reflexive pronouns	PHSE, Citizenship	• Discuss what kind of part-time job a new school could offer its older students. • Design a game screen providing a snapshot of the key information about the new virtual school.
5B Mi futuro: *Work experience, future study and jobs, working abroad*	Future career and study plans Work experience Find and apply for a summer job Job interviews	**Reading** Reading for gist Deciphering Spanish words False friends **Writing** Writing formal and informal letter Using accents and capital letters correctly Avoiding word-for-word translations	Revision of tenses Present participles Verbs with prepositions The phrase *lo que*	PHSE, Citizenship	• You are going to take a part in a hot air balloon debate. The balloon is sinking. One of you must be thrown out to save the lives of the others. • Research a chosen career or describe the life and career of a famous person/ celebrity.

Introduction

GCSE Spanish for OCR and the new GCSE specifications

Welcome to **GCSE Spanish for OCR**!

GCSE Spanish for OCR is a broad-ability course for 14–16 year-olds which prepares students for the new OCR GCSE Spanish specifications. The course offers a single-tier **Students' Book** and is accompanied by differentiated **Exam Skills Workbooks**. The course has been written in response to a need for more motivating and relevant content to prepare students for Controlled Assessments and to inspire them to pursue Spanish to GCSE level and beyond.

How does GCSE Spanish for OCR differ from other courses on the market?

GCSE Spanish for OCR has been designed to take account of:
- the introduction of Controlled Assessment to examine speaking and writing
- a renewed emphasis on Personal Learning and Thinking Skills, and cross-curricular links in the new National Curriculum
- a reduction in the uptake of GCSE languages
- a greater range of ability in non-tiered classes
- the findings of the Dearing Review regarding the need for more motivating topic coverage at Key Stage 4
- increased demands on teacher time in terms of planning, presentation and assessment.

To achieve this, **GCSE Spanish for OCR** offers:
- differentiation within the activities on each double-page spread, with material that will be within reach of students of all abilities
- motivating themes and topics that will be of greater relevance to teenagers, presented in a 'hands-on' manner and including more real world and vocational links
- activities on every spread that are designed to help students to prepare for the kind of tasks that they will need to perform in a Controlled Assessment
- an emphasis on transferable skills, so that if teachers choose to set Controlled Assessments on topics that are not on the prescribed topic list for listening and reading, students will have the tools to approach them with confidence
- material which will appeal to a variety of different learning styles, flagged up in this Teacher's Book with the PLTS icon
- a more personalised approach to assessment, including on-screen assessment *of* and *for* learning, supported by the **Assessment OxBox CD-ROM**

- Record & Playback activities and a video-based pronunciation guide in an integrated multimedia package (**Resources and Planning OxBox CD-ROM**)
- fully editable lesson plans to allow teachers to customise and deliver exciting structured lessons with minimal hassle (**Resources and Planning OxBox CD-ROM**).

How does GCSE Spanish for OCR make it easier for you to meet the needs of your students?

Firstly, **GCSE Spanish for OCR** provides *clarity*:
- **a clear structure**
  - There are ten units in total, each pair covering one of the prescribed topics from the OCR GCSE specification.
  - Each unit is designed to cover one half-term's work, with six units being covered in Year 10, and four units covered in Year 11, to allow time for mock exams and Controlled Assessments during teaching time in Year 11.
  - Each unit has five main teaching spreads, and a grammar spread (*Gramática en acción*), which makes it easy to teach one double-page spread per week.
  - Additional pages provide further work on skills (*Habilidades*), a speaking and writing task which takes a similar form to a Controlled Assessment (*Escenario*), additional reading material (*Lectura A/B*), and a vocabulary résumé.
  - The assessment sheets provide material for end-of-term tests at the end of each unit. There are also regular formative and summative assessments on the **Assessment OxBox CD-ROM**.
- **clear presentation**
  - In the Students' Books, scene-setting unit opener pages provide clear contexts and a preview of the skills and grammar that will be covered in each unit.
  - Activities are tagged with listening, speaking, reading, writing, pairwork and groupwork icons, so that students can find their way around a spread easily and know what they will need to do in each activity at a glance.
  - Core grammar and skills are highlighted in *Gramática en acción* and *Habilidades* boxes, and revisited in greater detail on the *Gramática en acción* and *Habilidades* pages.
- **clear progression**
  - Clear learning objectives for grammar (G), vocabulary (V) and skills (K) at the top of each spread show students exactly what they will learn.
  - Key grammar and skills are presented and practised carefully and systematically.
  - Students are able to check their progress and identify areas for improvement via each unit's *Habilidades* page and the *Checklist* page in the **Exam Skills Workbooks**.

In addition, **GCSE Spanish for OCR** provides *comprehensive and flexible support* to ensure that *lesson planning and teaching are as easy as possible*:

- this Teacher's Resource Book provides a clear, at-a-glance Lesson Planner page for each core spread, with ideas for starter and plenary activities to help you save preparation time.

- the teaching notes make extensive suggestions for how activities can be differentiated for different ability ranges, and indicate which other course components can be used to reinforce and extend the material covered on a particular spread.

- on the **Resources and Planning OxBox CD-ROM**, you'll find an editable electronic version of these Lesson Planners, with links to the resources required for each lesson, allowing you to build and modify your lessons to suit your students' needs.

- other useful features on the **Resources and Planning OxBox CD-ROM** include a lesson plan builder, audio recordings in MP3 format, and the facility to incorporate all your own lesson resources, including worksheets and photos.

To find out more about individual components, please read on!

The components of GCSE Spanish for OCR

Students' Book

The 224-page Students' Book consists of ten main units, plus an *Introduction* which introduces students a range of learning strategies to employ while studying for their GCSE. This allows roughly one unit per half-term's work. Each unit is divided into an opening page, presenting the themes, skills and grammar coverage of the unit, five core teaching spreads, a grammar spread and a skills page. Each spread offers a range of different activities to suit different levels of ability and the course has been written to enable teachers to select those activities that will suit individual groups and students. **GCSE Spanish for OCR** is designed to build on Key Stage 3 Spanish and provides the necessary programme of teaching, practice, revision and reference materials. Full attention has been given throughout the course to the Subject Criteria for Modern Foreign Languages.

The Students' Book contains the following sections:

Unidades 1A–5B

There are ten 16-page units structured around the contexts from the OCR prescribed topic list. Each unit has been planned to be interesting and motivating, as well as to provide a coherent and systematic approach to language development in terms of grammar and skills. An outline of the content of each unit is given on pages 4–5 of this book. For a detailed description of the features of a **GCSE Spanish for OCR** unit, see pages 10–11.

Lectura

GCSE Spanish for OCR features a 20-page section of differentiated reading material towards the back of the Students' Book, consisting of one reinforcement page (*Lectura A*) and one extension page (*Lectura B*) for each unit. The *Lectura A* pages provide opportunities for extra practice of core language from the unit, while the *Lectura B* pages provide extension material for students who are confident with the core language.

Gramática en acción /Grammar Bank

A grasp of grammar and structure lies at the heart of language learning, but grammar is too often perceived by learners as boring, unnecessary drudgery, rather than as a tool which enables them to express themselves with greater freedom and variety. In **GCSE Spanish for OCR**, grammar is introduced on a 'need' basis, in grammar boxes on each spread, and presented with a clear purpose in mind. Grammar is thus integrated into the core aims and productive outcomes of each spread, rather than being treated as a separate aspect of language learning. A more in-depth treatment of the grammar points covered is then provided in the *Gramática en acción* spread at the end of the unit, which focuses on 3-4 core grammar areas. This is supported by a series of detailed grammar presentations on the **Resources and Planning OxBox CD-ROM**, which are designed to provide a point of reference for students who would like to deepen or revise their knowledge of a particular aspect of grammar.

The grammar explanations within the main teaching units are complemented by the detailed grammar reference section at the back of the Students' Book, the *Grammar Bank*. Here, additional grammar practice activities are integrated into the corresponding grammatical explanations, enabling students to consolidate or revise further their knowledge of grammar.

Exam Practice

The *Exam Practice* section at the back of the Students' Book provides students with a complete set of sample exam questions for each of the four key skill areas, which can either be used at the beginning of the course to ascertain the level needed to obtain a GCSE, or close to the end of the course as revision material.

Vocabulario

A Spanish–English and English–Spanish glossary contains useful words from both the Students' Book and the OCR prescribed vocabulary list for students' reference. Vocabulary flashcards for each unit are also provided on the *Resources and Planning OxBox CD-ROM*.

Teacher's Book

Each unit contains the following detailed teaching notes:
- a unit overview grid, providing a summary of the skills, grammar and language coverage of the unit
- notes to accompany the unit opening page, including unit objectives and assessment opportunities
- a Planner section for each core teaching spread for ease of lesson planning, including suggestions for starter and plenary activities
- ideas for presenting and practising new language
- detailed notes on the Students' Book material, including answers to all activities
- suggestions for further activities to reinforce and extend the content of the Students' Book
- cross-references to other course components, indicating where corresponding resources are available on the **Resources and Planning OxBox CD-ROM**, in the **Activity Sheets** supplied with this book or in the **Exam Skills Workbooks**
- transcripts for all listening material from the Students' Book.

Audio CDs and MP3 files

The CDs provide the listening material to accompany the Students' Book and **Activity and Assessment Sheets**. The listening material was recorded by native Spanish speakers. The material is scripted and contains a range of text types, including monologues, dialogues and longer conversations. Sound files are also available in MP3 format on the **Resources and Planning OxBox CD-ROM**. All recorded material may be copied within the purchasing institution for use by teachers and students.

CD contents:

CD 1	Units 1A–2A
CD 2	Units 2B–3B
CD 3	Units 4A–5B
CD 4	Exam Practice section; Assessment Papers

Activity and Assessment Sheets

The Activity Sheets, located on the CD that accompanies this Teacher's Resource Book, are designed to be used in parallel with the **GCSE Spanish for OCR** course and there are cross-references to them throughout. Answers for each unit's Activity Sheets are provided on the CD and on the **Resources and Planning OxBox CD-ROM**. The Activity Sheets provide opportunities for further practice and extension of the language, grammar and skills covered in the unit.

Each unit has the following Activity Sheets:
- *Leer*: a page of reading extension material with comprehension activities
- *Escribir*: a page of writing activities, offering advice on how to use a range of different expressions and structure writing
- *Escuchar*: listening activities
- *Hablar*: speaking activities
- *Gramática en acción*: consolidation and practice of key grammar points

- *Habilidades*: a page on which students can record their responses to the language learning skills and strategies page at the end of the Students' Book unit
- *Vocabulario*: a list of key vocabulary from the unit, which students can use as a reference or as an aid to learning

Exam Skills Workbooks (Foundation and Higher Tier)

The **Exam Skills Workbooks** are divided into two sections: practical advice and worksheets. The first section offers targeted advice for how students can prepared for and approach the GCSE exams and Controlled Assessments for each skill. There is a detailed pronunciation guide, followed by practice listening material which follows the same format at the listening exam. There then follows a section on strategies for learning vocabulary.

In the worksheets section, the following sheets are provided for each unit of the Students' Book:
- *Gramática en acción*: a page focusing on key grammar covered in the unit
- *Escenario:* two worksheets offering advice and strategies for approaching the written and spoken Controlled Assessment-style tasks from the *Escenario* page of each unit of the Students' Book.
- *Checklist*: a checklist of the core language and skills covered in the unit, providing an opportunity for students to review their progress and reflect on areas for improvement.

The Workbooks are designed for students to write in, so they are ideal for homework and individual study. Rubrics are provided in English throughout so that students can work independently. The activities can be completed with minimal teacher input.

Grammar Workbook

The **GCSE Spanish for OCR Grammar Workbook** provides comprehensive coverage of the QCA prescribed grammar content for GCSE. It includes:
- clear explanations of all grammar points
- extensive practice activities
- answers (in a detachable answer booklet).

OxBox CD-ROMs

See **An integrated approach: How OxBox works** on page 11 of this book.

Course progression

Review of GCSE specifications

The new specifications for GCSE Modern languages introduced in September 2009 respond directly to the need to make language learning and assessment reflect more closely the needs and interests of students, changing patterns of learning at KS2 and KS3, and the increasing use of ICT to enhance learning.

The specifications impact on the way tasks are assessed – most notably speaking, which is assessed internally; on the selection of topics and contexts for learning – speaking and writing tasks may be selected by teachers and students if they wish, and are no longer tiered; and on the way tasks are submitted – as up to 60% of the final marks can be achieved prior to a terminal exam by using unitised assessment. We include a brief summary of course details, assessment objectives and changes below, but you should refer to the official OCR website http://www.ocr.org.uk/qualifications/gcsefor2009/Spanish for full details.

Course summary		
Unit title and description	**Assessment and duration**	**Weighting**
Listening (tiered)		
Learners: • listen for, identify and note main points, and take details from spoken target language of increasing length, speed and complexity • demonstrate an understanding of target language using a range of non-verbal responses, and some short answers in English.	Written examination	20%
	Foundation tier – 35 minutes	Spoken short course 40%
	Higher tier – 45 minutes	
Speaking (untiered)		
Using target language, learners: • communicate in target language on at least two topics – from a specified list, or of their own choice • interact with target language speakers, expressing and justifying opinions where appropriate.	Controlled assessment	30%
		Spoken short course 60%
Reading (tiered)		
Learners: • read, identify and note main points, and take details from target language text of increasing length, speed and complexity • demonstrate an understanding of target language using a range of non-verbal responses, and some short answers in English.	Written examination	20%
	50 minutes	Written short course 40%
Writing (untiered)		
Using the target language, learners: • communicate on at least two topic areas – from a specified list, or of their own choice • express and justify points of view in target language where appropriate.	Controlled assessment	30%
		Written short course 60%

The above table shows the increased relative value of speaking and writing in the new exams – 60%, as compared to 40% total for reading and listening. The table below summarises all the key changes in the new specification.

	What changes?	**What stays the same?**
Structure	• Speaking tasks are now assessed internally, and externally moderated by OCR. • There are now only two speaking tasks. • Written tasks are all moderated by OCR. • There are now only two written tasks. • GCSE short courses are now available. • Listening and reading remain tiered.	• The four skills – reading, writing, listening and speaking – are still assessed separately.
Content	• Updated choice of topics. • Teachers and learners can now choose your own topics for speaking and writing. • Listening and reading questions are no longer in the target language.	• Most topics cover areas that are essential in language learning contexts.
Assessment	• Speaking no longer needs to be taken as a final exam. • Not all speaking tasks have to be recorded. • Spoken and written work can be submitted via the OCR website repository, a secure website designed specifically for uploading portfolios electronically. • Short courses are available, so learners can choose to be assessed on just their strongest skills.	• The four assessment objectives remain the same.

Completing the GCSE programme in one year

Until recently, the general assumption in course construction was that students benefited from a relatively predetermined course progression over a fixed period of time, typically two years, to ensure that 'prescribed content' was covered in full. The advent of primary languages, fast-tracking, competition for timetable allocation, etc., means that courses may need be delivered over different lengths of time and even in different Key Stages. The revised GCSE specifications, which have a reduced emphasis on pre-defined content (at least for the Controlled Assessments in speaking and writing, which account for the majority (60%) of the total marks), also create opportunities for more streamlined approaches to learning. **GCSE Spanish for OCR** is designed to be used flexibly as regards time allocation, content coverage and also content sequencing. Here are some suggestions to consider if you wish to prepare students for GCSE over one year:

- Encourage learners to identify, analyse and plan responses to their own learning needs from the outset. They can construct personal study plans for regular review.
- Select contexts for Controlled Assessments at the outset by asking students to vote for interest areas – e.g. sport, shopping, music, etc. (Remember only two submissions are required.) Focus on these units.
- Focus on developing and reviewing skills and grammar rather than lots of topics. The introductory section in the Students' Book provides some useful pointers. The **Exam Skills Workbooks** and **Resources and Planning OxBox** provide key points of support and are ideal for independent study.
- Prepare for listening and reading assessments by homing in on the most useful associated skills and strategies: prediction, gist and detail, sound/spelling links, applying grammatical knowledge, personalised vocabulary lists, etc. Avoid lengthy detours through topics not on your priority list and long decontextualised word lists.
- Plan intensive sessions on some/all of the above at regular intervals, with specially timetabled half or whole days to review and embed skills and grammar leading to *Escenario* assessments or other motivating outcomes.

Detailed plans are included on the **Resources and Planning OxBox** so that lesson planning and delivery can be done flexibly and adapted to fit timetable allocations.

Teaching across the abililty range using GCSE Spanish for OCR

There is an extensive literature on differentiation, with many excellent ideas available in print and on the internet. The Framework for KS3 supports entitlement and enablement for all learners of a Modern Foreign Language. The purpose here is to provide a few ideas and pointers as to how **GCSE Spanish for OCR** supports the spirit and practice of the new specifications across the ability range. Several of the points have already been made in the precediing section *Completing the GCSE programme in one year* – please refer back to this for further ideas.

Some key points:
- Differentiated teaching and learning is a response to the needs of learners of *all* abilities, to be planned for at the outset once the composition of the teaching group is known, and implicit in each lesson and activity. It should not be seen as a bolt-on activity for remedial work.
- The two OxBoxes provide unique, flexible tools to help with planning, resourcing and assessing your learners at each stage (see page 11).
- 60% of marks are available for Speaking and Writing Controlled Assessments, which are both untiered. As candidates are no longer pre-classified into Foundation and Higher-tier entrants, they can accede to any grade on the day.
- The course is constructed to support untiered whole class teaching and learning using the coursebook, whilst providing for individual needs and independent study in other components, particularly the two **Exam Skills Workbooks**.
- There are now only two Speaking and two Writing tasks, which allows for a greater focus on both content and skills.
- Sharpen your focus through selection: content can be selected at unit and even spread level if desired, and adapted to meet specific interests and local environments.
- Focus on skills: regular and imaginative review of skills and strategies for learning are needed throughout KS4. Make sure your students work through the ideas in the *Introduction*, as well as the *Habilidades* pages.

What about the listening and reading exams?
- The focus on skills and strategies should also reduce the need for exhaustive coverage of all content and vocabulary – especially for learners who find memorising vocabulary difficult. There is provision through the course for regular and varied practice of these skills. (See also *Lectura A* and *B* in the reading section.)

And grammar?
- Grammar, traditionally seen as threatening or tedious by some learners (and teachers?) is treated pragmatically through on-the-page help boxes in English, and regular *Gramática en acción* reviews designed to be accessible to all students.

Teaching with GCSE Spanish for OCR

Features of a GCSE Spanish for OCR unit

Unit opening page
Each unit begins with an opening page which is designed to set the scene for the unit. A list of contexts, skills and grammar points provides a preview of what is to come, and each opening page encourages students to think ahead to the extended *Escenario* tasks that they will be performing at the end of it. The opening pages can also be used as the basis for plenary activities: at the end of work on each unit, students

can return to the opening page to answer the questions, review what they have learned and reflect on areas for improvement. Each unit takes two primary skills as its main focus: listening, speaking, reading or writing.

Activity spreads

There are five activity spreads per unit, via which the key language is presented and practised. Each double-page spread includes:
- a clear statement of what students are going to learn on the spread, given in Spanish to encourage students to reflect on their learning in the target language
- activities in all four skills to practise the key language of the spread: the majority of rubrics on the core spreads are in Spanish; English is used for the *Remate* section in which students bring all of their acquired knowledge together in two extended tasks
- icons to identify each skill (listening, speaking, reading, writing) and highlight pairwork and groupwork activities
- clearly identified vocabulary and skills panels, providing support and reference for students
- clearly presented grammar boxes to introduce and recap on grammar points. Key grammar is then further developed on the *Gramática en acción* spread (see below).

The first activity spread in each unit is designed to review prior knowledge, and draws on language and topics that are likely to have been touched upon in Key Stage 3. These are then taken and translated into more relevant and advanced contexts over the following spreads. Throughout the book, there is an emphasis on the cross-curricular aspects of language learning: how a knowledge of the Spanish-speaking world feeds into students' studies of geography and citizenship, and equips them for the world of work. There is a concerted attempt to demonstrate how a knowledge of Spanish and other foreign languages can be useful for different jobs, lifestyles and travel, and a focus on the cultural differences and similarities between Spanish-speaking countries and the UK.

Gramática en acción

Each unit features a *Gramática en acción* spread, focusing on key grammar points that have been introduced on the five core teaching spreads. Further grammar practice activities are provided in the grammar reference section (*Grammar Bank*) at the back of the Students' Book, in the **Activity Sheets**, **Exam Skills Workbooks** and **Grammar Workbook**. An overview of the grammar points covered in each unit of **GCSE Spanish for OCR** is provided on pages 4–5 of this book.

Habilidades

This page recaps the language learning skills and strategies introduced in the unit. The development of language learning skills is considered to be an integral part of the language learning process and should be given sufficient time during whole-class work. Students who are given opportunities to practise these skills from the start will develop into effective independent language learners. An

overview of the skills coverage of **GCSE Spanish for OCR** is provided on pages 4–5 of this book.

Escenario

This page presents two extended tasks or projects of a similar type to those that students will be expected to perform for the GCSE Speaking and Writing Controlled Assessments. Additional support and advice on how to approach these tasks is provided in the **Exam Skills Workbooks**.

Lectura

This section, coming after Unit 5B in the Students' Book, has additional reading material designed to encourage students to work independently and practise their reading strategies. There are two pages per unit, with the first page *Lectura A*, more suited to learners working at Foundation level, and *Lectura B* pitched at Higher-level learners

Vocabulario

This summary of the key language covered on each spread of the unit can be used by students as a reference or as an aid to learning. The '*Vocabulario*' list is also provided as an **Activity Sheet** and in the **Exam Skills Workbooks**.

An integrated approach: How OxBox works

What is OxBox?

OxBox is a 'toolkit' of electronic resources that is designed to facilitate lesson planning and delivery, and to provide an effective way of assessing students' progress through the **GCSE Spanish for OCR** course. Think of OxBox as a virtual filing cabinet with three main folders: one for lesson plans, one for teaching materials and one for tests.

Each folder comes filled with pre-prepared resources to

supplement and support the **GCSE Spanish for OCR** course, ranging from electronic lesson plans that make it easy for you to plan and deliver your lesson, to stimulating interactive activities that will motivate your students as they learn. In developing the OxBox resources, the main areas of anxiety and difficulty at GCSE level have been focussed on: speaking, pronunciation, grammar, and vocabulary learning. There are motivating resources to help students to develop their skills in each of these areas (see 'Resources' section below). OxBox also contains a 'User Management' folder, into which you can import class registers and create user accounts for your students.

Fully customisable

OxBox is compatible with all standard Microsoft Office® programs so, as well as being able to create new plans and assessments using the OxBox interface, you can also import your own Word® or Excel®-based lesson plans and materials into OxBox and file them in one centralised location. Many of the resources included in OxBox are themselves fully editable Word® and PowerPoint® files, permitting you to adapt them to the needs of a particular class or combine them with your own materials as you see fit. Because OxBox comes with a site licence, it can be installed on your school's local network, thereby additionally enabling you to share materials with other teachers if you wish to do so.

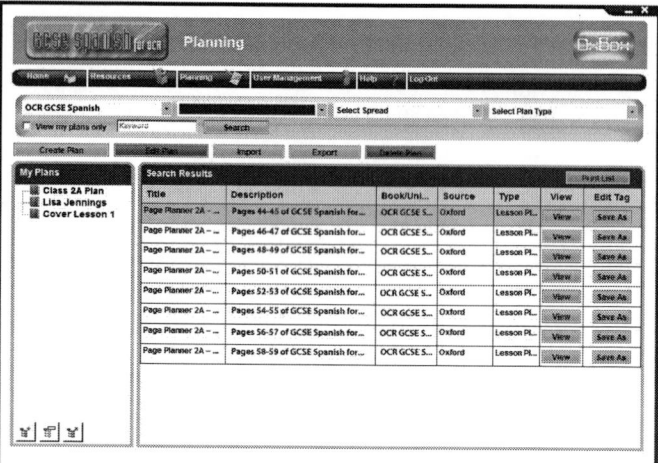

Different access levels for teachers and students

OxBox provides two separate environments, one for teachers and one for students, giving access to different resources. If you log in as a teacher, you have complete access to all of OxBox's resources: you can import class registers, add new exercises and assessments, and assign assessments to particular groups of students. You can also see individual or aggregated test results for any assessments you have set. Students, on the other hand, can only run interactive activities and resources that have been tagged specifically for student access and take the tests that you have assigned to them. This means that students can work on OxBox activities and assessments at individual workstations in the classroom using individual log-in IDs.

Lesson planning

The planning section in the OxBox contains a variety of resources designed to help you teach the **GCSE Spanish for OCR** course, and reduce the burden of time-consuming lesson conception and planning:

- Course overviews and unit plans familiarise you with the objectives and contents of each unit, allowing you to map out the term's work quickly and easily.

- Lesson plans offer ideas and strategies for delivering the **GCSE Spanish for OCR** course, and suggestions on how you can combine the different resources available in the **GCSE Spanish for OCR** Students' Book and on OxBox. They also point to extension activities from the **Exam Skills Workbooks** and **Activity Sheets**. The Lesson Player automatically launches each of the resources required for a lesson, so you don't need to waste any time finding and opening them while teaching.

- The Lesson Planner provides a simple template in which you can write additional lesson plans which link to resources in OxBox. Using the lesson planner, you can also customise existing plans, tailoring them to different classes by changing the materials used in the lesson.

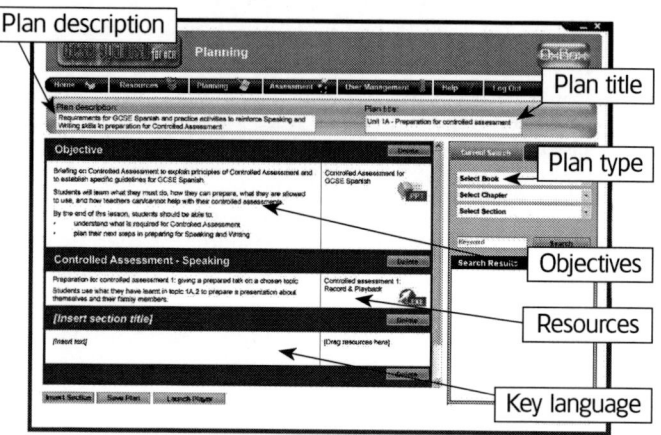

Resources

Record & Playback Activities

On the **Resources and Planning OxBox**, there is one interactive activity to accompany each of the spoken *Remate* tasks from the main teaching spreads, and each of the spoken *Escenario* tasks from the end of each unit of the Students' Book. The activities, which take three different formats, enable students to record their verbal responses to each task and save them to disc so that they can analyse their own strengths and weaknesses and gain valuable practice for the speaking controlled assessments. The three types of activity available are:

- **Interview** (single user activity)
  Users hear a series of recorded questions, in Spanish, or see a series of English prompts on screen, and record their responses to them. At the end of the activity, users can play back the entire conversation, including the answers they recorded.

- **Role play** (single user activity)
  Users hear a recorded conversation between two people, and are then invited to play the part of one of the two speakers. At the end of the activity, they can play back a new version of the conversation, which includes the parts that they recorded.

- **Debate** (two-user activity)
  Two users take part in a debate on a given topic and record their arguments on alternate screens. At the end of the activity, they can play back a recording of their discussion.

To make use of the record functionality, simply connect a microphone or microphone headset to your student's computer microphone socket, and press the 'Record' button on screen to start recording. Remind students to click on the disc icon at the end of each activity to save all of the recorded audio clips to disc.

The audio files from the Record & Playback activities are saved as MP3s, so can easily be e-mailed from student to teacher, imported back into the OxBox, or saved to disc to create a portfolio of speaking tasks enabling you to monitor students' progress throughout the course.

Pronunciation presentations

On the OxBox, you'll find one pronunciation presentation for each unit of the **GCSE Spanish for OCR** course. Each presentation addresses the main pronunciation issues that arise from the content of the unit. They include clear explanations of how to form the Spanish sounds described, and video clips of native speakers making each sound, offering students a model to emulate.

The video clips can be started simply by clicking on the video still on screen.

Grammar reference presentations

The **Resources and Planning OxBox** also contains animated grammar presentations for each unit of the course, covering key grammar topics from the QCA prescribed grammar content for GCSE. These presentations offer clear explanations of each

point, with ample examples, and are intended to be used by students for reference and revision. They are best viewed in 'Slide Show' mode.

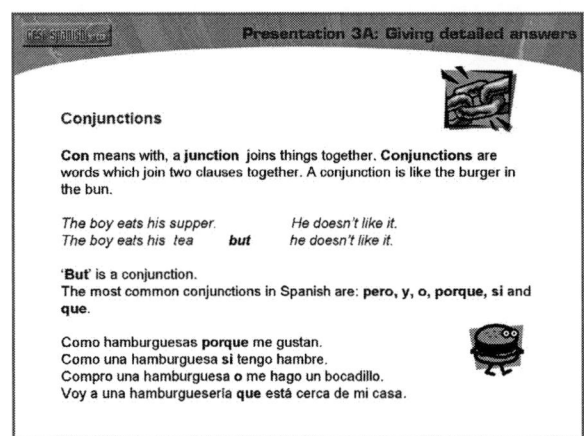

The topics covered in each presentation are:

1A Getting the basics right
1B Making comparisons
2A Introducing verbs
2B Working with verbs
3A Giving detailed answers
3B Questions and exclamations
4A Understanding past tenses
4B Working with other tenses
5A Developing accuracy
5B Improving your style

Interactive vocabulary flashcards

The **Resources and Planning OxBox** also provides a set of interactive flashcards for each unit of the course. Each set covers selected vocabulary from the OCR Vocabulary List and contains integrated sound clips so that students can test both their recall and their pronunciation.

The 'text' and 'clue' features help students to learn words that they are having difficulty with and use the flashcards formatively.

Zoomable opening page presentations

An interactive presentation of the opening page of each unit is provided on the **Resources and Planning OxBox**. Each presentation consists of an image of the relevant page from the Students' Book, which is intended to be displayed on an interactive whiteboard. Key parts of the image have been predefined as zoomable areas. The magnified areas can be taken as the focus of class discussion surrounding the skills and grammar knowledge listed, or used as a springboard for vocabulary extension.

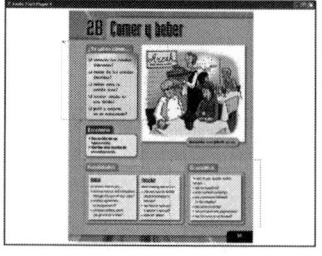 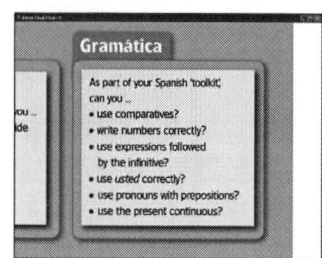

Assessment

The **Assessment OxBox CD-ROM** contains a series of formative and summative tests in each of the key skill areas, many of them auto-marked, for each unit of the course. The tests loosely mirror the structure of the OCR exams in terms of the number of tasks per test, and two different versions of each summative listening and reading test are provided: one for foundation-tier candidates and one for higher-tier candidates.

- **Formative assessments**
  Formative assessments are designed to be completed by students as they progress through the course, helping them to master what they have learned and improve any areas of weakness. In auto-marked tests, students are asked to predict how well they will answer each question before attempting it, and are given two chances to get it right. If they answer incorrectly, they are given feedback on why their answer was wrong and, ultimately, told the right answer. At the end of the test, they are not given an overall score.

- **Summative assessments**
  Summative assessments provide you with a simple and effective way to chart your students' progress at regular intervals throughout the **GCSE Spanish for OCR** course. Summative assessments are provided as end-of-term and end-of-year tests. In the auto-marked summative assessments, students may only attempt each question once and are given an overall result at the end of the test. Once all the members of a class have sat a summative test, the results are aggregated automatically so that you can identify any areas that caused particular difficulty.

Presentation and practice of new language

In the Students' Book, new language is presented via the core spreads in a variety of ways, through photos, illustrations and different types of text. Recorded material is provided on CD or as MP3 files on the **Resources and Planning OxBox CD-ROM**, and may be used for repetition by students in order to ensure the best possible pronunciation and intonation.

Once presented, the key language of each unit is developed through a wide variety of mixed-skill practice, with activities to ensure language development from supported/guided to more open-ended. **GCSE Spanish for OCR** intends each activity to have a purpose for students, and to be interesting

and motivating as well as promoting linguistic development. Students should be encouraged to learn by heart on a regular basis, not only items of vocabulary but also short conversations. This promotes good language learning habits and ensures that students are able to transfer language learned to new contexts.

Additional reinforcement and extension activities are provided on the *Lectura* pages, with further consolidation and practice on the **Activity Sheets**, in the **Exam Skills Workbooks** and on the **Resources and Planning OxBox CD-ROM**, in the form of interactive flashcards. Extra grammar practice is available at the end of the Students' Book in the grammar reference section.

Target language in the classroom

GCSE Spanish for GCSE builds on good practice at KS3, providing support through rubrics and examples to maximise the use of Spanish as the means of communication in the classroom. Comprehension questions for listening and reading activities are given in English, however, mirroring the style of the OCR exams, as are the more complicated instructions for the Controlled Assessment-style tasks in the *Remate* and *Escenario* sections.

It is worth spending time on a regular basis revising classroom language, so that students are reminded of the key phrases and encouraged to use them as much as possible.

Differentiation

Particular features of **GCSE Spanish for OCR** that make it easier to differentiate work include:
- Two levels of **Exam Skills Workbooks** and foundation and higher-level *Lectura* pages in the Students' Book for fast- and slow-tracking learners.
- Record & Playback activities including examples of sample answers at different levels, with activities that will be accessible to all ranges of ability.
- The earlier activities on each core teaching spread of the Students' Book provide more accessible tasks for less able students. The activities towards the end of the spread are more challenging.
- The teaching notes for individual activities often provide suggestions for differentiation, e.g. varying the amount of support offered and adapting the tasks slightly to suit different students.

Independent learning

The following features of **GCSE Spanish for OCR** are designed to encourage learner independence:
- The *Gramática en acción* and *Lectura* pages in each unit are ideal for independent work.
- Each unit's *Habilidades* page/Activity Sheet and the Checklist worksheet in the **Exam Skills Workbooks** encourage students to take responsibility for their own learning by providing opportunities for them to review what they have learned and reflect on areas for improvement.

- The *Vocabulario* pages at the end of each unit and on an Activity Sheet can be used independently by students as a reference source or as an aid to learning.
- The *Grammar Bank* section at the back of the Students' Book provides full explanations of all the grammar points in English together with additional practice activities, so that students are able to use it independently as a reference source.
- A strong emphasis on language learning strategies throughout (via the *Tipp* boxes and pages in the Students' Book and associated Activity Sheets) encourages students to progress as independent learners.
- The **Exam Skills Workbooks** are designed for independent work, with rubrics in English throughout.

PLTS and creativity

One of the key aims of **GCSE Spanish for OCR**, and indeed of the new National Curriculum, is that students should be able to learn in a meaningful way. This means, for example, thinking flexibly, analysing language and problem-solving, justifying answers, and making predictions based on previous knowledge. It encourages students to move towards becoming independent learners. Once students take a more active role in their language learning, they make quicker progress and the thinking skills learned can be applied to other curriculum areas.

Creativity in language learning is not simply imaginative use of language, such as poetry, creative writing, etc. It also refers to resourcefulness, e.g. finding ways to express oneself using only a limited range of language, taking risks and experimenting with language.

See **Independent learning** above for examples of features of **GCSE Spanish for OCR** that encourage students to take a more active role in their learning. In addition, the following types of activity used in the course help to promote thinking skills and creativity:

- Encourage students to deduce new language for themselves (e.g. verb endings, adjective endings) by working from what they already know.
- Ask students to spot the odd-one-out in a group of words/phrases, giving a reason. All appropriate answers should be accepted, provided that students can justify them, e.g. answers may be based on meaning, grammar, pronunciation, etc.
- Encourage students to apply previously learned language in different contexts.
- Provide opportunities for students to use language spontaneously. This promotes the development of coping strategies, since students need to find ways of communicating when they don't know the word for something, dealing with unpredictable situations, etc.
- Ask students to write something within an exact word count, e.g. 100 words exactly. This type of task encourages students to experiment with language and take risks, because in order to arrive at the precise word count they will need to paraphrase.
- Provide opportunities for students to share their knowledge in pairs/groups or during whole-class feedback.

Assessment

Assessment of learning

Regular assessment of student progress is an integral part of the learning process. **GCSE Spanish for OCR** offers an approach to assessment in line with the National Curriculum and OCR GCSE syllabus.

A range of formative and summative assessment opportunities are provided on the **Assessment OxBox CD-ROM**: for details of this, see *An integrated approach: How OxBox works* on pages 11–12 of this book. In addition, **GCSE Spanish for OCR** provides the following assessment opportunities:

- The *Escenario* page at the end of each unit in the Students' Book can be used as a practice Controlled Assessment task and graded using GCSE marking criteria
- At the start of the teaching notes for each unit in this book, the **Assessment opportunities** section suggests activities from the forthcoming unit that may be suitable for formative assessment. Two skills are suggested for assessment in each unit.
- The **Assessment Sheets**, supplied on the CD accompanying this book, provide material for end of unit texts to help you monitor students' progress in the four key skill areas throughout the course.

Assessment for Learning

Assessment for Learning (AfL) helps students to know and understand the standard they are aiming for, and also to understand what they need to do in order to achieve their objectives. It involves not only sharing learning goals with students, but also involving them in both peer- and self-assessment. AfL stresses the importance of ensuring that the information gained about students' progress is used, by both teachers and learners, to identify the next steps for learning. This might involve giving students opportunities to talk about what they have learned and what they have found difficult.

In **GCSE Spanish for OCR**, each unit's *Habilidades* page/ Activity Sheet and accompanying Checklist in the **Exam Skills Workbooks** is specifically designed to encourage students to review their progress and reflect on areas for improvement. Formative assessments on the **Assessment OxBox CD-ROM** also include colour-coded confidence buttons, prompting students to reflect on how well they have absorbed the material covered in the Students' Book as they answer each question.

Further guidance on AfL can be found in *Training Materials for the Foundation Subjects* (Module 1 "Assessment for learning in everyday lessons"), which is available to download from The Standards Site (managed by the Department for Children, Schools and Families) (www. standards.dfes.gov.uk). For further guidance on AfL, see also the website of the Qualifications and Curriculum Authority (QCA) (www.qca.org.uk).

Unit 1A Mi vida			Overview grid	
Spread	**Contexts**	**Skills**	**Grammar**	**Vocabulary**
Spread title	• Topic areas covered within the unit	• Key skills focus	• Grammar covered in the unit	Key vocabulary
pages 12–13 **Cómo dar tus datos personales**	• Describing yourself	• Pronunciation of vowels and consonants	• Present tense Interrogatives	¿Cómo te llamas? ¿Cuál(es)? ¿Cuándo? ¿Cuánto/a/os/as? ¿Dónde? ¿Qué? ¿Quién(es)? el baile, el/la cantante, el domicilio, la edad, el noreste, el país aspirar a, mezclar, seguir en los pasos, tener éxito chiquito/a, oriundo/a actualmente
pages 14–15 **Cómo describir a tu familia y a tus amigos**	• Describing other people	• Reading aloud • Writing more complex sentences	• Adjectives (1)	el campo, la cara, la finca, la nariz, un novio/a, los ojos, las orejas, el pelo alto/a, bajito/a, bonito/a, delgado/a, demasiado/a, encantado/a, feo/a, largo/a, mayor(es), mismo/a, redondo/a, travieso/a
pages 16–17 **Cómo hablar de tu rutina diaria**	• Daily routine	• Practise what you are going to say	• Reflexive verbs Immediate future	aburrirse, acostarse (ue), alistarse, despertarse (ie), divertirse, ducharse, madrugarse, maquillarse, peinarse, relajarse, tener hambre, vestirse (i) en seguida, por la mañana, por la noche, por la tarde, siempre, tarde, temprano vago/a
pages 18–19 **Cómo sobrevivir a las tareas domésticas**	• Describing the home and the chores	• Gain time when you speak Check your written work	• Prepositions The contraction of *al* / *del*	un armario, la cama, el dormitorio, un escritorio, un espejo, los muebles, la ventana al lado de, al pie de, debajo de, delante de, encima de, enfrente de, entre, junto a, por el suelo, sobre compartir, quejarse, desordenado/a
pages 20–21 **Cómo hablar de la vida en casa**	• Personal characteristics	• Speaking strategies	• Possessive adjectives	cariñoso/a, dulce, egoísta, mimado/a, pesado/a, quieto/a, ruidoso/a, trabajador(a) aconsejar, ayudar, dejar, llevarse bien con, parecerse a, tomar una copa, tratar de ambos, buena suerte, el equipo, al igual que
pages 22–23 **Gramática en acción**	• Writing full descriptions • Using adjectives and verbs correctly		• Using question words • Using *al* and *del* correctly • Using the present tense of regular, reflexive, radical-changing and irregular verbs • Using the immediate future • Using adjectives, comparing things and showing possession	
page 24 **Habilidades**	• Increasing your language skills for fluency	• Sounding as Spanish as possible • Starting the conversation • Using fillers to keep the conversation going • Extending your sentences • Checking your work carefully		
page 25 **Escenario**	• Interview the family member of a contestant on a TV programme. • Write a horoscope and write a letter to a problem page.			
page 26 **Vocabulario**	• Summary of key vocabulary for the unit.			
pages 171–172 **Reading Pages**	Describing your ideal partner, talking about a volunteer job: • to encourage independent reading and to develop reading strategies. • to provide alternative class and homework material for students who finish other activities quickly.			

1A Mi vida

Unit Objectives

Contexts: yourself and your family, daily routine, housework and life at home
Skills focus: sounding Spanish, starting a conversation and using fillers, rehearsing what you want to say, extending your sentences and checking accuracy
Grammar: gender of nouns, interrogatives, *al* and *del*, the present tense, the immediate future, adjectives, comparisons, possession

Controlled assessment opportunities

Writing: Students' Book, page 13, activity 12
Writing: Students' Book, page 15, activity 11
Speaking: Students' Book, page 17, activity 9
Writing: Students' Book, page 19, activity 9
Speaking: Students' Book, page 21, activity 7

See also **GCSE Spanish for OCR Assessment OxBox CD-ROM.**

An introduction to the unit   página 11

- *Aim*: To introduce the themes of the unit and encourage students to think about the reasons for learning Spanish.
- The opening page is designed with captions, pictures and page cross-references to provide a preview of what is to come:

	Students' Book
Cómo dar tus datos personales	page 12
Cómo describir a tu familia y a tus amigos	page 14
Cómo hablar de tu rutina diaria	page 16
Cómo sobrevivir a las tareas domésticas	page 18
Cómo hablar de la vida en casa	page 20
Gramática en acción – improving your use and understanding of Spanish	page 22
Habilidades – increasing your language skills for fluency	page 24
Escenario – una entrevista con un miembro de la familia de uno del los participantes en un programa de tele Escenario – escribir un horóscopo sobre Jorge, Mari Ángeles, Lorena o Isidoro	page 25

- Allow time for students to read the questions and cross-refer to the relevant pages of the Students' Book. They could do this individually or in pairs / small groups, followed by whole-class discussion.
- This spread also provides an opportunity for students to recap on familiar language. Ask them to think about language they already know that might be useful when working on the themes of the unit.

- Mindmap any language they produce, and if possible, keep it on display as reference as you progress through the unit. It can be added to at intervals as new language becomes familiar.
- At the end of work on the unit, allow time for students to return to this spread and repeat the mind-mapping process, this time including what they have learned over the course of the unit. Get them to answer the questions in their own words, and encourage them to use the results for revision purposes.
- Ask them what they found difficult, interesting etc. What do they think are the important things they have learned in this unit? What do they still need to improve on?
- If time permits, get the students to redesign the page. How would they set it out so it reflects the unit? How would they make it attractive to other learners of their age? How would they make it easy to follow? What would they include in terms of text, pictures, captions, page references? Ask them to imagine they are producing material for next year's class who will be learning the same thing – what would they have found it useful to know?

¿Por qué aprender el español? Para hablar con otros de tu familia y la vida en casa.

- Students share any experiences they have had of speaking to Spaniards about themselves e.g. on holiday or on an exchange.
- Ask them to consider what sort of language they would need to describe themselves, their family and home life to someone in Spanish.

Cómo dar tus datos personales

Planner

➤ Objectives
- Describing yourself

➤ Resources
Students' Book, pages 12–13
CD 1, tracks 2–4
Grammar Workbook, pages 19, 32–37
Activity sheets 1–4

➤ Key language
¿Cómo te llamas? ¿Cuál(es)? ¿Cuándo? ¿Cuánto/a/ os/as? ¿Dónde? ¿Qué? ¿Quién(es)?
el baile, el/la cantante, el domicilio, la edad, el noreste, el país
aspirar a, mezclar, seguir en los pasos, tener éxito
chiquito/a, oriundo/a
actualmente

➤ Skills
- Pronouncing vowels and consonants in a more Spanish manner

➤ Grammar
- Present tense and interrogatives

➤ PLTS
Student's Book, page 13, activity 11,
Team Workers
Students' Book, page 13, activity 12,
Creative Thinkers

➤ Starters
- Revise the alphabet and how to pronounce the different letters. Remind students that every letter is pronounced in Spanish, and there are no exceptions to the rules of pronunciation, unlike in English.
- Get students to pick a random word from the Students' Book and write it on the board. Another student has to pronounce it.
- Students' Book page 13, activity 1. Students practise saying the words given, then reading

the text about Jorge. They should read it several times over to a partner until they feel confident and can read it fluently. Volunteers can read it out to the class and receive feedback on their pronunciation.
- Students' Book, page 13 activity 3. Students practise searching a text for specific information. Before they complete the form, ask them to pick out what they consider to be the main points of the text. How much of it can they understand without looking up any words? What can they work out from what they already know?

➤ Plenaries
- Have any students ever taken part in a talent competition? Get them to describe it as though for a live report (so they can use the present tense). They can prepare what they are going to say in advance. Or they could "report" on a friend who is taking part in a competition while that person mimes what is happening.
- Students' Book, page 13 activity 11. Students interview each other, replying as if they are one of the competition candidates. They can use the information about the four characters, or they can pick their favourite celebrity and answer as them.
- Students' Book, page 13, activity 12. Students write a full and fanciful description of themselves and their talent, as though applying for a talent show. They should pick a stage name and provide pictures of their costume. The rest of the class will decide if they will get into the competition.
- Play consequences with the competition form. One person writes a name, another an age, the next the nationality etc. They should be as inventive as possible, and include the special talent this person has. At the end, they have to read out the information e.g. *Victoria Beckham tiene 89 años y es cubano* etc., *su talento es cantar mientras bebe limonada* or some other absurd skill. They could illustrate these bizarre personalities.

---

1 **Practica las vocales y los consonantes difíciles.**

- Students practise pronunciation by listening and then repeating. This can be done on a whole class or pairwork basis, with one student listening to and correcting another.

1-3

Note: Urubicha is an amazing town in Bolivia where they make violins like Stradivarius and all young people learn to play.
http://www.institutodemusicaurubicha.org/main.html

CD 1, track 2   **página 13, actividad 1**

Jorge Hola a todos. Me llamo Jorge Cifuentes y soy boliviano, oriundo de Urubichá en el noreste del país donde todos los jóvenes aprenden a tocar el violín desde chiquitos. Ahora vivo en Madrid con mis tíos. Tengo dieciocho años y mi cumpleaños es el nueve de octubre, así que soy Libra. Me encanta toda clase de música y aspiro a seguir los pasos de mis padres y abuelos de modo que por ahora me dedico a mis estudios musicales en el conservatorio.

2 **Empareja las respuestas (a–j) de Isidoro con las preguntas 1–10 en la página 12.**

- Students match Isidoro's answers with the questions on page 12.

Answers: **a** 4, **b** 6, **c** 1, **d** 3, **e** 7, **f** 10, **g** 2, **h** 9, **i** 5, **j** 8

4–6

3 **Copia y completa la ficha para Jorge.**

- Students fill out the form with Jorge's details.

Answers: **Apellido**: Cifuentes; **Nombre**: Jorge; **Edad**: 18; **Nacionalidad**: boliviano; **Cumpleaños**: 9 octubre; **Domicilio**: Madrid (oriundo de Urubicha, Bolivia); **Otra información**: soy Libra, toco el violín, me encanta la música.

4–5

4 **Escucha a Mari Ángeles. Completa una ficha para ella.**

- Students listen to Mari Ángeles and fill out a form with her details.

4–6

 CD 1, track 3   **página 13, actividad 4**

Buenas noches. Mi nombre es Mari Ángeles Valverde y tengo veintiún años. Cumplo años el dieciséis de mayo, entonces soy Tauro. Actualmente vivo en Barcelona pero soy argentina de Bariloche en lo alto de los Andes. Trabajo en un banco pero los sábados o domingos soy parte de un grupo roquero. Mi ídolo es Shakira, y yo también quiero tener éxito como cantante de la música rock.

Answers: **Apellido**: Valverde; **Nombre**: Mari Ángeles; **Edad**: 21; **Nacionalidad**: argentina; **Cumpleaños**: 16 mayo; **Domicilio**: Barcelona (oriundo de Bariloche, Argentina); **Otra información**: soy tauro, trabajo en un banco, soy parte de un grupo roquero, mi ídolo es Shakira.

5 **Copia y aprende de memoria las palabras interrogativas. ¿Qué tienes que recordar cuando escribes una pregunta en español?**
Grammar reference page 204–205

- Students write out and learn the question words. Highlight that all question words in Spanish have an accent, whilst their equivalent non-question words do not.

4–6

6 **Usa las mismas preguntas y responde con tus datos personales.**

- Students personalise the activity by responding to the questions with their own information. A Mastermind type scenario can be set up, with students having to answer the questions against the clock, to increase fluency and confidence.

4–7

7a **Escucha la entrevista con Lorena. Verdadero, falso o no mencionado.**

- Students listen to the interview with Lorena and decide if the statements are True (V), False (F) or Not Mentioned (NM).

4–7

 CD 1, track 4   **página 13, actividad 7**

- Hola Lorena. Queremos saber algo de ti – cuéntanos primero de dónde eres.
- Pues soy de Ávila al oeste de Madrid, la capital, pero mis padres son de Murcia y casi toda la familia vive allí.
- Y tienes un ídolo a quien sigues?
- Claro – quiero ser como Mónica Cruz y bailar como Joaquín Cortés. Soy fanática del baile y me gusta mezclar lo moderno con lo tradicional.
- Bueno ya veremos – y ¿cuántos años tienes?
- Voy a cumplir dieciocho la semana que viene.
- Y tienes trabajo?
- No en el momento porque quiero seguir estudiando baile hasta poder formar parte de un grupo.

Answers: **1** F, **2** V, **3** V, **4** NM, **5** V

7b **Escucha la entrevista otra vez y escoge la respuesta adecuada.**

- Students listen to the interview again and choose the correct answer.

4–7

Answers: **1** diecisiete, **2** oeste, **3** bailar, **4** Ávila, **5** bailando

8 **Inventa unas respuestas para Lorena a las preguntas no contestadas de la página 12. Haz la entrevista con un(a) compañero/a y grábala. ¿Quién pronuncia mejor?**

- Students make up replies to the questions Lorena hasn't answered in her interview. Discuss in class a couple of likely answers to get students started. Students record the interview and play it back so they can hear their own pronunciation.

4–7

9 **Escribe los verbos completos: cant<u>AR</u>, com<u>ER</u>, viv<u>IR</u>.**
Grammar reference page 201

- Students write out in full the three verbs. Ask students how many other verbs belonging to the three categories they can think of.

4–6

10 **Lee la presentación de Jorge en la página 12 otra vez y analiza los verbos resaltados en rojo. Escribe la forma del infinitivo para cada verbo. ¿Son regulares, irregulares, reflexivos o radicales?**

- Students analyse the verbs in Jorge's presentation on page 12. Discuss in class why / how they know which verbs fall into which categories. They could write them out in full, and use them in sentences of their own devising for further practice.

4–8

Answers:
regular   aprender, vivir, encantar (impersonal), aspirar
irregular   ser, tener
reflexive   llamarse, dedicarse
radical changing   tener

Remate

11 Imagine that you are one of the celebrities. Find the facts to answer the questions from page 12 in an interview. A asks the question and B answers as the celebrity.

* Students interview each other, replying as if they are one of the competition candidates. If they don't give their name, the rest of the class can guess which person they are from the information they give.

Success criteria activity 11:
* *students communicate effectively and accurately*
* *students express personal opinions and justify points of view*
* *students use a variety of vocabulary and structures*
* *students deal with unpredictable elements*
* *students use different tenses or time frames*

12 Imagine that you want to go in for *Telón Abierto*.
* Encourage students to write as positively as possible about themselves and their abilities (NB in MFL it is permissible and sometimes desirable to lie with enthusiasm if it produces better language!). Entries can be displayed in the classroom and voted on to see who would be let through into the competition.

Success criteria activity 12:

* *students give information accurately*
* *students express personal opinions and justify points of view*
* *students use a variety of vocabulary and structures*
* *students use different tenses or time frames*

Cómo describir a tu familia y tus amigos

páginas 14 y 15

Planner

➤ Objectives
* Describing other people

➤ Resources
Students' Book, pages 14–15
CD 1, tracks 5–8
Grammar Workbook, pages 7–9
Activity sheets 1–4

➤ Key language
el campo, la cara, la finca, la nariz, un novio/a, los ojos, las orejas, el pelo
alto/a, bajito/a, bonito/a, delgado/a, demasiado/a, encantado/a, feo/a, largo/a, mayor(es), mismo/a, redondo/a, travieso/a

➤ Skills
* Reading aloud to improve confidence with speaking
* Writing more complex sentences using conjunctions

➤ Grammar
* Adjectives

➤ PLTS
Students' Book, page 15, activity 10,
Independent enquirers
Students' Book, page 15, activity 11,
Self-managers

➤ Starters
* Students look at the photos on page 14 and use whatever language they can remember to describe them. You can ask them questions to jog their memories.
* Students' Book, page 14, activity 1. Students listen to the audio script and then call out any words or phrases they have understood, before going on to the more specific tasks.
* Students' Book, page 14, activity 2a. Before doing the listening activity and filling in the grid, students listen to the audio script and use it as revision for physical descriptions.
* Students' Book, page 15, activity 3a. Before they read out the text, remind students of the rules of intonation, where emphasis falls in words etc. Give students a copy of the text that they can write on, and go through the first paragraph with them, underlining each syllable where the emphasis falls. Get them to do the same with the second paragraph, then check their answers.

➤ **Plenaries**

- Students' Book, page 15, activity 10. Ask one or two of the questions round the class before students engage in the question and answer activity, and show them in what form you want them to note their answers. For more able students, you can encourage them to ask the questions from memory, with just a word or a couple of letters as prompts.
- Students' Book, page 15, activity 11. Remind students of verb endings by writing a few sentences of a description on the board, and highlighting the 1st person endings. Show them how to turn it into

a 3rd person description, if that is what you want them to do, by changing the verb endings; ask students to supply a few more changes, then start them off doing the activity individually.

- Use the list of antonyms from activity 7. Draw up a list of people – celebrities, teachers, class members as appropriate. One student calls out a word e.g. *alegre*, and another student calls out someone who fits the description. A further layer can be added by the first student saying *sí* or *no* until the class guesses who it is the student is thinking of when they say *alegre* etc.

1a Escucha. ¿Se trata de la familia A, B o C?

- Students listen and decide which family is being talked about.

	CD 1, track 5	página 14, actividad 1
Entrevistador	Muy buenas noches a todos. Vamos a comenzar con unas preguntas acerca de vuestras familias. A ver Jorge ¿Qué me cuentas? ¿Dónde vive tu familia?	
Jorge	Bueno pues mi familia vive en Urubichá en el noreste de Bolivia.	
Entrevistador	Y ¿cuántos hay en tu familia?	
Jorge	Pues somos tres nada más. Mi madre es enfermera y trabaja en el hospital local.	
Entrevistador	¿Tienes hermanos o hermanas?	
Jorge	Sí, tengo un hermano pequeño que se llama Manuel.	
Entrevistador	Y ¿Cuántos años tiene?	
Jorge	Tiene apenas once.	
Entrevistador	¿Tu madre cómo se llama?	
Jorge	Se llama Angelines	
Entrevistador	Y tu hermano Manuel ¿Cómo es?	
Jorge	Manuelito estudia el violín también pero no es tan dedicado como yo.	
Entrevistador	Bueno gracias – ahora Mari Ángeles. ¿De dónde eres tú?	
Mari Ángeles	Soy argentina de Bariloche.	
Entrevistador	¿Cuántas persona hay en tu familia?	
Mari Ángeles	Hay tres – mi padre, mi madre y yo – soy hija única.	
Entrevistador	Claro. Descríbeme tu madre ¿Es bonita como tú?	
Mari Ángeles	¡Qué va! Es mucho más bella que yo; tiene el pelo largo y rizado y los ojos bonitos y grandes. Tengo suerte porque mis padres son jóvenes todavía.	
Entrevistador	Me permites preguntar ¿Qué edad tienen?	
Mari Ángeles	Eso no se pregunta – ¡es un secreto!	

Answers: B, C

1b Escucha otra vez y anota las preguntas.

- Students listen again and make a note of the questions. They should compare their list with a partner, and go through it in class to make sure they've got everything in preparation for 1c below. Think of how to ask questions in a different way. For example: *¿De dónde son? ¿Dónde viven?*

Answers: ¿Qué me cuentas? ¿Dónde vive tu familia? ¿cuántos hay en tu familia? ¿Tienes hermanos o hermanas? ¿Cuántos años tiene? ¿Tu madre cómo se llama? ¿Cómo es? ¿De dónde eres tú? ¿Cuántas persona hay en tu familia? ¿Es bonita como tú? ¿Qué edad tienen?

1c Usa las preguntas de 1b para hacer preguntas a un(a) compañero/a sobre la tercera familia.

- Students use the questions they have noted down to ask each other about the third family pictured, Isidoro's. They will need to look back at the previous spread for some of the information.

2a Escucha y rellena la tabla. ¡Ojo! – los adjetivos concuerdan.
Grammar reference page 203

- Students listen and complete the table. Highlight the agreement of the adjectives and make sure students understand it.

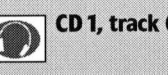

	CD 1, track 6	página 14, actividad 2
Mari Ángeles	Ay Lorena, me encanta tu pelo negro tan largo. Tienes una cara linda y redonda con la nariz pequeña y los ojos grandes y bonitos.	
Lorena	Bueno, tú también tienes los ojos grandes y bonitos. Claro tu pelo corto y rizado es otra cosa ¿verdad? Pero tienes una nariz bonita y una cara guapísima – me parece a mí.	
Jorge	Ahora amigo Isidoro, que cara tan fea tienes con estos ojos pequeños y nariz tan larga. ¡Y de tu pelo ni hablar – tan rizado y despeinado!	
Isidoro	¡Que guay, amigo Jorge! Tú no puedes hablar con tu cara larga y ojos marrones, tu pelo liso y negro y esa nariz enorme!	

Answers:

nombre	pelo	cara	nariz	ojos
Lorena	larg**o**	redond**a**	pequeñ**a**	negr**os**
Mari Ángeles	corto y rizado	guapísima	bonita	grandes y bonitos
Isidoro	rizado y despeinado	fea	larga	pequeños
Jorge	liso y negro	larga	enorme	marrones

2b **Escucha otra vez y escoge la palabra correcta.**

- Students listen again and choose the correct word. Tell them to pay particular attention to the agreements.

Answers: **2** bajito, **3** andaluz, **4** bonitos, **5** feas

4–7

2c **Explica por qué has eliminado cada palabra.**

- Students explain their choices. This is a useful exercise to do in class to reinforce the formation and use of agreements.

4–7

2d **Ahora describe a tí mismo/a.**

- Students describe themselves. If written down, this can be used as the basis for a guessing game where the class decides who the individual descriptions are of.

4–8

3a **Lee en voz alta la inscripción de Lorena y graba tu voz. ¿Qué tal tu pronunciación?**

- Students record themselves reading the description. This is a good opportunity to revise rules of pronunciation and intonation, looking for examples in the text.

1–4

3b **Escucha las preguntas y busca las respuestas en el texto de 3a.**

- Students listen and look for the answers in the previous text. Lower ability students can be given a transcript with bits missing which they then complete. They do the listening comprehension later when they are familiar with the text.

5–8

🎧 **CD 1, track 7** **página 15, actividad 3b**

1 ¿Cómo se llama la muchacha?
2 ¿De dónde es?
3 ¿Cómo es?
4 ¿Cuántos años tiene su novio?
5 ¿Cuántas personas hay en su familia?
6 ¿Dónde viven?
7 ¿Cómo son los animales que tiene en casa?
8 ¿Cómo sabe usted que le gusta el baile?
9 ¿Cómo describe a sus padres?
10 ¿Qué comenta sobre la vida en su ciudad?

Answers: **1** Se llama Lorena Villalba **2** Es de Ávila. **3** Es alta y delgada con el pelo moreno y largo. **4** Su novio tiene diecisiete años también. **5** Hay siete personas en su familia.

6 Viven en una finca en Ávila. **7** Los perros son traviesos. **8** Dice que es un fanático de baile. **9** Dice que sus padres son un poco estrictos pero simpáticos y generosos. **10** Comenta que en Ávila siempre lo pasan bien.

4 **Lee el email otra vez y señala los conectores.**

- Students look for conjunctions in the email.

Answers: y, porque, así que, donde, pero

5–6

5 **Completa las frases con un conector.**

- Students complete the sentences with a connecting word from the box. Students can use these to write three sentences describing their own home life.

Answers: **a** porque, **b** pero, **c** que, **d** donde, **e** con quienes

4–7

6 **Describe oralmente a tu mejor amigo/a. Usa las preguntas para ayudarte.**

- Orally, students describe a friend. This consolidates physical descriptions and should be done as far as possible from memory.

6–8

7 **Busca las parejas de antónimos. ¿Cuántos conoces ya? Anota lo que significan en inglés.**

- Students find the pairs of antonyms and work out their meanings. They can play a game of opposites, either in pairs or as a whole class; A says a word and B has to give opposite meaning.

5–8

Answers: reservado – sociable, perezoso – trabajador, agradable – desagradable, cobarde – valiente, generoso – egoista, alegre – triste, paciente – impaciente, formal – informal, tonto – inteligente, hablador – callado, serio – divertido

8 **Piensa en una persona de la clase. Tus compañeros/as tienen que hacer preguntas alternativas para adivinar en quién piensas.**

- Play this in pairs or small groups, or on a whole class basis. It can be extended to include a list of celebrities or other well known people locally.

7–9

9a **Escucha. ¿Quién es?**

- Students listen and decide who is being described.

🎧 **CD 1, track 8** **página 15, actividad 9a**

Siempre ha tenido el pelo largo y muy bonito, pero antes era negro y ahora creo que es rubio.

Tiene una cara linda y llamativa con grandes ojos negros y una nariz distinguida. Es alta y delgada y tiene una disposición risueña y dulce.

Siempre sonríe y canta alegre. Además escribe sus propias canciones con una letra muy interesante – casi es poesía.

Answer: Shakira

9b **Ahora describe a otro ídolo. Tu compañero/a tiene que adivinar quién es.**

- Students use the other photos as prompts, or choose another well known celebrity, and describe them to their partner who has to guess who is being described.

5–8

Remate

10 **Ask and answer these questions.**

PLTS

- If students speak to class members they don't know so well, or ones chosen randomly, they will have to listen properly for the answers.

Success criteria activity 10:
4–9
- *students communicate effectively and accurately*
- *students express personal opinions and justify points of view*
- *students use a variety of vocabulary and structures*
- *students deal with unpredictable elements*
- *students use different tenses or time frames*

11 **Write a text about your real or imaginary family, using the final paragraph of Lorena's e-mail as a model. Try to write at least 100 words.**

PLTS

- Students can write about their own family, or could write in the third person about one of the people they spoke to in activity 10.

Success criteria activity 11:
4–9
- *students give information accurately and in the appropriate style*
- *students express personal opinions and justify points of view*
- *students use a variety of vocabulary and structures*
- *students use different tenses or time frames*

Cómo hablar de tu rutina diaria
páginas 16 y 17

Planner

➤ **Objectives**
- Talking about your daily routine

➤ **Resources**
Students' Book, pages 16–17
CD 1, tracks 9–10
Grammar Workbook, pages 37, 47
Activity sheets 1–4

➤ **Key language**
aburrirse, acostarse (ue), alistarse, despertarse (ie), divertirse, ducharse, madrugarse, maquillarse, peinarse, relajarse, tener hambre, vestirse (i)
en seguida, por la mañana, por la noche, por la tarde, siempre, tarde, temprano

➤ **Skills**
- Practise what you are going to say

➤ **Grammar**
- Reflexive verbs and the immediate future

➤ **PLTS**
Students' Book, page 16, activity 3,
Reflective learners
Students' Book, page 17, activity 9,
Effective participators

➤ **Starters**
- Write a phrase about daily routine on the board e.g. *me levanto*. Call out some times e.g. *las siete, las siete y media* etc. and get students to put their hands up when they hear the time they do that activity. Continue with further activities. If possible, elicit the activities from the students, or get a student to call out the times to encourage involvement.
- Students' Book page 16, activity 1. Before they do the reading activity, give students a list of phrases in English about their daily routine and ask them to find the equivalent in Spanish in the text.
- Students' Book page 17, activity 5. Before students write the sentences, either ask them to find a verb for each picture, or provide less able students with a list of verbs in the infinitive to match to the pictures.
- Students' Book page 17 activity 6. Explain to students that the competition is the next day, and ask them (in English) what they think the four friends are likely to do. Then brainstorm / look up any vocabulary to do with this, and finish by doing the listening activity.

23

➤ **Plenaries**

- Students' Book, page 16, activity 2a. After doing the activity, or before doing activites 9 & 10, give students a copy of the audio script and ask them to pick out certain colloquial expressions e.g. *bueno, lo que pasa es...* etc.
- Students look back through the unit and make a list of all the reflexive verbs. They choose 3 and write sentences about what they are going to do after school / this evening / at the weekend. They read them out or give them to a partner who decides if they are true or false.

- Students' Book page 17 activities 8 and 9. Students prepare and perform a role play as if they are about to take part in the final of the competition, describing their preparations. Discuss in class first what such preparations are likely to be, and pick out vocabulary and structures from the unit to use.
- Students write predictions for what people are going to do in the near future. This can include such things as what their friend is going to eat for lunch, what their mother will do when they get home, what the head teacher will say when he walks into assembly etc. They read them out if they want, and the next lesson re-read them and say how many predictions were correct.

---

1 Lee el texto e indica si las frases son verdaderas, falsas o no mencionadas.

- Students read the text and decide if the statements are True (T), False (F) or Not Mentioned (NM).

Answers: **a** F, **b** NM, **c** V, **d** V, **e** V, **f** F, **g** V, **h** NM

5–8

2a Escucha la conversación y contesta a las preguntas. ¿Quién ...

7–9

- Students listen and decide which person each question applies to. If necessary, provide a copy of the transcript to less able students here as this is quite a complex text and requires students to think about the questions very carefully.

🎧 **CD 1, track 9**	**página 16, actividad 2a**
Mari Ángeles	Oye Isidoro, tú eres vago. Te levantas tarde ¿verdad?
Isidoro	Bueno lo que pasa es que me acuesto tarde sobre todo cuando toco con un grupo.
Mari Ángeles	Yo también me acuesto tarde cuando me divierto con mis amigos los fines de semana.
Isidoro	Claro y cuando te quedas en casa te aburres un montón.
Mari Ángeles	De verdad que no porque siempre me gusta practicar el baile o a veces me peino diferente o me maquillo o veo qué ropa voy a ponerme para la noche ¿sabes?
Isidoro	Pero durante la semana a qué hora te acuestas normalmente?
Mari Ángeles	Pues a eso de las once porque me gusta dormirme temprano.
Isidoro	Yo no puedo porque como demasiado. Durante el día no como casi nada, y luego por la noche tengo mucha hambre.
Mari Ángeles	¡Vaya que tío tan complicado eres! Yo en cambio soy muy sencilla y práctica y sigo mis rutinas todos los días sin variar mucho.

Answers: **1** Isidoro, **2** Mari Ángeles, **3** Mari Ángeles, **4** Mari Ángeles, **5** Mari Ángeles, **6** Isidoro, **7** Isidoro, **8** Mari Ángeles

2b Completa las frases con un verbo adecuado de la lista de abajo.

- Students complete the text using the verbs given.

Answers: **1** es, **2** se levanta, **3** se acuesta, **4** toca, **5** se divierta, **6** se aburre, **7** maquillarse / peinarse, **8** peinarse / maquillarse, **9** acostarse, **10** tiene

6–8

3 Practica solo/a. Piense en lo que vas a decir para describir lo que haces por la mañana antes de ir al cole. Usa despertarse, levantarse, ducharse, peinarse etc.

PLTS

4–9

- Students practise what they will say about daily routine. Discuss a list of questions in class first, and elicit a couple of sample answers to get students started. Give them time to make notes (not write it out in full) and ask questions about their daily routine. This can also be done in pairs or small groups.

4 Lee el texto 1 otra vez e indica los verbos reflexivos.
Grammar reference page 202

4–6

- Students re-read text 1 and note down all the examples of reflexive verbs they find there. They could also write out the verb *levantarse* in full to practise forming reflexive verbs, then change the questions in activity 2 above to be in the *tú* form and answer them for themselves.

Answers: despertarse, levantarse, ducharse, ponerse, vestirse, encontrarse

5 ¿Qué va a hacer Isidoro? Escribe cinco frases.
Grammar reference page 203

4–6

- Students use the pictures as prompts to write sentences about what Isidoro is going to do. They can also use it as a class speaking activity, taking it in turns to speak for Isidoro e.g. "*Voy a ...*" The teacher asks the questions round the class and pupils answer as if they are Isidoro.
- It is acceptable to say *te vas a levantar* – but only teach this if it is unlikely to cause confusion.

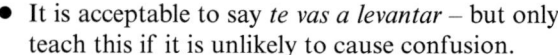

6 **Escucha a Lorena y a Mari Ángeles y contesta a las preguntas.**

- Students listen to Lorena and Mari Ángeles and answer the questions.

🎧 CD 1, track 10	página 17, actividad 6
Lorena	Mañana es la final – voy a levantarme temprano, a eso de las seis, y voy a practicar unos pasos de mi baile preferido un poco para relajarme.
Mari Ángeles	Buena idea. Yo pienso cantar sólo unas notas para no estresar la voz pero voy a hacer ejercicios de respiración que dicen que es bueno cuando uno quiere cantar.
Lorena	Vamos a desayunar en la cantina antes de bañarnos porque quiero ponerme mi traje de baile en seguida para estar lista.
Mari Ángeles	Yo no voy a alistarme en seguida; tengo la intención de esperar hasta el último momento para vestirme porque mi traje es largo e incómodo y además ¡voy a llevar tacones muy altos!

Answers: **a** Lorena va a levantarse a las seis; **b** Va a practicar unos pasos de su baile preferido; **c** Van a tomarse el desayuno en la cantina; **d** Mari Ángeles piensa cantar sólo unas notas y hacer ejercicios de respiración; **e** Van a bañarse después de desayunar porque quieren vestirse; **f** Lorena va a esperar porque su traje es largo e incómodo, y va a llevar tacones muy altos;

7 **Lee y complete la nota usando las palabras de la casilla.**

- Students complete Jorge's sarcastic note using the words given. They can then write an indignant reply from the girls suggesting what is going to happen to Jorge in the morning.

Answers: **1** temprano, **2** la mañana, **3** estamos, **4** beber, **5** real

Remate

8 **Prepare an interview about what you are going to do for the finals of the competition.**

PLTS

- Students can make notes individually or work with a partner. They can choose one of the four contestants to role play, or act as though they are taking part themselves.

9 **Your partner thinks of the questions and you prepare the answers.**

PLTS

- Students role play their interview. Discuss possible questions in class first. The class can score them on how many reflexive verbs they use correctly, how many time frame words (*temprano* etc.) and how well prepared they are likely to be for the competition.

Success criteria activity 9:
- *students communicate effectively and accurately*
- *students express personal opinions and justify points of view*
- *students use a variety of vocabulary and structures*
- *students deal with unpredictable elements*
- *students use different tenses or time frames*

10 **Write a brief paragraph about what your family is going to do.**

PLTS

- Students write a short text, possibly in the style of an email to a friend who cannot attend the final, explaining what their families are going to be doing on the day of the competition.

Success criteria actvity 10:
- *students give information accurately and in the appropriate style*
- *students express personal opinions and justify points of view*
- *students use a variety of vocabulary and structures*
- *students use different tenses or time frames*

Cómo sobrevivir a las tareas domésticas

páginas 18 y 19

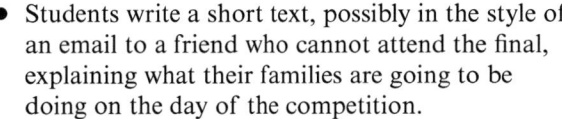

Planner

➤ **Objectives**
- Describe the home and daily chores

➤ **Resources**
Students' Book, pages 18–19
CD 1, tracks 11–13
Grammar Workbook, pages 6, 66
Activity sheets 1–4

➤ **Key language**
un armario, la cama, el dormitorio, un escritorio, un espejo, los muebles, la ventana
al lado de, al pie de, debajo de, delante de, encima de, enfrente de, entre, junto a, por el suelo, sobre
compartir, quejarse, desordenado/a

➤ **Skills**
- How to gain time to think when you speak
- Checking your written work for errors

➤ **Grammar**
- Prepositions
- The contraction of *al / del*

➤ **PLTS**
Students' Book, page 19, activity 7b,
Independent enquirers
Students' Book, page 19, activity 9,
Creative thinkers

➤ **Starters**
- Students' Book page 18, activity 1. Students write a list against the clock of all the vocabulary they already know in the pictures. They tick or underline any items they have in their own rooms.
- Students' Book page 19, activity 5. Before doing the listening activity, students work in small groups to compile a list in Spanish of the chores shown. They must do this relying only on their own and each other's memory, no reference materials. They swap their lists with another group to be marked, and see how many they got right.
- Play 'I went to the market' with furniture. A student says "*En mi dormitorio tengo una cama*", and the next student says "*En mi dormitorio tengo una cama y un armario*" etc until someone cannot think of something. To make it more difficult, work your way round the different rooms in the house, or insist that each item be in alphabetical order.
- Play 'Against the Clock'. Students work in groups. The teacher calls out the beginning of a chore e.g. "*Pongo*", and the first group to call out / write down and hold up / run to the board

and write down "*Pongo la mesa*" wins a point. The phrase has to be completely correct.

➤ **Plenaries**
- Students' Book page 19, activity 6. After carrying out the survey, students write up and analyse their results. What is the difference between male and female chores (if any)? Who does most housework – the boys or the girls? Who does most out of their parents? What do they think of this?
- Students pick the person in their house (or someone else they know) who does the most housework, and interviews them about what they do during a typical day, including every single task. They write it up as a third person story.
- Students interview each other about life at home. They should include opinions and where appropriate justification for their statements e.g. "*No saco al perro porque es el perro de mi hermano y no es muy simpático conmigo.*"
- Students imagine their future room and describe it orally or in written form. "*Cuando he ganado la lotería, voy a tener un dormitorio enorme con un jacuzzi en la esquina...*"

---

1 Mira las imágenes. ¿Cuántos membres de muebles conoces ya? ¿Quién tiene la lista más larga en menos tiempo?

1–3

- Students brainstorm furniture, either individually or in pairs or small groups. You can turn this into a game – who knows the most words in the shortest time.

2 Escucha. ¿De quién es este dormitorio?

4–8

- Students listen and decide which picture matches the description of the bedroom.

🎧 **CD 1, track 11**   **página 18, actividad 2**

Pues os cuento que mi dormitorio es como el centro de mi mundo – para mí sola. No tengo que compartirlo con hermanos ni hermanas porque soy hija única. Mi madre siempre se queja porque dice que es el cuarto más desordenado de la casa pero no me importa.

Tengo mi cama debajo de la ventana de donde puedo ver los picos de los Andes y los lagos de Bariloche y mi escritorio está al lado del armario. Hay una silla junto al escritorio donde tengo el ordenador portátil. Paso horas en Facebook con mis amigos o me acuesto sobre la cama y charlo o mensajeo con el móvil. ¡Mi ropa siempre está por el suelo porque nunca tengo tiempo suficiente para guardarla en el armario! Claro esta foto es de mi casa en Argentina y ya que estoy en una residencia en Barcelona todo es diferente.

Answer: D

3a Lee y empareja las notas con una imagen. Haz una lista de todas las preposiciones.

4–8

- Students read the notes and match them to the pictures. They note down all the prepositions used in the texts.

Answers: **1** C, **2** A, **3** B
al lado de, entre, en, encima del, al pie de, enfrente del

3b Por turnos con tu compañero/a pregunta y contesta. Trata de usar todas las preposiciones en su lista de 3a.

4–9

- Students take it in turns to ask their partner about their bedroom. They can draw a rough plan or picture as they talk to make sure they understand what the other person is saying.

3c Compara los dormitorios.

4–9

- In class, compare the different rooms. It may be useful to provide a transcript of Mari Ángeles' description at this point. Students could draw plans or pictures as suggested above to accompany the comparisons.
- Students also write about their own bedroom, or about the room of the person they interviewed in activity 3b. As a whole class activity, you could do a comparison of who has the tidiest bedroom in the class.

4a Escucha la conversación y anota el orden en que se usan las frases.

* Students listen and note down the order in which they hear the given phrases.

4–9

 CD 1, track 12   **página 18, actividad 4a**

Jorge	Bueno, Isidoro, dime cómo es tu casa – debe ser grande ¿verdad? porque sois una familia grande.
Isidoro	Pues no tanto, no tanto, – es de dos pisos y, claro, la cocina y la sala son amplias y cómodas.
Jorge	¡Qué guay! ¿Y tiene jardín?
Isidoro	Vaya eso sí que es grande con árboles frutales y hortaliza.
Jorge	¿De veras? Y, pues – me parece que debe ser bonito vivir allí.
Isidoro	Sí, tienes razón; me gusta pasar un rato con mi familia en la terraza que siempre es tranquila y fresca.
Jorge	De acuerdo; eso me encanta a mí también – pasarlo bien con la familia.
Isidoro	Vale – debes echar de menos a los tuyos ¿verdad?
Jorge	Pues claro. Pero mis tíos son buena gente y el apartamento está en la planta baja de modo que hay un pequeño jardín enfrente.

Answers: **1** bueno, **2** claro, **3** guay, **4** vaya, **5** ¿de veras? **6** pues, **7** me parece que, **8** tienes razón, **9** de acuerdo, **10** vale

4b Inventa una conversación sobre tus rutinas diarias y tu casa y dormitorio. Sigue el ejemplo escuchando y trata de usar cada palabra o frase de arriba.

* Students prepare their own discussion about their home. Provide a template of the transcript from 4a to help students requiring support to invent a conversation of their own.

4–9

5a Escucha y anota en qué orden se mencionan.

* Students listen and note down the order in which the pictures are mentioned.

4–6

 CD 1, track 13   **página 19, actividad 5a**

Normalmente me levanto y primero arreglo mi cama; segundo paso la aspiradora; después hago las compras y, si es necesario, después lavo el coche; entonces riego las plantas por la tarde; más tarde pongo la mesa para la cena y, después de cenar, friego los platos y, ¡por último, saco la basura! ¡Phew, y me acuesto porque estoy ya tan cansada y agotada!

Answers: g, d, f, a, h, c, e, b

5b Ahora mira la lista para mañana y empareja los dibujos con las frases.

* Students match the items on the list to the pictures from 6a.

Answers: **1** g, **2** c, **3** h, **4** a, **5** d, **6** b, **7** e, **8** f

2–4

---

6 Encuesta de clase. Pregunta a tus compañeros/as: ¿Qué haces para ayudar en casa? ¿Cuántas veces a la semana? ¿Cuál es la faena que más se hace y cuál menos? ¿Qué opinas?

* Discuss questions in class first, and compare results. Students can write a paragraph explaining who does which tasks, why / not and what they think of it all.

4–9

7a Lee lo que Jorge escribe sobre su vida en casa. ¡Ojo que hay unos errores!

* Students read Jorge's letter.

5–8

7b Ahora hay que chequear la carta. Indica cuáles son los errores y explica por qué son errores.

* Students find the mistakes in the letter and explain what the problems are, orally in class, and written down to make sure they have understood the problems.

5–8

PLTS

Answers: V=verb, adj=adjective, S=spelling, acc=accent

Querida madre y hermanito,
    Os cuento que aquí todo voy (**V**) bien en casa de los tíos. Todo me parece muy modernos (**adj**): el apartamento (**S**), los muebles y la cocina también. Tiene dos banos (**acc**), dos dormitios (**S**) y sala comedor mediano. La cocina soy (**V**) bastante pequeño (**adj**) y tiene aparátos (**acc**) domésticos como lavadora de ropa pero no de platos. Yo siempre ayudamos (**V**) a la tía en la cocina – o friego o secar (**V**) los platos y los guardo en su sitio.
    Por la mañana hago el cafe (**acc**) y desayunamos juntos. Voy a pintar mi dormitório (**acc**) de azul claro con blanco. ¿De qué color tienen (**V**) su dormitorio ahora el travieso de Manuelito?
    ¿Cómo sigue todo el mundo en Urubicha? Me los imagino sentados tranquilas (**adj**) en la terraza después de la cena. Mañana es la finales (**S**) del concurso de modo que voy a madrugar y alistarme antes de las seis para tocar el violín un poco antes de comenzar la (**S**) día.

Remate

8 Sit or stand back to back with a partner – one describes their bedroom and the other draws what they hear. Show it to your partner so that they can check what is right and what is wrong

* Go back over what has been covered so far in the unit and choose 10 questions to ask. If students talk to several people and note down their responses they will have good material for an extended piece of written work on life at home.

4–9

Success criteria activity 8:
* *students communicate effectively and accurately*
* *students express personal opinions and justify points of view*
* *students use a variety of vocabulary and structures*
* *students deal with unpredictable elements*

9   Write five sentences about the chores that you are going to
     do tomorrow. Don't forget to check your sentences carefully!

4–6

- Students practise writing about future plans in the
  context of life at home. They can compare their
  plans with the rest of the class and see how many
  people plan to do the same thing.

Success criteria activity 9:
- *students give information accurately and in the
  appropriate style*
- *students express personal opinions and justify points
  of view*
- *students use a variety of vocabulary and structures*
- *students use different tenses or time frames*

Cómo hablar de la vida en casa   páginas 20 y 21

Planner

> **Objectives**
- Personal characteristics

> **Resources**
Students' Book, pages 20–21
CD 1, track 14
Grammar Workbook, page 16
Activity sheets 1–4

> **Key language**
*cariñoso/a, dulce, egoísta, mimado/a, pesado/a,
quieto/a, ruidoso/a, trabajador(a)
aconsejar, ayudar, dejar, llevarse bien con, parecerse
a, tomar una copa, tratar de
ambos, buena suerte, el equipo, al igual que*

> **Skills**
- Avoid uncomfortable silences when speaking

> **Grammar**
- Possessive adjectives

> **PLTS**
Students' Book, page 21, activity 7,
Effective participators
Students' Book, page 21, activity 8,
Reflective learners

> **Starters**
- Students' Book page 20, activity 1. Students
  look at the words in the box and classify them
  as positive or negative characteristics. They may
  need to use a dictionary. They then describe
  a member of their family or a friend e.g. *Mi
  madre es extrovertida y mi padre es organizado.*
- Put a number of short phrases in Spanish and
  English on the board and ask students to match
  them up e.g. *mis padres, nuestros abuelos, tu*

*casa, su elefante – my parents, our grandparents,
your house, his elephant.* Draw attention to the
possessive adjectives, ask what they notice about
masculine and feminine agreements, and get
them to explain how that differs from English.
- Students' Book page 21, activity 6. Before
  matching the letters and the replies, ask
  students to find all examples of people and
  characteristics in the letters. This will help them
  understand the texts more easily.
- Brainstorm types of problems before writing the
  problem page letters. Draw up columns headed
  by people e.g. *padres, hermanos, amigos, novios.*
  Under each one write some typical problems
  *no me dejan salir, entran en mi dormitorio sin
  permiso* etc.

> **Plenaries**
- The teacher writes a number of sentences on the
  board, and the students have to put the personal
  a in the correct place. As an extension, write up
  a verb and a person and the students have to
  write a sentence with it, including the personal *a*
  where necessary.
- Write an alphabet of personal characteristics,
  and see who finds the most unusual words e.g.
  A – abatido, B – babieca etc. If they write the
  English separately, it can be given to another
  group / pair / student to match up.
- Discuss which person on page 21 has the most
  serious problem, and which the most trivial.
  Which problem is the easiest to solve?
- Students' Book page 21, activity 7. Students
  write and reply to problem letters. This is a
  particularly good opportunity for students to
  use Spanish for something they are directly
  interested in – themselves and their problems,
  but try to keep the tone fairly light as not all
  problems can be dealt with in the course of a
  language lesson.

1a Escucha, copia y rellena la tabla.

7–9

- Students listen and complete the table. Pause after each section if necessary to allow students to take notes. Alternatively, you could play it in full several times, each time asking the whole class for what they have understood and gradually building up the answers.

🔊 **CD 1, track 14**   **página 20, actividad 1**

Entrevistador	Buenas noches a todos – vamos a hablar de vuestras familias. ¿Cómo son? ¿Quién se parece a quién? ¿Y con quién o quiénes os lleváis bien o al contrario no os lleváis bien? Jorge vamos a comenzar contigo.
Jorge	Pues, a ver, cierto que me llevo bien con mi madre, pero muy bien porque es una persona dulce y cariñosa. Creo que me parezco a mi padre porque no soy muy paciente y tengo la nariz grande como él. Normalmente me llevo bien con mi hermano menor Manuelito también pero lo que pasa es que es muy mimado y a veces no me llevo bien con él porque es bastante travieso.
Entrevistador	Vale – gracias. Aquí vives con tus tíos ¿verdad?
Jorge	Claro y me llevo bien con ambos porque son una pareja muy simpática y generosa
Entrevistador	Muy bien, muy bien, vamos a hacer la misma pregunta a Lorena.
Lorena	Vaya vaya, me parece que nuestras madres son similares – yo me llevo bien con mi madre porque es honrada y la respeto mucho al igual que a mi padre, pero a veces él es un poco severo no siempre conmigo pero sí con mis hermanos porque se levantan tarde y son vagos y no ayudan en casa. ¡Parezco a mi madre porque soy trabajadora!
Entrevistador	El cuento de siempre no es así – ¡los hombres vagos y las mujeres trabajadoras! Bueno tú que dices Isidoro?
Isidoro	Bueno no sé, pero creo que me llevo bien con todos – sobre todo con mis abuelos que son dos personas muy amables y tranquilas pero no sé si me parezco a ellos. Lástima porque creo que parezco más a mis hermanos que son extrovertidos y alegres. Mis padres a veces se quejan de nosotros por ser tan ruidosos en casa con la música alta.
Entrevistador	Bueno por último pero no menos importante te toca a ti Mari Ángeles.
Mari Ángeles	¡Fenomenal – porque yo sé que parezco a mi padre por lo inteligente que es – una persona organizada y es guapo! En cambio me llevo muy bien con mi madre porque es tan suave conmigo, no es estricta y siempre es servicial. Yo no me quejo de nadie porque sé que no soy una persona perfecta!
Entrevistador	¡Qué suerte tienes, niña!

Answers:

Jorge – Persona(s)	Jorge – Razón
se lleva bien con su madre	es dulce y cariñosa
parece a su padre	no es paciente, tiene una nariz grande
se lleva bien a veces con su hermano	es mimado y travieso
se lleva bien con sus tíos	son simpática y generosa

Lorena – Persona(s)	Lorena – Razón
se lleva bien con su madre	es honrado y la respeta
se lleva bien con su padre	la respeta, pero es un poco severo

Isidoro – Persona(s)	Isidoro – Razón
se lleva bien con sus abuelos	son amables y quietas
parece a sus hermanos	son extrovertidos y alegres

Mari Ángeles – Persona(s)	Mari Ángeles – Razón
parece a su padre	es intelegente, organizado y guapo
se lleva bien con su madre	es suave y servicial

1b Escucha otra vez. ¿Quién se queja de quién? ¿Por qué razón?

7–9

- This time, students listen to understand who is complaining about whom and why.

Answers:

Jorge – Persona(s)	Jorge – Razón
su hermano menor	es mimado y travieso

Lorena – Persona(s)	Lorena – Razón
su padre	es un poco severo
sus hermanos	son vagos y se levantan tarde

Isidoro – Persona(s)	Isidoro – Razón
sus padres se quejan de los niños	hacen demasiado ruido en casa

Mari Ángeles – Persona(s)	Mari Ángeles – Razón
nadie	sabe que no es una persona perfecta

2 ¿A quién te pareces tú? ¿A quién te gustaría parecerte?
Grammar reference page 203

4–9

- Orally or written, students describe who in their family they are like and why, or who they would like to be like.

3 Con tu compañero/a prepare una entrevista formal sobre la familia. Usa cada frase de arriba para ganar tiempo cuando no sabes lo que vas a decir.

4–9

- Students prepare an interview about their family with a partner. They should have a check list of items to use including the phrases for gaining time. Other students could mark them on how many items on the check list they cover. They can take notes on each interview and give feedback to check understanding.

4 ¡A jugar! La clase entera. Cada persona debe escribir una respuesta. Tomen turnos para leer en voz alta tu respuesta. Si tienes la misma respuesta que la persona anterior – sal del ciclo.

6–7

- Students write answers to the questions, and take it in turns to give their answers. If they have the same answer as the person before them, they are out of the game.

5   Escribe una lista de palabras que describen características buenas y otra lista de características malas. Compara tu lista con la de tu compañero/a.

4–7

- Students write and compare a list of good and bad characteristics, preferably from memory. They could then compare lists with other students to see who has the longest list or the most original words. Play a game; shout out a characteristic, and the students have to call out the name of someone (friend, family member, celebrity) who is like that.
- Discuss ways of learning all these words e.g. *Mire – pronuncie – grabe – escriba*

6a Lee y empareja cada carta con una solución adecuada.

- Students read the letters and match them to the answers.

6–9

Answers: **1** d, **2** c, **3** a

6b Busca en las cartas frases que signifiquen:

5–8

- Students search the letters for the phrases. Depending on the ability level, these letters could be further exploited for grammar use and vocabulary.

Answers: he doesn't like me – no le gusto, they come home late – regresan tarde, I don't have any privacy – no tengo nada de privacidad, don't let me go out at night – no me dejan salir de noche, at my age – a mi edad, between the two of you – entre las dos, go straight to the point – ir directo al grano

Remate

7   Invent a problem and, following the example above, write a letter to *Corazón abierto*. Swap letters with a partner and write a reply.

PLTS

4–9

- Students write a letter to a problem page like the ones in activity 6. They swap letters with another student, and write a reply to the other person's letter.

8   Take it in turns to read the replies aloud. Who has the best accent? Correct any mistakes in the replies. Who made fewer mistakes?

PLTS

4–6

- Students read out the reply they have written for pronunciation practice. If the problem letters were given out randomly, students could then identify which is the answer to "their" letter. Or, after the reading out loud part of the activity, you could do a whole class matching activity like that in activity 6.

Success criteria activities 7&8:
- *students give information accurately and in the appropriate style*
- *students express personal opinions and justify points of view*
- *students use a variety of vocabulary and structures*
- *students use different tenses or time frames*

Gramática en acción

páginas 22 y 23

Planner

➤ **Objectives**
- Writing full descriptions using adjectives and verbs correctly

➤ **Resources**
Students' Book, pages 22–23
Exam Skills Workbook, page 25 (F and H)
Grammar Workbook, pages 4–9
Activity sheet 5
Resources and Planning OxBox CD-ROM

➤ **Grammar**
- Nouns and adjectives

➤ **Verbs**
The present tense

➤ **PLTS**
Students' Book, page 23, activity 13,
Reflective learners
Students' Book, page 23, activity 16,
Team workers

➤ **Nouns and adjectives**

1   Choose the correct word from the box below and complete the text.
- Do the first one or two in class, selecting and discarding options, and explaining why. For further practice, students can re-write the text so it says the opposite of what it says now, or so that it describes their own house.

Answers: **1** bonita, **2** cultivado, **3** varios, **4** azules, **5** organizada, **6** domésticos, **7** amplio, **8** redonda, **9** segundo, **10** muchas

➤ **Verbs**

2   What kind of verbs are these – a, b, c, or d?
- Students classify the verbs given. They could also make up sentences using these verbs for practice.

Answers:
a comer, escribir, hablar, correr, estudiar, vivir;
b levantarse, llamarse;
c querer, tener, jugar, preferir, poder;
d ir, tener, hacer, ser, estar.

3 Complete the verb table with the correct part of the verb (a-h).
- Students will use their answers in the following activities.

Answers: **a** quiero, **b** eres, **c** tiene, **d** vamos, **e** jugamos, **f** sois, **g** queréis, **h** tienen

4 Choose the correct verb.
- Encourage students to write out the whole sentence to set the correct part of the verb in context.

Answers: **a** tiene, **b** vive, **c** sois, **d** vamos, **e** quieren

5 Complete the sentences with the correct reflexive pronoun.
- Less able students may need a list of reflexive pronouns to choose from.

Answers: **1** me, **2** se, **3** se, **4** se, **5** nos, **6** te, **7** nos, **8** se

➤ The present tense

6 How do you form the present tense of regular verbs? Choose three regular verbs, one for each group (-ar, -er, -ir) from the box in question 2 and write them out in full, showing the endings clearly. How many more can you add to this list for each group from memory?
- Students revise the forming of regular verbs. They can work individually to see how much they can remember, or you can start with a whole class session.

7 How do the pronouns change in reflexive verbs? Write out *levantarse* in full and show the pronouns clearly.
- Students can write out a series of sentences using the different parts of the verbs e.g *Me levanto a las ocho. Papá se levanta a las seis.*

8 How is the vowel change for radical-changing verbs shown in the dictionary? Show examples from the box in question 2. Choose one for each type of radical change (ue l lie) and write them out.
- Students practise using a dictionary to help them adapt the language they look up. Encourage students to build up a word bank of similar types of verbs.

9 There are five common irregular verbs in the box in question 2. Write them out in full on cards. Use the first letter of each verb to make up a rhyme to help you remember which they are.
- Emphasise that students will need these verbs again and again.

Answers: ir, ser, hacer, tener, estar
(e.g. I Should Have Three Eggs)

10 Play a game of 'guess the infinitive'.
- This can be done orally around the class, or as a pairwork snap-type card game if resources permit,

or in a team game by taking small cards with e.g. *soy, va, tiene* written on them to infinitives displayed on larger pieces of card around the room against the clock.

11 Complete the questions with the correct form of the verb.
- Further verb practice.

Answers: **a** despertáis, **b** prefieres / preferéis, **c** tienes / tenéis que, **d** vas / vais, **e** sales / saléis

12 In pairs ask and answer the questions above correctly giving your own information.
- Students can do this orally or written. Point out that this type of question is good practice for the oral exam.

13 What two things do you have to remember when asking a question in Spanish?
- Elicit answers from the class.

Answers: Writing – the upside down question mark at the beginning of the question, Speaking – intonation that goes up at the end of the question.

14 Remember what you learnt about writing longer sentences! Complete the sentences with a word from the box below.
- Further practice of connecting words.

Answers: **a** porque, **b** pero, **c** que, **d** donde, **e** con quienes

15 Write a list from memory of the chores you are going to do tomorrow.
- Students can then compare with a partner.

16 Write descriptions of these people. Ask a partner to check them for you.
- Checking others' work encourages students to check their own more carefully. Give a list of items to look out for. Do one or two as a whole class as an example.

Success criteria activity 16:
- *students give information accurately and in the appropriate style*
- *students express personal opinions and justify points of view*
- *students use a variety of vocabulary and structures*
- *students use different tenses or time frames*

17 In pairs, each make up the personal facts for a contestant in a TV show.
- Students draw together much of the language of the unit in this interview activity.

Success criteria activity 17:
- *students communicate effectively and accurately*
- *students express personal opinions and justify points of view*
- *students use a variety of vocabulary and structures*
- *students deal with unpredictable elements*
- *students use different tenses or time frames*

Habilidades

Planner

➤ Objectives
- Learning techniques for being more confident in speaking and more accurate in writing

➤ Resources
Students' Book, page 24
CD 1, tracks 15–16
Exam Skills Workbook, page 26 (F), page 27 (H)
Activity sheet 6
Resources and Planning OxBox CD-ROM

➤ Skills
- Sounding as Spanish as possible
- Asking questions to keep a conversation going
- Rehearsing what you want to say
- Extending your sentences
- Checking your work carefully

➤ PLTS
Students' Book, page 24, activity 1, *Self-managers*
Students' Book, page 24, activity 2, *Team Workers*

➤ Hablar

1 Sound as Spanish as possible.

❒ Practise in front of a mirror and watch the way your mouth and lips move. Now exaggerate the movements and check how this improves the sound you make. Practise with all the names you have used in this unit.

- This can be done by students at home.

❒ If one of the letters has an accent, that letter is strongest, as in Mari Ángeles. Listen and repeat.

- Students might find it easier if the poem is broken down, line by line, or even phrase by phrase.

🎧 CD 1, track 15　　　**página 24, actividad 1**

Bea la fea, tenía diecisiete años y fue al baile con su novio Juan.

Bailó veinte tangos y cuatro fandangos, luego fueron a la tienda [a] por pan.

Le cogió de la mano y le dio un gran abrazo y volvieron a casa juntitos.

Te quiero amor mío dijo Bea la fea y se dieron un montón de besitos.

❒ Practise saying different consonants. Listen and repeat. Then make up more examples of your own.

- Do one or two examples as a whole class first to pool ideas. Pay particular attention to consonants that sound different in English; *c, ll, qu, z, g, j* etc.

🎧 CD 1, track 16　　　**página 24, actividad 1**

Celia come cinco cerezas pero Cecilio se zampa diez.
Jorge Jiménez, el general juega con Jacinta, la girafa de Jaén.
Victor es mi perro pequeño y Vicente Núñez es cómo me llamo.

❒ Practise reading aloud. Read as much as you can aloud to practise sounds and hear yourself speaking Spanish. Take turns to read aloud Jorge's text on page 12 again. Give each other marks out of ten and comment on which words need more practice.

PLTS　● It is helpful to record yourself as it can be quite hard to really listen to yourself while you are speaking. When students are marking each other, give them a check list of things to listen out for.

2 Ask questions to keep a conversation going.

❒ How many question words can you remember that begin with the letter 'C?' Make a list. Then write down all the other question words that you have learnt in this unit. Make up a jingle or rap to help you remember them or sing them to your favourite tune.

PLTS　● Students can work in pairs or small groups, then compare what they have come up with.

❒ Practise intonation. As soon as you see the question mark at the beginning of a sentence, think about the intonation of your voice. Practise and listen to the difference.

- Students can practise the statements and questions with a partner.

3 Rehearse what you want to say in advance.

❒ Revise the *Remate* sections and repeat your answers in your head.
- Students draw on material from the unit to prepare for the next activity.

❒ Prepare a conversation about what you're going to do this afternoon after school.
- Students can work in pairs or small groups, using a variety of material from the unit, and incorporating the techniques they have been practising on this spread. They could gain marks every time they use a specific piece of information or technique from this unit.

4   Avoid awkward silences.

❒ Listen to the conversation 5a on page 18 again. How many fillers can you hear?
- Go through the conversation in class to check they have heard all the fillers.

❒ Make up another conversation like the one on page 18, using as many fillers as you can.
- It is helpful to supply students with a copy of the transcript at this point.

➤ **Escribir**

5   Extend your sentences.

❒ How many linking words can you remember in Spanish? Make a list. Think of some more in English and look them up in a dictionary.
- Start this off as a whole class mind-map activity, to be continued individually or in pairs, with the end results pooled together.

❒ Now write the longest sentence you can. Compare yours with the rest of the class. Who has managed to write the longest sentence? Can you spot any mistakes in it?
- Remind students to stick to simple language they are familiar with, and to re-use material they have covered, not to be tempted to think of a sentence in English and attempt to translate it.

6   Check your work carefully.

❒ What two main points do you need to remember when you check verbs? Write down a list of the other parts of a sentence you need to keep an eye on when checking your work. Make up a poster to remind you, and use it regularly until you know it by heart.
- Ask students to come up with as many different things as they can that they think are important when writing correctly in Spanish. If necessary define the grammatical terms in simple language e.g. "*Gender – is it male (el) or female (la)?*" Ask them to think of examples.

Escenario

página 25

Planner

➤ **Objectives**
- Talking about character traits of different people

➤ **Resources**
Students' Book, page 25
Exam Skills Workbook, pages 23–24 (F),
pages 24–25 (H)
Resources and Planning OxBox CD-ROM

➤ **Skills**
- Writing practice
- Speaking practice

➤ **PLTS**
Students' Book, page 25, Escenario Oral,
Creative Thinkers
Students' Book, page 25, Escenario Escrito,
Team Workers

➤ **Oral**

Interview the family member of a contestant on *Telón Abierto*.

PLTS
4–9

- Students can do the dialogue as though interviewing the family member for one of the celebrity magazines, or a TV chat show.
- *GCSE Grades A*–C*
- *Grade C Students use past, present and future tenses. They express opinions, and deal with some unpredictability.*
- *Grade A Students express and justify opinions. They use a variety of vocabulary and structure in longer speech sequences.*

➤ **Escrito**

Write a horoscope for Jorge, Mari Ángeles, Lorena or Isidoro.

PLTS
4–9

- If it helps students find a starting point, get them to research what personality traits are typical for which star sign, but remind students that in MFL it is good to be inventive and not stick to the rigid truth if it produces better and more interesting language.
- For the *Corazón Abierto* letter, ask students what kind of things they grumble about other family members for. Be aware that Problem Page activities might be a sensitive issue for some, and offer a humorous slant on the subject.
- *GCSE Grades A*–C*
- *Grade C Students use opinions and past, present and future tenses, both factually and imaginatively. Register is appropriate and style is basic.*
- *Grade A Students write factually and imaginatively using longer sequences and a range of vocabulary and structure. They express and justify opinions in an appropriate style.*

Vocabulario

> This is a summary of key language from the unit, organised by spread and theme. Students can use it for reference while working on the unit, and as an aid to learning vocabulary.

Lectura

Planner

> ### Objectives
> - Describing your ideal partner, talking about a volunteer job.
> - To encourage independent reading and develop reading strategies.
> - These pages also provide alternative class and homework material for students who work quickly and require extension work.

> ### Resources
> Students' Book, page 171–172

> ### PLTS
> Students' Book, page 171, activity 5, *Team Workers*
> Students' Book, page 172, activity 5, *Self-managers*

> ### Lectura A – Mi pareja ideal

1 **Lee el artículo y busca cómo se dice ...**
- Students look for these useful phrases in the text.

Answers: **a** sobre todo, **b** mejores cualidades, **c** no busco la perfección, **d** los defectos graves, **e** llevarse bien con, **f** pasarlo bien

2 **Escribe un texto parecido sobre tu pareja ideal.**
- Students use and adapt the text to write about their ideal partner.

3 **¿A ver cuánto recuerdas de lo que has escrito? Cambia tu papel con el de tu compañero/a y por turnos haced las siguientes preguntas.**

- Students question each other and see how much they can remember about what they have written – their partner corrects them if necessary.

4 **Ahora piensa de otras cinco preguntas.**

- Students decide what other information they would like to find out about their friend's perfect partner.

5 **¿Cuál de los/las dos tiene mejor memoria?**
PLTS
- Students mark each other on how much each can remember about their perfect partner.

> ### Lectura B – Diario de un voluntario en un refugio de animales

1 **Lee el diario y empareja un titular con cada párrafo.**
- Students match each heading to one of the paragraphs in the text.

2 **¿Qué significan las palabras resaltadas en negrita?**
- Students decide what the phrases in bold mean. Discuss how they reached their conclusions (use of cognates, previous knowledge etc.)

Answers: **1** my favourites, obedient, abandoned; **2** wash and dry, take them home; **3** where they play, important to train them, to adopt, get on well with the family; **4** say goodbye, a caretaker (guardian), at night

3 **Busca las frases y palabras en el texto que signifiquen:**
- Students look for these phrases in the text.

Answers: **a** a tiempo, **b** cambiar el agua, **c** a veces, **d** tienen hambre y sed, **e** demasiado pequeñitos, **f** sacar la basura, **g** cuatro por cuatro, **h** lo que menos me gusta, **i** lo que me encanta, **j** hasta mañana

4 **Lee el diario y contesta a las preguntas en inglés.**
PLTS
- Students answer the questions in English.

Answers: **a** She changes all the animals' water. **b** She likes to say hello to all the animals and make sure they are all ok; she tries not to have favourites but it is difficult. **c** All the animals are there because they have been abandoned, mistreated, or their owners no longer want them. **d** This morning there were two new kittens whose mother could not be found. **e** They have to be trained to be obedient and get on well with people for when someone comes to adopt them. **f** She doesn't like saying goodbye to the animals at night, and having to shut them up. **g** The way the parrot always says goodbye to her.

5 **Imagine que tú trabajas en el refugio. Escribe una entrada para el diario de dos días más de la semana. Explica lo que tienes que hacer, cómo son los animales y por qué te gusta trabajar allí.**
- Students write their own diary entries, as if they are working at the refuge.

Unit 1B Nuestro entorno		Overview grid		
Spread	**Contexts**	**Skills**	**Grammar**	**Vocabulary**
Spread title	• Topic areas covered within the unit	• Key skills focus	• Grammar covered in the unit	Key vocabulary
pages 28–29 **Cómo describir donde vives**	• Describing where you live	• Increasing comprehension of written and spoken texts	• The imperfect tense	las afueras, un bosque, el casco histórico, los jóvenes, el mundo, un pueblo, su pueblo natal bello/a, concurrido/a, feo/a, hermoso/a, tranquilo/a, turístico/a echar de menos ahora, bastante, como, me recuerda, mucho que hacer, nadie, siempre, tan
pages 30–31 **Cómo comparar diferentes lugares**	• Comparing and contrasting different places	• Comprehension of spoken and written texts • Improving a text with key phrases and new vocabulary	• Comparatives, the preterite tense	una calle, una ciudad gemela, un edificio, una fuente de ingresos, un municipio, el patrimonio amistoso/a, bonito/a, caro/a, conocido/a por, de moda, deprimente, impresionante, precioso/a, ruidoso/a, sucio/a a diferencia de, a pesar de, actualmente, aunque, en comparación con, en lugar de, mientras, tal vez, tanto
pages 32–33 **Cómo solicitar información sobre una ciudad**	• Asking questions and giving directions	• Using prediction as a listening skill	• Using *tú* and *usted* appropriately, the imperfect tense	¿a qué punto? ¿cómo? ¿cuándo? ¿cuánto? ¿dónde? ¿por qué? ¿qué? ¿quién? a la derecha, a la izquierda, al final de la calle, al lado de, cerca, delante de, detrás de, enfrente de, en la plaza, entre, lejos cruzar la calle, recordar, seguir todo recto tanta gente
pages 34–35 **Cómo solucionar problemas de transporte**	• Using and finding out about public transport	• Transfering language known from one situation to a new one	• Answering questions	un andén, un avión, un billete de ida y vuelta, un billete sencillo, un horario, una señal, una taquilla, un torniquete, un tren cambiar, llegar, salir está a … metros
pages 36–37 **Cómo describir un viaje**	• Discussing the pros and cons of various means of transport	• Using different techniques to improve reading skills of longer texts	• Comparatives and superlatives	un barco, un caballo, una camioneta, un coche, una moto, el problema, un viaje emocionante, juntos/as, peligroso/a caminar, hacer autostop a pie, cualquier, más tarde, todavía
pages 38–39 **Gramática en acción**	• Using verbs more confidently in the past tense		• *Tú* and *usted* • Preterite and imperfect tenses • Comparatives and superlatives	
page 40 **Habilidades**	• Developing reading skills and learning strategies	• Finding the right information to answer a question • Identifying specific details • Deciphering the meaning of a sentence without understanding every word • Identifying people's opinions • Predicting what you are going to hear • Making accurate inferences • Predicting and keeping track		
page 41 **Escenario**	• A humorous scene where everyone wants to help a confused traveller. • An email to a Spanish friend who is going to visit.			
page 42 **Vocabulario**	• Summary of key vocabulary for the unit.			
pages 173–174 **Reading Pages**	Talking about transport, and what your local area is like: • to encourage independent reading and to develop reading strategies. • to provide alternative class and homework material for students who finish other activities quickly.			

1B Nuestro entorno

Unit Objectives

Contexts: describing and comparing different places, asking for local information, journeys and solving transport problems
Skills focus: reading when you don't understand every word, predicting and keeping on track when listening, using efficient strategies to learn
Grammar: *tú* and *usted*, the preterite and the imperfect, using the comparative and the superlative

Controlled assessment opportunities

Writing: Students' Book, page 29, activity 9
Speaking: Students' Book, page 31, activity 10
Writing: Students' Book, page 33, activity 13
Speaking: Students' Book, page 35, activity 8
Writing: Students' Book, page 37, activity 11

See also GCSE Spanish for OCR Assessment OxBox CD-ROM.

An introduction to the unit   página 27

- *Aim*: To introduce the themes of the unit and encourage students to think about the reasons for learning Spanish.
- The opening page is designed with captions, pictures and page cross-references to provide a preview of what is to come:

	Students' Book
Cómo describir donde vives	page 28
Cómo comparar diferentes lugares	page 30
Cómo solicitar información sobre una ciudad	page 32
Cómo solucionar problemas de transporte	page 34
Cómo describir un viaje	page 36
Gramática en acción – improving your use and understanding of Spanish	page 38
Habilidades – increasing your language skills for fluency	page 40
Escenario – una escena cómica donde todos quieren ayudar a un viajero confuso Escenario – un correo electrónico a un amigo español que va a visitar	page 41

- Allow time for students to read the questions and cross-refer to the relevant pages of the Students' Book. They could do this individually or in pairs / small groups, followed by whole-class discussion.
- This spread also provides an opportunity for students to recap on familiar language. Ask them to think about language they already know that might be useful when working on the themes of the unit.

- Mindmap any language they produce, and if possible, keep it on display as reference as you progress through the unit. It can be added to at intervals as new language becomes familiar.
- At the end of work on the unit, allow time for students to return to this spread and repeat the mind-mapping process, this time including what they have learned over the course of the unit. Get them to answer the questions in their own words, and encourage them to use the results for revision purposes.
- Ask them what they found difficult, interesting etc. What do they think are the important things they have learned in this unit? What do they still need to improve on?
- If time permits, get the students to redesign the page. How would they set it out so it reflects the unit? How would they make it attractive to other learners of their age? How would they make it easy to follow? What would they include in terms of text, pictures, captions, page references? Ask them to imagine they are producing material for next year's class who will be learning the same thing – what would they have found it useful to know?

¿Por qué aprender el español? Para describir donde vives y poder viajar.

- Students share any experiences they have had of travelling in or to Spain e.g. different types of transport used.
- Ask them to consider what sort of language they would need to find their way around on public transport, or to describe where they live to another person.

Cómo describir donde vives

Planner

➤ Objectives
- Describing where you live

➤ Resources
Students' Book, pages 28–29
CD 1, tracks 21–22
Grammar Workbook, page 45
Activity sheets 8–11

➤ Key language
las afueras, un bosque, el casco histórico, los jóvenes, el mundo, un pueblo, su pueblo natal
bello/a, concurrido/a, feo/a, hermoso/a, tranquilo/a, turístico/a
echar de menos
ahora, bastante, como, me recuerda, mucho que hacer, nadie, siempre, tan

➤ Skills
- Increasing comprehension of written and spoken texts

➤ Grammar
- The imperfect tense

➤ PLTS
Students' Book, page 29, activity 8,
Team Workers
Students' Book, page 29, activity 9,
Independent Enquirers

➤ Starters
- Students' Book page 27. Students look at the pictures and brainstorm vocabulary that goes with them. What is the unit going to be about? Write down their predictions, and review them at the end of the unit.
- Students' Book page 28, activity 1. Students look at the photos and say which one they like the look of best and why.
- Play "word association" in Spanish. Put the name of the students' home town on the board, and ask for the first word in Spanish they can think of that goes with it. Then ask for a word which goes with the first word, and so on, seeing how long a chain of associations you can make.

➤ Plenaries
- Students' Book page 28, activity 8. Students work in pairs to describe the photos. In addition, they could write out their sentence on a piece of paper and display these in the classroom.
- Students' Book page 28, activity 9. Play a Consequences style game with descriptions of where they live. The Teacher writes pointers on the board e.g. *Vivo en... Me gusta porque..., sin embargo es bastante...* The idea is to create an absurd description.
- Students research their home town and produce a brief before-and-now description like the one of San Vicente de la Barquera.

---

1   En el texto sobre San Vicente de la Barquera, busca:

- Students read through the text several times, scanning for specific information, looking for different things each time. If they work in pairs, the teacher can "hear" them finding things without having to write everything down.

Answers:
personas y lugares San Vicente de la Barquera, pueblo, restaurantes, bares, playas, bosques, castillo, costa, jóvenes, instituto, mi tío, una ciudad, casas, el mundo, lugares
adjetivos para describir lugares pequeño, turístico, nuevos, bello, verde, pintoresco, tranquilo, ruidosa, preciosas
opiniones me encanta, me gusta
palabras que denominan el tiempo hoy, cuando yo era joven, a los dieciséis años, ahora
palabras para conectar o separar ideas con, y, pero

2   Escucha y lee a la vez.
- Students listen to the text, reading it at the same time. After locating things in different parts of the

text, the next step is to read it through accurately and carefully. The listening means they read it and hear the correct pronunciation.

> **CD 1, track 21   página 29, actividades 2 y 3**
>
> Realmente me encanta San Vicente de la Barquera. En mis viajes por el mundo, siempre echo de menos a mi pueblo pequeño. Hoy es un pueblo bastante turístico, con nuevos hoteles, restaurantes, bares y actividades en las playas. Cuando yo era joven, San Vicente era muy bello y muy verde, con los bosques, su castillo pintoresco y la costa sin nadie. Pero no había mucho que hacer para los jóvenes. Yo dejé el instituto a los dieciséis años y fui a trabajar para mi tío en su empresa de construcción. No había futuro para mí como cantante en San Vicente, pero no quería abandonar el pueblo. Me gusta porque es tan tranquilo, no quiero vivir en una ciudad ruidosa. Ahora tengo varias casas preciosas en diferentes partes del mundo, pero siempre en lugares que me recuerdan a San Vicente.

3 Escucha otra vez y contesta a las preguntas.

- Students listen to the text more carefully looking for the answers to the questions. Answers which are not full sentences are acceptable.

Answers: **a** David es de San Vicente de la Barquera. **b** Le encanta su pueblo. **c** Es muy pintoresco. **d** Es bastante turístico. (**Note:** Though you could argue that's a good thing!) **e** En el pasado no había nada para los jóvenes.

4 ¿Que significan esas palabras? Luego haz frases sobre San Vicente de la Barquera.

- Students write sentences using the words in the box, and adapting the language of the text. Encourage them also to write the opposite of what appears in the text to increase their use of language.

5 Mira las cuatro fotos (página 28). Haz una lista del vocabulario necesario para describirlas. Escucha y haz corresponder las tres descripciones con las fotos.

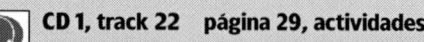

- Students work in groups, recalling vocabulary from KS3. Their lists can be pooled and displayed before listening to the CD.

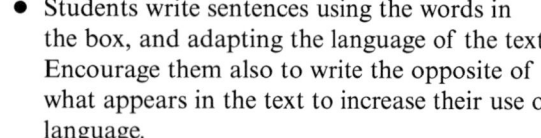

> 🔊 **CD 1, track 22   página 29, actividades 5, 6 y 7**
>
> **a** No me gusta mucho vivir en la ciudad, es bastante ruidosa, concurrida, sucia. Hay parques, pero siempre hay tanta gente y movimiento. Mi sueño sería ir a vivir en una isla tropical, pero quiero seguir con mis estudios y luego encontrar un buen trabajo en una oficina o una fábrica aquí.
>
> **b** Es muy conveniente vivir aquí. Tengo las ventajas de poder ir al centro cuando quiero, pero donde vivo, todo es muy tranquilo. Hay buenos institutos, tiendas y parques. El único problema es que es muy caro comprar una casa aquí. Pero mientras vivo con mis padres está bien. Más tarde, no sé, será difícil.
>
> **c** Me aburro aquí. Es demasiado tranquilo, y no hay jóvenes de mi edad. Para ir al instituto, tengo que ir en autobús. Los fines de semana no veo a nadie. Es bastante feo, y deprimente.

Answers: **a** 3, **b** 2, **c** 4

6 Escucha y deduce quién va a quedarse allí donde vive, y quién va a abandonar el lugar.

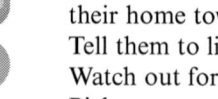

- Students listen again and decide who will stay in their home town and who is likely to move away. Tell them to listen out for sentences with "pero". Watch out for red herrings like the tropical island. Pick up on positive and negative tones of voice.

Answers: **a** stay, **b** leave, **c** leave

7 Apoderarse de vocabulario: Escucha otra vez y apunta estas palabras en español.

- Students listen again for specific words. Play the CD section by section. Encourage students to listen and remember and not write while listening.
- Differentiation: Let pupils have a copy of the transcript; listen for the words, then check in the unit glossary; or listen for the words and put your hand up when you think you hear one – the teacher can pause so you can say what you thought you heard.

Answers: dirty – *sucia*, so many people – *tanta gente*, a good job – *un buen trabajo*, convenient – *conveniente*, advantages *ventajas*, when I want – *cuando quiero*, the only problem – *el único problema*, expensive – *caro*, I get bored – *me aburro*, too – *demasiado*, nobody – *nadie*, ugly – *feo*, depressing – *deprimente*

Remate

8 Use the expressions in the *Habilidades* box to help you talk about the places in the photos.

- Students work in pairs to describe the photos. They have to keep talking until the teacher says stop. More able students can compete against each other (in Just a Minute style) to see who can talk the longest. Students can then write it up and as a challenge try to use all the words in the grid. They will have to supply more of their own ideas to avoid repetition.

Success criteria activity 8:
- *students communicate effectively and accurately*
- *students express personal opinions and justify points of view*
- *students use a variety of vocabulary and structures*
- *students deal with unpredictable elements*

9 Write a description of the place where you live. Make it possible to guess from this description whether you're intending to stay there or not.

- Students give all the good and bad points of where they live as they see it. The reader (class mate or teacher) has to decide whether they think the pupil is planning on living there for ever or leaving.

Success criteria activity 9:
- *students give information accurately and in the appropriate style*
- *students express personal opinions and justify points of view*
- *students use a variety of vocabulary and structures*

Cómo comparar diferentes lugares

Planner

➤ Objectives
- Comparing and contrasting different places

➤ Resources
Students' Book, pages 30–31
CD 1, tracks 23–24
Grammar Workbook, pages 9, 43
Activity sheets 8–11

➤ Key language
una calle, una ciudad gemela, un edificio, una fuente de ingresos, un municipio, el patrimonio
amistoso/a, bonito/a, caro/a, conocido/a por, de moda, deprimente, impresionante, precioso/a, ruidoso/a, sucio/a
a diferencia de, a pesar de, actualmente, aunque, en comparación con, en lugar de, mientras, tanto

➤ Skills
- Improving a text with key phrases and new vocabulary

➤ Grammar
- Comparatives, the preterite tense

➤ PLTS
Students' Book, page 31, activity 9,
Creative Thinkers
Students' Book, page 31, activity 10,
Effective Participators

➤ Starters
- Students do some pre-unit research on the three main places. Ask them to find out where the places are, how big they are (and compare that with their home town) and what you would visit as a tourist.

- Pick out some words from each of the three texts on page 30 activity 1 and get the students to find which text they belong to. Make them words the students should already understand so they begin to build up a picture of these places.
- Students' Book page 30, activity 1. Students complete the "dating agency" form for Madrid and the other cities. After they have done activity 2, they can complete similar forms for the British cities described.
- Students' Book page 31, activity 6. Brainstorm a list of adjectives with the class and a list of places. In small groups, make as many simple comparison sentences as possible.

➤ Plenaries
- Students' Book page 30, activity 4. Give students a selection of appropriate verbs (e.g. *comprar*) and ask them to make the 1ˢᵗ person preterite form. Then ask them to make up brief sentences, serious or amusing, using the verbs (*Compré un elefante*).
- Students' Book page 31, activity 9. Students can type up their descriptions and publish them on the school web site if available. They can illustrate and display the descriptions.
- Students' Book page 31, activity 10. Students use the language they have learnt to debate the merits of different places. They could record their speeches on video.
- Have a Best Town competition. Students choose any place they know, have visited, or would like to visit, and prepare an oral presentation with visual back up. The class votes for the person who gives the most informative, interesting and convincing presentation.

1a Lee el texto sobre Madrid. Copie y completa la ficha.

5–8

- Students read about Madrid and complete the form. Apply some of the reading strategies from the previous page: look for names of people and places, find numbers, look for words that describe a town, find words you know, read through pronouncing the words in your head.

Answers: (suggested)

Nombre: MADRID, **Situación:** Capital de España, **Población:** 3 000 000, **Características:** Contrastes: cultura, historia, moda, **Puntos de Interés:** Galerías, teatros, vida nocturna, bares, **Deporte/Recreación:** fútbol – Real Madrid (Note: there is also Atlético Madrid), **Título:** Ciudad de los Árboles, **Personajes:** none mentioned – students could research some

1b Aohara lee los textos sobre Alta Gracia y San Vicente de la Barquera y escribe una ficha parecida.

5–8

- Students read about Alta Gracia and San Vicente de la Barquera and complete the forms.
- Extension – discuss (possibly in English) which of these places the students would be interested in visiting and why – or why not. If they're not enthused by heritage and UNESCO, they could research on the internet what there is for young people to do in these places, or find out more about the famous people mentioned.

Answers: (suggested)

Nombre: SAN VICENTE DE LA BARQUERA, **Situación:** Costa Cantábrica, **Población:** 4 000, **Características:** Contrastes: cultura, historia, turismo, **Puntos de Interés:** pueblo viejo, edificios y monumentos interesantes, Parque Natural de Ovambre, **Deporte/Recreación:** caminar en el Parque Natural, **Título:** bien de Interés Cultural, **Personajes:** David Bustamente

Nombre: ALTA GRACIA, **Situación:** Provincia de Córdoba, Argentina, **Población:** 43 000, **Características:** Contrastes: cultura, historia, turismo, **Puntos de Interés:** museos, monumentos, **Deporte/Recreación:** none mentioned – students could research some, **Título:** Patrimonio de la Humanidad, **Personajes:** Ernesto "Che" Guevara

2 Escucha las descripciones de cuatro lugares en Inglaterra. Intenta identificar una ciudad 'gemela' para los tres lugares de arriba.

5–8

- Students listen to the descriptions and try to find a suitable twin town from the three above.

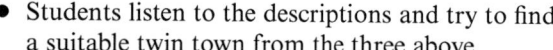
 CD 1, track 23   página 31, actividades 2 y 3

1 Alonso Visité la ciudad hace tres años, y era muy impresionante. Tiene nueve millones de habitantes y hay gente de todas partes del mundo que viven o que están allí de visita. El centro de la ciudad es muy interesante, con monumentos importantes, y museos. También puedes hacer una excursión en un barco por el río. Es bonito, pero hay demasiado tráfico y mucha gente. Y muchas veces llueve. Es la capital, y está en el sur del país. Es famoso por la familia real y sus palacios.

2 Ana Hice un intercambio con un instituto en esta ciudad. No es un lugar muy turístico, pero es muy típico de la vida moderna. El centro histórico ha cambiado mucho, y hoy hay muchas tiendas modernas, bares y restaurantes. En las afueras hay supermercados grandes. No fui mucho al centro porque mi amigo inglés vive en las afueras. Está en el norte del país y tiene unos cincuenta mil habitantes.

3 Rafa Era una ciudad importante en la historia, pero hoy depende del turismo y sus instalaciones deportivas para atraer a los visitantes. Tiene 39 mil habitantes, así que no es una ciudad muy grande. Es famosa por su arquitectura y hay varios museos que se pueden visitar por ejemplo la casa de Mary Wollstonecraft. Además, se puede pasear por el campo y las montañas.

4 Marta Es un pueblo que vi en la televisión. Me gustaría visitarlo porque parece muy bonito. Está en el norte, entre la montaña y el mar, y sólo tiene tres mil habitantes. Antes era un puerto pequeño, pero hoy es más turístico. Se puede pescar o explorar la naturaleza. No conozco a nadie famoso en ese pueblo, porque es tan pequeño.

Answers: **1** Madrid, **2** Alta Gracia, **3** Alta Gracia, **4** San Vicente

3 Escucha otra vez. ¿Quién o quiénes? (Alonso, Ana, Rafa, Marta).

5–8

- Students listen again to decide which person or people are the answers to questions a – e.

Answers: **a** Alonso, Ana, **b** Rafa, **c** Alonso, Rafa, Marta, **d** Alonso, **e** Alonso

4 Haz corresponder.

4–6

- Students match and complete the sentences to practise the use of the preterite.

Answers: **a** 2, **b** 1, **c** 4, **d** 3

5 Mira las fichas sobre las tres ciudades (página 30). Usa algunos de estos verbos para hablar de una de las ciudades.

4–9

- Students look again at the forms they filled in for the three Hispanic cities. They use the words in the box to talk about one of them. If they don't use *fui a*, their partner has to decide which city they are talking about, and can respond to their description with *fuiste a...*

6 ¿Qué piensas? Decide si estás de acuerdo.

4–5

- Students decide if they agree with the statements or not. It doesn't matter if they know or not – they are making predictions to be checked.

7 Escucha y verifica.

5–8

- Students listen and check the answers they discussed in activity 6.

 CD 1, track 24   página 31, actividades 7 y 8

Madrid no es tan grande como Londres. Mientras que Londres tiene nueve millones de habitantes, Madrid solo tiene tres millones. Además, en comparación con el Támesis, el río Manzanares es mucho más pequeño. A pesar de ser una ciudad más pequeña, Madrid tiene más vida que Londres, porque se concentra en el centro histórico. Las dos ciudades son conocidas por su vida cultural, sus museos y sus excepcionales galerías. Para los turistas tal vez Madrid no es tan caro como Londres, pero para vivir allí cuesta mucho dinero.

8 Escucha otra vez. ¿Cuáles de estas frases oyes?

4–8

- Students listen for the given phrases. They will need to check their meanings to be able to use them in the next activities, and improve the quality of the language they use.

Answers: como ✓, a diferencia de x, en comparación con ✓, a pesar de ✓, mientras x, aunque x, en lugar de x, tal vez ✓

Remate

9 Write a comparison between the place where you live and the places on page 30. Mention: the size of the place, any specific features or important monuments it has, and what there is to do there.

- It is helpful to give students the transcripts for this spread here, to increase vocabulary. They can compare their home town with one or more of the given places to extend their work.

4–9

Success criteria activity 9:
- *students give information accurately and in the appropriate style*
- *students express personal opinions and justify points of view*
- *students use a variety of vocabulary and structures*

10 Choose one of the three places. Prepare a debate in which you defend your preference against a partner who chooses another place.

- Students defend their chosen place to a partner, or in a class debate. Some additional research (e.g. homework, internet) would enable them to know the place better and speak with more confidence. Two local "rival" towns could produce a fierce debate.

4–9

Success criteria activity 10:
- *students communicate effectively and accurately*
- *students express personal opinions and justify points of view*
- *students use a variety of vocabulary and structures*

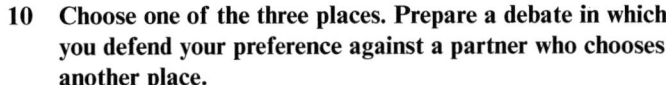

Cómo solicitar información sobre una ciudad

páginas 32 y 33

Planner

➤ Objectives
- Asking questions and giving directions

➤ Resources
Students' Book, pages 32–33
CD 1, tracks 25–28
Grammar Workbook, pages 22, 45
Activity sheets 8–11

➤ Key language
¿a qué punto? ¿cómo? ¿cuándo? ¿cuánto? ¿dónde? ¿por qué? ¿qué? ¿quién?
a la derecha, a la izquierda, al final de la calle, al lado de, cerca, delante de, detrás de, enfrente de, en la plaza, entre, lejos
cruzar la calle, recordar, seguir todo recto
tanta gente

➤ Skills
- Using prediction as a listening skill

➤ Grammar
- Using *tú* and *usted* appropriately
- The imperfect tense

➤ PLTS
Students' Book, page 32, activity 4, *Reflective Learners*
Students' Book, page 33, activity 13, *Self Managers*

➤ Starters
- Direct students to http://en.wikipedia.org/wiki/The_Motorcycle_Diaries or http://www.spartacus.schoolnet.co.uk/COLDguevara.htm so they can find out about Che Guevara and understand the references in the unit.
- Write *tú* and *Usted* on the board, and get students to explain what they mean and when they would use them. Ask them to produce some examples.
- Students' Book, page 33 activity 9. Make up a story as a whole class using the directions vocabulary before setting students off on the vocabulary task.
- Students' Book page 33, activity 11. If students need more support give them a copy of the transcript and ask them to highlight all the vocabulary to do with directions.

➤ Plenaries
- Students' Book page 33, activity 13. Students design a leaflet of their home town with a guided tour marked on it.
- Students return to their list of questions from activity 1 and use them as the basis to conduct an interview with a famous person about their place of birth.
- Give students a set of directions to follow and send them off round the school to find out where they end up. They have to finish in the correct place to win. An envelope at each destination can contain part of a sentence that when put together describes the school or a well known local place.

1 **Haz una lista de preguntas para entrevistar a una 'celebridad' sobre su ciudad.**

- Students work individually or as a whole class to produce a list of questions.

4–6

2 **Escucha sin apuntar, luego intenta recordar las preguntas que hace Malcolm.**

- Students listen without taking notes. Remind them that they can listen multiple times, and do not have to try to remember everything at once. For more support, do the listening before writing the list of questions in activity 1.

4–8

> **CD 1, track 25   página 32, actividad 2**
>
> Bueno, aquí estoy en Alta Gracia, la ciudad donde vivía la familia Guevara. Quiero explorar la ciudad y conocer más sobre la juventud de Ernesto. Quiero saber:
>
> ¿Cómo es la ciudad? ¿Qué se puede visitar? ¿Dónde está la casa de la familia Guevara? ¿Por qué vivían aquí? ¿Cómo era la ciudad en los años 30, y cómo ha cambiado?

Answers: ¿Cómo es la ciudad? ¿Qué se puede visitar? ¿Dónde está la casa de la familia Guevara? ¿Por qué vivían aquí? ¿Cómo era la ciudad en los años 30, y cómo ha cambiado?

3 **Malcolm entrevista a Gabriela. Con un(a) compañero/a, haz el diálogo, utilizando la información siguiente.**

- Students complete the dialogue with the information given. More able students do it directly from the stimulus box while less able ones write the dialogue down and perform it.

4–8

4 **Escucha y verifica.**

PLTS

- Students listen and check their conversations against the model. Those needing more help could listen first, and do the speaking activity second, though this does not practise the skill of predicting.

4–8

> **CD 1, track 26   página 32, actividad 4**
>
> **Malcolm** ¿Cómo te llamas?
> **Gabriela** Me llamo Gabriela Rentería.
> **Malcolm** ¿Desde hace cuanto tiempo vives aquí?
> **Gabriela** Nací aquí, así que vivo aquí desde hace 16 años.
> **Malcolm** ¿Qué piensas de la ciudad?
> **Gabriela** Es una ciudad muy bonita pero no muy moderna.
> **Malcolm** ¿Qué puedes hacer aquí?
> **Gabriela** Puedes jugar al golf, ir al cine, caminar, visitar los parques o el casino.
> **Malcolm** ¿Cómo puedes explorar la ciudad?

> **Gabriela** Todo está muy cerca, así que puedes explorar a pie sin problema.
> **Malcolm** ¿Puedes ver la casa de Che Guevara?
> **Gabriela** Sí, es un museo. Está abierto desde las nueve de la mañana hasta las siete de la tarde.
> **Malcolm** ¿Sabes dónde está el museo?
> **Gabriela** Está en la calle Avellaneda.
> **Malcolm** ¿Qué puedes ver en el museo?
> **Gabriela** Puedes ver fotos, documentos, su bicicleta y el coche de la familia Guevara.

5 **Malcolm entrevista a la abuela de Gabriela. Escucha sin apuntar, luego intenta recordar sus respuestas.**

- Students listen without taking notes and try to answer the questions. Listen several times and ask the whole class to give whatever information they can remember each time; they may be pleasantly surprised at how much they can produce.

5–8

> **CD 1, track 27   página 32, actividad 5**
>
> **Malcolm** ¿Cómo se llama usted?
> **Lourdes** Me llamo Lourdes García Leal.
> **Malcolm** ¿Desde hace cuánto tiempo vive aquí?
> **Lourdes** Vivo aquí desde hace setenta y cinco años.
> **Malcolm** ¿Qué piensa de la ciudad?
> **Lourdes** Ya es una ciudad muy grande, con nuevos barrios y mucha gente.
> **Malcolm** ¿Cómo era antes?
> **Lourdes** Era una ciudad preciosa, que mucha gente visitaba para escapar de la capital. Venían con el tren, había hoteles lujosos, bailes, el club de golf, y mucho dinero.
> **Malcolm** ¿Cómo ha cambiado?
> **Lourdes** Las casas grandes ya son museos, el hotel es un casino, vienen turistas pero vienen a ver los monumentos, no a convivir.
> **Malcolm** ¿Quién venía aquí?
> **Lourdes** Mucha gente famosa… El músico Manuel de Falla tenía una casa aquí, la familia de Ernesto Guevara vivía aquí.
> **Malcolm** ¿Por qué?
> **Lourdes** El joven Ernesto tenía asma, y Alta Gracia era famosa por su aire pura.

Answers: **1** Me llamo Lourdes García Leal. **2** Vivo aquí desde hace setenta y cinco años. **3** Ya es una ciudad muy grande, con nuevos barrios y mucha gente. **4** Era una ciudad preciosa, que mucha gente visitaba para escapar de la capital. Venían con el tren, había hoteles lujosos, bailes, el club de golf, y mucho dinero. **5** Las casas grandes ya son museos, el hotel es un casino, vienen turistas pero vienen a ver los monumentos, no a convivir. **6** Mucha gente famosa… El músico Manuel de Falla tenía una casa aquí, la familia de Ernesto Guevara vivía aquí. **7** El joven Ernesto tenía asma, y Alta Gracia era famosa por su aire pura.

6 Compara la forma de los verbos en las preguntas que hace Malcolm a Gabriela y a su abuela. ¿Cómo es diferente? ¿Por qué?

3–6

● Students compare the difference in the questions Malcolm asks Gabriela and her grandmother. Copies of the transcript are helpful here. Get the students to explain the differences, what the two forms of address are, and when they would be used. Extension: students adapt the questions to ask the same things to a group of people, formally and informally.

7 Utiliza las preguntas para hacer la entrevista con dos compañero/as. Una persona hace el papel de Gabriela y la otra de su abuela. A ver si contesta la persona correcta.

4–8

● Students take on the roles of Malcolm and either Gabriela or Lourdes to practise asking and answering questions. More advanced students can complete the task from memory, with other class members checking on a transcript how correct they are.

8 Separa las frases para hacer dos descripciones de Alta Gracia – cómo es hoy, y cómo era antes.

4–8

● Students separate out the "before" and "now" statements about Alta Gracia to form two descriptions. If there is time, they can refer back to the previous spread for examples of how to extend their work and make it more interesting.

Answers: **before** a, c, e, f, h, j; **now** b, d, g, i

9 Haz dibujos para illustrar el vocabulario. Inventa una historia en inglés.

4–6

● Students make up a picture story / cartoon strip to record and learn the vocabulary. The pupils ideally do this in their own vocabulary books – they will have a story mainly in English, punctuated by the pictures and the Spanish phrases. e.g. *James Bond was **delante del** hotel* (pic). *Little did he know, his enemy was waiting **detrás del** hotel* (pic). They can stick to the original order of the words, or change it around. Explain this is a useful technique for learning vocabulary.

10 Copia y completa una tabla así:

4–6

● Students copy and complete the table.

Answers:

Palabras equivalentes		Palabras opuestas	
torcer a la derecha	girar a la derecha	subir	bajar
seguir todo recto	continuar	a la izquierda	a la derecha
calle	avenida	detrás de	delante de
cruzar	atravesar	lejos de	cerca de
rodar	dar la vuelta	ir	volver

11 Mira el mapa. Escucha a Malcolm en el Centro de Información. Identifica los lugares A–G en el mapa.

5–8

● Students listen to Malcolm and follow the route marked on the map, identifying the places mentioned. The emphasis here is on following the route – "keeping track" – not finding the places.

 CD 1, track 28   **página 33, actividad 11**

Malcolm	Hola, quiero ir al Museo de la Casa de Ernesto Guevara. ¿Por dónde se va?
Chica	Pues, mira aquí en el mapa, te voy a enseñar varios lugares de interés aquí en Alta Gracia.
Malcolm	¿Dónde estamos nosotros?
Chica	El centro de información está aquí en el Reloj Público, mira.
Malcolm	Ah, sí, ya veo. Así que tengo que ir todo recto y luego a…
Chica	Pues, primero tienes que ver el Tajamar que está aquí delante del Reloj Público.
Malcolm	¿Qué es el Tajamar?
Chica	Es un lugar muy bonito. Es como un lago artificial en medio de la ciudad. Es perfecto para ir a caminar o a sacar fotos.
Malcolm	Bueno, el Tajamar, delante del Reloj Público, gracias
Malcolm	Y de allí, puedo ir a la casa de Che Guevara?
Chica	Antes, vale la pena visitar el Museo de la Ciudad. Está aquí detrás del Reloj Público.
Malcolm	Bueno, entonces ¿por dónde se va?
Chica	Sales de aquí, y tienes que torcer a la izquierda y cruzar la plaza.
Malcolm	Entonces, el Museo de la Ciudad, detrás del Reloj Público, al cruzar la plaza…
Chica	Y después, muy cerca del Museo de la Ciudad, está la Iglesia de los Jesuitas y su museo, en la esquina.
Malcolm	Ya veo, La Iglesia aquí, muy cerca del Reloj Público.
Chica	Luego hay que volver al Reloj Público y tomar la Avenida del Tajamar. Pasando el Tajamar, hay que ir a la derecha, luego a la izquierda para tomar la Avenida Sarmiento. En la calle Velez Sarsfield, se tuerce a la izquierda y luego otra vez se tuerce a la izquierda en el Bulevar Carlos Pellegrini. Tienes que seguir todo recto hasta llegar al Museo de Manuel de Falla. El museo está a la izquierda, enfrente del Club de Golf.
Malcolm	¿Cómo? El Museo de Manuel de Falla está enfrente del Golf. El museo está a la izquierda, y el club de golf a la derecha.
Girl	Después, puedes continuar y torcer a la derecha para caminar entre el Parque García Lorca, a la izquierda, y el golf, a la derecha.
Malcolm	Sí, El parque está a la izquierda, y el golf a la derecha. ¿Y está muy lejos la casa de los Guevara?
Girl	No, está cerca, a unos dos cientos metros. Puedes dar la vuelta al golf, o sea, tienes que seguir todo recto, luego torcer a la derecha para rodar el campo de golf, luego otra vez a la derecha y bajar por la Avenida Avellaneda. La Casa de Ernesto Guevara está a la derecha.

Answers: Students should follow the directions and come across the places in the following order:
1 Reloj Público, **2** E El Tajamar, **3** F El Museo de la Ciudad, **4** G La Iglesia, **5** D La Casa de Manuel Falla, **6** A El Club de Golf, **7** B El Parque García Lorca, **8** C La Casa de Ernesto Guevara

Remate

12 Can you show Malcolm a more direct route? With a partner, practise guiding him to different places on the map.

5–8

- Students choose a more direct route and explain it to a partner who has to follow it on the map. With a large copy of the map, students can take it in turns to give directions from the class to one student following the route on the board – if a "direction giver" makes a mistake someone else takes over. Or students can compete in pairs against the clock to complete the route in the shortest time.

Success criteria activity 12:
- *students communicate effectively and accurately*
- *students use a variety of vocabulary and structures*
- *students deal with unpredictable elements*

13 Design a leaflet with a route for exploring the place where you live. Include instructions, descriptions and interesting information.

PLTS

4–9

- Students design a leaflet of their home town with a guided tour marked on it. To one side there should be a "You have to go left/right" directions section. There should also be a section describing places en route, or this can be simpler labels with arrows to the places marked. The information can be opening times etc.

Success criteria activity 13:
- *students give information accurately and in the appropriate style*
- *students express personal opinions and justify points of view*
- *students use a variety of vocabulary and structures*

Cómo solucionar problemas de transporte

páginas 34 y 35

Planner

➤ **Objectives**
- Using and finding out about public transport

➤ **Resources**
Students' Book, pages 34–35
CD 1, tracks 29–31
Grammar Workbook, pages 19–21
Activity sheets 8–11

➤ **Key language**
un andén, un avión, un billete de ida y vuelta, un billete sencillo, un horario, una señal, una taquilla, un torniquete, un tren
cambiar, llegar, salir
está a … metros

➤ **Skills**
- Transfering language known from one situation to a new one

➤ **Grammar**
- Answering questions

➤ **PLTS**
Students' Book page 35, activity 7, *Creative Thinkers*

Students' Book page 35, activity 8, *Effective Participators*

➤ **Starters**
- Students' Book page 34, activity 1. Before doing this activity, discuss metros with the class. Who's been on what and where? How do they work? Which one did you like the best?
- Students' Book page 34, activity 1. Pre-reading activity. Reproduce the text on a board. Read through out loud and tell students to stop you whenever they recognise a word. Try and place the word in context e.g. they may recognise *sistema*; ask them to extrapolate what *sistema de Metro*, then *sistema de Metro de Madrid* is. Draw lines and write notes on the board. Only tackle words they already recognise.
- Produce a mindmap of different types of transport, the journeys you use them for, their advantages and disadvantages.
- Students' Book page 35, activity 5. Discuss – in English or Spanish – the differences between travel by train and by air. Get students to look back through the spread so far and pick out any language they could use in these situations, and list them where they can be seen.

1 Lee y contesta a estas preguntas.

- Students read the text and answer the questions.

Answers: **a** 7, **b** Zona A, **c** billete sencillo, billete Metrobús, Abono Turístico, **d** billete sencillo – 1€, billete Metrobús – diez viajes – 7€, Abono Turístico – de 1 a 7 días, **e** billete sencillo y billete Metrobús – taquillas en estaciones, máquinas o kioscos de prensa, Abono Turístico – taquillas, **f** no – para niños de 4 a 11 años, **g** no – de las 6:30 a la 1 de la madrugada, **h** mapas y señalización en los andenes

5–8

2 Busca estas palabras clave. Tendrás que buscar en la página completa.

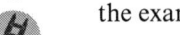

- Students search the page for the key words in the box. Explain that these are key words to learn for the exam.

Answers: **ticket office** taquilla, **ticket** billete, **line** línea, **station** estación, **platform** andén, **turnstile** torniquete, **machine** máquina, **map** mapa, **sign** señalización, **discount** descuento

5–8

3 Lee y escucha al Señor. Descubre los cuatro errores según la información.

- Read and listen to the dialogue, and find the four errors according to the information in activity 1.

5–9

> 🔊 **CD 1, track 29**   **página 34, actividad 3**
>
> **Hombre** Necesito ir al Parque del Retiro. ¿Cuál es la estación de metro más cerca?
> **Empleado** Necesita ir a la estación Retiro.
> **Hombre** Está en la línea 7. ¿Verdad?
> **Empleado** No, señor, está en la línea 13, la roja.
> **Hombre** ¿Necesito cambiar de tren?
> **Empleado** No, es directo. Está a unos 5 minutos de aquí.
> **Hombre** ¿Es más barato si compro diez billetes?
> **Empleado** Un billete para diez viajes cuesta 8€ o un abono para un día cuesta 5€.
> **Hombre** ¿Vale la pena comprar un abono?
> **Empleado** Sólo si se va a hacer más de cinco viajes en un solo día.
> **Hombre** Bueno, compro un billete sencillo. Es 1€50, ¿no?
> **Empleado** Aquí tiene

> **Hombre** Gracias. ¿Tengo que validar el billete en la máquina?
> **Empleado** No, eso es para los abonos. Solo hay que cancelarlo en el torniquete.
> **Hombre** ¿Cuándo es el próximo tren?
> **Empleado** Llegan cada tres minutos.
> **Hombre** Ah, sí, claro. ¿Voy por aquí a la izquierda?
> **Empleado** No señor, es el sentido contrario. Hay que seguir las señales para la línea roja, próxima estación Banco de España.

Answers: **1** un billete para diez viajes cuesta 7€, no 8€, **2** no se sabe si un abono para un día cuesta 5€, **3** un billete sencillo cuesta 1€, no 1€50, **4** los trenes llegan cada 5 minutos, no cada 3 minutos

4 Escucha y apunta los datos en un billete.

- Students listen and fill in the information on the ticket. Giving them the information printed out on a ticket sized piece of paper or card makes the activity seem more realistic.

5–9

> 🔊 **CD 1, track 30**   **página 35, actividad 4**
>
> **Cliente** Quiero comprar un billete.
> **Empleada** ¿A dónde quiere ir?
> **Cliente** A Barcelona.
> **Empleada** ¿Es para qué día?
> **Cliente** Para el dos de noviembre.
> **Empleada** ¿Y a qué hora?
> **Cliente** Tengo que estar en Barcelona a las diez de la mañana.
> **Empleada** El tren sale a las siete y llega a las nueve cincuenta y siete.
> **Cliente** Bien. ¿Cuánto cuesta el billete?
> **Empleada** ¿En club, preferente o turista?
> **Cliente** En Turista
> **Empleada** ¿Es para una persona?
> **Cliente** Sí.
> **Empleada** Son € 20.

Answers: **Origen:** Madrid; **Destino:** Barcelona; **Fecha:** 2 noviembre; **Hora de salida:** 07:00; **Clase:** Turista; **Número de personas:** 1; **Precio:** 125 € 20.

5 Lee y utiliza la información de abajo y haz seis frases en inglés sobre el AVE.

- Students prepare six sentences about the Spanish train.

4–9

6 Escucha y completa la información.

- Students listen and complete the information. Again, an actual form to fill in makes the task more interesting. The students listen for the details, then the teacher asks them for the answers in Spanish and writes it up on the board in full sentences with the help of class.

5–9

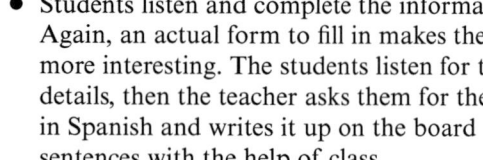

CD 1, track 31	página 35, actividad 6

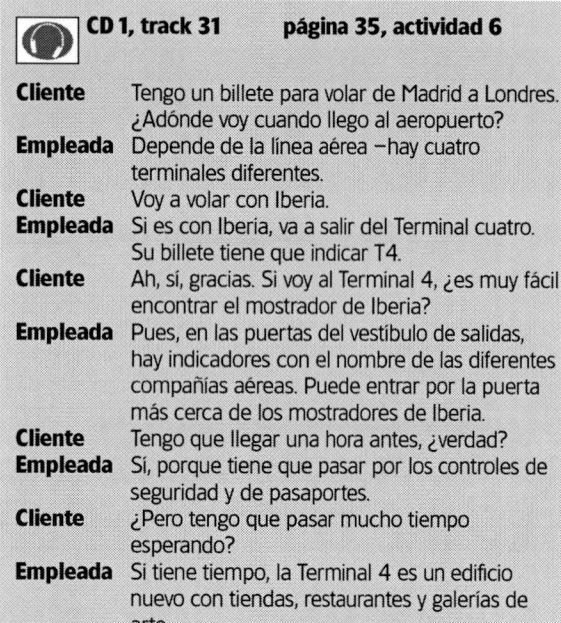

Cliente	Tengo un billete para volar de Madrid a Londres. ¿Adónde voy cuando llego al aeropuerto?
Empleada	Depende de la línea aérea –hay cuatro terminales diferentes.
Cliente	Voy a volar con Iberia.
Empleada	Si es con Iberia, va a salir del Terminal cuatro. Su billete tiene que indicar T4.
Cliente	Ah, sí, gracias. Si voy al Terminal 4, ¿es muy fácil encontrar el mostrador de Iberia?
Empleada	Pues, en las puertas del vestíbulo de salidas, hay indicadores con el nombre de las diferentes compañías aéreas. Puede entrar por la puerta más cerca de los mostradores de Iberia.
Cliente	Tengo que llegar una hora antes, ¿verdad?
Empleada	Sí, porque tiene que pasar por los controles de seguridad y de pasaportes.
Cliente	¿Pero tengo que pasar mucho tiempo esperando?
Empleada	Si tiene tiempo, la Terminal 4 es un edificio nuevo con tiendas, restaurantes y galerías de arte.

Answers: **Terminales** 4, **Terminal para Iberia** 4, **Acceso** puertas en el vestíbulo de salidas más cerca de los mostradores de Iberia, **Tiempo requerido** 1 hora, **Controles** seguridad y pasaportes, **Facilidades** tiendas, restaurantes y galerías de arte

Remate

7 Write a guide about how to use the transport in the place where you live. Follow the style of the information given on this page.

  PLTS

- Collate some information as a whole class first – types of transport, routes, cost etc. Tell the students to set it out as if explaining to someone with no previous knowledge of the area how to use the local transport system. Differentiation: they can personalise it with anecdotes to make it more interesting.

5–9

Success criteria activity 7:
- *students give information accurately and in the appropriate style*
- *students express personal opinions and justify points of view*
- *students use a variety of vocabulary and structures*

8 Test your partner's knowledge. Ask them about the transport in Madrid. Who knows the most?

  PLTS

- Students prepare a list for a partner using the questions from this page or make up their own own based on the information. They shut the books and ask a partner. See who knows the most. This can be done in pairs or as a whole class / small groups quiz if more appropriate.

5–9

Success criteria activity 8:
- *students communicate effectively and accurately*
- *students use a variety of vocabulary and structures*
- *students deal with unpredictable elements*

Cómo describir un viaje

páginas 36 y 37

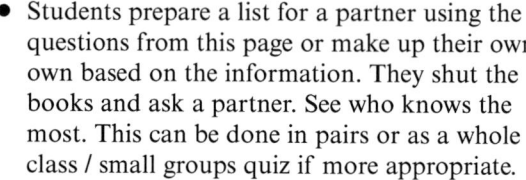

Planner

➤ **Objectives**
- Discussing the pros and cons of various means of transport

➤ **Resources**
Students' Book, pages 36–37
CD 1, track 32
Grammar Workbook, pages 9–12
Activity sheets 8–11

➤ **Key language**
un barco, un caballo, una camioneta, un coche, una moto, el problema, un viaje
emocionante, juntos/las, peligroso/la
caminar, hacer autostop
a pie, cualquier, más tarde, todavía

➤ **Skills**
- How to improve reading skills of longer texts

➤ **Grammar**
- Comparatives and superlatives

➤ **PLTS**
Students' Book, page 36, activity 4,
Team Workers
Students' Book, page 37, activity 11,
Creative Thinkers

➤ **Starters**
- Display a large map of South America, and ask students if they can name any of the countries, and if they know where they are. Alternatively supply them with a list of the country names and get them to decide in pairs or groups which country goes where. If possible, display a map of the UK to scale alongside to give students an idea of the size of the place. This could be done as a pre-unit homework.
- Ask students to research a list of statements (in Spanish if possible) about South America and the rest of the class have to decide if they are true or false, e.g. *There are X countries, X countries speak Spanish, Argentina is X times bigger than the UK, country X won the World Cup in X*, etc. Each student or pair could produce just two or three statements to make up the whole quiz.
- Watch a part of the film. If you can't easily find a copy, it is always possible to search for clips on the internet.
- Play preterite tense word association. The teacher calls out or writes on the board part of a verb in the preterite, and students have to call out or write down the first thing they can think of to make a short sentence e.g. *comió – patatas fritas, nadé – en la piscina*. Make sure you choose familiar verbs for this activity.
- Reading strategies: It is a good idea to get to grips with a difficult text by reading through it quickly, looking for different things each time.

This way students build up a picture of the text, and avoid getting stuck. It focuses on what you DO understand. It is not necessary to write down all the words – working in pairs works well, as the teacher can "listen in" and monitor what pupils are finding.
This strategy is then followed by focusing on identifying the most important points, then focusing on specific details.
Later, there should be a linear (word-by-word) reading, making sure pupils focus on pronunciation.

➤ **Plenaries**
- The teacher gives students a few words, and they have to produce a statement in the superlative e.g. *deporte – peligroso – el puenting es el deporte más peligroso que conozco.*
- Students write a mini-story with six provided verbs in the preterite e.g. *Fui a la playa y nadé en el mar. Comí una hamburguesa y bebí una coca-cola etc.* For added complexity, throw in some unrelated nouns e.g. *elefante, garaje* etc which have to be included to make the story absurd. Students could illustrate their story as a kind of surreal cartoon strip.
- Students' Book, page 37, activity 11. Students write about the South American journey. Make a list in class first of the reasons for doing such a journey, what type of people would be interested in it, the potential problems they might encounter, and why they might prefer a different type of journey. Get them to draw up lists or make spidergrams of useful vocabulary and structures from the spread to accompany these reasons before they start writing.
- Students' Book, page 37, activity 12. Students decide who wrote which text. They should give reasons for their choice e.g. *Pienso que Mark ha escrito el texto A por que le gusta mucho la aventura.*

1 **Busca rápidamente en el texto.**

5–9

- Students scan the text for the following information. To make it easier, if they have the text on paper, they can underline the different aspects in different colours, or this can be done on the board after they have reaad it in pairs.

Answers:
a Alta Gracia, América del Sur, Argentina, Chile, Perú, Ecuador, Colombia, Venezuela y Panamá, Chuquicamata, hospital para leprosos, el río Amazonas, Miami, Ernesto Guevara, Alberto Granado, la gente de los países, los obreros, moto, caminar, autostop, camionetas, camionetas para el transporte de animales, barco, avión

b 1952, catorce mil kilómetros, 500cc, 1936, tres mil kilómetros, cuatro kilómetros

c para, y, pero, entonces, Empezaron, después, entonces, Más tarde, Una noche, Al fin

d joven, romántico, nuevas, algunos, mecánicos, grandes, extrema, peligrosa, para, por, De, a, con, en

e salió, acompañó, recurrieron, fueron, Empezaron, empezó, Tuvieron que, hicieron, conocieron, visitaron, viajaron, compartieron, trabajaron, cruzó, Salieron, se separaron, voló, Era, podían, trabajaban, Viajaban

2 Identifica los aspectos básicos.

- Students focus on the main aspects of the text.

Answers:
la ruta y el viaje De Argentina, fueron a Chile, luego al Perú, Ecuador, Colombia, Venezuela y Panamá, era un viaje de dos jóvenes en busca de nuevas experiencias
el tema principal de cada párrafo la ruta, como cambiaba el viaje, la visita a la mina, Perú y el final del viaje

6–9

3 Identifica detalles específicos.

- Students search for specific information.

Answers:
incidentes que ocurrieron la moto empezó a tener problemas mecánicos, visitaron la mina de Chuquicamata, trabajaron en un hospital para leprosos en Perú, Ernesto cruzó el río Amazonas nadando
opiniones o valores dos jóvenes llenos de esperanza, El contacto con los obreros y campesinos empezó a cambiar la filosofía de los dos amigos

6–9

4 Con un(a) compañero/a, lee los párrafos en voz alta, poniendo atención en la pronunciación.

- Students now take it in turns to practise pronunciation by reading the text aloud to each other. The teacher can model a sentence or two first, then the students practise, and the listener of the pair says where the reader differs from the model and how. The first person in the pair then listens to see if the second person can improve on this, having heard the first person.

4–6

PLTS

5 Mira las frases con palabras en negrita. Decide si son palabras que ya conoces, puedes adivinar, puedes ignorar o hay que buscar en el diccionario.

- Students look back at the highlighted words and classify them as described.

5–8

6 ¿Puedes descifra cada frase?

- Students give a loose translation of the phrases with the highlighted words. They can do this individually or collaborate in pairs and feed back to the class.

5–8

7 Evalúa en inglés tu nivel de comprensión: ¿Cuánto entiendes? ¿Qué grado de dificultad tiene el texto? ¿Cuáles son las estrategias más efectivas?

- This is an opportunity to discuss with the students how to deal with a text of this length and complexity, and which of the above strategies they found most useful.

5–9

8 Lee el texto, y escoge el adjetivo mejor para cada forma de transporte que menciona.

- Students read the text and fill in the gaps with the best adjective.

Answers: **1** práctico, **2** conveniente, **3** emocionante, **4** incómodo, **5** peligrosa

5–9

9 Estas frases están revueltas. Escríbelas de forma correcta.

- Students re-write the sentences correctly.

Answers: **a** El avión es la forma de transporte más rápido. **b** La mejor manera de viajar es en coche. **c** Ir a caballo es la manera menos cómoda. **d** El mejor momento fue llegar a mi casa.

5–7

10 Escucha a los cuatro jóvenes. ¿A quiénes les gustaría hacer este viaje?

- Students read the advert – check they understand it – and listen to decide which people would like to go on this journey.

5–9

 CD 1, track 32   **página 37, actividad 10**

1 Paco ¿Viajar por América Latina en moto? Pues, me gustaría conocer los países de América del Sur, pero en moto parece bastante incómodo y hasta puede ser peligroso. Ya sé que tendría problemas con mi madre para poder ir. Creo que prefiero esperar y viajar cuando sea, mayor, y de una manera más práctica.

2 Raquel Me parece bastante emocionante, y supongo que puedes escoger cómo vas a viajar. Me gusta la aventura, y un viaje así puede cambiar tu vida. ¡Tienes que hacerlo!

3 Estéban ¿A quién no le gustaría una experiencia así? Puede ser difícil, peligroso o incómodo, pero así es viajar, y hay que hacerlo cuando eres joven. No puedes pasar toda tu vida en un solo lugar.

4 Isabel A mí me gusta la aventura verdadera. Me gustaría salir de mi propia puerta y a ver hasta dónde llego. No necesito seguir en los pasos de nadie, ni una compañía para organizarlo todo. Así no lo hizo Ernesto Guevara, y yo tampoco.

Remate

11 **Write your own opinion about the trip around South America. Compare the trip with you own experiences, or mention your ambitions or dreams.**

5–9

- Encourage students to make use of all the language on the spread; a copy of the above transcript may be useful. Remind them to give reasons. Tell them to personalise their work with a journey they have done / would like to do.

Success criteria activity 11:
- *students give information accurately and in the appropriate style*
- *students express personal opinions and justify points of view*

- *students use a variety of vocabulary and structures*
- *students use different tenses or time frames*

12 **Now read the opinions of the rest of the class and try to guess who wrote what.**

5–9

- This can be done individually, or with pairs or groups looking at a selection of texts and identifying them.

Success criteria activity 12:
- *students communicate effectively and accurately*
- *students express personal opinions and justify points of view*
- *students deal with unpredictable elements*
- *students use different tenses or time frames*

Gramática en acción   páginas 38 y 39

Planner

➤ **Objectives**
- Using verbs more confidently in the past tense

➤ **Resources**
Students' Book, pages 38–39
Exam Skills Workbook, page 29 (F), page 30 (H)
Grammar Workbook, pages 9–12, 22, 43–47
Activity sheet 12
Resources and Planning OxBox CD-ROM

➤ **Grammar**
- *Tú* and *usted*
- Preterite and imperfect tenses
- Comparatives and superlatives

➤ **PLTS**
Students' Book, page 39, activity 4,
Reflective Learners, Effective Participators
Students' Book, page 39, activity 11, *Self Managers*

➤ **The preterite and the imperfect**

1 **Separate these verbs into preterite or imperfect.**
- Students should read through the grammar box and explanation before doing this activity.

Answers:
preterite: decidió, viajaron, compró
imperfect: trabajaba, era, vivíamos

2 **Use them to complete these sentences. Then translate the sentences into English.**

Answers: **a** viajaron, **b** vivíamos, **c** era, **d** trabajaba, **e** compró, **f** decidió

a They travelled from Argentina to Colombia.
b We used to live in Madrid.
c The journey was long and difficult.
d He used to work in his uncle's company.
e He bought houses in different countries in the world.
f He decided to move to the city.

3 **Translate these sentences into Spanish.**

Answers:
a Compramos un billete par el avión.
b Viajabas del Terminal 3.
c Hicieron un Terminal neuvo.

d Viajaba en el tren.
e Iba en coche.

➤ **Ser and estar**

4 **Explain the choice of *ser* or *estar* in these sentences.**

PLTS   *Answers:* **a** permanent quality, **b** temporary status, **c** permanent quality, **d** position, **e** temporary status

5 **Translate these sentences into Spanish. Warning: One of them is not *ser* or *estar*!**

Answers:
a El pueblo es muy concurrido.
b El colegio está en el centro del pueblo.
c ¿Hay un museo en el pueblo?
d Es un pueblo viejo.

➤ **The comparative**

6 **Write out comparative sentences.**
- Students use the prompts to complete the sentences.

Answers: **b** El autobús es más lento que el avión. **c** El tren es más fácil que el autobús. **d** La bici es tan lento que el autobús. **e** Viajar en tren es menos sana que caminar. **f** Viajar en tren es tan caro que viajar en avión.

➤ The superlative

7 Translate the following sentences into Spanish, using the superlative.

Answers: **a** Es el viaje más peligroso del mundo. **b** Es la frase más ridícula posible. **c** Es el transporte menos cómodo. **d** Es el mejor conductor. **e** Es la situación peor que se puede imaginar.

8 Write sentences to describe somewhere you have visited a couple of times. Use the preterite to say what you did there. Use the imperfect to talk about what it used to be like. Use the comparative and the superlative to make comparisons with other places.

PLTS • Do some whole class work with students first if necessary, modelling a decription, or giving the

students some bullet points and asking them to put them into full sentences in Spanish, using some examples of past tense verbs, comparatives and superlatives. Ask for ideas from the class for trips done in the past, then tell them to write their own descriptions.

Success criteria activity 8:
- *students give information accurately and in the appropriate style*
- *students express personal opinions and justify points of view*
- *students use a variety of vocabulary and structures*
- *students use different tenses or time frames*

Habilidades

página 40

Planner

➤ Objectives
- Developing reading skills and learning strategies

➤ Resources
Students' Book, page 40
CD 1, track 29
Exam Skills Workbook, page 30 (F), page 31 (H)
Activity sheet 13
Resources and Planning OxBox CD-ROM

➤ Skills
- Finding the right information to answer a question
- Identifying specific details
- Deciphering the meaning of a sentence without understanding every word
- Identifying people's opinions
- Predicting what you are going to hear
- Making accurate inferences
- Predicting and keeping track

➤ PLTS
Students' Book, page 40, activity 1,
Team Workers
Students' Book, page 40, activity 6,
Reflective Learners

➤ Leer

1 Read for gist.

❏ Read the following passage through once and discuss what it is about with a partner. What title woud you give it based on your first impressions?

 • Remind students that at this stage they do not need to understand it all, but focus on what they *do* understand.

2 Read for specific details.

❏ If there are comprehension questions, you only need to understand enough of the text to answer them. Read the text again before attempting these.
- Encourage students to focus just on the answers to the questions.

Answers: **a** safe and peaceful, **b** gangs come and race cars in the streets, **c** in violence, fighting and shouting, **d** they run away and the police arrive too late

3 Deal with words you don't know.

❏ If you try to read every sentence, you need to decide whether to guess, ignore, or look up words. Look at the sentences in which the following words are used. Write down how you are going to deal with each of the words that you don't know.
- Students should tackle this is pairs or groups and share their techniques with the rest of the class.

➤ Escuchar

4 Listen for gist.

❏ Listen to the recording once to get the gist and see if the order of the questions is the same as the order in which things are mentioned in the recording. Concentrate on picking upt important information, not answering the questions as you go.

CD 1, track 33   **página 40, actividad 4**

> Pues donde yo vivo, antes era un lugar súper tranquilo, pero ya ha cambiado totalmente. Se ha vuelto muy inseguro, aun de día. Roban en los supermercados y en las tiendas como si nada. Quiero mudarme a otro barrio, pero ya nadie quiere vivir aquí y no puedo vender mi casa.

5   Focus on the questions.

❏ Look at the comprehension questions and predict what you may hear in the recording. For each question, make a list of any nouns, verbs and phrases that are likely to come up, as well as more general things like 'expressions of time'.

Answers: **a** very peaceful, **b** very unsafe, **c** there's lots of shop lifting, **d** move to another area, **e** nobody wants to live here and she can't sell her house

➤ **Aprender**

6   Use targeted strategies to learn new vocabulary.

❏ Put the strategies below in order of how frequently you use them. Be honest!

PLTS   ● Remind students that these techniques make it easier to learn, and are not just more work.

Put them to the test. Try out different strategies as you work through this book and see which gets the best results.

● You could draw up a class list of techniques most used, and one of techniques likely to be most useful, and look at the differences.
● Students can pick a couple of techniques each week to try out, or you can divide the class up into small groups who all use a different technique on the same items to compare what actually works best.

Escenario   página 41

Planner

➤ **Objectives**
● An email to a Spanish friend who is going to visit.
● A humorous scene where everyone wants to help a confused traveller.

➤ **Resources**
Students' Book, page 73
Exam Skills Workbook, pages 27–28 (F), pages 28–29 (H)
Assessment sheets 1–8
Resources and Planning OxBox CD-ROM

➤ **Skills**
● Writing practice
● Speaking practice

➤ **PLTS**
Students' Book, page 41, Escenario Oral, *Effective Participators*
Students' Book, page 41, Escenario Escrito, *Independent Enquirers*

➤ **Oral**

Act out a sketch about a tourist who asks for advice about transport but ends up totally confused.

PLTS   ● Students follow the instructions to create the sketch. Parallel classes can perform it to each other. Afterwards, the audience have to be able to say what was going on.
● *GCSE Grades A*-C*
● *Grade C Students use past, present and future tenses. They express opinions, and deal with some unpredictability.*
● *Grade A Students express and justify opinions. They use a variety of vocabulary and structure in longer speech sequences.*

➤ **Escrito**

Write an email to a Spanish friend who is coming to visit.

PLTS   ● Students follow the instructions to write the email. They can do a research homework first where they try to find somewhere in Spain similar to where they live in the UK. Remind them to refer back through this and previous units for vocabulary and structures.
● *GCSE Grades A*-C*
● *Grade C Students use opinions and past, present and future tenses, both factually and imaginatively. Register is appropriate and style is basic.*
● *Grade A Students write factually and imaginatively using longer sequences and a range of vocabulary and structure. They express and justify opinions in an appropriate style.*

Vocabulario   página 42

This is a summary of key language from the unit, organised by spread and theme. Students can use it for reference while working on the unit, and as an aid to learning vocabulary.

Lectura

Planner

➤ **Objectives**
- Talking about transport and your local area
- To encourage independent reading and develop reading strategies.
- These pages also provide alternative class and homework material for students who work quickly and require extension work.

➤ **Resources**
Students' Book, page 173–174

➤ **PLTS**
Students' Book, page 173, activity 2, *Independent Enquirers*
Students' Book, page 174, activity 4, *Reflective Learners*

➤ **Lectura A – La Carretera Nacional**

1a Lee la caricatura y busca estas palabras en español.
- Students read the cartoon and look for the words.

Answers: **a** tráfico, **b** hoy, **c** averiado, **d** atasco, **e** funciona

1b Lee y deduce el significado de noticias, sin, bajo control, todo va bien, no entiendo.

PLTS
- Students work out from context the meaning of the given words.

Answers: **a** news, **b** without, **c** under control, **d** everything is going fine, **e** I don't understand

1c Explica la situación en inglés y por qué ha ocurrido la confusión.
- You can put the students into groups, and time them to see who works it out first.

4 Lee el texto sobre la Carretera Nacional rápidamente varias veces, buscando palabras asociadas con transport, weather, numbers, places.
- Students look for groups of words in the text.

Answers: **a** carretera, coches normales, vehículos todo terreno, **b** tormentas, lluvias intensas, **c** Carretera Nacional 6, 24 kilómetros, 50 kilómetros, **d** Mogador, Tehuachinango, Rancho Seco

5 Lee el texto en voz alta, poniendo atención en la pronunciación.
- If possible, students record themselves speaking. They mark themselves, or another student, against a model recording.

6 Busca en español *National Road, all-terrain vehicles, intense rain, river, diversion.*
- Students look for the words in Spanish.

Answers: **a** Carretera Nacional, **b** vehículos todo terreno, **c** lluvias intensas, **d** el río, **e** una desviación

7 Decide si es *a weather report, a warning about a closed road, directions to get to Mogador.*
- Students decide what type of text it is.

Answer: b

8 Haz corresponder con las palabras en negrita.
- Students match the phrases to the highlighted ones in the text.

Answers: **a** can't get past – no pueden pasar, **b** has burst its banks – se ha desbordado, **c** is closed – está cerrada, **d** cross by the bridge – cruzar el río por el puente, **e** have destroyed – han destruido

9 Contesta en inglés.
- Students answer in English.

Answers: **a** The National Route 6 is closed. **b** The storms and intense rains caused it. **c** The river Nazas has flooded and destroyed part of the road. **d** You have to take a 50 km detour via the bridge at Rancho Seco.

➤ **Lectura B – Donde vivo**

1 Escoge tres de estas estrategias para ayudarte a leer el texto.
- Students decide which strategies to use to help them understand the text.

2 Contesta en inglés.
- Students answer the questions in English.

Answers: **a** He lives in a flat. **b** No, he has to go to the town centre on the bus for that. **c** He goes to the café on the corner. **d** He would like a park. **e** They get bored and cause trouble. **f** He would like to live in the centre so he could visit the shops and walk along the river.

3 Lee en silencio las cartas de arriba. ¿Cuánto entiendes?
- Students read the letters to see how much they can understand.

4 Escoge tres estrategias de actividad 1 para entender mejor las cartas.

PLTS
- Students look back at the reading strategies. They can highlight the parts that they now also understand.

5 Escribe un resumen en inglés.
- Students write a summary of the texts in their own words in English.

Unit 2A Una vida sana y activa   Overview grid

Spread	Contexts	Skills	Grammar	Vocabulary
Spread title	• Topic areas covered within the unit	• Key skills focus	• Grammar covered in the unit	Key vocabulary
pages 44–45 **Cómo decidir el mejor deporte para ti**	• Choosing the best sport for you	• Adding emphasis when speaking to sound more convincing	• Impersonal verbs	un casco, los discapacitados, el equipo, la escalada, la espeleolgía, el estilo libre, la mariposa, la natación, el nivel, el puenting, el piragüismo, el pulmón, las ruedas, el tobillo apretado/a, convencional, emocionante, innovador(a), orgulloso/a, peligroso/a zambullir
pages 46–47 **Cómo comparar a deportistas 'héroes'**	• Comparing sporting heroes	• Adding emphasis when speaking to sound more convincing	• The preterite	la carrera, los competidores, un deportista, un disparate, el entrenador, el ganador, el palmarés, el piloto despeinado/a, muerto/a, mundial apoyar, despedir(se) de, enfadarse con, morirse, murió, tener éxito, tener razón además, a pesar de
pages 48–49 **Cómo elegir un estilo de vida sano**	• Talking about a healthy lifestyle	• Writing longer texts	• *desde hace*, imperative	el almuerzo, la cena, los dulces, la merienda, el plátano, una régimen perezoso/a adelgazar, dejar de, descansar, estar en forma, llevar tiempo, ponerse a dieta, relajarse, seguir en los pasos de, solía comer desde hace, en cambio, enhorabuena, nunca
pages 50–51 **Cómo explicar lo que te duele**	• Talking about being ill and injured	• Emphasising key words	• The perfect tense	el césped, una cita, el codo, el consejo, la cruz roja, el dedo gordo, el dolor de cabeza, la espalda, un esparadrapo, la garganta, el hombro, el jarabe, la muela, los primeros auxilios mareado/a, torpe sangrar de la nariz, tropezar contra, trotar de madrugada
pages 52–53 **Cómo disfrutar de actividades al aire libre**	• Talking about activities you do in the open air	• Using memory aids to make learning easier	• Adverbs	la altura, el buceo (con tubo), el buzo, un potro, el senderismo encerrado/a, miedoso/a gozar, pasarlo bomba, lanzarse, lograr, quedarse adentro, afuera, al principio, anteayer, pasado mañana aunque, de modo que, también qué lástima
pages 54–55 **Gramática en acción**	• Reviewing and learning verbs		• Using verbs impersonally like *me interesa(n)* • Using reflexive constuctions like *se juega(n)* • Using the irregular form of the preterite tense • Using time clauses like *desde hace* • Using the perfect tense • Using adverbs and phrases of time and place	
page 56 **Habilidades**	• Sounding convincing when you speak	• Using intensifiers to sound convincing • Stressing certain words / using stress to sound convincing • Using descriptions and linking words to avoid short sentences • Using quantifiers and expressions of frequency to add colour to your writing • Using determiners correctly		
page 57 **Escenario**	• Give an oral presentation on healthy living, and a written one on outdoor activities. • Write a diary entry about what you did on your sporting holiday.			
page 58 **Vocabulario**	• Summary of key vocabulary for the unit.			
pages 175–176 **Reading Pages**	A new Olympic sport, a star tennis player: • to encourage independent reading and to develop reading strategies. • to provide alternative class and homework material for students who finish other activities quickly.			

2A Una vida sana y activa

Unit Objectives

Contexts: sports and sporting heros, healthy lifestyle, saying where it hurts, activities in the open air
Skills focus: using intensifiers, stressing certain words and using stress to sound convincing; using descriptions, linking words, quantifiers, expressions of frequency and determiners; how to learn new words and verb tenses
Grammar: impersonal verbs, reflexive constructions, irregular preterites, time clauses, perfect tense, adverbs and phrases of time and place

Controlled assessment opportunities

Writing: Students' Book, page 45, activity 5
Speaking: Students' Book, page 47, activity 6
Writing: Students' Book, page 49, activity 6
Speaking: Students' Book, page 51, activity 4
Speaking: Students' Book, page 53, activity 4

*See also **GCSE Spanish for OCR Assessment OxBox CD-ROM**.*

An introduction to the unit página 43

- *Aim*: To introduce the themes of the unit and encourage students to think about the reasons for learning Spanish.
- The opening page is designed with captions, pictures and page cross-references to provide a preview of what is to come:

	Students' Book
Cómo decidir el mejor deporte para ti	page 44
Cómo comparar a deportistas 'héroes'	page 46
Cómo elegir un estilo de vida sano	page 48
Cómo explicar lo que te duele	page 50
Cómo disfrutar de actividades al aire libre	page 52
Gramática en acción – improving your use and understanding of Spanish	page 54
Habilidades – increasing your language skills for fluency	page 56
Escenario – promociona la vida saludable Escenario – describir un incidente al centro de actividades	page 57

- Allow time for students to read the questions and cross-refer to the relevant pages of the Students' Book. They could do this individually or in pairs / small groups, followed by whole-class discussion.
- This spread also provides an opportunity for students to recap on familiar language. Ask them to think about language they already know that might be useful when working on the themes of the unit.

- Mindmap any language they produce, and if possible, keep it on display as reference as you progress through the unit. It can be added to at intervals as new language becomes familiar.
- At the end of work on the unit, allow time for students to return to this spread and repeat the mind-mapping process, this time including what they have learned over the course of the unit. Get them to answer the questions in their own words, and encourage them to use the results for revision purposes.
- Ask them what they found difficult, interesting etc. What do they think are the important things they have learned in this unit? What do they still need to improve on?
- If time permits, get the students to redesign the page. How would they set it out so it reflects the unit? How would they make it attractive to other learners of their age? How would they make it easy to follow? What would they include in terms of text, pictures, captions, page references? Ask them to imagine they are producing material for next year's class who will be learning the same thing – what would they have found it useful to know?

¿Por qué aprender el español? Para hablar de deporte y la vida sana.
- Students share any experiences they have had of taking part in sport and outdoor activities, and discuss what a healthy lifestyle involves in terms of eating and activity.
- Ask them to consider what sort of language they would need to discuss these topics with someone in Spanish, or how they could participate in sporting activities in Spain e.g. finding out information in a sports' centre.

Cómo decidir el mejor deporte para ti

páginas 44 y 45

Planner

➤ **Objectives**
- Choosing the best sport for you

➤ **Resources**
Students' Book, pages 44–45
CD 1, track 37
Grammar Workbook, page 66
Activity sheets 15–18

➤ **Key language**
un casco, los discapacitados, el equipo, la escalada, la espeleolgia, el estilo libre, la mariposa, la natación, el nivel, el puenting, el piragüismo, el pulmón, las ruedas, el tobillo
apretado/a, convencional, emocionante, innovador(a), orgulloso/a, peligroso/a
zambullir

➤ **Skills**
- Adding emphasis to sound more convincing

➤ **Grammar**
- Impersonal verbs

➤ **PLTS**
Students' Book, page 45, activity 4,
Effective Participators
Student's Book, page 45, activity 5,
Independent Enquirers

➤ **Starters**
- Students' Book page 44, activity 1. Students brainstorm sports and classify them into types. Broaden this out to include any sports they know, not just the ones in the pictures. This can also be a pre-unit homework.

- Not every student is a sports fan. Give students the opportunity to set up a 2nd Life type alter-ego, through whom they carry out the activities in the unit. Encourage them to create a profile and portrait of this person.
- Students' Book page 45, activity 2. Before listening to the phone calls, ask students to write down / look up three words for each picture connected to that sport that they might expect to hear. After, ask how many they heard.
- Play sports hangman in pairs, groups or as a class. Encourage students to use the more unusual ones, not just *tenis*. Students get a point for each sport guessed correctly, or if no one guesses, the "hangman" gets the point.

➤ **Plenaries**
- The class produces a sports guide. They choose or are given at random one or more sports, and produce an illustrated description of the sport. The results should be collated and displayed on a "sports wall".
- Students write short, inaccurate statements about sport e.g. *El fútbol se juega con una raqueta.* Other students have to correct them.
- Give out a transcript of the activity 2 phone calls, cut up into separate statements. Students re-make the conversation jigsaw, and listen to see if they are correct.
- Students' Book page 45 activity 5. Students answer questions on their prepared presentation about a chosen sport. The Teacher could give out a list of questions in advance so students can prepare possible answers. If students have not necessarily chosen a sport they do like, the others could guess if they are telling the truth or not.

1a **Mira los iconos en la página 44. ¿Cuántos deportes conoces ya en español? Escribe una lista.**

- Students list all the sports shown that they already know in Spanish. They could do this individually and pool the answers, or they could work in groups against the clock.

2–4

Answers: la canoa, el todo terreno, el golf, la equitación, el surf, la vela, el parapente, el monopatín, el trampolín, el voleibol, el go-karting, el fútbol, el tenís, el hockey en silla de ruedas, el rugby, la baile, el patinaje

1b **¿De memoria, cuántos deportes puede nombrar que se juegan con ...?**

- Students classify the sports, and any others they can remember, according to how they are played.

2–4

1c **Usa tu diccionario para completar tu lista.**

- Students use a dictionary to complete their lists if necessary.

4–7

2a **Escucha las llamadas telefónicas e identifica el deporte.**

- Students listen and identify the sport. Ask what clues students used to make their choice e.g. *natación* in the first one.

5–8

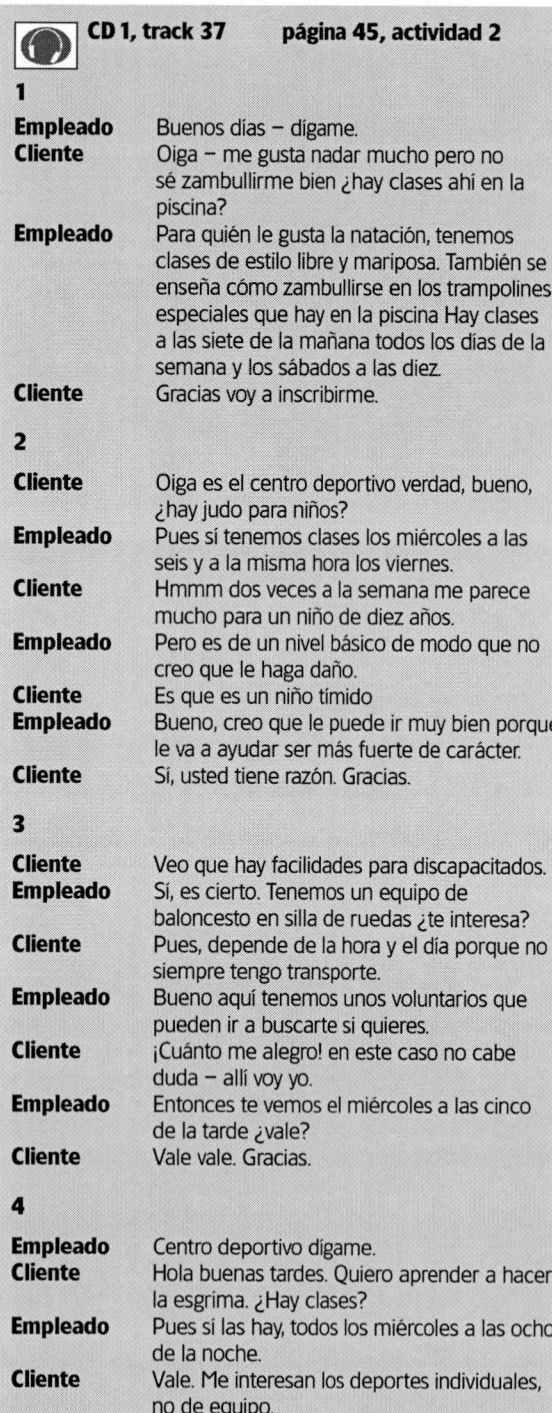

CD 1, track 37 **página 45, actividad 2**

1

Empleado	Buenos días – dígame.
Cliente	Oiga – me gusta nadar mucho pero no sé zambullirme bien ¿hay clases ahí en la piscina?
Empleado	Para quién le gusta la natación, tenemos clases de estilo libre y mariposa. También se enseña cómo zambullirse en los trampolines especiales que hay en la piscina Hay clases a las siete de la mañana todos los días de la semana y los sábados a las diez.
Cliente	Gracias voy a inscribirme.

2

Cliente	Oiga es el centro deportivo verdad, bueno, ¿hay judo para niños?
Empleado	Pues sí tenemos clases los miércoles a las seis y a la misma hora los viernes.
Cliente	Hmmm dos veces a la semana me parece mucho para un niño de diez años.
Empleado	Pero es de un nivel básico de modo que no creo que le haga daño.
Cliente	Es que es un niño tímido
Empleado	Bueno, creo que le puede ir muy bien porque le va a ayudar ser más fuerte de carácter.
Cliente	Sí, usted tiene razón. Gracias.

3

Cliente	Veo que hay facilidades para discapacitados.
Empleado	Sí, es cierto. Tenemos un equipo de baloncesto en silla de ruedas ¿te interesa?
Cliente	Pues, depende de la hora y el día porque no siempre tengo transporte.
Empleado	Bueno aquí tenemos unos voluntarios que pueden ir a buscarte si quieres.
Cliente	¡Cuánto me alegro! en este caso no cabe duda – allí voy yo.
Empleado	Entonces te vemos el miércoles a las cinco de la tarde ¿vale?
Cliente	Vale vale. Gracias.

4

Empleado	Centro deportivo dígame.
Cliente	Hola buenas tardes. Quiero aprender a hacer la esgrima. ¿Hay clases?
Empleado	Pues sí las hay, todos los miércoles a las ocho de la noche.
Cliente	Vale. Me interesan los deportes individuales, no de equipo.
Empleado	Pues en este caso la esgrima te va bien ¿verdad?
Cliente	Sí, creo que es el mejor deporte para mí.

5

Cliente	Muy buenas tardes. Quiero inscribirme en clases de yoga.
Empleado	Está bien. Tenemos clases a las once los sábados por la mañana.
Cliente	Esto me va bien de hora y día. ¿No es demasiado complicado verdad?
Empleado	No, es bastante fácil si se concentra bien.
Cliente	Fenomenal, es lo que necesito – concentrarme en algo saludable.
Empleado	Entonces, le inscribo para este sábado que viene.
Cliente	Vale gracias.

6

Cliente	Hola me interesa hacer deporte pero no sé cuál.
Empleado	Bueno a ver –¿te interesan los deportes que se juegan con raqueta o con palo, o prefieres hacer algo diferente?
Cliente	Pues me gustaría jugar a la pelota vasca pero no se cómo se juega.
Empleado	Caramba – es sí un poco difícil para una persona tan jóven se juega con dos o cuatro jugadores y se necesita una cesta o chistera para lanzar la pelota y se pega la pelota contra una pared que se llama el frontón.
Cliente	Me parece emocionante y se juega muy rápido ¿verdad?
Empleado	Así es – se dice que es el juego más rápido del mundo.
Cliente	Me interesa mucho ¿cuando puedo empezar?
Empleado	Lo siento mucho pero aquí no se puede jugar. Hay que ir al Club Deportivo de Pelota Vasca.

Answers: **a** 3, **b** 5, **c** 6, **d** 1, **e** 4, **f** 2

2b **Escucha otra vez y copia y completa la tabla.**

- Students listen again and complete the table.

Answers:

Deporte	Cuándo	Veces
la zambullida	las 7h por semana, las 10h el sábado	6
el judo	las 18h los miércoles y los viernes	2
el baloncesto en silla de ruedas	las 17h los miércoles	
la esgrima	las 20h los miércoles	
la yoga	las 11h los sábados	
la pelota vasca	Hay que ir al Club Deportivo de Pelota Vasca.	

2c **Escucha otra vez y apunta estas palabras en español.**

- Students listen a third time and note down the Spanish for the given words. Differentiation: some students may need the transcript for support at this stage.

6–8

Answers: **1** estilo libre, la mariposa, la zambullida; **2** dos veces a la semana, de un nivel básico; **3** un discapacitado, una silla de ruedas, no cabe duda; **4** los deportes individuales, los deportes de equipo; **5** inscribirse en un club, bastante fácil, saludable;

2d Escucha la última llamada otra vez y explica cómo se juega.

7–9

- Listen to the last call again, and explain how this sport is played. Again, some students may need to follow the transcript as they listen here.

Answer: Se juega con dos o cuatro jugadores y se necesita una cesta o chistera para lanzar la pelota y se pega la pelota contra una pared que se llama el frontón.

3a Lee las descripciones y empáréjalas con una imagen.

4–8

- Students read the descriptions and match them to the correct pictures.

Answers: **a** 3 escalada, **b** 4 puenting, **c** 1 ciclismo, **d** 2 carrera libre

3b Escribe un párrafo similar para los dos deportes ilustrados que sobran.

5–8

- Students write similar paragraphs for the two extra pictures. Tell them to use structures and vocabulary from 3a where helpful.

Remate

4 Guess the sport!

 PLTS

4–9

- Students take it in turns to describe a sport to their partner who has to guess what it is.

5 Choose a different sport and write a brief paragraph about it.

- Students write a short paragraph about an unusual sport.

Success criteria activities 4 & 5:

 PLTS
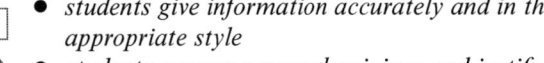

4–8

- *students give information accurately and in the appropriate style*
- *students express personal opinions and justify points of view*
- *students use a variety of vocabulary and structures*

Cómo comparar a deportistas 'héroes'

páginas 46 y 47

Planner

➤ Objectives
- Comparing sporting heroes

➤ Resources
Students' Book, pages 46–47
CD 1, tracks 38–39
Grammar Workbook, page 43
Activity sheets 15–18

➤ Key language
*la carrera, los competidores, un deportista,
un disparate, el entrenador, el ganador, el palmarés,
el piloto
despeinado/a, muerto/a, mundial
apoyar, despedir(se) de, enfadarse con, morirse,
murió, tener éxito, tener razón
además, a pesar de*

➤ Skills
- Adding emphasis when speaking to sound more convincing

➤ Grammar
- The preterite

➤ PLTS
Students' Book, page 47, activity 5b,
Reflective Learners
Students' Book, page 47, activity 7,
Self-Managers

➤ Starters
- In class, draw up a spidergram with the words *héroes de deporte* in the middle, surrounded by names, which in turn are surrounded by their sport and achievements.
- Students' Book page 46. Students look at the photos, and say what the sports are in Spanish. They guess a date for each picture, and after doing the listening, see how close they were.
- Students' Book page 47, activity 4. Before doing the gap fill activity, students read through the text and underline (on a paper copy) or note down any words they already understand. Get them to summarise in English what they think the text is about, and if they think the experience was a success or not.
- The teacher says a few short sentences with the emphasis in the wrong place, and asks the students why they sound wrong. Write a number of similar phrases on the board and ask the students to pick where the emphasis should go, then read them out to see if they sound right.

➤ **Plenaries**

- Quick-fire quiz. Give students a few minutes to re-read the section on spelling changes in the preterite, then call out verbs in quick succession. Students have to write down the correct form of the verb.
- Students' Book page 47, activity 5. After doing the activity, write *Los futbolistas ganan demasiado dinero hoy en día* on the board, and underneath draw two columns headed *Sí* and *No*. Students give reasons supporting either point of view which are added to the table. Students use the table to write a paragraph either agreeing or disagreeing with the statement.

- Students' Book page 47, activity 6. Students prepare a presentation on a sporting hero (or anti-hero), explaining and justifying their choice. The teacher can give them questions to help structure their presentation.
- Students Book page 47, activity 7. Students write a comparison between a past and a present sporting hero. Aim for a variety of sports and personalities. Ask how many of the people featured the students recognise or know about.

1a **Escucha y anota los nombres y el deporte.**

6–9

- Students listen and note down the answers in the grid. Listening for names is quite hard, and it would help students to write the names randomly on the board to choose from.

CD 1, track 38   **página 46, actividad 1**

1 Jóven Señorita, por favor ¿Quién es ese tipo tan viejo en la photo?

Señorita Un poco de respeto por favor – este señor fue el mejor piloto de todos los tiempos. Se llamaba Juan Manuel Fangio y vivió en Argentina.

Jóven ¿Está vivo todavía?

Señorita No, murió en 1995 todavía con su récord intacto – ganó la Fórmula 1 cuatro veces consecutivos de 1954 a 1957 y la quinta vez unos años más tarde, de modo que se le dice pentacampeón mundial.

Jóven ¿Con qué marca corrió?

Señorita Corrió con las marcas Alfa Romeo, Maserati, Ferrari y Mercedes Benz.

Jóven Y hoy es Michael Schumacher quien lleva la corona; pero mi favorito por supuesto es Alonso – él también es supercampeón.

2 Jóven Yo soy tenista de modo que sigo a Rafa – no hay – nadie mejor y va a ser el mejor deportista español de todos los tiempos.

Señorita Bueno puede, pero este otro aquí se llama Manolo Santana y fue el mejor amateur en los años sesenta.

Jóven ¿A ver, qué hizo comparado con Rafa?

Señorita Ganó dos veces Roland Garros el Open de los EEUU y también fue ganador de Wimbledon en 1966 además todavía sigue dirigiendo el tenis español.

Jóven De verdad tuvo bastante éxito entonces.

3 Jóven ¿Y ese ciclista quién es?

Señorita Es Miguel Induraín otro héroe español – su lista de triunfos es fenomenal. Ganó el Tour de Francia cinco años consecutivos de 1991 a 1995.

Jóven Y hoy en día es Sastre quien gana las carreras de ciclismo.

Señorita Claro, pero en los tiempos pasados cuando corría Federico Bahamontes (en los años 50) estaban solos, no tenían ni las facilidades que tienen hoy, ni los entrenadores, que les apoyan hoy.

4 Jóven Ni los modernos equipos Esas dos mujeres, ¿que hicieron?

Señorita Fueron las dos primeras tenistas femeninas españolas, Lili Álvarez y Rosa Torras, que participaron en los Juegos Olímpicos de 1924, cuando todavía no permitían a las mujeres participar oficialmente.

Jóven ¿Qué dijo? ¿Que no les permitían tomar parte?

Señorita No, a pesar de que los Juegos Olímpicos modernos empezaron en 1896, la mujer no pudo participar de manera oficial hasta 1928.

Jóven Como dice mi abuela en aquellos tiempos las mujeres solían quedarse en casa a cuidar a la familia …

Señorita ¡No seas tan pesado niña!

Answers:

nombre	pasado	presente	deporte
Juan Manuel Fangio	✓		Fórmula 1
Michael Schumacher		✓	Fórmula 1
Alonso		✓	Fórmula 1
Rafa		✓	tenís
Manolo Santana		✓	tenís
Miguel Induraín	✓		ciclismo
Sastre		✓	ciclismo
Federico Bahamontes	✓		ciclismo
Lili Álvarez		✓	tenís
Rosa Torras		✓	tenís

1b Escucha el último diálogo otra vez y escribe estos verbos en el tiempo correcto.

- Students listen to the last conversation again and put the verbs into the correct tense.

Answers: eran, participaron, permitieron, empezaron, pudo

6–9

1c Contesta a las preguntas en inglés.

- Students answer the questions in English. They may need to listen again, or look at a copy of the transcript.

Answers: **1** Juan Manuel Fangio, **2** 1995, **3** He won Formula 1 five times, **4** Miguel Induraín, **5** Manolo Santana, **6** tennis,

2 De memoria ¿A cuántos deportistas hispanohablantes conoces? Escribe una lista. ¿Quién tiene la lista más larga?

- Students see how many Spanish speaking sportspeople they can name. This activity is suitable for a research homework. Students can then bring their answers to class and explain in Spanish who the people are and what they did or do.

4–8

3 Escribe en español.

- Students write the sentences in Spanish, practising the preterite tense. The teacher can then give students a list of verbs in the preterite, and some other words, which the students have to use to make sentences which could be logical or illogical e.g. *durmió – perro – El perro durmió debajo de la mesa toda la noche.*

5–7

Answers: **a** Yo jugué al tenis, pero él jugó a rugby. **b** Empezé yo primero, luego ellos empezaron más tarde. **c** El gato durmió en la silla.

4a Lee el texto y complétalo usando los verbos de abajo.

- Students read the text and complete it with the given verbs.

Answers: **1** jugué, **2** llegué, **3** dijo, **4** empecé, **5** vistieron, **6** sintió, **7** saqué, **8** toqué, **9** comencé, **10** despidieron

5–8

4b Escribe cinco frases usando cinco de los verbos de arriba. Imagina un incidente que te pasó con un deporte que no te gusta. Explica lo que pasó, cómo y cuándo y lo que hiciste al final.

- Students write about themselves using some of the verbs from the previous exercise.

5–8

5a Primero lee la conversación en voz alta.

- Students read out the conversation in pairs and predict where the emphasis in the sentences will fall. A paper copy of the conversation would be useful so they can underline the emphasis.

3–6

5b Ahora escucha y lee la conversación. Anota dónde se pone el énfasis.

PLTS

- Students listen and see if they predicted correctly. They note where the emphasis actually falls.

3–6

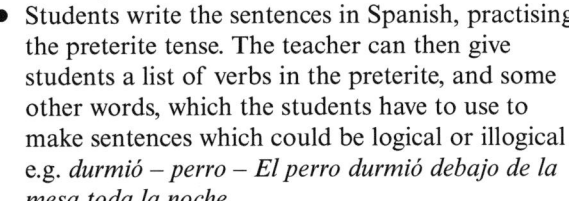

CD 1, track 39   página 47, actividad 5b

A – Los futbolistas ganan **demasiado** dinero hoy en día ¿no te parece?

B – **Pues** comparado con lo que ganaban el siglo pasado tienes **bastante razón**.

A – **Claro** si comparas el estilo de vida **de antes** con lo de **hoy** no es **mucha** la diferencia.

B – **¡Qué disparate!** No hay punto de comparación; **antes** no tenían las facilidades que tienen hoy y entrenaban **muchas horas** y era **mucho más** complicado viajar.

A – Eso es lo que dice todo el mundo pero **yo** no veo mucha diferencia.

B – **No me lo puedo creer**. Parece que no te importa el deporte.

A – **Jugar no**, pero **verlo** en la tele **sí**, y sobre todo porque España tiene **muchos** jugadores **fenomenales** hoy en día ¿no te parece lo mejor?

B – **Al contrario – es mucho más** saludable practicar deporte que estar sentado delante de la tele.

A – **¡Cada loco con su tema!**

5c Trata de imitar lo que oyes.

- Students practise the conversation again, this time trying to imitate what they heard.

3–6

Remate

6 Make an oral presentation about a sportsman or woman who you admire or don't admire. Describe the person – physique and character – and explain why you admire them (or not).

- Students must give reasons. If they're non-sporty, they may need some encouragement to come up with someone they admire. Remind them that in MFL it is perfectly permissible to *lie with enthusiasm* – they can choose to describe someone, then others have to decide if they really do admire them or not – how convincing can they be?

5–8

Success criteria activity 6:
- *students communicate effectively and accurately*
- *students express personal opinions and justify points of view*
- *students use a variety of vocabulary and structures*
- *students use different tenses or time frames*

7 Do some research about two great sportspeople, one from the last century and the other from today. Then write a brief comparison between the two.

PLTS

5–9

- Students compare two sporting heros, one past, one present, such as Di Estéfano (Real Madrid 1956–60), Cesc Fábregas (Arsenal 2005–), Bobby Charleton and Rooney or Walcott, Seve Ballesteros and Sergio García, Steve Cram and Usain Bolt. Non-sporty students may be interested in researching some of the more bizarre and obscure sports – trampolining, hang-gliding, base-jumping etc. You could run a competition to see who comes up with the most unusual people.

A copy of the listening script for the previous listening on old / new sportsmen will help with vocabulary and structures here.

Success criteria activity 7:
- *students give information accurately and in the appropriate style*
- *students express personal opinions and justify points of view*
- *students use a variety of vocabulary and structures*
- *students use different tenses or time frames*

Cómo elegir un estilo de vida sano

páginas 48 y 49

Planner

➤ Objectives
- Talking about a healthy lifestyle

➤ Resources
Students' Book, pages 48–49
CD 1, track 40
Grammar Workbook, pages 62, 74
Activity sheets 15–18

➤ Key language
el almuerzo, la cena, los dulces, la merienda, el plátano, una régimen
perezoso/a
adelgazar, dejar de, descansar, estar en forma, llevar tiempo, ponerse a dieta, relajarse, seguir en los pasos de, solía comer
desde hace, en cambio, enhorabuena, nunca

➤ Skills
- Writing longer texts

➤ Grammar
- *desde hace*, simple imperative

➤ PLTS
Students' Book, page 49, activity 5,
Team Workers
Students' Book, page 49, activity 6,
Creative Thinkers

➤ Starters
- Students' Book page 48. Students look at the pictures of the animals and say which they think is healthy and why (not). Keep a note of any vocabulary that comes up for reference throughout the spread.
- Students' Book page 48, activity 2. Before

listening, the students read through the statements and predict if it is the man or the woman who does these things. They then listen and see if they are correct in their assumptions.
- Do students think they have a healthy or unhealthy lifestyle? Why? Get them to make a note of their statements, and at the end of the spread ask if they have changed their opinion at all.
- Students' Book page 49, activity 6. Before students write their advice for their partners, spend some time putting forward problems, and eliciting advice e.g. *Como comida rápida cinco días a la semana – Debes cocinar bien por lo menos tres días durante la semana.*

➤ Plenaries
- Students' Book page 48, activity 2. After doing the listening, students use the expressions of time to write sentences about themselves e.g. *Hace diez años vivía en Nueva York.* You can also play the true / false game with these statements.
- Students' Book page 48, activity 3. Ask students to summarise (in English or Spanish depending on ability) what the writer thinks are the problems with his grandparents' and parents' lifestyles. They write a paragraph commenting on their own family's lifestyle, and what they would change in the future.
- Students' Book page 49 activity 5. Students question their partner or survey the class about the healthiness of their lifestyle. They should write up their findings in the third person.
- The teacher calls out or writes on the board a number of short statements that students have to classify as *Sana, Malsana* or *Depende* e.g. *estar de régimen* is healthy, but it depends on the diet, and how unfit or overweight the person was to start with. The more advanced students are, the more they should be made to justify their choices.

1a Lee el póster e identifica la imagen.

- Students read the poster and match the text to the pictures. Only three out of the five animals are written about.

Answers: **1** d, **2** c, **3** b

1b Escoje una instrucción para cada animal (1–3).

- Students choose a piece of advice to give to each animal from those in the list. This revises language from unit 1B.

Answers (possible): **1** dormir menos, **2** ponerse a dieta, **3** tener más disciplina

1c Inventa otras instrucciones para los dos animales que sobran.

- Students invent descriptions for the remaining two animals.

2a Escucha la conversación y contesta a las preguntas.

- Students listen to the conversation and answer the questions in English.

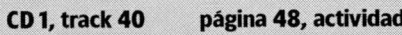

CD 1, track 40   página 48, actividad 2

F – ¿Tú crees que estás en forma? ¿Qué ejercicio haces?

M – Pues yo sé que no estoy en forma, antes comía chocolate todos los días pero ya llevo seis meses que no como tanto y ahora hago deporte.

F – Bueno desde hace diez años corro tres veces a la semana y ya hace dos años que corrí el maratón de modo que estoy en plena forma ¿verdad?

M – Pues ya yo llevo un mes recibiendo clases de yoga para relajarme porque me dijo mi profe que la relajación es tan importante como el deporte.

F – Claro que sí; y yo suelo ir a la piscina antes de desayunar y nado veinte minutos mínimo. Además sigo una régimen estricta desde hace tres años y como lo necesario nada más.

M – ¡Enhorabuena – tienes que ser la mujer más sano y saludable del planeta!

Answers: **1** woman, **2** man, **3** woman, **4** man, **5** woman

2b Escucha la conversación otra vez y anota todas las expresiones que indican tiempo.

- Students listen to the conversation again and note down all the expressions of time. Differentiation: some students will benefit from having the transcript at this point.

Answers: antes, llevo seis meses, ahora, hace diez años, hace dos años, llevo un mes, suelo, antes de, hace tres años

3a Lee y analiza el texto.

- Students read and analyse the text.

Answers:
1 ni, porque, y, que, por ejemplo, de modo que, pero, para
2 demasiado, muy bien
3 tan queridos, eficientes, aburridas, buena, adecuada, modernas, largas, apropiada, nutritiva, necesario, sana, saludable
4 no, ni, nada

3b Anota las palabras que son similares a palabras inglesas.

- Students make a note of words that are similar in English.

Answers: sinceramente, opinión, eficiente, dieta, nutrición, adecuada, facilidades, moderna, apropiada, nutritiva, necesario, atención, horas, manera

3c Busca en un diccionario palabras contrarias a:

- Students use a dictionary to find the opposite for the following words. To further build vocabulary, you could see who can produce the longest list of opposites.

Answers: **1** malsana, **2** ayer / mañana, **3** mala, **4** cortas, **5** poco, **6** inapropiada

4a Lee las frases. Usa las palabras conectores para escribir una sola frase.

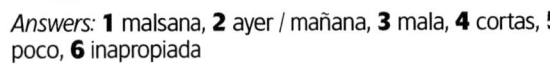

- Students use the connecting words to write longer sentences.

Answers: **1** …porque…, **2** …donde…, **3** …entonces…, **4** …mientras que…, **5** … en cambio…, **6** …pero…

4b Añade unas palabras (adjetivos o adverbios) a las frases de arriba para hacerlas aun más largas e interesantes.

- Students add more detail to the sentences, drawing on the words and phrases on this spread. Spend some time in class first drawing up spidergrams or word families of useful vocabulary, and do a couple of examples with the students first. See who can come up with the most inventive adaptations.

Answer (example): Desde hace tres meses voy a clases de yoga donde aprendo a relajarme que es muy buena para una vida sana.

Remate

5 Ask your partner about their healthy and unhealthy routines.

PLTS

- Students ask their partner how healthy their lifestyle is. More advanced students could survey several people, and use the results to compare what they are like. Once again, students don't have to be strictly truthful, and their questioner could have to decide if they are as healthy as they claim to be.

Success criteria activity 5:
- *students communicate effectively and accurately*
- *students express personal opinions and justify points of view*
- *students use a variety of vocabulary and structures*
- *students deal with unpredictable elements*

6 What advice can you give them? Write down the advice with a programme of healthy activities.

4–9

- Students write down advice for their classmates, based on the results they gave to the survey. If this is likely to be a sensitive issue, students could assume an alternative personality for these activities, maybe a sporting star or a TV personality. NB avoid using negative imperatives as they will not be covered until Unit 4b.

Success criteria activity 6:
- *students give information accurately and in the appropriate style*
- *students express personal opinions and justify points of view*
- *students use a variety of vocabulary and structures*
- *students use different tenses or time frames*

Cómo explicar lo que te duele
páginas 50 y 51

Planner

➤ Objectives
- Talking about being ill and injured

➤ Resources
Students' Book, pages 50–51
CD 1, tracks 41–42
Grammar Workbook, pages 51–52
Activity sheets 15–18

➤ Key language
*el césped, una cita, el codo, el consejo, la cruz roja, el dedo gordo, el dolor de cabeza, la espalda, un esparadrapo, la garganta, el hombro, el jarabe, la muela, los primeros auxilios
mareado/a, torpe
sangrar de la nariz, tropezar contra, trotar de madrugada*

➤ Skills
- Emphasising key words

➤ Grammar
- The perfect tense

➤ PLTS
Students' Book, page 51, activity 4,
Team Workers
Students' Book, page 51, activity 5,
Creative Thinkers

➤ Starters
- Before opening the spread, draw a large body on the board and get students to name as many parts as they can remember. When they run out of words, put them in pairs to find as many parts as possible in a dictionary against the clock.

- Students' Book page 50, activity 1. Without looking at the labelled body above, students list the parts shown in the pictures before listening.
- Students' Book page 51, activity 3. Before reading the text with a partner, students should read it through in silence. The teacher asks them to summarise (probably in English) what the conversation is about and who the different speakers are – you don't need to go into details. This knowledge makes it easier for students to decide where the emphasis should fall.
- Match scenarios to possible injuries e.g. *Mi hermano jugaba al fútbol en el parque – se ha torcido el tobillo*. Either the teacher or a student can provide the situations, and this can be done orally or as a written activity.

➤ Plenaries
- Students' Book page 50, activity 1. After doing the listening activities, give students a copy of the transcript with many key words and phrases blanked out. Students complete the story either from memory or with reference to the material in the spread.
- Students find examples of the irregular past participles in Señor Habichuela's story. The teacher provides a few examples, then students write their own sentences using them. More advanced students can turn it into a story – the more absurd the better, because more memorable.
- Write out the problems and solutions from activity 2 on pieces of card, and play Pairs with them in small groups.
- Students' Book page 51, activity 5. Using Señor Habichuela's story as inspiration, students write a sequel incident. Various scenarios can be discussed in class first, and vocabulary explored.

1a Mira los dibujos y haz una lista del vocabulario necesario. Escucha el cuento del Señor Habichuela y anota las partes del cuerpo mencionadas.

3–5

- In class, work on a list of vocabulary to go with the pictures so that students can understand the listening activity more easily. Then listen to the story and note down the body parts mentioned.

 CD 1, track 41   página 50, actividad 1

Érase una vez un señor muy distinguido pero algo torpe a la vez a quien le gustaba salir a correr todas las mañanas muy de madrugada.

Un buen día se levantó como siempre a las seis en punto y se puso los pantalones cortos y la camiseta y salió a correr muy contento.

Primero se cortó el dedo gordo con la llave de la puerta. ¡No importa! dijo y siguió corriendo.

Segundo al salir por el jardín se golpeó el codo con un arbol grande. ¡Ay qué dolor! dijo pero siguió corriendo.

En tercer lugar cuando ya estaba en la calle tropezó contra un coche y se dislocó el hombro. ¡Qué dolor! dijo pero siguió corriendo.

Después de un rato llegó al parque y se cayó en el césped y se dobló el tobillo, luego se golpeó la cabeza contra el suelo. ¡Dios mío que torpe soy!– dijo pero siguió corriendo.

Entonces vio a unos niños que jugaban al futbol y cuando los niños lanzaron la pelota, le golpeó en la cara y sangró de la nariz y se le rompieron dos dientes.

Al final, trató de dar una patada a la pelsta con el pie pero se lo fracturó. ¡Me rindo! dijo y ya no pudo seguir corriendo.

El pobre Señor Don Habichuela llegó a casa sin dientes, con el hombro dislocado, la cabeza golpeada, el dedo gordo cortado, el tobillo torcido, el codo lastimado, el pie fracturado y sangrando por la naríz.

Answers: el dedo gordo, el codo, el hombro, el tobillo, la cabeza, la cara, la nariz, los dientes, el pie

1b Escucha otra vez y pon las imágenes en el orden correcto.

3–5

- Students listen again and put the pictures in the order they are mentioned in the story.

Answers: **a** 6, **b** 3, **c** 8, **d** 4, **e** 2 **f** 1, **g** 5, **h** 7

1c Escucha otra vez y describe lo que ha pasado para cada imagen.

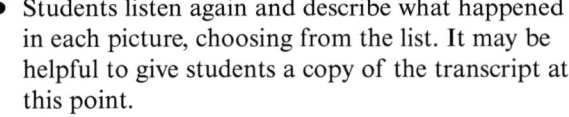

5–7

- Students listen again and describe what happened in each picture, choosing from the list. It may be helpful to give students a copy of the transcript at this point.

Answers: **a** la nariz sangra, **b** se ha dislocado el hombro, **c** se ha fracturado el pie, **d** se ha torcido el tobillo, **e** se ha lastimado el codo, **f** se ha cortado el dedo, **g** se ha golpeado la cabeza, **h** se ha roto los dientes,

1d Escucha otra vez y explica por qué.

5–8

- Students listen again and find the explanations for the injuries from the list.

Answers: **1** g, **2** e, **3** a, **4** c, **5** b, **6** f, **7** d, **8** f

1e ¿Qué se hace? Escribe ocho frases para explicar lo que hay que hacer en cada caso.

3–6

- Students give advice for all the injuries. They could form the sentences in a variety of ways.

Answers (examples): **1** Se ha fracturado el pie, entonces hay que llamar a una ambulancia. **2** Se ha torcido el tobillo, entonces hay que ponerle una venda. **3** Se ha golpeado la cabeza, entonces hay que ir a buscar a un médico. **4** Se ha lastimado el codo, entonces hay que llevarle a la clínica. **5** Se ha cortado el dedo gordo, entonces hay que darle primeros auxilios. **6** Se ha roto los dientes, entonces hay que llamar al dentista. **7** Se ha dislocado el hombro, entonces hay que llevarle al hospital. **8** La nariz sangra, entonces hay que darle primeros auxilios.

2a Consejos de salud – hay que encontrar una solución a cada problema.

4–8

- Students match the solutions to the problems. You can also play a true / false game where students have to say if the sentence you have given makes sense or not.

Answers: **1** c, **2** h, **3** i, **4** f, **5** g, **6** e, **7** a, **8** j, **9** b, **10** d

2b Por turnos con tu compañero/a, A dice lo que tiene y B da un consejo.

4–6

- Students practise using the language from activity 2a, taking it in turns to pick a problem, and the other person giving them a solution.

3a Por turnos con tu compañero/a, lee la conversación en voz alta. Practicad poniendo énfasis. ¿Quién lee mejor?

3–6

- Students practise reading the conversation with a partner, and predict where the emphasis will fall. A copy of the transcript to underline or otherwise mark up is useful here.

3b Escucha para verificar.

- Students listen to the conversation and check if they were correct.

 CD 1, track 42   página 51, actividad 3b

3–6

Enfermo	Oiga.
Recepcionista	Dígame. ¿En qué puedo ayudarle?
Enfermo	Necesito pedir cita con el médico.
Recepcionista	¿Es urgente?
Enfermo	Pues no exactamente pero tengo algo que consultarle.
Recepcionista	Bueno lo siento pero no tengo hora mañana, sólamente queda para pasado mañana.
Enfermo	Vale ¿A qué hora por favor?
Recepcionista	A las diez en punto … pero ¿qué tiene usted?
Enfermo	Hace dos días que tengo 42 fiebre de y me duele la garganta.
Recepcionista	¡Caramba por qué no lo dijo antes! Venga en seguida.

Remate

4 Imagine that Mr Bean wants a doctor's appointment. Person A is the doctor, and person B is Mr Bean. Invent a dialogue similar to the one above.

* This should be quite a long and involved conversation.

5–9

Success criteria activity 4:
* *students communicate effectively and accurately*
* *students express personal opinions and justify points of view*
* *students use a variety of vocabulary and structures*
* *students deal with unpredictable elements*
* *students use different tenses or time frames*

5 Write a brief paragraph about an amusing accident which happened to Mr Bean when he left the doctor's.

* Students write a continuation of the story when Mr Bean leaves the doctor's surgery. Encourage them to use a wide variety of the language from this spread.

6–9

Success criteria activity 5:
* *students give information accurately and in the appropriate style*
* *students express personal opinions and justify points of view*
* *students use a variety of vocabulary and structures*
* *students use different tenses or time frames*

Cómo disfrutar de actividades al aire libre

páginas 52 y 53

Planner

➤ Objectives
* Talking about activities you do in the open air

➤ Resources
Students' Book, pages 52–53
CD 1, tracks 43–44
Grammar Workbook, page 18
Activity sheets 15–18

➤ Key language
la altura, el buceo (con tubo), el buzo, un potro, el senderismo
encerrado/a, miedoso/a
gozar, pasarlo bomba, lanzarse, lograr, quedarse
adentro, afuera, al principio, anteayer, pasado mañana
aunque, de modo que, también
qué lástima

➤ Skills
* Using memory aids to make learning easier

➤ Grammar
* Adverbs

➤ PLTS
Students' Book, page 53, activity 4,
Effective Participators
Students' Book, page 53, activity 5,
Independent Enquirers

➤ Starters
* Brainstorm in class the different activities students do outside school, both active and sedentary, then underline or highlight the outdoor-fresh-air ones.
* Students' Book page 52, activity 2. Students read the email and underline or note down any words they already know. Ask them to say what they think the email is about.
* Students' Book page 53, activity 1. Before listening, students write out a statement for each person.
* Students' Book page 53, activity 3. Go through the email first and make sure students understand what attitude Anita had to each activity. Explain the telephone message is different, and elicit predictions as to how it might be so.

➤ Plenaries
* Students use the adverbs in the grammar box on page 52 (and any others) to write sentences about activities. They get one point for each adverb used within the sentence.
* Students' Book page 53, Habilidades. Give students an activity word and ask them to make a spidergram from it. This end-of-lesson activity can be repeated with different vocabulary many times.
* Students' Book page 53, activity 4. Students role play a telephone conversation with Anita.
* Students' Book page 53, activity 5. Students write a reply to Anita's email. Spend some time setting it up – how do you begin? What did you think about Anita's holiday? What did you think about the individual activities and why? What is your decision?

1a Empareja cada icono con una palabra adecuada.

- Students match the pictures to the names of the sports.

Answers: **Dani** espeleología, volar a cometa, **Maya** todo terreno, senderismo, **Pepe** equitación, esquiar sobre arena, **Tere** buceo (con tubo), surf

3–5

1b Antes de escuchar lo que dice cada persona decide quién va a decir cada una de las frases a–f.

- Students read the sentences and predict which person they apply to.

4–6

1c Escucha e identifica la actividad o actividades.

- Students listen and identify the activities.

5–7

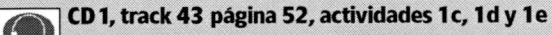

CD 1, track 43 página 52, actividades 1c, 1d y 1e

1 Maya: ¿Tú qué opinas, Pepe? ¿Es mejor salir en bici o a pie hoy?
Pepe: Pues no te puedo decir Maya – depende del tiempo – si va a llover mejor te vas en bici para poder volver más rápidamente.
Maya: Tienes razón y en efecto me gusta más montar a bici que ir a pie.
2 Dani: Dime Tere, ¿Hoy voy a ir por el aire o ir por debajo de la tierra?¿Cuál de los dos es preferible?
Tere: Yo prefiero siempre ir a las cuevas porque hace mucho frío al aire libre y hay demasiado viento hoy, Dani.
Dani: Pues cuando hay viento es mejor para volar alto, muy arriba en el aire – además prefiero estar al aire libre que encerrado bajo tierra.
3 Pepe: No importa cuál escojo hoy porque voy a estar afuera al aire libre.
Tere: Si pero con el tiempo que hace hoy creo que es mejor que vajas a trotar y a galopar con tu caballo favorito.
Pepe: No creo Tere, prefiero subir a las dunas de arena y bajar rápido, rapidísimo sobre los esquis.
4 Tere: De todos modos me voy a mojar en el mar así que no me importa el tiempo.
Maya: Claro no te importa porque vas vestida de buzo ¿verdad?
Tere: Pues sí, pero no voy a nadar sobre el mar sino por debajo, voy al fondo, a ver lo que encuentro allí abajo – es más emocionante.

Answers: **a** Tere, **b** Dani, **c** Tere, **d** Pepe, **e** Tere, **f** Maya

1d Escucha otra vez ¿Cuáles prefieren y por qué?

- Students listen again. Which activities do the speakers prefer and why? Some students may need a copy of the transcript from here on.

5–8

Answers: **Maya** todo terreno – le gusta más montar a bici que ir a pie; **Dani** volar a cometa – prefiere estar al aire libre; **Pepe** esquiar sobre arena – prefiere subir a las dunas y bajar rapidísimo sobre los esquis; **Tere** buceo – es més emocionante ver lo que hay debajo del mar.

1e Apunta estas palabras en español, luego escucha otra vez y verifica.

- Students write down the Spanish for the following words, and then listen again to check if they are right.

3–5

Answers: **under the ground** por debajo de la tierra, **you're right** tienes razón, **it's too windy** hay demasiado viento, **fly high in the air** volar alto, muy arriba en el aire, **on horseback** montado sobre caballo, **the top of the dunes** el tope de las dunas de arena, **in a wetsuit** vestida de buzo, **to the bottom** al fondo

1f Ahora escribe dos frases para resumir lo que dicen cada persona. Usa las frases de la actividad 1c y el vocabulario del 1a.

- Students write two sentences to summarise what each person is going to do.

5–7

2a Lee el email y busca: actividades, palabras o frases que expresan emoción o que expresan tiempo.

- Students read the email and look for the different types of information.

5–8

Answers: **actividades** la escalada, el puenting, senderismo, exploramos unas cuevas; **emoción** gozando, lo pasamos bomba, me pareció fenomenal, estuve un poco miedosa, esto te digo me dio miedo, ¡¡guay y más que guay!!; **tiempo** el año pasado, al principio.

2b Contesta a las preguntas en inglés.

- Students answer the questions in English.

5–8

Answers: **1** How are you all in Britain? Would you like to do these activities? **2** It's summer. **3** She enjoyed rock climbing, hiking and caving. **4** She was frightened. **5** They have asked her to invite her friend along next year.

3a Antes de escuchar el mensaje relaciona estas frases.

- Before doing the listening activity, students match up the phrases describing various activities.

5–8

Answers: **1** d, **2** e, **3** a, **4** c **5** b

3b Ahora escucha el mensaje telefónico y anota tres diferencias entre lo que escribió Anita en el email y lo que dice por teléfono.

- Students listen to the telelphone message and note the differences between that and the email. They may need to listen several times.

5–8

CD 1, track 44 página 53, actividades 3b y 3c

Oye oye, soy yo Anita – mira contéstame rápido a mi email porque quiero organizar el viaje. Te cuento que lo que hicimos fue fenomenal – lástima que no pude subir a las rocas porque me dio mareo y sentí miedo de la altura pero sí fui a pasearme por las montañas – espectacular – muchos se lanzaron del puente pero yo no – prefiero quedarme en tierra firme. Lo de las cuevas me dió miedo y aunque logré entrar, no llegué hasta el fondo. De todos modos lo pasamos de maravilla y quiero repetir la aventura de modo que me tienes que contestar en seguida – me oyes?

Answers:
1 Hice la escalada y me pareció fenomenal – no pude subir las rocas porque me dio mareo
2 Otra cosa que hicimos fue el puenting – muchos se lanzaron del puente pero yo no
3 Exploramos unas cuevas muy profundas –¡¡guay y más que guay!! – lo de las cuevas fue miedoso pero sí logré entrar pero no al fondo

3c Escucha otra vez y escribe V (verdadero) o F (falso) para cada frase en inglés.

● Decide if the sentences are true or false.

Answers: 1 V, 2 F, 3 V, 4 F, 5 F

5–8

3d Explica en inglés las diferencias entre lo que escribió y lo que dijo.

● Explain the differences between the email and the telephone message in English.

5–8

Remate

4 Imagine the telephone conversation between Anita and her penpal. Invent a list of questions and answers. Then have the conversation and record it.

 PLTS

5–8
● In class, first brainstorm some questions that either person might ask – when is the holiday, do you have to participate in all activities, which is the best activity etc. Decide if Anita succeeds in persuading her friend to accompany her or not. The friend must give their reasons.

Success criteria activity 4:
● *students communicate effectively and accurately*
● *students express personal opinions and justify points of view*
● *students use a variety of vocabulary and structures*
● *students deal with unpredictable elements*
● *students use different tenses or time frames*

5 Write a reply to the email.

PLTS

4–9
● Students write a reply to the email. In addition to accepting or refusing the invitation, they can describe an activity holiday they have been on, an activity day they have done with school, or similar. Maybe they think their idea is better and want to persuade Anita to join them. They must explain why and be as persuasive as possible.

Success criteria activity 5:
● *students give information accurately and in the appropriate style*
● *students express personal opinions and justify points of view*
● *students use a variety of vocabulary and structures*
● *students use different tenses or time frames*

Gramática en acción

páginas 54 y 55

Planner

➤ **Objectives**
● Reviewing and learning verbs

➤ **Resources**
Students' Book, pages 70–71
Exam Skills Workbook, page 33 (F and H)
Grammar Workbook, pages 18, 44–45, 51–52, 66, 74
Activity sheet 19
Resources and Planning OxBox CD-ROM

➤ **Grammar**
● Using verbs impersonally like *me interesa(n)*
Using reflexive constuctions like *se juega(n)*
Using the irregular form of the preterite tense
Using time clauses like *desde hace*
Using the perfect tense
Using adverbs and phrases of time and place

➤ **PLTS**
Students' Book, page 54, activity 3b,
Reflective Learners
Students' Book, page 55, activity 5,
Team Workers

➤ Verbs

1   Look back over the unit and write down a list of all the verbs for these two categories. How many more can you think of? Check them out in your dictionary first and then add them to your list.

> *Answers:*
> **third person verbs**: me gusta/me gustan, me interesa, me encanta, me parece, me duele
> **impersonal verbs**: se juega, se reconoce, se puede, se necesita, se pega, se hace, se lleva, se parece, se construye, se aprende, se practica, se pone, se lanza, se permite, se suele, se prohíbe, se debe, se ha fracturado, se ha torcido, se ha golpeado, se ha lastimado, se ha cortado, se ha roto, se ha dislocado, se ha tropezado, se ha caído

2   Make up five sentences using different verbs from the list in activity 1 to show that you know how to use them. Ask your teacher to check them to make sure they are correct and then learn them and keep them for revision purposes as good examples which you made up.

- Encourage students to make up memorable, and possibly silly, sentences as they are more likely to remember them.

➤ Radical and spelling changes in the preterite

3a   Look at these sentences and decide which will need verbs that are radical changers and which need a spelling change.

- When they write down the answers, students could colour code the different types of verbs to help them remember.

> *Answers:* **1** compitieron – radical change; **2** llegó, llegué – spelling change; **3** busqué – spelling change; **4** se sintió, se divirtió – radical change; **5** se durmió, se despirtó – radical change.

3b   Check the spelling in the grammar section of the Students' Book.

PLTS
- Students can mark each other's work.

3c   Write the sentences in English.
- Translating examples adds to their memorability.

> *Answers:* **1** They competed in all the sports that day. **2** Pedro arrived early but I arrived late. **3** When the games began, I looked for my team. **4** Suddenly Luisa felt ill, but even so she enjoyed the match. **5** María fell asleep in the car and only woke up on arriving home.

➤ Imperatives

4   Write down the infinitive and the meaning for each one of the verbs above.

Imperatives		Infinitives	Translation
tú	vosotros/as		
toca	tocad	tocar	to touch
come	comed	comer	to eat
sube	subid	subir	to go up
levántate	levantaos	levantarse	to get up
pon	poned	poner	to put
ten	tened	tener	to have
sal	salid	salir	to go out
haz	haced	hacer	to do/make
ve	ven	ver	to see

➤ The perfect tense

5   That's a lot to remember so make up a jingle or rhyme to help you remember them all.

PLTS
- More advanced students could make up an absurd mini-story in Spanish e.g. *He **abierto** la puerta y he **cubierto** el perro con una toalla.* The verbs don't need to go in alphabetical order but it helps to remember them that way and make sure all are included.

6   Practise question and answer sessions using the perfect tense of these verbs.

- Students use the verbs in the box to practise the perfect tense in the form of an interview about activities. Differentiation: more able students could be given random verbs they have to respond to from a list held by their partner e.g. *montar – ¿Has montado en caballo?* Less able students could pre-prepare questions with a partner, and ask them of another person.

7   Now revise household chores by writing a list of chores you have or have not done today. Use the perfect tense.

- If students don't wish to be too serious, they could write a mixture of sensible and silly chores for their partner or others to identify. e.g. *He sacado la basura – bien; he regado el perro – ¡qué va!*

8   Then use the imperative to give a list of instructions telling your partner what to do.

Habilidades

Planner

➤ **Objectives**
- Sounding convincing when you speak

➤ **Resources**
Students' Book, page 56
Exam Skills Workbook, page 34 (F), page 35 (H)
Activity sheet 20
Resources and Planning OxBox CD-ROM

➤ **Skills**
- Using intensifiers to sound convincing
- Stressing certain words / using stress to sound convincing

- Using descriptions and linking words to avoid short sentences
- Using quantifiers and expressions of frequency to add colour to your writing
- Using determiners correctly

➤ **PLTS**
Students' Book, page 72, activity 3, *Reflective Learners*
Students' Book, page 72, activity 4, *Creative Thinkers*

➤ **Hablar**

1 Sound convincing. Use intensifiers to sound convincing. How many can you remember?

❏ How can you sound more convincing using them in these sentences?
- Discuss how different intensifiers can totally change a sentence e.g. *Es importante hacer un poco de deporte. Es importante hacer mucho deporte.* Elicit examples from the students.

❏ Stress certain words to sound convincing. Which words would you choose to stress in the following sentences? Check with the teacher or assistant.
- Again, discuss how a change in emphasis can change the meaning of the sentence. This is a useful communication tool to be aware of in English as well.

Answers:
a En **mi** opinión **usted** es un poco **perezoso**.
b Ellos **sí** son ambiciosos.
c No me respetan **nada** – de **ninguna manera**.

➤ **Escribir**

2 Add colour to your writing.

❏ Revise page 15 of Unit 1A. Write five sentences about sports you can do and the facilities where you live.
- Differentiation: more able students can write longer sentences or short paragraphs. Do an example or two with the class to show them how to build up their texts.

3 Use strategies to learn new words.

❏ Draw spidergrams to link these words together, and add as many more as you can remember.
PLTS
- Linking words in a pattern helps students memorise them.

❏ Link these words into word families, and add as many more as you can remember.
- Another technique to aid memory is to group words together in types.

4 Use strategies for learning verbs and tenses.

❏ Sequence the tenses of new verbs in a timeline. Make up a learning card to show the sequence these verbs follow, and what each tense means.
PLTS
- Show an example on the board first then get students to do their own, possibly in small groups or pairs, and discuss some of the examples in class. Who has produced a memorable time line?

Escenario

Planner

➤ Objectives
- Give an oral presentation on healthy living, and a written one on outdoor activities

➤ Resources
Students' Book, page 57
Exam Skills Workbook, pages 31–32 (F),
pages 32–33 (H)
Resources and Planning OxBox CD-ROM

➤ Skills
- Writing practice
- Speaking practice

➤ PLTS
Students' Book, page 57, Escenario Oral,
Effective Participators
Students' Book, page 57, Escenario Escrito,
Self-Managers

➤ Oral

Create a television advert promoting healthy living.

- Students follow the instructions to work in groups and create their advert. Explain to students what they have to present. They can choose to cover all the issues, just focus on one or two or aim for a balanced view e.g. talking about both the dangers of not enough or too much sport.
- *GCSE Grades A*-C*
- *Grade C Students use past, present and future tenses. They express opinions, and deal with some unpredictability.*
- *Grade A Students express and justify opinions. They use a variety of vocabulary and structure in longer speech sequences.*

➤ Escrito

Imagine you went to this activity centre. Write a diary entry about what you did on one particular day on your sporting holiday.

- Refer students back to the email exchange between Anita and her friend on pages 52 and 53 and encourage them to draw on any experiences they may have had in this area. Discourage them from trying to re-tell a personal experience precisely; they need to make the story fit the language they can use rather than the other way round. Remind them that the quality of the language is more important than the truth of the story.
- *GCSE Grades A*-C*
- *Grade C Students use opinions and past, present and future tenses, both factually and imaginatively. Register is appropriate and style is basic.*
- *Grade A Students write factually and imaginatively using longer sequences and a range of vocabulary and structure. They express and justify opinions in an appropriate style.*

Vocabulario

This is a summary of key language from the unit, organised by spread and theme. Students can use it for reference while working on the unit, and as an aid to learning vocabulary.

Lectura

Planner

➤ **Objectives**
- A new Olympic sport, a star tennis player
- To encourage independent reading and develop reading strategies.
- These pages also provide alternative class and homework material for students who work quickly and require extension work.

➤ **Resources**
Students' Book, page 175–176

➤ **PLTS**
Students' Book, page 175, activity 4, *Independent Enquirers*
Students' Book, page 176, activity 2, *Self-Managers*

➤ **Lectura A – Deporte**

1 Lee el texto y busca las palabras que significan.
- Students read the text and find the equivalent words in Spanish.

Answers: **a** las carreras, **b** los saltos, **c** un freno, **d** un cambio de velocidad, **e** la silla

2 Busca cinco palabras técnicas más.
- Students find five more words.

Answers (possible): **1** circuitos, **2** los corredores, **3** entrenar, **4** aterrizar, **5** esquinas, **6** una colina, **7** los ciclistas, **8** la puerta

3 Contesta a las preguntas en inglés.
- Students answer the questions in English.

Answers:
a This is the first time this sport had taken part in the Olympic Games.
b Contestants compete in groups of eight around a course with lots of difficult corners and jumps.
c It is important to leave the gate first and quickly so as not to become muddled up with the other cyclists.

4 Escribe un texto parecido sobre un deporte que te interesa a ti.

PLTS
- Students write a smiliar text about a sport that interests them, or the teacher could deal out Olympic Sports at random to the class so that you end up with a variety of texts that could be used for a compare and contrast exercise. What are the particular challenges of each sport? Which are most interesting to watch? Which are team sports, and which individual ones? What different types of skill are required for each? etc.

➤ **Lectura B – Rafa, el tenista de oro de 2008**

1 Lee el texto y decide cuál de los parrafos lleva los siguientes títulos.
- Students read the paragraphs and find the appropriate title for each.

Answers: **a** 2, **b** 5, **c** 1, **d** 3

2 Inventa otro título para el párrafo extra.

PLTS
- Students decide how to title the remaining paragraph.

Answer (possible): su fisica

3 ¿En cuál de los párrafos se encuentra la respuesta a estas preguntas?
- Students find which paragraph contains the answer to the questions.

Answers: **a** 5, **b** 4, **c** 1, **d** 2, **e** 3

4 ¿Cuál de estas frases es verdadera o falsa o no se menciona?
- Students decide which statements are true, false, or doesn't say.

Answers: **a** V, **b** F, **c** V, **d** NM. **e** NM

Unit 2B Comer y beber			Overview grid	
Page, reference	Contexts	Skills	Grammar	Vocabulary
Spread title	• Topic areas covered within the unit	• Key skills focus	• Grammar covered in the unit	Key vocabulary
pages 60–61 **Cómo comparar las comidas diferentes**	• Comparing food and drink in different cultures	• Descriptions • Making comparisons	• Comparatives and impersonal expressions	yo pienso que, prefiero comer, a mí me gusta, me encanta delicioso/a, fuerte, ligero/a, pesado/a, picante, sabroso/a, sano/a, soso/a, variado/a acostumbrarse a, echar de menos, encontrar estar acostumbrado/a, ser adicto/a a, ser aficionado/a, ser cierto
pages 62–63 **Cómo hablar de sus comidas favoritas**	• Talking about your favourite food	• Expressing interest when talking	• Structures followed by the infinitive	los fideos, los guisantes, la mezcla, la receta, la sartén, la sidra asqueroso/a, crudo/a, grasiento/a, innovador(a), sabroso/a, salado/a, saludable añadir, batir, dar forma, dar la vuelta, echar, estar entusiasmado con, pelar, preparar con antelación, probar, quemarse
pages 64–65 **Cómo hablar sobre la comida sana**	• Talking about healthy and less healthy food	• Expressing yourself in a more natural way	• Present continuous	a menudo, de vez en cuando, dos veces al mes, por lo menos, todos los días los lácteos, el sobrepeso apetecer, cuidarse, engordar, evitar, hacer un esfuerzo, hacer una locura, intentar (+ infinitivo), llevar tiempo a dieta, parar de (+ infinitivo), perder peso, adelgazar, tener ganas de (+ infinitivo) ¿de veras?, haga lo que haga, no me diga
pages 66–67 **Cómo comprar comida en una tienda**	• Shopping for food • Markets vs supermarkets	• Remembering vocabulary	• *tú* and *usted*	el cierre, una docena, los embutidos, la frutería, la manifestación, la naranjada, la panadería, la pastelería, la pescadería, la tableta de chocolate, la tarrina de helado impersonal, incómodo/a, limpio/a, pasado/a de moda, práctico/a estar de acuerdo Me parece que …, Creo que … , Pienso que …
pages 68–69 **Cómo pedir y quejarte en un restaurante**	• Ordering in a restaurant and complaining politely	• Asking questions	• Pronouns	la chuleta con patatas, los cubiertos, el flan, el helado, las judías con jamón ¿Adónde vamos a comer?, Adonde queráis, Me apetece, No me importa, ¿Qué queréis tomar?, Tengo mucha hambre frío/a, libre, sucio/a Disculpe, ¿podría cambiarme el tenedor, por favor?, Perdone, pero se ha olvidado mis cubiertos. Perdone, pero creo que se ha equivocado de pedido. Perdone, pero hay un problema con la cuenta. ¿Podríamos cambiarnos de mesa? ¿Podría revisar la cuenta, por favor? ¿Podría traerme …?
pages 70–71 **Gramática en acción**	• Using comparatives		• Comparatives and superlatives • Impersonal phrases followed by infinitive • Present continuous • Polite form of verbs • Pronouns with prepositions (emphatic pronouns) • Number	
page 72 **Habilidades**	• Expressing yourself in a more natural way	• Express interest and enthusiasm through the tone of your voice • Express agreement or disagreement • Behave politely when you go out for a meal • Pick out the clues to decide which information is relevant • Use tone to work out a speaker's opinion		
page 73 **Escenario**	• Use the language of food both orally and written to interview a chef and customers in a restaurant. • Write the webpage of a 3-star restaurant for the Michelin Guide.			
page 74 **Vocabulario**	• Summary of key vocabulary for the unit.			
pages 177–178 **Reading pages**	Food and drink in Spanish speaking countries: • to encourage independent reading and to develop reading strategies. • to provide alternative class and homework material for students who finish other activities quickly.			

2B Comer y beber

Unit Objectives

Contexts: food and drink – shopping, eating out, cultural differences

Skills focus: expressing interest, enthusiasm, agreement or disagreement; complaining politely using adverbs, making points for or against using clues to find relevant information.

Grammar: comparatives, writing numbers correctly, expressions followed by the infinitive, using usted, pronouns with prepositions, the present continuous

Controlled assessment opportunities

Speaking: Students' Book, page 61, activity 9
Speaking: Students' Book, page 63, activity 12
Writing: Students' Book, page 65, activity 15
Writing: Students' Book, page 67, activity 12
Speaking: Students' Book, page 69, activity 8

*See also **GCSE Spanish for OCR Assessment OxBox CD-ROM**.*

An introduction to the unit   página 59

- *Aim*: To introduce the themes of the unit and encourage students to think about the reasons for learning Spanish.
- The opening page is designed with captions, pictures and page cross-references to provide a preview of what is to come:

	Students' Book
Cómo comparar las comidas diferentes	page 60
Cómo hablar de tus comidas favoritas	page 62
Cómo hablar sobre la comida sana	page 64
Cómo comprar comida en una tienda	page 66
Cómo pedir y quejarte en un restaurante	page 68
Gramática en acción – improving your use and understanding of Spanish	page 70
Habilidades – increasing your language skills for fluency	page 72
Escenario – entrevistar a un jefe de cocina Escenario – escribir una reseña de un restaurante para la guía Michelin de gastronomía	page 73

- Allow time for students to read the questions and cross-refer to the relevant pages of the Students' Book. They could do this individually or in pairs / small groups, followed by whole-class discussion.
- This spread also provides an opportunity for students to recap on familiar language. Ask them to think about language they already know that might be useful when working on the themes of the unit.

- Mindmap any language they produce, and if possible, keep it on display as reference as you progress through the unit. It can be added to at intervals as new language becomes familiar.
- At the end of work on the unit, allow time for students to return to this spread and repeat the mind-mapping process, this time including what they have learned over the course of the unit. Get them to answer the questions in their own words, and encourage them to use the results for revision purposes.
- Ask them what they found difficult, interesting etc. What do they think are the important things they have learned in this unit? What do they still need to improve on?
- If time permits, get the students to redesign the page. How would they set it out so it reflects the unit? How would they make it attractive to other learners of their age? How would they make it easy to follow? What would they include in terms of text, pictures, captions, page references? Ask them to imagine they are producing material for next year's class who will be learning the same thing – what would they have found it useful to know?

¿Por qué aprender el español? Para comer y beber bien en España.
- Students share any experiences they have had of eating in Spain e.g. in restaurants, in Spanish homes, buying food in a shop or market.
- Ask them to consider what sort of language they would need to survive in Spain e.g. how to order in a restaurant, how to buy food, how to say if they like or dislike something.

Cómo comparar las comidas diferentes

páginas 60 y 61

Planner

➤ Objectives
- Comparing food and drink in different cultures

➤ Resources
Students' Book, pages 60–61
CD 2, tracks 2–4
Grammar Workbook, pages 9, 66
Activity sheets 22–25

➤ Key language
Yo pienso que, prefiero comer, a mí me gusta, me encanta
delicioso/a, fuerte, ligero/a, pesado/a, picante, sabroso/a, sano/a, soso/a, variado/a
acostumbrarse a, echar de menos, encontrar
estar acostumbrado/a, ser adicto/a a, ser aficionado/a, ser cierto

➤ Skills
- Using adverbs and adjectives to write more detailed sentences

➤ Grammar
- Comparatives and impersonal expressions

➤ PLTS
Students' Book, page 61, activity 8,
Team workers
Students' Book, page 61, activity 9,
Effective participators

➤ Starters
- Students' Book page 60. Students look at the cartoons and guess, without reading the speech bubble (cover it with a scrap of paper or reproduce it as an OHT or on an interactive whiteboard), which country each pictures represents. What helped them make their decision? What do they see as typical about the food of any particular country? Then read the speech bubble and see if they got the country correct.
- Students' Book, page 61, activity 1. Students read the cartoons and, with their partner, decide if they agree or disagree with the captions. Why? What do they think of the food shown in the cartoons? Have they tried any of it?
- Students' Book, page 61, activity 5. Ask students to think of or look up as many different drinks in Spanish as they can. Classify them into alcoholic, non-alcoholic, for adults, for children etc. Ask them, if appropriate, which they have tasted and / or like or dislike and why.

➤ Plenaries
- Students' Book, page 61, activity 7. Students discuss who does most of the cooking in their homes. Is it the men or the women? Why? Is this fair? Do they cook, or only their parents? Why? Is it important to know how to cook? How has who does the cooking changed over the past two or three generations? When they have completed their survey and discussion, they can turn their results into a piece of written work e.g. *Cocina en casa*.
- Students' Book, page 61, activity 8. Students orally review the language of the spread by quizzing their partner, or a number of students, about their food likes and dislikes, what they like to cook and what they know about foods from other countries. You can provide students with a list of questions, or ask them to make up their own.
- Students' Book, page 61, activity 9. Spend time in class collecting ideas for different culinary traditions, or ask the students to research these first. Discuss the language of advertising and persuading, and ask students how they will deal with this in Spanish. What positive words and phrases do they know?

1 **Mira el dibujo en la página 60. ¿Estás de acuerdo o no con las afirmaciones? Habla con tu compañero/a.**
- Students look at the cartoon and discuss with their partner if they agree or disagree with the statements.

4–9

2 **Escucha y decide si las frases en la página 60 son verdaderas (V) o falsas (F).**
- Students listen to the CD. They read the sentences and decide which of them are true or false.

Answers: **a** V, **b** V, **c** V, **d** F, **e** F, **f** V

4–8

CD 2, track 2 página 61, actividad 2

Las diferencias entre España e Inglaterra son bastante grandes, aunque ahora Inglaterra tiene más productos españoles en los supermercados y por eso la comida española es mucho más popular que antes. Sin embargo, hay algunas diferencias grandes, como por ejemplo, cómo cocinamos: los españoles siempre cocinan con aceite, normalmente de oliva. El pan es muy importante y todo el mundo come pan en las comidas; en Inglaterra es algo muy inusual. Nosotros los españoles comemos a la una y media aproximadamente, ¡y hay personas que comen a las tres! A los españoles nos gusta comer, y nos encanta nuestra comida. Comemos comida de otros países en restaurantes, sobre todo comida italiana, pero no es algo tan normal como en Inglaterra.

3 Lee otra vez las frases y escribe los adverbios de frecuencia de cada frase. Con tu compañero/a, escribe una frase para cada uno relacionada con la comida.

- Students read the sentences and write down all the adverbs of frequency. Working with their partner, they write their own sentences about food using each of the adverbs they have found.

Answers: Adverbs of frequency – nunca, muy de vez en cuando, siempre, normalmente, casi nunca, de vez en cuando

4 Lee las opiniones de los estudiantes de 'Erasmus' en la página 60 y decide de qué países hablan las frases a–g.

- Students read the opinions of the Erasmus students and decide which country is being talked about.

Nota: "Erasmus" is a study programme for students to study abroad (es una beca para estudiar en el extranjero).

Answers: **a** Portugal, **b** México, **c** México, **d** Cuba, **e** Inglaterra, **f** Inglaterra, **g** Cuba

5 Une las bebidas con sus descripciones. Después escucha las respuestas.

- Students match the descriptions of the drinks to the names in the word box below. They then listen to the CD and check their answers.

 CD 2, track 3 página 61, actividad 5

a Es la bebida más consumida en los pubs ingleses. (la cerveza)
b Es una de las bebidas españolas más típicas del verano. (la sangría)
c En los restaurantes italianos, esta bebida es la especialidad (el café)
d Es la mejor bebida que produce Chile. (el vino)
e Es la bebida más sana de todas, la más natural, ideal para el desayuno. (la leche)
f Es una bebida típica de España, mucho más fuerte y espesa que en Inglaterra (el chocolate)

Answers: **a** la cerveza, **b** la sangría, **c** el café, **d** el vino, **e** la leche, **f** el chocolate

6 Lee las entrevistas y decide a qué persona se refieren las frases de abajo.

- Students read the interviews and decide which person is being referred to in the sentences below.

Answers: **a** Jordi, **b** Laura, **c** Poli, **d** Jordi, **e** Laura, **f** Poli

7 Escucha a Graciela hablar sobre las comidas en su casa y escribe la información adecuada.

- Students listen to Graciela talking about meals and answer the questions.

 **CD 2, track 4** página 61, actividad 7

– Graciela, cuéntanos un poco sobre la comida en tu casa.
– Bueno, normalmente, durante la semana, cocina mi madre y el fin de semana mi padre. Los dos son amantes de la cocina y se les da bien pero tienen especialidades diferentes; por ejemplo, a mi padre se le da fenomenal cocinar los platos principales, la paella, la carne asada ... y mi madre es la experta en dulces. Hace unas tartas de chuparse los dedos, y su arroz con leche es famoso entre nuestros amigos. Cuando éramos pequeños, mis padres siempre hacían las fiestas de cumpleaños en casa, y mi padre hacía la comida y mi madre los postres. Yo intento aprender de ellos pero no tengo tanto talento y por ahora mi especialidad es la tortilla de patatas – no es mucho pero al menos es un comienzo ...

Answers: **a** la madre, **b** las tartas, **c** porque aún está comenzando a cocinar, **d** el arroz con leche de la madre, **e** la madre, 5 días a la semana

Remate

8 Take it in turns to ask your partner questions about the food they like and dislike, what they like to cook, and what typical foods they know about in another country.

PLTS

- In pairs, students practise the language orally by question and answer. Teachers could brainstorm questions with the whole class first.

Success criteria activity 8:
- *students communicate effectively and accurately*
- *students express personal opinions and justify points of view*
- *students use a variety of vocabulary and structures*
- *students deal with unpredictable elements*

9 Choose a country with your partner and write an advertisement about the food and traditions of that country. Try to be convincing!

PLTS

- Students work with their partner to produce a piece of written work. This could be shared with the class and commented upon by the other students.

Success criteria activity 9:
- *students give information accurately and in the appropriate style*
- *students express personal opinions and justify points of view*
- *students use a variety of vocabulary and structures*

Cómo hablar de tus comidas favoritas

Planner

➤ Objectives
- Talking about your favourite food

➤ Resources
Students' Book, pages 62–63
CD 2, tracks 5–7
Grammar Workbook, pages 62, 74
Activity sheets 22–25

➤ Key language
los fideos, los guisantes, la mezcla, la receta, la sartén, la sidra
asqueroso/a, crudo/a, grasiento/a, innovador(a), sabroso/a, salado/a, saludable
añadir, batir, dar forma, dar la vuelta, echar, estar entusiasmado con, pelar, preparar con antelación, probar, quemarse

➤ Skills
- Using different phrases and structures to express interest when talking

➤ Grammar
- Structures followed by the infinitive

➤ PLTS
Students' Book, page 63, activity 12,
Self-managers
Students' Book, page 63, activity 13,
Creative thinkers

➤ Starters
- Do a whole class mind map of any food items in Spanish that the students can remember. Get students individually to classify them into items they like and items they dislike. How many ways of expressing positive and negative reactions to something can they remember?
- Students' Book page 62, activity 1a. Before listening, ask students if they can remember what the different foods are in Spanish. If they don't know all the words, what other things might they listen out for to help them? (e.g. nationality)
- Students' Book, page 62, activity 1b. Get students to classify the pictures from activity 1a in order of preference, and make statements about them using the language in 1b e.g. *Me encanta la paella, no soporto la ensalada* etc.
- Students' Book, page 62, activity 5. As above, ask students how many of the items they can name in Spanish before looking at the questions for activity 5. Then get them to read the instructions. What words don't they know? Can they work out what the instruction is about anyway? How? Now get them to check any words they don't know in a dictionary or glossary.

➤ Plenaries
- Students' Book page 63, activity 10. Using the language practised in activity 9, students write about what they like and dislike eating and drinking. They should include their most and least favourite dishes and reasons for their likes and dislikes. Do their friends have similar tastes? What about their family – are they similar or different in their likes to anyone? Does their family have an influence on what they eat?
- Students' Book page 63, activity 13. Students demonstrate a recipe to the class. As an alternative to real or acted demonstrations, students could take photos / draw pictures of a dish in preparation at home or in a Food Technology lesson, and use these to explain to the class how the dish is prepared. The name of the dish should not be given, and students have to write down guesses as to what is being prepared at various stages of the demonstration.
- Students prepare an interview with a famous person in their restaurant, and write it out, magazine-style. Alternatively, they could interview someone they know (family friend, relative, another teacher) and write the interview up in Spanish to provide a critics' guide to local restaurants.

1a Escucha y mira los dibujos y ponlos en orden según las descripciones.

- Students look at the pictures and put them in the order they hear their descriptions.

🎧 **CD 2, track 5**   **página 62, actividad 1**

1 Mi comida favorita es, por supuesto, la comida oriental. Me encantan los fideos, y además es una comida muy baja en calorías. No soporto la comida rápida, ¡es asquerosa!

2 ¿Mi plato favorito? El pescado con patatas fritas de la tienda al lado de mi casa. Es grasiento y por eso no lo como todos los días, pero me chifla la comida rápida. ¡De todos modos, es mejor que una hamburguesa!

3 Mi comida favorita es el pollo asado que cocina mi madre los domingos. ¡Es la mejor cocinera del mundo!

4 Mi plato favorito es siempre el postre, ¡me gustan tanto los dulces! La comida no me interesa tanto como las tartas, o los pasteles. ¡Soy muy goloso!

5 Soy vegetariana y por eso mi comida favorita es la ensalada. Odio la carne y el pescado pero me encantan las verduras.

6 Me apasiona la comida española, y el arroz, así que prefiero la paella con verduras y carne o pescado porque es una comida completa.

Answers: **1** e, **2** a, **3** c, **4** f, **5** b, **6** d

1b Escucha otra vez y trata de escribir el equivalente español de estas opiniones sobre la comida.

- Students listen again and try to find out the Spanish equivalents of the English opinion phrases.

2 Lee el correo electrónico de Tomás y escribe verdadero (V) o no mencionado (NM).

- Students read Tomás' email and decide if the statements are True (V) or Not Mentioned (NM).

Answers: **a** V, **b** NM, **c** V, **d** V, **e** V, **f** NM, **g** NM

3 Lee otra vez el correo electrónico de la actividad 2 y busca los antónimos de los siguientes adjetivos.

- Students re-read the email, looking for antonyms of the given adjectives.

Answers: **asqueroso** sabroso, **fresca** rápida, **sosa** salada, **saludable** grasienta, **auténtica** artificial

4 Habla con tu compañero/a sobre tus gustos personales. ¿Qué te gusta? ¿Qué prefieres? ¿Qué comida no soportas?

- With their partners, students discuss the food they like and dislike. They could note down their answers, and discuss them with the rest of the class.

5 Mira los dibujos y pon las instrucciones en orden.

- Students have to put the recipe instructions in order following the pictures.

Answers: **1** d, **2** c, **3** g, **4** a, **5** e, **6** f, **7** b

6 Utilizando el vocabulario de la actividad anterior, describe una receta a tu compañero/a. Tu compañero tiene que adivinar qué plato es.

- Students describe a recipe to their partner, who has to guess which dish they are describing. Partners can mark each other for describing a recipe correctly.

7 Escucha esta receta y escribe verdadero (V), falso (F) o no mencionado (NM).

- Students listen to the recipe and decide if the statements are True (V), False (F) or Not Mentioned (NM).

🎧 **CD 2, track 6**   **página 63, actividad 7**

Para hacer una ensaladilla rusa tiene que tener dos patatas grandes, una lata pequeña de atún, guisantes y zanahorias y unas aceitunas verdes. También puede añadir pimiento rojo si es de su gusto.

Lo primero que hay que hacer es pelar las patatas y ponerlas en agua caliente. Cuando ya están cocidas, hay que dejarlas enfriar antes de cortarlas. Después debe añadir el atún y los guisantes, zanahorias y el pimiento rojo. Es importante cortar los ingredientes en trozos pequeños para que la ensaladilla quede más elegante. Finalmente, hay que hacer una mayonesa con aceite de oliva y un huevo fresco, sal y zumo de limón. Cuando todo está preparado, debe cubrir la ensaladilla con la mayonesa, darle forma en el plato y añadir las aceitunas. ¡Buen provecho!

Answers: **a** V, **b** NM, **c** V, **d** NM, **e** F, **f** F, **g** V

8 Mira la actividad 5 y escribe todas las estructuras seguidas de infinitivo que puedas encontrar.

- Students re-read activity 5, noting down all structures followed by the infinitive.

Answers: tiene que, debe, puede, para, hay que, es importante, y

9 **Utiliza las estructuras de la caja para completar las frases. Algunas aceptan más de una opción. ¿Recuerdas todos sus significados?**

- Students use these structures to complete the sentences. Point out that some have more than one correct answer. Check that they understand all the phrases before they begin.

Answers:
a No soporto comer a las doce: ¡es demasiado temprano!
b Me encanta salir a los bares y comer tapas los domingos, ¡es perfecto!
c Es importante comer sano todos los días.
d Odio comer los calamares fritos, ¡son asquerosos!
e No me interesa cocinar y por eso solamente **f** puedo preparar huevos fritos.
g Debes desayunar bien antes de ir al colegio.
h Tengo que preparar la cena los martes para mis hermanos.
i Me apasiona comer el sushi y toda la comida oriental.

10 **¿Qué te gusta comer y beber? ¿Qué odias? Escribe algunos ejemplos y utiliza las estructuras de la actividad 9.**

- Students write about what they like and dislike eating and drinking.

11a **Escucha la entrevista a Marina, chef del restaurante 'El novillo' y contesta a las preguntas en inglés.**

- Students listen to the interview and answer the questions in English.

  CD 2, track 7   **página 63, actividad 11**

Entrevista con Marina Cerezo, chef del restaurante 'El Novillo.'
– Marina, usted es famosa por su combinación de ingredientes inusuales. Dígame, aquí entre usted y yo, ¿le gusta todo lo que cocina?
– ¡Por supuesto! Todos los platos que cocino los pruebo y puedo decir que sí. Claro que tengo mis comidas favoritas: no soy vegetariana pero me encantan las verduras. También me gusta el pescado aunque no soporto el sushi porque es pescado crudo.
– ¿Qué le gusta beber?
– Un poco de todo – los zumos naturales, el agua sin gas, los batidos ... no me gusta el alcohol y casi nunca bebo, pero, sin embargo, en fiestas o celebraciones especiales siempre pido un cóctel, ¡cómo no! Me gustan las bebidas dulces. Para mis clientes habituales siempre tenemos un buen vino de Rioja bien seco y sidra bien fresca, ¡para eso estamos en Asturias!
– ¿Y por qué le gusta cocinar?
– Me apasiona la cocina. No sólo cocino, sino que también preparo la mesa. Para mí, es importante crear un buen ambiente para los invitados. En 'El Novillo' cada detalle es vital.
– ¿Y cuáles son sus proyectos?
– Ahora estoy entusiasmada con trabajar otra vez para un programa de televisión y además, voy a tener una sección en una revista de cocina muy moderna donde hablaré de mis mejores platos.

Answers: **a** because she combines unusual ingredients, **b** she likes them a lot; she tries them all, **c** sushi, because it's raw fish, **d** a bit of everything; fruit juice, a little alcohol, **e** cider, **f** set the tables, **g** writing a column in a magazine about modern cookery

11b **Escucha otra vez y escribe las palabras clave de cada pregunta.**

- Students listen again, and note down the key words that enabled them to answer the questions at 11a.

Answers: **a** combinación /inusuales, **b** por supuesto, puedo decir que sí, probar, **c** sushi, no soporto, crudo, **d** un poco de todo, cóctel, **e** sidra, **f** no sólo... sino también, preparo, **g** trabajar otra vez

11c **Escribe las expresiones que Marina usa para afirmar algo, y expresar acuerdo o desacuerdo. ¿Cómo es el tono de sus respuestas?**

- Students make a note of the expressions Marina uses to confirm something, and to express agreement and disagreement. Discuss how the tone of voice gives clues to what she is saying.

Answers: por supuesto, cómo no, no soporto, puedo decir que sí

11d **En la pregunta 5, hay dos bebidas que se mencionan. ¿Cómo sabes cuál es la respuesta apropiada?**

- Students decide how they arrived at the correct answer for e.

Answer: seco is masculine, but *fresca* is feminine so the drink has to be *sidra* (f)

11e **Mira la transcripción y trata de leer el texto con la entonación apropiada.**

- Give students copies of the transcript and get them to practise the conversation. Encourage them to think about intonation as they speak.

Remate

12 **Work with a partner. They hate a particular food and you try to persuade them to change their mind.**

- First, brainstorm a list of hated foods with the class. Choose one, and get them to give some reasons, in Spanish, why you should like it. Then students work with their partners.

PLTS

13 **Choose a recipe with your partner. Rehearse and then demonstrate how to cook it in front of the rest of the class. The class votes for the best demonstration. Use the phrases in activity 5 to help.**

PLTS

- Encourage students to use activity 5 as a model. If actual demonstrations are not practical, a comedy version could be done, using unlikely props e.g. extra large wooden spoons, toy saucepans etc.

Success criteria activities 12 & 13:
- *students communicate effectively and accurately*
- *students express personal opinions and justify points of view*
- *students use a variety of vocabulary and structures*
- *students deal with unpredictable elements*

Cómo hablar sobre la comida sana

Planner

➤ Objectives
- Talk about healthy and less healthy food

➤ Resources
Students' Book, pages 64–65
CD 2, tracks 8–10
Grammar Workbook, page 41
Activity sheets 22–25

➤ Key language
a menudo, de vez en cuando, dos veces al mes, por lo menos, todos los días
los lácteos, el sobrepeso
apetecer, cuidarse, engordar, evitar, hacer un esfuerzo, hacer una locura, intentar (+ infinitivo), llevar tiempo a dieta, parar de (+ infinitivo), perder peso, adelgazar, tener ganas de (+ infinitivo)
¿de veras?, haga lo que haga, no me diga

➤ Skills
- Sounding more natural in Spanish by using different expressions and tones of voice

➤ Grammar
- The present continuous

➤ PLTS
Students' Book, page 65, activity 13
Independent enquirers
Students' Book, page 65, activity 16,
Team workers

➤ Starters
- Use the mind map of food you prepared at the beginning of the previous spread. Get students to classify the foods on it into *sana* and *malsana*. This can be done in a Venn diagram, with an overlap in the middle for foods which fall between the extremes of healthy and unhealthy.
- Students' Book page 64, activity 1. Before listening, check the students know what the different foods are in Spanish. Ask them which ones they like, and which ones they think are healthy.
- Read the letters to the problem page on page 65, and get the students to explain, in English or Spanish, what the problems are that are being described. Pick out key vocabulary.

- Students' Book page 65, activity 8. Students pick out all the verbs in the present continuous. Get them to note down the infinitive of each verb, and make up a sentence using each in the present continuous. They can do this in pairs or small groups. To make it more interesting, give them certain key words they have to include, so that you end up with strange sounding sentences e.g. *Estoy comiendo patatas en el patio con el perro*. Explain that unlikely associations can aid memory.

➤ Plenaries
- Students' Book page 64, activity 4. Students write about what they eat and how often. Encourage them to expand on their written work by explaining why they eat certain items e.g. *Como cereales cada mañana porque me gustan y son bastante sanos. También son fáciles a preparar.*
- Students' Book page 65, activity 15. Students write a special diet for a sportsperson. They should say what type of sports the person does, as this will have a bearing on what they eat e.g. a dancer will want to stay small and light, while a rugby player will want to be fit but strong. Consider if all sports are good for the body, and what the problems of special diets might be.
- Display some pictures of celebrities chosen for their obvious healthiness or lack of it. There could be sports people, the obese, the very underweight. (Be sensitive to local issues within the class.) Discuss which people are healthy and which are unhealthy, and what type of foods they probably eat. Get the students to pick a celebrity. Those with "unhealthy" celebrities describe what "their" problem is and the type of food they eat, while those with "healthy" ones describe why they are so, and give advice to the "unhealthy" on how to improve their lifestyle. This can be done individually, as pairwork, groupwork, or a whole class activity.
- Students' Book, page 65, activity 16. Students work with a partner to produce an interview with someone well known, discussing the secrets of their health and fitness. They can use any number of celebrity magazines for research, and do not have to be limited to sports people e.g. Madonna is well known for being very fit.

1 **Escucha a estos chicos hablando de las comidas. ¿Cuáles mencionan?**

- Students listen to the five boys talking about food and note down which ones each mentions.

> **CD 2, track 8**   **página 64, actividades 1 y 2**
>
> **1**
> – Martín, ¿qué comes?
> – Normalmente como ensaladas y verduras todos los días, pero a veces me apetece una hamburguesa y patatas fritas. Tomo comida rápida dos veces al mes, aproximadamente, no está mal, ¿no?
>
> **2**
> – ¿Y tú, Javi?
> – No me gusta el pescado, así que como carne prácticamente todos los días, y fruta y yogures. No como nunca pasteles porque no me gustan los dulces.
>
> **3**
> – ¿Y a ti, Mercedes?
> – A mí me encanta la comida italiana y como pasta por lo menos cuatro veces al mes. Me apasionan los helados, sobre todo el de chocolate. El pescado también me encanta, e intento comerlo al menos dos veces por semana.

Answers: **1** d, b, **2** a, c, e, f, **3** g, f, a

2 **Escucha la actividad 1 otra vez y escribe la frecuencia con que comen la comida que mencionan.**

- Students listen again and note down how often the speakers eat the food they talk about.

Answers:
Martín – ensaladas y verduras todos los días, comida rápida dos veces al mes
Javi – carne todos los días, pasteles nunca
Mercedes – pasta cuatro veces al mes, pescado dos veces por semana

3 **Con tu compañero/a, practica las siguientes preguntas.**

- In pairs, students practise asking each other the questions. Encourage them to pay particular attention to question intonation.

4 **Ahora escribe tus respuestas en tu cuaderno. Utiliza los adverbios de frecuencia.**

- Students write down their answers to activity 3, using the adverbs of frequency from activity 2 where appropriate.

5 **Lee los correos electrónicos y elige quién dice qué. ¿Quién ...?**

- Students read the emails and answer the questions.

Answers: **a** Marina, **b** Julio, **c** Rosa, **d** Gerardo, **e** Julio, **f** Gerardo, **g** Marina, **h** Rosa

6 **Escucha a los dos amigos hablando sobre su dieta y escribe las respuestas.**

- Students listen and answer the questions.

> **CD 2, track 9**   **página 64, actividad 6**
>
> – Ay Juan, me encuentro fatal, no duermo bien y estoy cansado todo el tiempo.
> – Manuel, trabajas demasiado y sufres de estrés. Dime, ¿qué comes?
> – No tengo mucho tiempo, así que no desayuno y normalmente como un bocadillo rápido y bebo una Coca-Cola, o una cerveza con los amigos en unos veinte minutos porque tengo que volver al trabajo urgentemente. Después estoy tan cansado cuando llego a casa que no cocino, así que compro una pizza o algo rápido, o voy a McDonald's.
> – ¡Estás loco! Yo tengo el mismo problema y por eso estoy cambiando mi dieta. Estoy siguiendo el consejo del médico, así que ahora estoy comiendo más fruta y verduras, y carne y pescado; es importante comer bien para tener energía. Es una cuestión de cambiar de hábitos. Por ejemplo, por las mañanas estoy bebiendo leche en lugar de café, y tomo cereales. Es importante comer por la mañana y tú no lo haces...

Answers: **a** porque trabaja demasiado y sufre estrés, **b** bocadillo y cerveza – pizza o McDonald's después para cenar, **c** más fruta y verduras, carne y pescado, **d** leche y cereales, **e** café, **f** no desayuna

7 **Lee el consultorio de salud de la revista *Saber vivir*.**

- Students read the problem page and the answers.

8 **Lee la actividad anterior y escribe en tu cuaderno todos los verbos que encuentres en el presente continuo. ¿Puedes recordar cómo se forma?**

- Students re-read the problem page and note down all examples of the present continuous.

Answers: estoy comiendo, estoy perdiendo, estoy pasando, estás haciendo, estás yendo, estamos hablando, estás comiendo, estás sintiéndote, estás corriendo un riesgo, estás tomando

9 **Busca en la actividad anterior el gerundio del verbo ir. ¿Cuál es?**

- Highlight the gerund of *ir* and the irregular verbs.

Answer: yendo

10 **El gerundio de 'sentir' es 'sintiendo'. ¿Cómo es el gerundio de los verbos radicales?**

- Revise how to form the gerund of radical changing verbs.

11 Mira la formación del presente continuo en la página 70 y cambia los siguientes verbos: **como, preparo, bebemos, lavan, dormís, llevas, cocina.**

- Students change the following forms into the present continuous.

Answers: estoy comiendo, estoy preparando, estamos bebiendo, están lavando, estáis durmiendo, estás llevando, está cocinando

6–9

12 Escucha la entrevista con Belén Rueda y escribe verdadero (V) o falso (F) o no mencionado (NM).

- Students listen to the interview and decide if the statements are True (V), False (F), or Not Mentioned (NM)

7–9

> **CD 2, track 10**　　　　**página 65, actividad 12**
>
> – Señoras y señores, aquí estamos en Cámara ... acción, el programa de cine de la 2 de TVE, y hoy tenemos con nosotros a la famosa Belén Rueda.
> – Buenas tardes Belén y gracias por estar esta tarde con nosotros en nuestro programa. Todo el mundo está deseando saber cuál es el secreto de su éxito. Una familia, un marido perfecto, una carrera meteórica ...¿cómo lo hace?¿Se cuida mucho?
> – ¡Claro que sí! Soy una actriz y vivo de mi imagen, pero no soy la única. **Que yo sepa**, todas las actrices llevan una dieta sana y hacen mucho ejercicio para mantenerse bien.
> – ¿Y usted tiene tiempo para el gimnasio además de para la familia?
> – Por supuesto. **Además, el que algo quiere, algo le cuesta**, así que tengo hacer el esfuerzo y pasar al menos dos horas en el gimnasio con mi entrenador personal.
> – ¡No me diga! ¿De veras? Yo pensaba que usted era así por naturaleza ...
> – Sí, soy delgada por naturaleza, pero tengo que cuidarme para estar lo mejor posible, así que hago deporte y como bien: mucha fruta y verdura, pocas grasas, mucha agua ...
> – Pero **haga lo que haga**, su marido la va a adorar igual ...
> – Sí, ¡ya lo sé!, pero aún así, me gusta cuidarme para mí misma.
> – Claro, no hay nada malo en tener autoestima. Pero dígame, ¿no le parece difícil **estar siempre en el ojo del huracán?**
> – ¡De eso nada! Me encanta. Me gusta ver que el público me quiere, aunque eso no implica que me encante tener mi privacidad y estar con mi familia.
> – Gracias, Belén.
> – De nada, ha sido un placer.

Answers: **a** V, **b** V, **c** F, **d** V, **e** F, **f** NM

13 Lee la transcripción de la entrevista y escribe las expresiones (subrayadas) que ayuden a transmitir entusiasmo e interés.

- Provide the students with a transcript of activity 13. They write out the underlined expressions and try to work out what they mean. There are many expressions like this in listening activities that students should try to become familiar with.

PLTS

7–9

14 Ahora busca también las frases en negrita. ¿Qué pueden significar?

- Students do the same with the bold expressions. Tell the students they will need these expressions later.

7–9

Remate

15 Write a special diet for a sportsperson. What should they eat and not eat, and why?

- Students should justify their choices, not just write a list of foods e.g. *Verduras – come por lo menos cinco porciones al día porque contienen muchas vitaminas.* They could also draw up a meal sheet for a day or a week. Encourage them to look back through the unit so far for language and structures.

4–9

16 Work with a partner and do an interview with someone well known. Talk about the secret of their success at keeping fit and well. Use the phrases in activities 13 and 14 to help.

PLTS

- Brainstorm in class a list of well-known fit and healthy people; either sports people or other obviously fit celebrities. Internet research would probably reveal some real facts about their fitness regimes.

Success criteria activities 15 & 16:
- *students communicate effectively and accurately*
- *students express personal opinions and justify points of view*
- *students use a variety of vocabulary and structures*
- *students deal with unpredictable elements*
- *students use different tenses or time frames*

4–9

Cómo comprar comida en una tienda

Planner

➤ Objectives
- Numbers and quantities

➤ Resources
Students' Book, pages 66–67
CD 2, tracks 11–14
Grammar Workbook, page 22
Activity sheets 22–25

➤ Key language
el cierre, una docena, los embutidos, la frutería, la manifestación, la naranjada, la panadería, la pastelería, la pescadería, la tableta de chocolate, la tarrina de helado
impersonal, incómodo/a, limpio/a, pasado/a de moda, práctico/a
estar de acuerdo
Me parece que…, Creo que…Pienso que…

➤ Skills
- Remembering vocabulary

➤ Grammar
- *tú* and *usted*

➤ PLTS
Students' Book, page 66, activity 3,
Reflective learners
Students' Book, page 67, activity 13,
Creative thinkers

➤ Starters
- Play bingo with big numbers. Set a limit for the game e.g. "10 numbers between 200 and 300".
- Ask the students what their favourite shop is, what type of shop it is, why they like it, if they like shopping and why / why not. Collect the information in a table, and get the students to write sentences using it.
- Look at the picture on page 66. Ask the class if they like supermarkets or not and why.
- Students' Book page 67, activity 10. Students revise in pairs when to use the *tú* and *usted* forms. Supply them with a list of verbs, and get them to produce a list of questions using both forms.

➤ Plenaries
- Shopping role play. Get students to write products and quantities on slips of paper. Some students write a shopping list, and have to "buy" the items on it from whichever students have them; sometimes the "seller" will have to explain they don't have the item, or have a lesser quantity. Swap roles.
- Collect opinions about shopping experiences and explain them to the class.
- Get students to bring in a till receipt or shopping list from the family weekly shop and describe it in Spanish (orally or written).
- Students produce a poster of food vocabulary.
- Students' Book page 67, activity 12. Students prepare a formal letter, attempting to persuade a neighbourhood of the benefits of a new supermarket. As a further extension, those against the development could write a reply.

---

1 **Escucha la entrevista con los vecinos de Marhuenda y escribe verdadero (V) o no mencionado (NM).**

- Students listen to the interview and decide if the statements are True (V), or Not Mentioned (NM).

5–9

| CD 2, track 11 | página 66, actividad 1 |

Estamos en Marhuenda, en el barrio 'Las flores', donde hoy hay una manifestación en contra del nuevo supermercado. Buenos días señora, ¿por qué está aquí hoy?
- No entiendo por qué quieren poner otro supermercado. Tenemos cinco o seis en cada calle, y son todos idénticos. No necesitamos otro más, eso está claro.

- Gracias, señora. ¿Y usted, señor?
- Los productos de los supermercados son más caros – no comprendo por qué esta obsesión de cerrar el mercado que llevamos utilizando toda la vida. Soy un jubilado con una pensión pequeña, ¿cómo voy a comer todos los días?
- Gracias, señor. ¿Y tú, cómo te llamas?
- Soy Sonia Torres.
- Dime, Sonia, ¿qué piensas tú del cierre del mercado?
- Pues sinceramente, es un escándalo. Mi padre trabaja en el mercado y vende carne, y si tiene que cerrar su puesto se queda sin trabajo, y lo mismo con mis amigos. Todos trabajamos en el mercado, es nuestra vida.
- Muchas gracias, Sonia. Y esto es todo, señoras y señores, desde Marhuenda.

Answers: **a** V, **b** V, **c** NM, **d** V, **e** NM, **f** NM

2 Julio va con su madre al supermercado. Mira la lista y escribe en cuál sección van a comprar cada cosa.

- Students match the items on the shopping list to the sections in the supermarket.

Answers: **1** E, **2** B, **3** G, **4** f, **5** A, **6** D, **7** C

3 Escucha y comprueba tus respuestas.

PLTS

- Students listen and check the answers to activity 2.

CD 2, track 12   **página 66, actividad 3**

– Vamos a ver ... ¿dónde compramos las manzanas?
– En la frutería, claro.
– Y a ver ... las zanahorias.
– Ah, mamá, mira, están en la sección de las verduras.
– ¿Y dónde está el chorizo para los bocadillos? No entiendo esta tienda.
– En la sección de embutidos ...
– Anda, Julio, vamos a comprar la leche y los yogures de la semana. Venga, están en la sección de productos lácteos. Y no te olvides de comprar los pasteles y el chocolate en la pastelería, y ahí en la panadería el pan. ¡El pescado en la pescadería, claro!
– Sí, mamá ...

4 Escucha y elige la opción adecuada. ¿Qué compran los dos?

- Students listen and choose the correct option.

CD 2, track 13   **página 66, actividad 4**

– Buenos días señora, ¿Qué desea?
– Quisiera un kilo de tomates.
– Y tú, ¿qué deseas?
– Quisiera doscientos cincuenta gramos de jamón, y huevos también.
– ¿Cuántos huevos quieres?
– Una docena, por favor.
– Mamá, ¿qué compras?
– Pues una bolsa de patatas para la tortilla.
– Y esa botella, ¿qué es?
– Pues una botella de Coca-Cola para todos, para tomar mientras veis el partido de fútbol en la tele.

Answers: **a** 1 kg, **b** 250 gramos, **c** 12, **d** una bolsa, **e** una botella

5 Escucha y escribe las cantidades.

- Students listen and write down the quantities.

CD 2, track 14   **página 66, actividad 5**

– ¡Tenemos el coche lleno! Todo el maletero lleno de comida. ¡Cómo pesa esto!
– Claro, son tres kilos de cebollas ... Mira, he comprado también 200 gramos de chorizo y una barra de pan para tus bocadillos. Una bolsa de patatas fritas y dos botellas de naranjada son para cuando vengan tus amigos a ver el fútbol, . ¡Ah! Y para desayunar un cartón de leche. Nunca tenemos bastante en casa ...

Answers: **a** 3 kgs, **b** 200 gramos, **c** un cartón, **d** dos botellas, **e** una barra, **f** una bolsa

6 Practica estos números con tu compañero. ¿Cómo se dicen en español?

- In pairs, students practise saying numbers. Get the students to write out the numbers as words first, then test their partner.

7 Lee los siguientes números y elige la opción correcta con tu compañero/a.

- Students read the numbers and choose the correct option.

8 Lee el artículo del periódico y habla con tu compañero/a. Escribe verdadero (V), falso (F) o no mencionado (NM).

- Students read the article and decide if the statements are True (V), False (F) or Not Mentioned (NM).

Answers: **a** NM, **b** V, **c** NM, **d** F, **e** V, **f** V, **g** V

9 Habla con tu compañero/a y da tu punto de vista. ¿Qué prefieres tú, mercado o supermercado? Utiliza las estructuras para ayudarte.

- In pairs, students discuss which type of shopping experience they prefer. Tell them to note down useful words and phrases from the newspaper article to help them explain their views.

10 Habla con tu compañero/a. ¿Con quién utilizas 'tú' y con quién 'usted'? ¿Por qué?

- In pairs, students discuss when to use tú and usted. Ask them to produce some examples, and then check with the whole class, and revise use of formal and informal structures if necessary.

11 Pon en práctica tus conocimientos y rellena los espacios.

- Students complete the sentences with the appropriate form of the verb.

Answers: **a** toma usted, **b** cocinas, **c** va usted, **d** está usted, **e** bebes

Remate

12 You are the manager of the supermarket in activity 8. Write a letter to the neighbours trying to convince them that the supermarket is ideal for the town.

- Revise the conventions of formal letter writing. Compare students' letters to see who is the most convincing.

13 In groups, design a leaflet to promote everything that is wonderful about your supermarket. Which is the best leaflet in the class?

- Brainstorm for supermarket names, special offers, location, and design what it looks like. Use comparatives and superlatives to convince readers. Think of slogans.

Success criteria activities 12 & 13:

- *students give information accurately and in the appropriate style*
- *students express personal opinions and justify points of view*
- *students use a variety of vocabulary and structures*
- *students use different tenses or time frames*

Cómo pedir y quejarte en un restaurante

páginas 68 y 69

Planner

➤ Objectives
- Ordering in a restaurant and complaining politely

➤ Resources
Students' Book, pages 68–69
CD 2, tracks 15–17
Grammar Workbook, pages 13, 17
Activity sheets 22–25

➤ Key language
la chuleta con patatas, los cubiertos, el flan, el helado, las judías con jamón
¿Adónde vamos a comer?, Adonde queráis, Me apetece, No me importa, ¿Qué queréis tomar?, Tengo mucha hambre
fría/o, libre, sucia/o
Disculpe, ¿podría cambiarme el tenedor, por favor?, Perdone, pero se ha olvidado mis cubiertos. Perdone, pero creo que se ha equivocado de pedido. Perdone, pero hay un problema con la cuenta. ¿Podríamos cambiarnos de mesa? ¿Podría revisar la cuenta, por favor? ¿Podría traerme…?

➤ Skills
- Asking questions

➤ Grammar
- Pronouns

➤ PLTS
Students' Book, page 68, activity 4, *Independent enquirers*
Students' Book, page 69, activity 9, *Reflective learners*

➤ Starters
- Look at the three menus on page 68 and ask the students which restaurant they would eat at and why. Ask them which restaurant serves the healthiest food, and which one they think serves the most typically Spanish food.
- Ask the students what they consider typical Spanish / Italian / French / German / American / British food to be. Get them to describe it.
- Students' Book page 68, activity 4. Discuss with students the kind of problems you might have at a restaurant and want to complain about.

➤ Plenaries
- Students look through the spread for pronouns, and classify them according to type.
- Students have a limited amount of time to place an order with a "waiter" and have it read back to check the order was taken correctly. Swap roles.
- Students' Book, page 69, activity 8. Students role play one of the situations. They have to place their order, find the problem, make the complaint and resolve the situation.
- Students' Book, page 69, activity 9. Students use and expand on the role-playing situation to produce a comic strip.

1 Mira los tres menús y escucha a los amigos. Decide qué menú eligen.

• Students listen and read the menus. They decide which restaurant the friends will visit.

> **CD 2, track 15**   **página 68, actividad 1**
>
> – Tengo mucha hambre, ¿adónde vamos a comer?
> – Adonde queráis. ¿Qué queréis tomar?
> – Me apetece pescado, ¿y a ti?
> – Yo prefiero la carne, ¿y tú, Mario?
> – Pues mira, no me importa, yo quiero tomar un café y un postre. La comida me da igual.
> – Entonces, lo mejor es que entramos aquí – tú puedes tomar la chuleta con patatas, yo los calamares y tú el flan. ¿Qué os parece?
> – Pues ya está.

Answer: **2** Restaurante La Marina

2 Escucha al camarero y al cliente y elige la opción correcta.

• Students listen and choose the correct option.

> **CD 2, track 16**   **página 68, actividad 2**
>
> – Buenas tardes, señor, ¿qué desea?
> – Quisiera comer unas tapas: tortilla, aceitunas, chorizo ...
> – ¿Y para beber?
> – Para beber, una Coca-Cola, y rápido – tengo solamente media hora para comer.
> – Y de postre tenemos helados, flan ...
> – No, gracias, no me gustan los dulces.
> – Muy bien. Se lo traigo todo ahora.

Answers: **a** española, **b** mucho tiempo, **c** refrescos, **d** postre

3a ¿Quién dice qué? Escribe las preguntas y las respuestas en la columna adecuada.

• Students complete the table, matching questions to responses.

Answers:

Camarero	Cliente
¿Qué desea?	Quisiera ...
¿Qué va a tomar?	Para mí ...
¿Qué va a beber?	Para beber ...
¿Qué va a tomar de postre?	De postre quisiera ...
¿Algo más?	¿Tiene ...?
No, lo siento.	
¡Que aproveche!	La cuenta, por favor
Ahora se la traigo.	

3b Haz una conversación con tu compañero/a. Uno es el camarero y otro el cliente. Utiliza las frases de 3a como apoyo.

• In pairs, students take it in turns to be the waiter and the customer. The waiter should note down the order so they can check they got it right.

4 Lee estas frases y decide cuáles de ellas son quejas.

PLTS

• Students decide which statements are complaints and which are not.

Answers: **a** no, **b** complaint, **c** no, **d** complaint, **e** complaint, **f** complaint, **g** complaint, **h** no

5a Lee las siguientes frases y compáralas con las de la actividad 4. ¿Cómo puedes quejarte más educadamente?

• Students use the statements to re-write the complaints in activity 4 more politely.

Answers (examples): **b** Perdón, pero estas patatas están frías. ¿Podría traerme otras, por favor? **d** Disculpe, ¿podría cambiarme el vaso, por favor? **f** Perdone, pero hay un problema con la cuenta. ¿Podría revisarla, por favor? **g** Perdone, pero creo que se ha equivocado de pedido. Yo pedí unas aceitunas.

5b Ahora reescribe estas frases para quejarte con mejores modales.

• Students re-write the statements more politely.

Answers (examples): **1** Perdone, pero hay un problema con la reserva. Reservamos una mesa para cuatro personas para las ocho. **2** Perdone, pero se ha olvidado mis cubiertos. **3** Perdone, pero hay un problema con la cuenta. ¿Podría revisarla, por favor?

6 Escucha esta conversación en el restaurante y decide si las afirmaciones son verdaderas (V) o falsas (F).

• Students listen to the conversation and decide if the statements are True (V) or False (F).

> **CD 2, track 17**   **página 69, actividad 6**
>
> – Buenas tardes. ¿Qué les pongo de beber?
> – Para mí, un vino tinto, ¿y para ti, Raúl?
> – Para mí una cerveza.
> – ¿Y para comer?
> – Quisiera esta sopa que tienen en el menú.
> – Lo siento, señor, pero no nos queda.
> – Qué mala suerte. Bueno, pues un pincho de tortilla.
> – Perfecto, señor. ¿y usted?
> – Unos calamares fritos.
> – Ahora mismo se los traigo.
>
> – ¡Uf! Estos calamares están muy calientes!
> – Espera un poco, hombre. ¿Quieres un poco de mi tortilla?
> – Ah, mira, la cuenta. Pero ...!?
> – Qué pasa?
> – Cuarenta euros. ¡Imposible!
> – ¡¿Cenar dos tapas por cuarenta euros?! Vamos a hablar con el camarero.
> – ¡Camarero, esta cuenta está mal!. Por veinte euros podíamos comer en el restaurante de al lado. Lo siento pero no pago una cantidad así.
> – Disculpe, señor. Creo que hay una equivocación. Ahora vuelvo.
> – Aquí tiene.
> – ¡Ah, esto está mejor! gracias.

Answers: **a** V, **b** F, **c** F, **d** V, **e** F, **f** V

7a **Lee este texto e indica los pronombres enfáticos.**

- Students find the emphatic pronouns in the text. Point out *conmigo* as being different and explain if necessary.

4–7

Answers: Vamos a Telepizza ... a ver qué queréis ... para mí una pizza margarita, y para papá una tropical. ¿Y para ti, Rita? Ah, una de cuatro quesos. Ana, ¿Vienes conmigo? No puedo llevarlas todas sola porque pesan mucho. Julio, ¿vais a ver a vuestros primos? Porque si vais a cenar con ellos no compro pizza para vosotros.

7b **Lee estas frases y une las frases de las dos columnas.**

- Students match the longer phrases with the shortened ones using the pronouns.

4–7

Answers: **1** f, **2** e, **3** i, **4** g, **5** b, **6** a, **7** d, **8** h, **9** c

Remate

8 **There is a problem in the restaurant. With two partners choose one of the three situations below. You are the waiter and they are the customers who are complaining.**

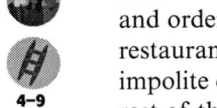
4–9

- Students use all the language of complaint and ordering to produce a conversation in a restaurant. They can choose to be polite or impolite customers. Groups could perform to the rest of the class, who have to decide what type of customer they are.

Success criteria activity 8:
- *students communicate effectively and accurately*
- *students express personal opinions and justify points of view*
- *students use a variety of vocabulary and structures*
- *students deal with unpredictable elements*
- *students use different tenses or time frames*

9 **Write a comic strip with a partner about a disastrous supper in a restaurant, using the menu above for ideas.**

PLTS

4–9

- Students revise all the language of this spread by writing a comic strip. Ideas for disasters could be brainstormed in class first.

Success criteria activity 9:
- *students give information accurately and in the appropriate style*
- *students express personal opinions and justify points of view*
- *students use a variety of vocabulary and structures*
- *students use different tenses or time frames*

Gramática en acción

páginas 70 y 71

> **Objectives**
- Review of comparatives and superlatives
- Use of the present continuous

> **Resources**
Students' Book, pages 70–71
Exam Skills Workbook, page 37 (F), page 38 (H)
Grammar Workbook, pages 9–11, 29, 41, 64, 66, 72
Activity sheet 26
Resources and Planning OxBox CD-ROM

> **Grammar**
- Comparatives and superlatives
- Impersonal phrases followed by infinitive
- The present continuous
- The polite form
- Pronouns with prepositions (emphatic pronouns)
- Number

> **PLTS**
Students' Book, page 70, activity 4,
Independent enquirers
Students' Book, page 71, activity 12,
Effective participators

> **Comparatives and superlatives**

1 **Use the comparatives in Spanish to compare the following:**

4–7

- Spend a short time revising how to form comparatives. The following answers are examples.

Answers: **a** La sopa es más sosa que la ensalada. **b** El café es más fuerte qu el té. **c** La tortilla española es menos pesada que el asado tradicional inglés. **d** La paella es más sano qye las tostadas con alubias. **e** La salsa de tomate es más picante que la mayonesa.

2 **With your partner, describe two famous dishes of your country and express opinions about them.**

4–9

- When students have produced their descriptions, the others can guess which dishes they are describing.

➤ **Impersonal phrases followed by infinitive**

3 **Translate the following sentences.**

6–8

● Students practise using impersonal structures in these sentences.

Answers:
a En España se puede comer tapas todas las tardes.
b En España se come más mariscos que en Inglaterra.
c Se hace la tortilla española con patatas y huevos.

4 **Write one sentence with each of the expressions from the box above. Can you do it if the verb is reflexive?**

PLTS

?–?

● Do a few examples in class first, then let students work independently before collating their answers to see how many different ideas they have come up with.

5 **Read the sentences 1–5 and match them up with sentences a–e.**

5–8

● Students practise recognising these structures followed by the infinitive.

Answers: **1** d, **2** e, **3** a, **4** c, **5** b

6 **Write down sentences using an impersonal structure, such as *me gusta, te gusta* etc. Use a different pronoun for each sentence. Make sure you get the pronouns right!**

7–9

● Brainstorm impersonal structures in class first. Give the students some titles to write sentences about.

➤ **The present continuous**

7a **Write the gerund of *e>ie* verbs following the example.**

6–7

● Get the students to use the grammar reference section or a dictionary to look for some more.

Answers: pedir – pidiendo, mentir – mintiendo

7b **Do the same with *o>ue* verbs.**

6–7

● Get the students to use the grammar reference section or a dictionary to look for some more.

Answer: morir – muriendo

➤ **Pronouns with prepositions (emphatic pronouns)**

8 **Fill the gaps with the appropriate emphatic pronouns.**

4–6

● Students use clues in the sentences to fill the gaps using emphatic pronouns.

Answers: **a** para él, **b** para mí, **c** para nosotros, **d** para ellos, **e** para ti

➤ **Numbers**

9 **Look at the order for a special celebration in a restaurant. Write down the numbers in Spanish. Make sure that you check the genders!**

1–3

● Students practise using large numbers. Get them to do the activity without looking at the table, then check back to see if they were right.

➤ **The polite form**

10 **How would you …**

4–6

● Students practise the use of familiar and polite forms of address. The following answers are examples. See how many different ideas the class can come up with.

Answers: **a** ¿Vienes al supermercado conmigo? **b** ¿Quiere usted beber algo? **c** ¿Quieres ir a comer un helado? **d** ¿Le apetece una taza de café? **e** ¿Puedes ayudarme a cocinar?

11 **Write to a problem page about somebody who has an addiction or a food allergy and give advice to that person.**

4–9

● In class, produce a list of problems to choose from. Give students the opportunity for a humorous take on a serious subject. Students work in pairs or groups to produce a list of useful phrases and vocabulary from the unit or other sources. Combine these lists for all the class to use. All students write a letter to the problem page, which another student has to write an answer for.

12 **Do an interview with a famous person about the food that they like and dislike using the polite form.**

PLTS

4–9

● Work on a list of questions to be asked. Practise the interview with their partner before performing for the class, who have to note what the person's likes and dislikes are. Students could also interview a real, mutually known, perform the interview in Spanish, and have the class guess who they interviewed.

Success criteria activities 11 & 12:
● *students communicate effectively and accurately*
● *students express personal opinions and justify points of view*
● *students use a variety of vocabulary and structures*
● *students deal with unpredictable elements*
● *students use different tenses or time frames*

Habilidades

Planner

➤ **Objectives**
● Express yourself in a more natural way

➤ **Resources**
Students' Book, page 72
CD 2, track 18–20
Exam Skills Workbook, page 38 (F), page 39 (H)
Activity sheet 26
Resources and Planning OxBox CD-ROM

➤ **Skills**
● Express interest and enthusiasm, agreement and disagreement through the tone of your voice
● Behave politely when you go out for a meal
● Pick out the clues to decide which information is relevant
● Use tone to work out a speaker's opinion

➤ **PLTS**
Students' Book, page 72, activity 2, *Creative thinkers*
Students' Book, page 72, activity 5, *Reflective learners*

➤ **Hablar**

1 Express interest and enthusiasm through the tone of your voice.

● One student picks a card that says *positivo* or *negativo*, and says a sentence in the appropriate manner. The others score him on how easily they understand his attitude.

2 Express agreement or disagreement.

● Tell students to look back through the unit for other useful expressions.

3 Behave politely when you go out for a meal.

● When they have completed the activities with their partner, students can combine their ideas with the whole class to see how many different ways of sounding polite they have come up with. They can get extra points for original ideas.

➤ **Escuchar**

4 Pick out clues to decide which information is relevant.

● Students listen and complete the activities.

> **CD 2, tracks 18 and 19**   **página 72, actividad 4**
>
> **1 Lo importante** no es la frecuencia o las horas de la comidas: para llevar una vida sana, hay que beber mucho agua – al menos un litro al día.
> **2 Solo me interesan** los precios. Es verdad que las tiendas locales forman parte de nuestra cultura tradicional, pero prefiero tener dinero para mi ocio.
> **3** Pues sí, comer alimentos azucarados pueden perjudicar seriamente la salud. Hacer deporte es aún mas importante. **No se puede negar** que la persona que hace deporte cinco veces a la semana vivirá más tiempo.

Answers: **1** drinking water, **2** the price of food, **3** taking exercise. For the second activity, students' answers will vary.

5 Use tone to work out a speaker's opinion.
● Students listen and complete the activity.

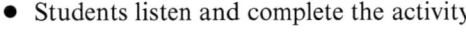

> **CD 2, track 20**   **página 72, actividad 5**
>
> **Jorge** ¡Huy! Este restaurante es increíble. Has visto cuántos camareros trabajan en este lugar! Al menos cinco por mesa!
> **Padre** Los precios también son increíbles! Creo que voy a hacer muchas horas extras en la oficina este mes.
> **Madre** Vale Luis... ¡Has de admitir que el ambiente de este restaurante es todo un logro! **[positive tone]** La decoración de las mesas, el lugar, los baños **[dreamily]**
> **Luisa** Sí sí... Nunca, en toda mi vida, he visto un lugar así.
> **Jorge** He comido mucho... qué pastel, qué pastel!
> **Padre** Sí sí... y qué sopa! Aún recuerdo la combinación de las espinacas y las fresas **[sarcastic]** No encontraréis una cena como esta en ningún otro restaurante...
> **Madre** Bueno, lo más importante es que toda la familia está disfrutando. Jorge, es tu día especial.
> **Padre** Sí, sí... ¡especial!

Answers: **Jorge** positive, **Jorge's mother** positive, **Jorge's father** negative, **Luisa** positive

Escenario

Planner

➤ Objectives
- Use the language of food both orally and written to describe a restaurant situation.

➤ Resources
Students' Book, page 73
Exam Skills Workbook, pages 35–36 (F),
pages 36–37 (H)
Assessment sheets 9–16
Resources and Planning OxBox CD-ROM

➤ Skills
- Writing practice
- Speaking practice

➤ PLTS
Students' Book, page 73, Escenario Oral,
Team workers
Students' Book, page 73, Escenario Escrito,
Self-managers

➤ Oral

Interview the chef in a restaurant.

 • Discuss the type of questions the critic would ask.
GCSE Grades A*-C
Grade C Students use past, present and future tenses. They express opinions, and deal with some unpredictability.
Grade A Students express and justify opinions. They use a variety of vocabulary and structure in longer speech sequences.

➤ Escrito

Write a webpage of a 3-star restaurant for the Michelin Guide.

PLTS • Explain what the Michelin Guide is if necessary.
GCSE Grades A*-C
Grade C Students use opinions and past, present and future tenses, both factually and imaginatively. Register is appropriate and style is basic.
Grade A Students write factually and imaginatively using longer sequences and a range of vocabulary and structure. They express and justify opinions in an appropriate style.

Vocabulario

This is a summary of key language from the unit, organised by spread and theme. Students can use it for reference while working on the unit, and as an aid to learning vocabulary.

Lectura

Planner

> **Objectives**
> - Food and drink in Spanish speaking countries.
> - To encourage independent reading and develop reading strategies.
> - These pages also provide alternative class and homework material for students who work quickly and require extension work.

> **Resources**
> Students' Book, page 177–178

> **PLTS**
> Students' Book, page 177, activity 1, *Reflective Learners*
> Students' Book, page 178, activity 2, *Team Workers*

> ## Lectura A – Las comidas y bebidas españolas y latino americanas

1   Lee el test y escribe lo siguiente:

PLTS

7–9

- Students do the test and find the answers to the questions.

Answers: **a** tomates / patatas / lechuga / zanahorias **b** aceitunas / aguacates / uvas / naranjas **c** sal / pimentón / chile **d** calimocho / vino / naranjada / Coca-Cola / sangría / chocolate caliente **e** saltamontes / chapulines **f** pollo / cuí / hámster

2   Habla con tu compañero/a. Usa las palabras de la caja para ayudarte.

4–9

- Students can work out their answers with a partner before discussing them in class.

3   Con tu compañero/a, escribe un test similar sobre la comida en tu país. Utiliza algunas de las frases de la primera lectura para ayudarte.

7–9

- Encourage students to think about foods and drink that are typical of this country, and possibly bizarre to foreigners.

> ## Lectura B – Un email de Mike!

1   Busca en el correo de Mike las frases equivalentes.

7–9

- Students find the Spanish equivalents in the text.

Answers: **a** nos llevamos bien, **b** todos se sentaban a la mesa para desayunar, comer y cenar, **c** El desayuno en España no es muy fuerte, **d** no estoy acostumbrado a comer tanto al mediodía, **e** Fran y yo tomábamos algo a las cinco de la tarde, **f** es muy caro comprar el alcohol en los bares, **g** Fran consideraba el botellón algo normal

2   Habla con tu compañero/a.

PLTS

7–9

- Students discuss the questions with a partner, which could develop into a class discussion on the differences and similarities between lifestyle in this country and Spain.

3   Eres un(a) chico/a español(a) que va a Inglaterra de intercambio. Escribe un correo hablando de las diferencias entre las comidas y las bebidas españolas, y los hábitos de los chicos. Utiliza el correo de Mike como referencia.

7–9

- Students imagine this country through the eyes of a visiting Spaniard, using Mike's email as a reference for Spanish customs.

Unit 3A Las fiestas			Overview grid	
Spread	**Contexts**	**Skills**	**Grammar**	**Vocabulary**
Spread title	• Topic areas covered within the unit	• Key skills focus	• Grammar covered in the unit	Key vocabulary
pages 76–77 **Cómo ponerse de acuerdo para salir**	• Arranging to meet someone and go out	• Listening for information	• Verbs followed by an infinitive	regalos ir a los bolos a lo mejor, conmigo, contigo lo siento, pero … no … sino …
pages 78–79 **Cómo organizar una fiesta**	• Organising a party	• Talking about the future	• Pronouns	un disfraz, un globo, la madrugada, un pastel adornar, traer gratis espero, sería una buena idea, te invito, tengo ganas de
pages 80–81 **Cómo hablar de las compras**	• Talking about going shopping	• Giving advice	• Pronouns	una blusa, una boda, un cumpleaños, el dinero,una falda, un pantalón, el precio, una tienda, un vestido, unos zapatos, unas zapatillas buscar, devolver, disfrutar, gastar, probarse ropa demasiado/a, demasiados/as de todas formas, no te va, ¡qué vergüenza!
pages 82–83 **Cómo describir una fiesta**	• Describing a party	• Listening for emotion • Increasing fluency when speaking	• The imperfect continuous	el Carnaval, la Navidad, los refrescos enfadado/a abrir, apagar, caer, cortar, golpear, llegar, romper, vestirse
pages 84–85 **Cómo describir un festival**	• Describing a festival	• Reading longer texts and understanding gist and detail	• The comparative	un colchón, los espíritus malvados, los invitados, un milagro, un muerto, la novia, los tambores ahuyentar, casarse, celebrar, emborracharse, entregar, festejar, mojarse, pelear, soltar, tirar alegre, lindo/a e, lo que me sorprendió fue que…, lo que pasa es…, tardamos casi una hora
pages 86–87 **Gramática en acción**	• Using pronouns		• Using pronouns • Using the continuous form of the imperfect	
page 88 **Habilidades**	• Reading with greater understanding	• Learn the words • Work out the meanings • Understand the sentence • Look out for red herrings • Keep your own personal vocabulary reference book • Think about accuracy		
page 89 **Escenario**	• Discuss organising a party. • Describe a special event to a Spanish friend.			
page 90 **Vocabulario**	• Summary of key vocabulary for the unit.			
pages 179–180 **Reading Pages**	Understanding about parties and festivals: • to encourage independent reading and to develop reading strategies. • to provide alternative class and homework material for students who finish other activities quickly.			

3A Las fiestas

Unit Objectives

Contexts: parties, festivals and going out
Skills focus: scanning for information, untangling language; looking out for red herrings; sharing strategies
Grammar: using pronouns, using the continuous form of the imperfect

Controlled assessment opportunities

Writing: Students' Book, page 77, activity 6
Writing: Students' Book, page 79, activity 8
Writing and Speaking: Students' Book, page 81, activity 11
Writing: Students' Book, page 83, activity 10
Writing: Students' Book, page 85, activity 9

See also GCSE Spanish for OCR Assessment OxBox CD-ROM.

An introduction to the unit   página 75

- *Aim*: To introduce the themes of the unit and encourage students to think about the reasons for learning Spanish.
- The opening page is designed with captions, pictures and page cross-references to provide a preview of what is to come:

	Students' Book
Cómo ponerse de acuerdo para salir	page 76
Cómo organizar una fiesta	page 78
Cómo hablar de las compras	page 80
Cómo describir una fiesta	page 82
Cómo describir un festival	page 84
Gramática en acción – improving your use and understanding of Spanish	page 86
Habilidades – increasing your language skills for fluency	page 88
Escenario – un correo electrónico a un amigo español que va a visitar. – explicar cómo se festeja y qué planes tienes	page 89

- Allow time for students to read the questions and cross-refer to the relevant pages of the Students' Book. They could do this individually or in pairs / small groups, followed by whole-class discussion.
- This spread also provides an opportunity for students to recap on familiar language. Ask them to think about language they already know that might be useful when working on the themes of the unit.

- Mindmap any language they produce, and if possible, keep it on display as reference as you progress through the unit. It can be added to at intervals as new language becomes familiar.
- At the end of work on the unit, allow time for students to return to this spread and repeat the mind-mapping process, this time including what they have learned over the course of the unit. Get them to answer the questions in their own words, and encourage them to use the results for revision purposes.
- Ask them what they found difficult, interesting etc. What do they think are the important things they have learned in this unit? What do they still need to improve on?
- If time permits, get the students to redesign the page. How would they set it out so it reflects the unit? How would they make it attractive to other learners of their age? How would they make it easy to follow? What would they include in terms of text, pictures, captions, page references? Ask them to imagine they are producing material for next year's class who will be learning the same thing – what would they have found it useful to know?

¿Por qué aprender el español? Para divertirse en España.
- Students share any experiences they have had of going out or going to parties and festivals in Spain e.g. on holiday, with friends and family.
- Ask them to consider what sort of language they would need to invite a Spanish person to join them for an evening out or a special event.

Cómo ponerse de acuerdo para salir

Planner

➤ **Objectives**
- Arranging to meet someone and go out

➤ **Resources**
Students' Book, pages 76–77
CD 2, tracks 24–25
Grammar Workbook, page 66
Activity sheets 29–32

➤ **Key language**
regalos; ir a los bolos; a lo mejor, conmigo, contigo; lo siento, pero …; no … sino …;

➤ **Skills**
- Listening for information

➤ **Grammar**
- Verbs followed by an infinitive

➤ **PLTS**
Students' Book, page 77, activity 3,
Team Workers
Students' Book, page 77, activity 6,
Creative Thinkers

➤ **Starters**
- In class or small groups, students draw up a list of things they do with their friends and classify them into categories such as *cada semana, de vez en cuando, raramente*.
- Students' Book, page 77, activity 1. Look at all the pictures on page 76 and see how many activities students can name in Spanish. Ask them to put them into short sentences.
- Students' Book, page 77, activities 1 & 2. Before students listen, ask them to also find out what month the conversation takes place in.
- Students' Book, page 77, activity 3. Before preparing the dialogue, give or elicit from the students some fillers such as *pues, no sé, lo siento pero* etc. Explain that when speaking they do not have to say *¿Qué haces el martes?*, but *Y el martes, ¿qué haces?* or *¿ Y el martes?* will do. The other students or a panel of judges could mark them out of 10 on how natural they sound, and explain what they awarded the marks for.

➤ **Plenaries**
- Students' Book, page 77, activity 3. Students perform the dialogue in the back-to-back telephone.
- Students' Book, page 77, activity 6. Students write each other invitation notes. Encourage them to be inventive; if students assume a celebrity identity they can tailor the invitation to the person's known tastes, or try to tempt them to try something different.
- Students' Book, page 77, activity 7. Students reply to the notes. Discuss possible excuses in class first, and make up some more inventive ones.
- Play a game. Groups take it in turns to come up with an invitation that they issue to the other groups for a point. The first group to come up with a correctly phrased acceptance or excuse gets a point.

---

1   Mira las imágenes a–g en la página 76. Escucha a Sergio y apunta cuando va a hacer cada actividad (lunes–domingo, mañana o tarde).

- Students listen and note down when Sergio is going to do the activities in the pictures. Students have to extrapolate *jueves* as the word itself is not used. Students should write down the activities in a list first, then fill in when Sergio is going to do them.

5–8

 CD 2, track 24   página 77, actividades 1 y 2

Julia	Sergio, ¿puedes salir conmigo algún día de la semana que viene? Podemos ir a tomar un café o algo.
Sergio	Pues, el lunes voy a estar todo el día en la playa, luego por la tarde tengo mi club de karate. El martes estoy libre por la tarde, pero el miércoles tengo que ir al dentista, luego hay un programa de televisión que quiero ver. El día veintidós es el cumpleaños de mi hermana, y le vamos a hacer una fiesta. Puedes venir si quieres. El viernes después de mi clase de violín por la mañana, podríamos hacer algo. El sábado estoy libre, no, espera, le prometí a mi madre, voy a ir con ella al centro comprar regalos. No tengo nada en mi agenda para el domingo.
Julia	El domingo es día de Navidad. Todo va a estar cerrado.

Answers: **a** lunes, **b** jueves, **c** lunes por la tarde, **d** viernes por la mañana, **e** miércoles, **f** miércoles, **g** sábado

2 Lee el correo de Julia y escucha otra vez. ¿Cuando pueden salir juntos?

5–8

- Students read Julia's email and listen again to find out when the two could meet. They may find it easier to draw up a grid and fill in the days and the activities, and see where Sergio and Julia are both free.

Answers: viernes por la tarde

3 Con un(a) compañero/a, haz un diálogo entre Sergio y Julia.

PLTS

5–8

- Students make up a conversation between Julia and Sergio. Do not give them a copy of the transcript. They should use the information from the listening and reading activities, but aim to make it different from the one on the recording. When they perform the dialogue, if they sit back to back so that they can't see each other's faces it feels like a real phone conversation.

4 Escucha 1–4. Decide quién realmente quiere aceptar la invitación. Desde "¡¡¡¡Sí!!!" (5 puntos) hasta "¡No! ¡No! ¡No!" (0 puntos).

4–8

- Students listen and decide who will accept the invitation. The answers could be up for debate.

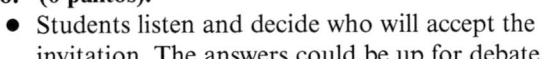

CD 2, track 25   página 77, actividad 4

1
A ¿Qué haces el viernes por la tarde?
B No sé, ¿por qué?
A ¿Quieres ir a los bolos?
B ¿A los bolos?
A Sí
B ¿Contigo?
A Sí.
B ¿Quién más va a ir?
A Nadie más, solo tú, y yo.
B Pues, tengo que verlo. A lo mejor tengo que hacer algo con mi familia. Te digo mañana.

2
A ¿Quieres ir con nosotros a los bolos?
B ¡A los bolos! ¿Cuándo vais a ir?
A Vamos el sábado por la tarde, como a las seis.
B ¡Yaya! el sábado tengo que visitar a mi abuela, lo siento, Javier.

3
A ¿Qué haces el miércoles por la tarde?
B El miércoles ... no tengo nada planeado
A ¿Quieres ir a los bolos conmigo?
B Pues, ¿por qué no?, buena idea, llámame antes de irte.

4
A Vamos a ir a los bolos el viernes, por si quieres ir.
B Claro, ¿a qué hora?
A Pues, como a las seis y media, no sé todavía.
B ¿Y dónde nos vemos?
A Te llamo el viernes para decirte.
B Bueno, y si no, te llamo yo.

Answers (probable): **1** 1 point, **2** 0 points, **3** 4 points, **4** 5 points

5 Trabaja con un(a) compañero/a. Una persona invita, la otra hace excusas y pone pretextos. Mira las ideas en la página 76 para ayudarte.

4–8

- Students take it in turns to issue invitations and offer excuses. Check they know the vocabulary for the pictures on page 76 first, and ask for any other ideas they have (*tengo que sacar al perro, tengo que cuidar de mi hermanito, tengo que ir a mi clase de baile* etc).

Remate

6 Write an invitation to the other members of the group. Explain what you are going to do, where, when and with whom.

PLTS

4–8

- Students use the language learnt so far to issue written invitation notes. They could assume an alternative identity for this exercise (e.g. a celebrity) or draw names out of a hat at random so no one gets left out.

Success criteria activity 6:
- *students give information accurately and in the appropriate style*
- *students express personal opinions and justify points of view*
- *students use a variety of vocabulary and structures*
- *students use different tenses or time frames*

7 Read the invitations of the others in the group and then talk to them, telling them if you can accept or if not, why not.

4–8

- The teacher can set conditions for more advanced groups; pupils pick a slip of paper which says if they accept gladly / accept reluctantly / refuse gladly etc.

Success criteria activity 7:
- *students communicate effectively and accurately*
- *students express personal opinions and justify points of view*
- *students use a variety of vocabulary and structures*
- *students deal with unpredictable elements*
- *students use different tenses or time frames*

Cómo organizar una fiesta

Planner

➤ **Objectives**
- Organising a party

➤ **Resources**
Students' Book, pages 78–79
CD 2, tracks 26–27
Grammar Workbook, pages 22–29
Activity sheet 29–32

➤ **Key language**
un disfraz, un globo, la madrugada, un pastel; adornar, traer; gratis; espero, sería una buena idea, te invito, tengo ganas de.

➤ **Skills**
- Talking about the future

➤ **Grammar**
- Pronouns

➤ **PLTS**
Students' Book, page 79, activity 8,
Independent Enquirers
Students' Book, page 79 activity 9,
Team Workers

➤ **Starters**
- Brainstorm any party vocabulary students already know. Classify it into groups such as places to have a party, things to do, things to eat, reasons to have a party etc. Keep the vocabulary for reference throughout this spread, and also for the Escenario activity later in the unit.
- Students' Book, page 78, activity 1. First, get the students to match up Spanish and English, or Spanish phrases and pictures to make sure they understand the vocabulary.
- Students' Book, page 79, activity 6. Display, in random order, some short possible answers to the questions (unrelated to the listening text). Give students a time limit to match them up, check their answers and their understanding of the questions
- Students' Book, page 79, activity 7. Before answering their partner's questions, students should go through their chosen text noting down or underlining (on a paper copy) key words and phrases that will help them answer the questions. Go through the first question for each text in class, or ask the students to read their text in silence and answer any vocabulary queries they have.

➤ **Plenaries**
- Students' Book, page 79, activity 5. Return to this activity at the end of a lesson or part way through it, and call out or write on the board *te invito* and ask students what it means. Do several Spanish to English, then several English to Spanish. Repetition increases familiarity.
- Students' Book, page 79, activity 8. Students write to their "Spanish exchange partner", offering suggestions for activities. Their pick a name out of a hat and write their suggestion to that person without knowing who that person really is, to increase realism.
- Students' Book, page 79, activity 9. Students can reply and question their partner either using the telephone simulation technique (back to back), or in written form. With the teacher acting as postman, or between two parrallel classes, the exchange of information could be extended for quite some time, especially if the identities are kept strictly secret.
- Students plan and organise a Spanish party for a group of younger children. This can be a theoretical exercise, but is most effective if done for real. In Spanish, they choose and prioritise what must be done, share out the responsibilities and tasks, decide on party activities.

1 **Pon las actividades en orden de importancia.**

- Students list the preparation activities in order of importance. They can do this individually, then discuss their ideas with a partner and feed back to the rest of the class. Discuss on what basis they made their choices – timescale, importance, enjoyment etc.

3-5

2 **Vuelve a escribir el texto, sin repetir siempre 'voy a'.**

- Students re-write the paragraph, replacing *voy a* with alternative vocabulary.

3-5

Answer (possible): Mi proyecto es hacer una fiesta para mi amiga inglesa. Quiero invitar a todos mis amigos. Me gustaría hacer un CD especial con mis canciones favoritas para bailar. Tengo que comprar mucha comida, bebida, y espero hacer un pastel de cumpleaños. Tengo ganas de adornar la casa con globos. Necesito comprar un regalo para ella.

3 **Escribe tus planes para otra fiesta, según las imágenes.**

- Students write about their plans for a party. Discuss in class what kind of an event it is, and what the preparations are going to be.

4–6

Answer (possible): Mi proyecto es hacer una fiesta para mi madre. Quiero invitar a toda la familia. Tengo que preparar mucha comida, y necesito comprar mucha bebida. Tengo ganas de comprar un regalo para ella.

4 **Escucha a los dos amigos discutiendo sobre una fiesta. Contesta a las preguntas en inglés.**

- Students listen and answer the questions. Encourage them to listen without taking notes first, then see what they can answer. Listen again.

3–5

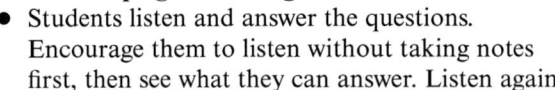 **CD 2, track 26**   **página 79, actividad 4**

Chico	Quiero hacer una fiesta para mi hermano menor.
Chica	¿Es su cumpleaños?
Chico	Sí, va a tener siete años.
Chica	¿Siete años? ¿Vas a invitar a muchos de sus amigos?
Chico	Sólo quiero invitar a cuatro o cinco. No puedo invitar a toda la clase.
Chica	¿Qué vas a hacer?
Chico	Eso es el problema. No sé.
Chica	Tengo una idea. ¿Ya le compraste un regalo?
Chico	No. Eso es otro problema. No sé qué voy a comprarle.
Chica	Pues, ¿por qué no le compras el nuevo juego de Matapinguinos Cinco para su consola de video juegos? Luego en la fiesta sus amigos pueden jugar juntos y hacer un campeonato.
Chico	Bien. El juego es bastante caro, pero si es su regalo y también es para la fiesta, puedo comprárselo. También puedo hacer el pastel en lugar de comprar uno. Perfecto.

Answers: **a** The boy's little brother. **b** It is his 7th birthday. **c** Four or five friends. **d** He doesn't know what to do, or what present to buy. **e** They will buy a new video game and the children can play it at the party.

5 **Haz corresponder las frases españoles y su traducción al inglés.**

Grammar reference page 210

- Students match up the Spanish and the English. They should write everything out in full, Spanish and English, and keep for reference. Remind them that it is the verb that shows who is doing the inviting. Also remind them that *te invito* can also mean I'm paying.

4–6

Answers: **1** g, **2** e, **3** a, **4** f, **5** c, **6** h, **7** d, **8** b

6 **Jesús organiza una fiesta. Escucha y contesta a las preguntas. ¿A cuáles de las preguntas no contesta Jesús?**

- Students listen and understand. Tell them to decide which details need to be noted down and which can be remembered before answering the questions.

5–8

 CD 2, track 27   **página 79, actividad 6**

Quiero hacer una fiesta para todos los estudiantes ingleses de intercambio que están aquí en el instituto. También los estudiantes españoles pueden venir. Es para todos. Incluso los profesores pueden venir si quieren. Va a ser en mi casa, porque tenemos un patio bastante grande. Va a empezar a las nueve y terminaremos a medianoche porque por la mañana tenemos que estar en el instituto. Voy a comprar las bebidas y mi mamá va a preparar algo de comer, tortilla, bocadillos, y cosas así. Si los españoles quieren traer también algo de comer sería buena idea. Podemos enseñar a los ingleses unos bailes y unas canciones. Voy a hacer una compilación en mi iPod.

Answers: **a** Va a hacer una fiesta para estudiantes de intercambio. **b** Pueden venir los estudiantes ingleses, los españoles y aun los profesores. **c** Va a ser en la casa de Jesús. **d** No contesta. **e** Va a ser a las nueve de la tarde. **f** Terminará a medianoche. **g** No contesta. **h** Los españoles tienen que traer algo de comer. **i** Sí, vamos a comer allí.

7 **Lee una de las propuestas (de Miguel o Rosa). Trabajo con un(a) compañero/a. A hace el papel del estudiante inglés y hace las preguntas de arriba. B hace el papel del español y explica qué va a pasar.**

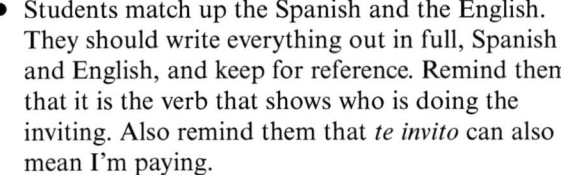

5–8

- Students choose a text to read. Their partner asks them questions about it, and notes down the answers to check later that their partner gave the correct information. The questioner should not look at the text while asking the questions. The first person must remember to answer questions about the text they read, and should try to get into character e.g. *"Miguel wants to invite us to... he's a friend in my class, he's really nice..."*

- If you have not done so before explain that in the context of a bar / restaurant etc "te invito" means "I'm paying". Discuss how Spanish eating out and going out hours are different to this country, and that it is not unusual for (adults) to meet for a meal at 10pm or later.

Remate

8 **Imagine that you are going to have a Spanish exchange student to stay in your house. Write to them and describe the different choices of things to do when you go out.**

PLTS

5–8

- Brainstorm some suggestions in class first to broaden the scope of activities. Categorise activities under *weekend, evening, daytime, in town, in the local area, longer trips* etc. Are there any unusual activities special to your area – caving, hot air ballooning, a wild animal park? Model how to offer some of the suggestions.

Success criteria activity 8:
- *students give information accurately and in the appropriate style*
- *students express personal opinions and justify points of view*
- *students use a variety of vocabulary and structures*
- *students use different tenses or time frames*

4–9

9 Ask a partner about the different suggestions you have written down. Play the role of the Spanish student, using the questions in activity 6.

- Students pick one or more of their partner's activities to question them about. They could prepare the list and find out genuine information before hand, or make it up as they go along,

maybe giving an activity outrageous prices or absurd opening hours if they wish to dissuade their visitor from that option. If they perform these dialogues, others can decide which activity the invitor really wants to do.

Success criteria activity 9:
- *students communicate effectively and accurately*
- *students express personal opinions and justify points of view*
- *students use a variety of vocabulary and structures*
- *students deal with unpredictable elements*
- *students use different tenses or time frames*

Cómo hablar de las compras

páginas 80 y 81

Planner

➤ Objectives
- Talking about going shopping

➤ Resources
Students' Book, pages 80–81
CD 2, tracks 28–29
Grammar Workbook, pages 22–29
Activity sheets 29–32

➤ Key language
una blusa, una boda, un cumpleaños, el dinero, una falda, un pantalón, el precio, una tienda, un vestido, unos zapatos, unas zapatillas
buscar, devolver, disfrutar, gastar, probarse ropa
demasiado/a, demasiados/las
de todas formas, no te va, ¡qué vergüenza!

➤ Skills
- Giving advice

➤ Grammar
- Pronouns

➤ PLTS
Students' Book, page 81, activity 8,
Self-Managers
Students' Book, page 81, activity 10,
Effective Participators

➤ Starters
- In class, brainstorm items students go shopping for. Do they buy these things with their own money, do their parents buy them, is it shopping for pleasure or duty.

- Students' Book, page 80, activity 1. Students search the texts simply for the different items to buy. Discuss if the class thinks the items are typical of male and female shopping habits or not.
- Students' Book, page 81, activity 7. Before deciding whether the characters on the spread are phobic or addicts, go through the statements and make sure students understand the vocabulary, possibly giving a loose translation, but not writing anything down at this point. Students pick one statement that applies to them.
- Play *Fui de compras*. One student says *Fui de compras y compré una falda*. The next says *Fui de compras y compré una falda y unos zapatos*, and so on. You can make it more complicated by doing it in alphabetical order, or limiting the subject matter to certain types of shopping, or cycling through the verb.

➤ Plenaries
- Students' Book, page 80, activity 6. Give students a copy of the transcript and tell them to find all the different verbs and say what tense they are in and, if possible, why.
- Students' Book, page 81, activity 10. Students carry out a questionnaire in class about people's shopping habits. This can be done with the aim of giving each student a score on the phobic / addict continuum, or analysing the class shopping habits in general.
- Students' Book, page 81, activity 11. Students write about going shopping and receive advice on their shopping habits from a partner. They can simply swap advice.
- The teacher reads out a statement and the students have to decide, without referring to the Students' Book, if it describes a shopping phobic or a shopping addict.

1 **Lee rápidamente los textos. Busca los diferentes tipos de artículos que mencionan comprar.**

- Students read the articles and note down the items the different people buy. A time limit can be set. On a paper copy of the articles, students can simply underline the items.

5–8

Answers: **Héctor** videojuegos, DVD, partido de fútbol
Carlos pilas, gafas de sol, chicle, bebidas, uniforme escolar
Elena zapatos, una falda, ropa
Virginia comida, carne, pescado, queso, ropa, un pantalón

2 **¿Quién menciona …**

- Students read again and decide who mentions what.

Answers: **a** Héctor, Carlos **b** Carlos, Elena, Virginia **c** Héctor, Carlos

4–7

3 **Busca estos datos específicos:**

- Students search the texts for the specific information.

Answers: **a** Héctor, **b** Carlos, **c** Virginia, **d** Elena

4–8

4 **Busca estas palabras en español:**

- Students look for the words in Spanish.

Answers:

I enjoy me encanta, **too many/too much** demasiado, **meat** carne, **batteries** las pilas, **to try on** probar, **to spend** gastar, **to take back** devolver, **skateboarding** el monopatín

5–8

5 **Haz corresponder:**

Grammar reference page 209

- Students match the Spanish and the English.

Answers: **1** b, **2** d, **3** c, **4** a

4–6

6 **Escucha (1–5) y decide de quién (Héctor, Carlos, Elena, Virginia) hablan.**

- Students decide who is being talked about; they look at the picture clues and listen.

4–8

> **CD 2, track 28**   **página 80, actividad 6**
>
> **1** Es mi mejor amigo, pero no me compró nada en mi cumpleaños. Dijo que no necesito nada.
> **2** Le voy a comprar algo de ropa. No tiene nada que ponerse porque sólo va de compras en los supermercados.
> **3** En mi cumpleaños me regaló una película en DVD – me la compró en Internet.
> **4** Lo bueno de tener una hermana mayor es que también compra ropa para mí. Encontró un vestido precioso que era demasiado pequeño para ella, y me lo compró. Le fascina la ropa.
> **5** Necesita una camisa o una gorra para llevar cuando va al estadio. Se las le voy a comprar y se las voy a regalar el sábado.

Answers: **1** Carlos, **2** Virginia, **3** Héctor, **4** Elena, **5** Héctor

7 **Decide si Héctor, Carlos, Elena y Virginia son adictos o tienen fobia a las compras.**

- Students decide if any of the four characters are shopping addicts or phobics. They need to look back at the original texts at activity 1, as well as taking into account any other information about them on this spread. Students can give reasons for their answers e.g. *Elena es adicta porque compra ropa que no necesita.*

5–9

Answers: **Héctor** no, **Carlos** fobia, **Elena** adicta, **Virginia** fobia

8 **Escucha los consejos de Azucena y Trinidad. Mientras escucha, apunta cuatro palabras (máximo) para cada consejo. Luego escribe los consejos en frases completas.**

PLTS

- Students listen for gist, making minimal notes, then reproduce the advice in their own words. They may need to listen several times. Emphasise they do not have to reproduce the exact language of the recording, but the meaning. This gives them confidence at adapting language.

6–8

> **CD 2, track 29**   **página 81, actividad 8**
>
> **A** Cuando vas de compras es importante ir con una lista.
> **B** Debes de tener una idea de qué quieres comprar y por qué.
> **A** Debes saber cuánto vas a gastar, y escoger la tienda que ofrezca el mejor precio.
> **B** Hay que comprar cosas que van bien con la ropa que ya tienes. Si ves una blusa bonita pero que no coordina con otra ropa que tienes, no puedes comprarla.
> **A** Tienes que probar la ropa en la tienda. Si te va bien, la puedes comprar. Sí no, no.

9 **Lee. ¿Quién respetó los consejos?**

- Students read the texts and decide who took the advice. If possible, they should explain their answers. Less able groups can give explanations after reading the transcript.

4–8

Answers: **Carlota** sí – no compró el vestido que no le gustó y no – compró unas zapatillas que necesitaba, **Cristina** sí – compró una blusa para el precio que quería, **Marco** no – compró un videojuego caro en vez de zapatos.

Remate

10 **Prepare a questionnaire to find out if there are shopping addicts or people with shopping phobia in your class. Interview members of the group.**

PLTS

- Students can use the statements before activity 7. Rather than just *sí* and *no* answers, they could add in *siempre*, *a veces*, *nunca*, and make up scores. Students can work in pairs, and collaborate with their partner to write up and analyse their answers.

4–9

Success criteria activity 10:

- *students communicate effectively and accurately*
- *students express personal opinions and justify points of view*
- *students use different tenses or time frames*

11 **Write down your opinion about going shopping. Include your habits, what happened the last time you went shopping, and your plans. Then read what your partner has written and offer them advice.**

- Students can do this as themselves, or in character as someone completely different or a celebrity. The scenarios can be realistic or humorous. The advice should fit the scenario, unless you want to add another layer by deciding who gave bad or good advice to the various people.

5–9

Success criteria activity 11:
- *students give information accurately and in the appropriate style*
- *students express personal opinions and justify points of view*
- *students use a variety of vocabulary and structures*
- *students use different tenses or time frames*

Cómo describir una fiesta

páginas 82 y 83

Planner

➤ Objectives
- Describing a party

➤ Resources
Students' Book, pages 82–83
CD 2, track 30
Grammar Workbook, pages 46
Activity sheets 29–32

➤ Key language
el Carnaval, la Navidad, los refrescos
enfadadola
abrir, apagar, caer, cortar, golpear, llegar, romper, vestirse

➤ Skills
- Listening for emotion
- Increasing fluency when speaking

➤ Grammar
- The imperfect

➤ PLTS
Students' Book, page 82, activity 1,
Reflective Learners
Students' Book, page 82, activity 5,
Team Workers

➤ Starters
- Ask students for what events people throw a party. Write the words on the board or a large piece of paper. Around each word make a spidergram of associated words. Groups or pairs could pick a type of party each and the vocabulary collected can be displayed to use for the Remate and Escenario activities.
- Students' Book, page 82, activities 1-5. It is helpful to provide students with a paper copy of this text so they can mark emphasis on it before reading out loud, highlight verbs in the preterite and imperfect etc. Copied onto a large piece of paper with space around the text, a group can make joint notes, and the class can compare their work.
- Students' Book, page 83, activity 7. Students look at the pictures and say (in English or Spanish) what is happening. If this happened to them, what would their reaction be on the *Humor – Horror* scale? What reaction do they think the people in the pictures will have? Then they listen to the CD and decide how close their predictions were.
- Students' Book, page 82, activity 10. Before students write their own decriptions, do one together as a class. Ask for someone to describe (in English) a real party. If possible, use a recent school event. Work as a class to write a simple paragraph describing the event, then look to see where it could easily be embellished. Point out verbs tenses, connectors etc. The students can use this as a model for their own work.

➤ **Plenaries**

- Students' Book, page 82, activity 6. Write on the board *Estaba bailando en el salón cuando encontré un insecto*. Ask the class if the sentence is *lógico* or *absurdo*. Do the same with a few more sentences, then get the students to take over the activity, either as a whole class, or in groups or pairs. They can use the phrases at activity 6 to start with, then make up their own.

- Students' Book, page 82, activity 8. When the students have done this activity, it can be re-used from memory by writing prompts on the board (*Event, when, what we did, connector, opinion, connector, someone said* etc. in Spanish or English as appropriate). It could be played again as a consequences game on paper, or students could be picked at random to give the next part of the story until it is completed.

- Students' Book, page 82, activity 9. The teacher reads out a complete and pre-prepared "story" from the table very quickly. Students will only have time to note down the number of each phrase. The first group or pair to conclude if the story is *ridículo* or *lógico* wins.

- Students' Book, page 82, activity 10. Students read each others' descriptions in silence and mark it from 1-5, 1 being *aburrido*, and 5 being *divertido*. The person who gets the highest score wins.

---

1   Lee el texto en voz alta, poniendo atención a la pronunciación.

PLTS

- Students read the text out loud to practise pronunciation. They can do it in groups of four, taking one paragraph each, and commenting on each other's reading, before volunteers read a paragraph out to a larger group or the whole class.

4-9

2   Busca los verbos en el pretérito (*I went, I saw, they said*) y en el imperfecto (*I was talking, they were dancing*).
Grammar reference page 205

- Students find all the verbs in the preterite and the imperfect in the text.

Answers:
preterite fui, cantamos, llegué, encontré, dije, dijo, subimos, vi, decidí, dijeron, entraron, fue
4-6
imperfect era, había, estaban escuchando, estaban hablando, estaban jugando, estaban haciendo, parecían, estaban bailando, hablaban, quería

3   Haz una lista en inglés de todas las actividades que hacían en la fiesta.

- Students write a list in English of all the different activities happening at the party.

Answers: listening to music, talking in the kitchen, playing a video game − having an interactive tennis match, dancing, talking in the garden / patio
5-8

4   Busca todas las opiniones y palabras referentes al tiempo.

- Students look for opinions and time phrases in the text.

Answers:
opiniones ridículos, divertido, relajada
4-8
palabras referentes al tiempo la semana pasada, cuando llegué, más tarde, momentos después

5   Explica a un(a) compañero/a todo lo que entiendes. Discute qué hacer con las palabras desconocidas.

PLTS

- Students explain what they understand of the text to a partner. Remind them that this does not mean they are trying to translate it. Students can then pool their ideas and discuss them in class, sharing techniques for understanding the text.

4-8
- Alternatively, each partner can be given an English version or a checklist for half the text, and as their partner tells them what they think, the one with the list says if they are right.

6   Haz frases completas y tradúcelas al inglés.

- Students match the two halves of the sentences and translate them into English.

Answers:
4-6
1 d   I was dancing in the living room when they turned the music off.
2 e   I was playing tennis on the PC when I hit my friend in the face.
3 b   I was talking to a girl when her boyfriend arrived.
4 a   I was drinking a drink when I dropped it and broke the glass.
5 f   I was eating a sandwich when I found an insect.
6 c   I was washing my hands when they opened the bathroom door.

7   Escucha y decide cuál es la actitud en cada caso. Desde 'Humor' (5 puntos) hasta 'Horror' (0 puntos).

- Students listen and decide if where the situations lie on the Humour to Horror scale. The CD provides a clue, but the answers are up for discussion.
4-6

Answers (possible): **a** 3, **b** 0, **c** 2, **d** 5, **e** 4.

CD 2, track 30 **página 82, actividad 7**

a Pues, yo estaba en el cuarto de baño cuando abrieron la puerta.

b Estaban cortando el pastel cuando cayó al suelo.

c Estaba jugando al tenis, cuando rompí el televisor.

d Mi hermano estaba cantando cuando le llamé en su teléfono móvil.

e Me estaba vistiendo para la fiesta cuando llegaron los invitados.

8 **Utiliza un dado para hacer frases sobre una fiesta. Decide si son ridículas o lógicas.**

4–7

- Students throw a dice to make up sentences from the table and decide if they are ridiculous or logical. Alternatively, one student writes the first phrase on the top of a piece of paper then folds it over as in Consequences, and passes it on to the next person in their group, who writes the next phrase and so on.

Remate

9 **Describe a party to your partner, using the table to help you.**

4–8

- For less able groups, the teacher can give them quick prompts e.g. *Christmas – last year – church – and – not fun* etc. The teacher can then give prompts for which they have to adapt the language of the table e.g. *My cousin's wedding – when I was 15 – they had a party* etc. Their partner has to note down the numbers of the phrases, or make notes in English, which they read back to the first person, who says if the listener is correct.

Success criteria activity 9:

- *students communicate effectively and accurately*
- *students express personal opinions and justify points of view*
- *students use a variety of vocabulary and structures*
- *students use different tenses or time frames*

10 **Write a description of a party like Rigoberto's, but with more incidents like those in activity 6.**

5–9

- Students use the phrases at activity 6 and the table at activity 8 to help them, as well as any of their own ideas. Alternatively, the teacher can provide certain incidents or vocabulary that have to be incorporated.

Success criteria activity 10:

- *students give information accurately and in the appropriate style*
- *students express personal opinions and justify points of view*
- *students use a variety of vocabulary and structures*
- *students use different tenses or time frames*

Cómo describir un festival

páginas 84 y 85

Planner

➤ **Objectives**
- Describing a festival

➤ **Resources**
Students' Book, pages 84–85
CD 2, track 31
Grammar Workbook, pages 9, 21
Activity sheets 29–32

➤ **Key language**
un colchón, los espíritus malvados, los invitados, un milagro, un muerto, la novia, los tambores
ahuyentar, casarse, celebrar, emborracharse, entregar, festejar, mojarse, pelear, soltar, tirar

alegre, lindo/a
e, lo que me sorprendió fue que …,
lo que pasa es …, tardamos casi una hora

➤ **Skills**
- Reading longer texts and understanding gist and detail

➤ **Grammar**
- The comparative

➤ **PLTS**
Students' Book, page 85, activity 9,
Independent Enquirers
Students' Book, page 85, activity 10,
Effective Participators

➤ **Starters**

- Discuss Spanish festivals with the class. Ask if anyone has ever been present at one, or heard of one. Describe one or two of the better known ones like Carnaval. Explain there are hundreds of festivals in Spain every year. Give every student a month, or even a date, and ask them to find a festival that happens then. Tell them they can use this at the end of the spread.
- Students' Book, page 84, activity 1. Before doing the activities, students read through the texts, individually or in pairs, and note down or underline (on a paper copy) anything they do understand. They write a brief resumé of the text in English, and after doing the activities refer back to it to see how much more they now understand.
- Students' Book, page 85, activity 6. Before reading the texts, students read statements a-g and predict which wedding they occurred at. Although the predictions are fairly obvious, it gives them something to look out for as they read the texts. More advanced groups can also find out why these things happened.
- Play word association. Say *fiesta*, the next person says e.g. *bailar* and so on. The aim is to get back to the word *fiesta*, but not before everyone has had a turn.

➤ **Plenaries**

- Students' Book, page 84, activity 5. After doing activities 1-5, tell students to read through the three texts one more time, very carefully, then close their books. The teacher makes statements, or reads phrases from the texts, and the students identify from which festival description they come.
- Students' Book, page 85, activity 8. After completing the reading activities about the weddings, give the students a copy of one of the descriptions with all the verbs blanked out. They have to complete the text. Supply a list of verbs (in the correct forms, or in the infinitive) if necessary.
- Students' Book, page 85, activity 9. Students research festival in Spain and Mexico and write about real or invented ones. As there are so many to choose from, each student could choose or be allocated a country, a region, or a time of year.
- Students' Book, page 85, activity 10. Students decide which festivals are real and which are invented. All the descriptions could be displayed around the class with accompanying pictures for students to look at and read, like an exhibition.

1 ¿De cuál/cuáles de las fiestas se trata?

- Students read the texts and decide to which each statement refers.

Answers: **a** 2 & 3, **b** 1, **c** 1 & 3, **d** 1

5–7

2 Busca estas palabras en español:

- Students look for the words in Spanish.

Answers: **bucket** el cubo, **hosepipe** la manguera, **drought** la sequía, **miracle** el milagro, **ducks** los patos, **toy** el juguete, **mattress** el colchón, **evil spirits** los espíritus malvados, **drums** los tambores

5–7

3 Ahora intenta leer las frases completas donde aparecen esas palabras.

- Students try to read and understand the whole sentences where these words appear. The teacher can ask for ideas from the class, combining what they understand.

6–8

4 Escucha e identifica la fiesta. ¿Qué ocurrió? Toma apuntes en inglés.

- Students listen and identify the festival. Tell them to listen for key words and to beware red herrings. When they have finished listening and said which festival they think it is, make two lists, one of key words, and one of red herrings.

5–8

 CD 2, track 31   **página 84, actividad 4**

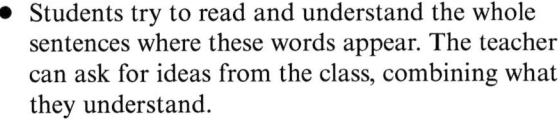

Fui a una fiesta en un pueblo pequeño. Por la mañana no había mucho para los turistas – era un pueblo muy tranquilo y normal. Luego más tarde fue muy divertido y un poco alarmante. Vi mucha gente mojada y vi alguna gente que peleaba. Lo que pasaba es que algunos tradicionalistas querían soltar unos patos vivos, y otros protestaban que era cruel y que ya no se hacía con pájaros vivos. Y mientras tanto, los participantes estaban en el agua, agarrando patos vivos y de juguete. Fue una experiencia inolvidable.

Answer: 2

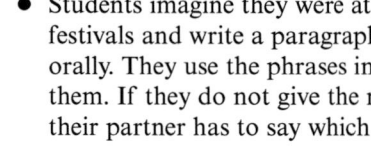

5 **Imagina que fuiste a una de las otras fiestas. Describe tu experiencia.**

5–8

- Students imagine they were at one of the other festivals and write a paragraph, or describe it orally. They use the phrases in the box to help them. If they do not give the name of the festival, their partner has to say which one they are describing.

6 **Lee sobre las dos bodas. Contesta a las preguntas en inglés.**

- Students read about the two weddings and answer the questions in English.

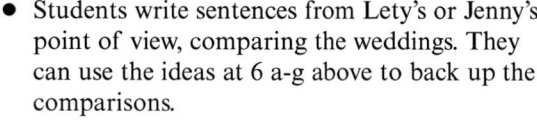

6–9

Answers: **a** England, **b** Mexico, **c** Mexico, **d** Mexico, **e** England, **f** England, **g** Mexico

7 **Lety y Jenny comparan las fiestas. Haz frases y explica por qué.**

5–8

- Students write sentences from Lety's or Jenny's point of view, comparing the weddings. They can use the ideas at 6 a-g above to back up the comparisons.

8 **Completa las frases.**

- Students read through the texts again and match up the sentences.

5–8

Answers: **1** e, **2** d, **3** a, **4** c, **5** b

Remate

9 **Find out on the Internet about some Spanish or Mexican festivals. Then write, in Spanish, a description of one of these festivals or invent one and write about it.**

PLTS

5–9

- Any of the travel guides to Spain and Mexico are good sources of information about festivals for tourists. Give some guidelines on what to include – where, time of year, origen, why, what happens, can tourists join in etc. They can use the words in the box to help them.

Success criteria activity 9:

- *students give information accurately and in the appropriate style*
- *students express personal opinions and justify points of view*
- *students use a variety of vocabulary and structures*
- *students use different tenses or time frames*

10 **Read the descriptions other people have written. Decide if you think they are real or invented festivals.**

PLTS

- Students will quickly realise that the more ridiculous the festival sounds, the more likely it is to be real.

Success criteria activity 10:

5–8

- *students communicate effectively and accurately*
- *students express personal opinions and justify points of view*
- *students deal with unpredictable elements*

Gramática en acción

páginas 86 y 87

Planner

> **Objectives**
- Use of pronouns

> **Resources**
Students' Book, pages 86–87
Exam Skills Workbook, page 41 (F), page 42 (H)
Grammar Workbook, pages 22–29, 46
Activity sheet 26
Resources and Planning OxBox CD-ROM

> **Grammar**
- Using pronouns
- Using the continuous form of the imperfect

> **PLTS**
Students' Book, page 86, activity 4,
Reflective Learners
Students' Book, page 87, activity 11,
Self-Managers

> **Imperfect and preterite**

1 **Look at these examples. Decide if the imperfect is being used to mean "was ... ing" or "used to...".**
Grammar reference page 205

Answers: Both can mean *was... -ing*, but imperfect can also mean *used to.*

2 **Translate these examples into English.**
Try and get the students to explain the difference in their own words as they are more likely to remember it that way.

Answers:

a I was talking to Juan. He invited me to a party.

b We were dancing in the garden when my parents arrived.

c We didn't play tennis because it was raining.

The imperfect is a longer and more continuous action in the past, while the preterite describes one completed action.

3a Use the imperfect to describe what was happening when you arrived at a party. Mention four things.

- Students can use a real party as a prompt for ideas.

3b Use the preterite to say what happened at the party. Mention five things.

- Encourage students to focus on the difference between the tenses. Ask them to give examples.

➤ Pronouns

4 Give a definition of a pronoun and think of some examples in Spanish. Check on page 210 of the Grammar section.

PLTS • Students can look for examples in the previous pages of this unit, especially pages 79 and 80.

5 Look at these examples and answer the questions.

Answers:

a Before the verb, or after an infinitive.

b The indirect object pronoun come first.

c The *le* pronoun becomes *se*.

6 Now translate the examples above into English.

Answers:

a I bought it for my teacher. I bought him a book in Spanish.

I decided to buy him a present.

I can't buy it, I don't have any money.

b He / she bought it for me.

I give it to you (I'm giving it to you).

I'm going to buy it for you.

He / She told (it to) us at the party.

c I gave it to him / her on his / her birthday.

I bought it for him / her because I liked it.

I told (it to) him / her but he / she wasn't listening to me.

I decided to buy them for him / her.

➤ Object pronouns

7 Write an explanation using the examples on this page, to show how to use object pronouns.

- Students can use Powerpoint to present their explanations.

8 Disjunctive pronouns follow a conjunction. What important points do you notice in these examples? Check on page 210 of the Grammar section.

Grammar reference page 210

Answers:

¿Es para mí? Sí, es para ti. Accent on *mí* but not on *ti* to distinguish it from *mi* (possessive)

No lo conozco pero tengo una foto de él. Accent on él to distinguish it from the article.

No me voy a sentar al lado de ella. / Fue a la fiesta con nosotros. / ¿Puedo ir con vosotros? Same as the subject pronoun but no accents.

¿Quieres salir conmigo? ¿Contigo? ¡Nunca! Conmigo/contigo not con mí/con ti. Don't introduce consigo unless it will not cause confusion.

➤ Possessive Pronouns

9 Rewrite these sentences using the possessive pronoun.

Answers:

a Mi teléfono es más caro que **el tuyo**.

b Sus padres son más ricos que **los nuestros**.

c Si te gustan los bocadillos, puedes comer **los míos**.

d No tengo bolígrafo. ¿Puedo utilizar **el tuyo**?

10 Don't forget how to use *lo* and *lo que*. Translate these sentences into English, and then write four more sentences beginning with '*lo*'.

Answers:

a The most important thing is to have fun.

b What I enjoy most is being with my friends.

11 Look at the description of an English wedding on page 85. Find all the sentences with pronouns, and translate them into English.

PLTS *Answers:*

a Fui a la boda de mi amigo inglés. *I went to my English friend's wedding.*

b Lo que me sorprendió fue que la boda no fue en una iglesia. *What surprised me was that the wedding wasn't in a church.*

c La hermana de mi amigo leyó un poema, firmaron el registro y fue todo. *My friend's sister read a poem, they signed the register, and that was it.*

d Lo que pasa es que todos se organizan como típicos ingleses, para fotos con la familia de la novia, fotos con los tíos, fotos con los niños, fotos con los amigos ... *What happens is that everyone is organised in a typically English way into photos with the family of the bride, photos with the aunts and uncles, photos with the children, photos with friends..*

e Los invitados compraron regalos para los novios, pero no se los presentaron en la boda. *The guests bought presents for the bride and groom, but didn't give them to them at the wedding.*

f Los compraron en Internet, y la tienda entrega los regalos directamente a la casa de los novios. *They bought them on the Internet, and the shop delivered the presents directly to the bride and groom's house.*

g Si no compras un regalo, no te invitan, creo. *If you don't buy a present, I think they don't invite you.*

h Luego hay una disco en el hotel y todo el mundo se emborracha. *Then there is a disco in the hotel and everyone gets drunk.*

i Para mí era una experiencia rara pero muy linda. *For me it was a strange experience, but very beautiful.*

12 Translate into Spanish:

Answers:

a – ¿Quieres ir de compras conmigo? Mi hermano tiene un teléfono nuevo que es mejor que el mío, y quiero comprarme uno. Si quieres, podemos comprarte uno también.

b – Bueno, tengo que decirtelo… sabía lo que querías, entonces ¡ya te lo he comprado!

Habilidades

página 88

Planner

➤ **Objectives**
- Reading with greater understanding

➤ **Resources**
Students' Book, page 88
CD 2, track 29
Exam Skills Workbook, page 42 (F), page 43 (H)
Activity sheet 34
Resources and Planning OxBox CD-ROM

➤ **Skills**
- Learning the words

- Working out the meanings
- Understanding the sentence
- Looking out for red herrings
- Keeping your own personal vocabulary reference book
- Recording vocabulary
- Thinking about accuracy

➤ **PLTS**
Students' Book, page 88, activity 3,
Independent Enquirers
Students' Book, page 88, activity 5,
Effective Participators

➤ **Leer**

1 Learn the words.

❏ Make sure you know what these words mean: *fiesta, sopresa, cruel, famoso, chico, chiste, nariz*
- Students work out the meanings.

Answers: party, surprise, cruel, famous, child, joke, nose

2 Work out the meanings.

❏ Try to use your knowledge of the endings to work out the meanings of the words. Or work out what the words mean in the sentence. Use this to work out what the ending does to the word.
- Students find the related words in the text and work out their meanings.

Answers: **festejar** celebrate, **sorprendente** surprising, **crueldad** cruelty, **fama** fame, **chiquillo** little child, **chistoso** jokey, **narices** nostrils

3 Understand the sentence.

❏ Translate these sentence into English. How much of the sentence do you need to read before you can translate even one word?
- Students analyse the sentences in detail to work out their meaning. This encourages greater accuracy.

Answers:
- You need the last word to work out that the giver is female. **SHE** gave me a book and **I** told her she was very kind.

- The writer is a boy; he went shopping with his sister, but the mother referred to them in the masculine plural.
- In the first sentence only the skirt is expensive, in the second, both items are.

4 Look out for red herrings.

❏ Students listen (a–c) and listen out for the red herrings. Then, they check with a partner and see if they missed anything.

 CD 2, track 32   página 88, actividad 4

a Me encanta ir de compras, me gusta ver la ropa, probar nuevos zapatos, sobre todo lo que está de moda, aunque ya no voy mucho porque no tengo dinero.

b ¿Compras? ¿Ir a caminar de tienda en tienda y pasar horas viendo nada mas que ropa? Puede que pienses que lo encuentro aburrido, sin embargo es lo que más me gusta.

c Me gusta ir de compras, sí, pero sólo una vez al año. Si tengo que ir más a menudo, es otra historia.

Answers: **a** sólo **b** pura, aburrido **c** sólo historia

➤ **Aprender**

5 Keep your own personal vocabulary reference book.

PLTS
- Students look at the different suggestions and decide which will be most helpful to them. The teacher could pick one technique per week or lesson and ask students how useful they found it.
- Alternatively, discuss techniques in class and try some out for effectiveness.

6   Think about accuracy.

❑ How much attention do you pay to detail when you are learning Spanish words?

● Students can do either or both these activities as a paired dictation – can they read it accurately

enough for their partner to write it down correctly? They should not read it word by word, but a few words at a time, and repeat. Remember punctuation marks.

Escenario   página 89

Planner

➤ **Objectives**

➤ **Resources**
Students' Book, page 89
Exam Skills Workbook, pages 39–40 (F),
pages 40–41 (H)
Resources and Planning OxBox CD-ROM

➤ **Skills**
● Writing practice
● Speaking practice

➤ **PLTS**
Students' Book, page 89, Escenario Oral,
Effective Participators
Students' Book, page 89, Escenario Escrito,
Creative Thinkers

➤ **Oral**

Your Spanish teacher wants to organise an evening activity for your group and your exchange partners when they come. Prepare some answers to his/her questions. Don't forget to talk about your own past experience and how it went.

4–9

● Students read the teacher's email first, identify the different suggestions made and comment on their suitability for such a party. They then respond to the questions using this material and their own ideas. They should draw on past experiences *En el cumpleaños de mi hermana, hicimos…* and use the language of opinions *En mi opinión, creo que sería una buena idea* etc. The activity should be carried out as a role play, but students can pre-prepare their answers in note form.

● *GCSE Grades A*–C*

● *Grade C Students use past, present and future tenses. They express opinions, and deal with some unpredictability.*

● *Grade A Students express and justify opinions. They use a variety of vocabulary and structure in longer speech sequences.*

➤ **Escrito**

Write an email to a Spanish friend who will be here during a special time of year.

4–9

● Discuss special events in class. Call out a month and ask students to think of an event that happens then e.g. January – New Year, February – Pancake Day etc. There may be some important local events as well. In groups, students pick one of the events and research vocabulary for it. They look through the unit for useful structures. Students then write the email. They can exchange it with their partner, who marks it according to if it answers the questions in the SB, and if the Spanish friend will be interested by the description i.e. is the writer enthusiastic or have they just written a list?

● *GCSE Grades A*–C*

● *Grade C Students use opinions and past, present and future tenses, both factually and imaginatively. Register is appropriate and style is basic.*

● *Grade A Students write factually and imaginatively using longer sequences and a range of vocabulary and structure. They express and justify opinions in an appropriate style.*

Vocabulario   página 90

This is a summary of key language from the unit, organised by spread and theme. Students can use it for reference while working on the unit, and as an aid to learning vocabulary.

Lectura

Planner

> **Objectives**
> - Understanding about parties and festivals
> - To encourage independent reading and develop reading strategies.
> - These pages also provide alternative class and homework material for students who work quickly and require extension work.

> **Resources**
> Students' Book, page 179–180

> **PLTS**
> Students' Book, page 179, activity 1,
> *Self-Managers*
> Students' Book, page 179, activity 2,
> *Reflective Learners*

> ## Lectura A – ¿Te gustan las fiestas?

1 **Utiliza estas estrategias para leer el texto.**

PLTS
- Students use the suggested strategies to read the quiz. If they have it on paper they can underline key words etc. They make notes on what the questions mean, and how they worked it out. You can split the class in half, and a "control" group reads the quiz "blind" without using the strategies, making notes as to what they understand. The two groups then compare what they understand – the "strategies" group should understand more!

2 **Con un(a) compañero/a, lee las preguntas en voz alta, poniendo atención en la pronunciación. A ver si podéis contestar a las preguntas.**

PLTS
- Students take it in turns with a partner to read out the questions and note their answers. They correct each other's pronunciation.

3 **Escribe tus respuestas. Cambia de la segunda persona (tú) a la primera (yo).**
- Students write out their answers in full to practise changing verbs from the 2nd to the 1st person e.g. *El fin de semana próximo* **voy** *a quedar***me** *en casa.*

4 **¿Puedes inventar más respuestas/opciones en español?**
- Students extend the quiz. Split the class into small groups, or each pair comes up with another question. Combine the questions, assign scores to the answers, and each student takes the quiz to find out how much of a party person they are. The marked quiz papers can be displayed with results comments written on them. e.g. *Mark es el rey de las fiestas – 45/50; Anna prefiere fiestas pequeñas con buenos amigos – 25/50* etc.

5 **Lee lo que dice Javier, y contesta a las preguntas del test para él.**
- Students respond to the quiz as if Javier.

Answers: **1** a, **2** b, **3** a, **4** b or c, **5** none, **6** c

> ## Lectura B – Las fiestas en Inglaterra

1 **¿Puedes deducir lo que significan estas palabras? Son similares a palabras que ya conoces en inglés, español u otro idioma: desnudos, crepas, microondas, mentir, oscuro, acercarse, amenazar.**
- Tell the students that the Spanish are not the only ones to have bizarre festivals; ask them if they can think of any in this country that are particularly strange. At the end of the reading activities, having looked at festivals from another point of view, ask if they can think of any other strange celebrations in this country.
- Students decide what the words mean without looking them up; ask them what clues they used, and go through the answers.
- (Point out *u* instead of *o* in the question and ask them why they think it is there. Can they think of another occasion when something similar happens? There's an example in text **a**.)

Answers: naked, pancakes, microwave (oven), to lie, dark, to get close, threaten

2 **Lee e interpreta las frases que contienen estas palabras.**
- Students read and translate the sentences containing these words.

Answers:
- Instead of putting on costume and dancing semi-naked through the streets to the sound of drums and salsa music..
- They eat pancakes at home with sugar and lemon.
- They even buy the pancakes in the supermarket and heat them in the microwave.
- Also, you have to lie and say you received sixteen anonymous cards.
- But on this night they go out, even though it's very cold, dark and raining.
- They build a big fire in the park, which is good, because it's so cold, but you're not allowed to get close in case you get burnt.
- This is a very nice celebration when parents allow their children to threaten old people.

3 **Con un(a) compañero/a, lee frases de los textos. A ver si podéis identificar las cinco fiestas.**

- Students take it in turns to read out a sentence from the text; their partner has to identify the celebration. Before they do this, check they know which festival is being talked about each in each text, and can say the name of the festival in Spanish.

4 **Busca opiniones, reacciones o comentarios irónicos.**

- Students look for opinions, reactions and ironic comments.

Answers:

a En lugar de disfrazarse, e <u>ir casi desnudos</u> bailando por la calle al sonido de tambores y música de salsa … ¿Qué es lo que hacen los ingleses? <u>Comen crepas en la casa con azúcar y limón. Aun compran las crepas en el supermercado y las calientan en el microondas.</u>

b <u>No sé</u> exactamente en que consiste su religión. <u>Creen que hay un conejo mágico que vive en el cielo.</u> Ese conejo va por todos los jardines y pone huevos. Pero no son huevos de gallina. Son huevos de chocolate.

c <u>Es un día muy especial cuando haces llorar a tus amigos feos.</u> Les mandas tarjetas para decirles que tienen una admiradora. Luego les dices que <u>es una broma</u> y que fuiste tú. También hay que mentir y decir que recibiste dieciséis tarjetas anónimas.

d Los ingleses normalmente pasan la tarde en sus casas viendo la televisión. Pero esa noche salen, aunque hace mucho frío, está oscuro, y llueve. <u>Hacen un fuego grande en el parque, lo que es bueno, porque hace tanto frío, pero no se permite acercarse al fuego porque pueden quemarse.</u>

e <u>Esa es una fiesta muy agradable donde los padres permiten a sus niños de amenazar a los ancianos.</u> Si no les dan caramelos, les rompen las ventanas. Los ancianos apagan todas las luces y no contestan a la puerta.

5 **Contesta en inglés.**

- Students answer the questions in English.

Answers: **a** Valentine's Day, **b** Hallowe'en, **c** Bonfire Night, **d** Pancake Day, **e** Easter

Unit 3B Cine y televisión			Overview grid	
Spread	**Contexts**	**Skills**	**Grammar**	**Vocabulary**
Spread title	• Topic areas covered within the unit	• Key skills focus	• Grammar covered in the unit	Key vocabulary
pages 92–93 **Cómo hablar sobre películas y programas**	• Discussing films and TV programmes	• Using synonyms and different structures to make writing more interesting	• Comparatives and superlatives	el desenlace, el documental, la estatuilla, el huérfano, la juventud, la película de guerra, la película de terror, el premio, el/la protagonista gracioso/a, inesperado/a, polémico/a, tetrapléjico/a cumplir, ganar, hacer el papel de, hacer gracia, luchar, merecer la pena, recomendar, tener lugar en … me aburre, me encanta(n)/me apasiona(n), me fascina(n), me vuelve(n) loco/a, se basa en …, se trata de …, termina mal
pages 94–95 **Cómo hablar sobre un artista famoso**	• Expressing opinions about famous singers, actors and other artists	• Understanding Spanish equivalents of English prefixes and suffixes	• Structures followed by an infinitive or a gerund	afable, altivo/a, atrevido/a, callado/a, camaleónico/a, cariñoso/a, contento/a, culto/a, dinámico/a, dulce, famoso/a, honrado/a, insoportable, inteligente, listo/a, mentiroso/a, parlanchín, simpático/a inagurar, fundar
pages 96–97 **Cómo hablar sobre las carreras artísticas**	• Talking about an actor's or a musician's career	• Using expressions of time to improve your written and spoken work	• The imperfect and the preterite tenses	al fin, desde entonces, desde hace …, hace ya …, más adelante estudioso/a, rico/a, soñador(a), tímido/a
pages 98–99 **Cómo hablar sobre diferentes actividades**	• Describing the pros and cons of different free time activities	• Adapting a model conversation for personal use and defending your point of view	• Negatives	el ajedrez, la escalada, el footing, el forofo, la pesca submarina, el senderismo bucear, comenzar a, dar comienzo, depender de, estar a favor, estar de buen humor, estar en contra, estar loco por, estar obsesionado con, ser frustrante nada, nadie, ni … ni, ninguno/a, nunca/jamás, raramente, también, tampoco, casi siempre, de vez en cuando, no me pierdo …, no soporto …, siempre que puedo
pages 100–101 **Cómo hablar sobre tus gustos**	• Discussing former and present tastes and preferences	• Finding out and discussing other people's opinions	• Verbs followed by prepositions	acabar de, aprender a, dejar de, empezar a, estar enganchado/a, hablar de, hartarse de, no parar de, volver a ahora, antes, en cuanto a … cuenta la historia de …, me obligaban a, me relaja, no me pierdo, suelo leer …
pages 102–103 **Gramática en acción**	• Practising the correct use of the imperfect and preterite tenses.		• Using the preterite and imperfect • Using comparatives and superlatives • Using negatives • Using verbs with prepositions	
page 104 **Habilidades**	• Improving learning skills and working out meaning from context	• Using synonyms • Avoiding repetition • Using the dictionary for unknown words • Recognising prefixes and suffixes • Recognising key words • Recognising false friends • Using games and strategies for learning		
page 105 **Escenario**	• Write a film review. • Research a Spanish festival.			
page 106 **Vocabulario**	• Summary of key vocabulary for the unit.			
pages 181–182 **Reading Pages**	The world of cinema: • To encourage independent reading and to develop reading strategies. • To provide alternative class and homework material for students who finish other activities quickly.			

3B Cine y televisión

Unit Objectives

Contexts: leisure activities and the arts
Skills focus: using the dictionary for unknown words, recognising prefixes and suffixes, recognising key words, recognising false friends; using games and strategies; using synonyms, avoiding repetition
Grammar: using the preterite and imperfect, using comparatives and superlatives, using negatives, using verbs with prepositions

Controlled assessment opportunities

Writing: Students' Book, page 93, activity 9
Speaking: Students' Book, page 95, activity 11
Writing and Speaking: Students' Book, page 97, activity 11
Writing: Students' Book, page 99, activity 13
Writing: Students' Book, page 100, activity 13

See also *GCSE Spanish for OCR Assessment OxBox CD-ROM*.

An introduction to the unit   página 91

- *Aim*: To introduce the themes of the unit and encourage students to think about the reasons for learning Spanish.
- The opening page is designed with captions, pictures and page cross-references to provide a preview of what is to come:

	Students' Book
Cómo hablar sobre películas y programas	page 92
Cómo hablar sobre un artista famoso	page 94
Cómo hablar sobre las carreras artísticas	page 96
Cómo hablar sobre diferentes actividades	page 98
Cómo hablar sobre tus gustos	page 100
Gramática en acción – improving your use and understanding of Spanish	page 102
Habilidades – increasing your language skills for fluency	page 104
Escenario – preparar y presentar una reseña sobre una película Escenario – buscar información sobre un festival de música	page 105

- Allow time for students to read the questions and cross-refer to the relevant pages of the Students' Book. They could do this individually or in pairs / small groups, followed by whole-class discussion.
- This spread also provides an opportunity for students to recap on familiar language. Ask them to think about language they already know that might be useful when working on the themes of the unit.
- Mindmap any language they produce, and if possible, keep it on display as reference as you progress through the unit. It can be added to at intervals as new language becomes familiar.

- At the end of work on the unit, allow time for students to return to this spread and repeat the mind-mapping process, this time including what they have learned over the course of the unit. Get them to answer the questions in their own words, and encourage them to use the results for revision purposes.
- Ask them what they found difficult, interesting etc. What do they think are the important things they have learned in this unit? What do they still need to improve on?
- If time permits, get the students to redesign the page. How would they set it out so it reflects the unit? How would they make it attractive to other learners of their age? How would they make it easy to follow? What would they include in terms of text, pictures, captions, page references? Ask them to imagine they are producing material for next year's class who will be learning the same thing – what would they have found it useful to know?

¿Por qué aprender el español? Para hablar de películas y tus artistas favoritos.

- Students share any experiences they have had of going to the cinema in Spain. Did they see an English film dubbed, or an original Spanish one?
- Ask them to consider what sort of language they would need to talk to a Spanish person about their favourite singer or actor.

Cómo hablar sobre películas y programas

Planner

➤ **Objectives**
- Discussing films and TV programmes

➤ **Resources**

Students' Book, pages 92–93
CD 2, tracks 37–39
Grammar Workbook, pages 9–11
Activity sheet 36–39

➤ **Key language**

el desenlace, el documental, la estatuilla, el huérfano, la juventud, la película de guerra, la película de terror, el premio, el/la protagonista graciosa/o, inesperado/a, polémico/a, tetrapléjico/a cumplir, ganar, hacer el papel de, hacer gracia, luchar, merecer la pena, recomendar, tener lugar en ... me aburre, me encanta(n)/me apasiona(n), me fascina(n), me vuelve(n) loco/a, se basa en ..., se trata de ..., termina mal

➤ **Skills**
- Using synonyms and different structures to make writing more interesting

➤ **Grammar**
- Comparatives and superlatives

➤ **PLTS**

Students' Book, page 93, activity 8,
Effective Participators
Students' Book, page 93, activity 9,
Independent Enquirers

➤ **Starters**
- Students look at the photos on page 92 and say if they have seen any of the films, if they liked them, why, why not etc. From memory, they try to say what types of films these are. When they do activity 1 they can check their previous ideas to see how much they remembered from previous learning.
- Students' Book, page 93, activity 4. Before answering the questions, tell students to read the texts, pick out the parts they understand and write a brief summary in English of what they think the film is about. You may need to provide a brief explanation of *la década de los 70 en Argentina, durante la represión militar* to put the film in context for them.

- Students' Book, page 93, activity 5. Before students do the activity in pairs, do one or two examples as a whole class. Ask for the name of a recent and well known film and write it on the board. Elicit opinions (good and bad) and write them on either side of the name. Write down *se trata de* and elicit a brief plot explanation. Ask students to find on the spread the words for *it's worth seeing it*. Is there any other information they can provide from the spread? They can use this as a guide for their discussion with their partner.
- Students' Book, page 93, activity 9. Before writing their resumé, ask students to pick out the information in the reviews on page 92 to complete the example sentences shown. Alternatively they can bring in a review from an English magazine, and pick out the relevant information to complete the sentences in Spanish. It does not have to be the film they will review in activity 9.

➤ **Plenaries**
- Students' Book, page 93, activity 2. After doing the listening activity, give students a copy of the transcript, and ask them to pick out one or two key words per text that gave them the clue they needed to identify the film. Were there any red herrings? Identify and deal with them.
- Students' Book, page 93, activity 7. At the end of the lesson, or sometime after doing activities 6 & 7, write the name of a TV programme on the board and elicit opinions e.g. *Me encanta porque es emocionante; Prefiero irme a la cama, es aburridísimo* etc. Add complexity by writing two names up and asking for a comparison. Students can win points as pairs or groups for producing a correct response / being the first to do so.
- Discuss bad films and / or TV programmes. Say or write up one of the negative expressions from activity 7, and ask for an example. Encourage disagreement!
- Students' Book, page 93, activity 9. If the school has an exchange programme or a partner school, the reviews could be sent or emailed to them for comments by the Spanish pupils – are the same films popular in Spain? Alternatively, they could be read by a parallel class, or just re-distributed between the students, who say or write if they agree or disagree with the reviews or why.

1 Mira los pósters de las películas en la página 92. ¿Qué tipo de películas son?

- Students match up the pictures and the types of films. They can compete in pairs against the clock.

Answers: **1** (*Tú la Letra, yo la Música*) e, **2** (*Expiación*) a, **3** (*Madgascar*) g, **4** (*Indiana Jones y el Reino de la Calavera de Cristal*) f, **5** (*Las Hermanas Bolena*) b, **6** (*Sexo en Nueva York*) c, **7** (*Una Verdad Incómoda*) d

2 Ahora escucha la definición de las películas y decide a cuál de ellas se refiere.

- Students listen and decide which film is being talked about.

 CD 2, track 37 **página 93, actividad 2**

a Es una comedia muy divertida que trata sobre varias amigas y que viven en la gran manzana. ¡Finalmente Carrie va a casarse con Big!

b Bueno, es una película de aventuras con el mayor héroe de los últimos veinte años, un profesor de Historia antigua, arqueólogo, que siempre lleva su sombrero y su látigo … ¡es genial!

c Es una película romántica en la que hay un chico compositor y una chica que limpia su casa y los dos tienen que crear una canción…

d Es la película histórica de la temporada y cuenta la relación entre dos hermanas, una muy dulce y la otra muy ambiciosa, y el rey Enrique octavo… ¡Inglaterra podría haber sido un país muy diferente! Es fascinante.

e Es una película documental, un reportaje sobre el medio ambiente y el calentamiento del planeta. Es muy interesante pero también preocupante, ¿cuántas cosas nos ocultan los políticos?

f Esta película de animación se centra en cuatro residentes del Zoológico de Central Park de Nueva York, que también son mejores amigos: un león, una cebra, una jirafa y una hipopótama embarazada. Cuando uno de ellos desaparece, los otros tres se escapan para buscarlo. Los cuatro son capturados y enviados de vuelta a África. Pero hay un accidente…

g Es una película de guerra y de amor en la que dos jóvenes se enamoran pero una serie de circunstancias y malentendidos con la hermana pequeña de la chica hace que tengan que estar separados para siempre.

Answers: **a** Película 6, **b** Película 4, **c** Película 1, **d** Película 5, **e** Película 7, **f** Película 3, **g** Película 2

3 Escucha las siguientes descripciones sobre estas dos películas españolas, *Mar Adentro* y *El Orfanato*, y elige la opción adecuada.

- Students listen to the descriptions of the two films and pick the sentences that describe them. When they have finished listening, they should write them out in full correctly, underlining and annotating any useful language. Explain these words first: *polémico* – controversial, *merece la pena* – it is worth, *huérfanos* – orphans, *desenlace* – the end, *candidatura* – nomination.

 CD 2, track 38 **página 93, actividad 3**

Mar adentro se basa en una historia verdadera y el protagonista es Ramón Sampedro, un hombre que tuvo un accidente durante su juventud y se quedó tetrapléjico, ¡treinta años en la cama, sin poder moverse! Leía mucho y escribía con la boca, y así escribió muchos poemas. El desenlace es trágico pero merece la pena ver esta película sobre un hombre que quería morir con dignidad y luchó por la eutanasia. El director, Alejandro Amenábar, es bastante joven pero muy famoso en España y *Mar adentro* ha ganado un Oscar.

El Orfanato trata de una mujer joven que decide crear un orfanato para acoger a niños sin padres. Para cumplir su sueño, va a vivir a una casa abandonada cerca de la playa, donde ella misma vivió cuando era pequeña con otros niños huérfanos. Pero en la casa hay un misterio y muchos secretos escondidos … y un día su hijo desaparece … el desenlace es inesperado …

Esta película ganó 14 candidaturas a los Goya, que son los equivalentes a los Oscar en España. ¡Me muero de miedo cuando la veo pero me encanta!

Answers: **a** de terror, **b** la vida de una persona real, **c** Mar Adentro, **d** mayor (**Note:** The man has the accident as a young man, but the film covers his life 30 years later.), **e** Mar Adentro, **f** Mar Adentro, **g** Mar Adentro

4 Lee las opiniones en la página 92 de dos personas sobre estas películas. ¿Quién dice que …

- Students read the texts on page 92 describing the two films and match the people to the statements.

Answers: **a** Julieta, **b** Julieta, **c** Julieta, **d** Manu, **e** Julieta

5 Habla con tu compañero/a sobre una película que te gusta y otra que no te gusta y explica por qué.

- Students discuss with their partner a film they have recently seen. Their partner can have a check list to fill in e.g. *título, actores, se trata de, tipo de película, premios ganados, opinión*

6 Mira la programación de la televisión en la página 92 y contesta a las siguientes preguntas.

- Students read the TV guide on page 92 and answer the questions. Tell them also to note down what words gave them the clues to the answers. This increases awareness when reading.

Answers: **a** 3, **b** Corazón de verano, **c** Todo sobre mi madre, 22.00, **d** Sobreviví

7 Escucha a estos dos amigos, Roberto y Mario, hablando de la programación de TVE2 y escribe sus opiniones.

- Students listen to Roberto and Mario and note their opinions about the different programmes. It may be helpful to draw up an answer grid for them to fill in as below.

CD 2, track 39   página 93, actividad 7

Roberto	Mario, ¿qué ponen en la tele esta tarde?
Mario	Pues primero los informativos territoriales. No están mal, al menos así sabemos qué pasa en nuestra parte de España.
Roberto	Hombre, la verdad es que es bastante útil oír las noticias regionales. ¿Y después?
Mario	Después echan "Corazón de verano"– ¡otra vez! ¡siempre lo mismo! No me interesan las vidas de los famosos. ¡Además, es que el programa es aburridísimo!
Roberto	Pues mira, a mí no me disgusta. Hay noticias divertidas y además, es mejor que escuchar las desgracias del mundo de los informativos. ¡Es verano y hay que relajarse!
Mario	Mira, Roberto, y después del telediario, el tiempo, ¡eso sí que es un tostón! No me importa si llueve o si hace calor, ¡qué obsesión con la meteorología!
Roberto	Tienes razón. Yo siempre cambio de canal cuando lo ponen. Oye, ¿has visto alguna vez "Sobreviví", Mario?
Mario	¡Es genial! Merece la pena quedarse tarde para verlo. Es como ver una película de aventuras. ¿Y tú?
Roberto	Bah, me aburre bastante – siempre prefiero irme a la cama que quedarme levantado para verlo.

Answers:
Roberto – opinión
Informativos territoriales: es bastante útil
Corazón de verano: no me disgusta,
El tiempo: –
Sobreviví: me aburre bastante, prefiero irme a la cama

Mario – opinión
Informativos territoriales: no están mal
Corazón de verano: siempre lo mismo, no me interesa, es aburridísimo
El tiempo: es un tostón, no me importa
Sobreviví: es genial, merece la pena

8 Escoge la opción adecuada para ti en estas frases. Justifica tu opinión con tu compañero/a.

- Students work in pairs, choosing the correct version for the sentence for themselves, and explaining why. They feed back to the class, either for themselves or for their partner.

4–9

PLTS

Remate

9 Choose a film you have seen and write a resumé of it. Explain why you like or dislike it.

PLTS

- Refer back to the Starter activity for activity 5, and give students a list of things to include. Tell them to look again at the descriptions on page 92, and give them a copy of the transcript for activity 3. Emphasise that they must include their opinion and give a reason for it. Tell them to imagine they are writing a review for a Spanish magazine or website read by people their age. Encourage them to expand upon the example sentences shown.

4–9

Success criteria activity 9:
- *students give information accurately and in the appropriate style*
- *students express personal opinions and justify points of view*
- *students use a variety of vocabulary and structures*
- *students use different tenses or time frames*

Cómo hablar sobre un artista famoso

páginas 94 y 95

Planner

➤ **Objectives**
- Expressing opinions about famous singers, actors and other artists

➤ **Resources**
Students' Book, pages 94–95
CD 2, tracks 40–41
Grammar Workbook, pages 59, 66
Activity sheet 36–39

➤ **Key language**
afable, altivo/a, atrevido/a, callado/a, camaleónico/a, cariñoso/a, contento/a, culto/a, dinámico/a, dulce, famoso/a, honrado/a, insoportable, inteligente,
listo/a, mentiroso/a, parlanchín, simpático/a inagurar, fundar

➤ **Skills**
- Understanding Spanish equivalents of English prefixes and suffixes

➤ **Grammar**
- Structures followed by an infinitive or a gerund

➤ **PLTS**
Students' Book, page 95, activity 10, *Creative Thinkers*
Students' Book, page 95, activity 11, *Team Workers*

➤ **Starters**

- Get students to research famous Spanish-speaking artists. Tell them especially to look out for people they have heard of but didn't realise were Hispanic.
- Ask students what they think *artista* means. Get them to find out synonyms (*músico, actor* etc.) and draw a spidergram in groups with examples.
- Students' Book, page 95, activity 6. Before doing the activity, ask students questions in English about the texts in preparation.
- Students' Book, page 95, activity 7. Split the class into groups or pairs, and give them a list of all the description words in activity 7. Give them 2 minutes to find out what they mean.

➤ **Plenaries**

- Students' Book, page 94, activity 1. After doing the activity, the teacher plays or reads the part of the text from "*Javier Bardem es mi actor preferido…*" When they have finished the students, as a whole class or in small groups or pairs, write down as much as they can remember. The teacher and the students repeat this until they have built up the whole paragraph. This encourages students to listen for detail, and builds up confidence.

- Students' Book, page 94, activity 4. Call out a characteristic, and students give the name of a famous actor or singer who fits it. This can be played in groups, where one group calls out an opinion, and the first group to call out a name wins a point. If no one can thnk of anyone within 5 seconds, the original group gets the point.
- Students' Book, page 95, activity 7. Ask the class for a controversial artistic figure (Pete Doherty, Amy Winehouse) and elicit opinions, using the phrases in activity 7. Encourage a heated exchange of views.
- Students' Book, page 95, activity 11. If students get into character (and costume) the interviews could be recorded on video and shown to another (younger) class who have to identify the stars; or the interviews could be performed for a school assembly (for Children in Need etc.) with a "simultaneous translator". The use of humour and the occasional celebrity-tantrum would enhance the performances.

---

1   **Escucha la opinión de Miranda sobre Juanes y Javier Bardem y decide si estas afirmaciones son verdaderas (V) o falsas (F) o no mencionadas (NM).**

- Students listen to Miranda talking about Juanes and Javier Bardem, and decide if the statements are True, False, or Not Mentioned. Students can find out more about these artists and what they have done for homework.

5–8

| CD 2, track 40 | página 94, actividad 1 |

Presenter   Miranda, ¿qué opinas de Juanes?
Miranda   Me gusta bastante. Es un cantante interesante y con una música muy pegadiza. Tiene canciones románticas, otras rockeras, algunas más tradicionales. Su estilo es muy variado y me parece también bastante guapo … ha ganado muchos premios por su música y toca la guitarra muy bien.
Presenter   ¿Y Javier Bardem?
Miranda   Javier Bardem es mi actor preferido. Es muy conocido en España porque su familia es una familia de actores también muy famosos por su talento. Javier no es guapo, pero tiene una cara con mucha personalidad y todo el mundo dice que tiene mucho sentido del humor. Tiene mucha experiencia como actor y creo que su trabajo en la película de los hermanos Cohen es el mejor de sus papeles ¡a pesar de su peinado!

Answers: **a** F, **b** V, **c** NM, **d** V, **e** V, **f** V, **g** NM

2   **Escucha la conversación entre Miranda y Bruno y contesta a las preguntas.**

- Students listen to the conversation and answer the questions. Listening for names can be very hard; ask students for their best guess, write down the correct parts, and listen again until they have built the name up.

5–9

| CD 2, track 41 | página 94, actividad 2 |

Miranda   Oye, Bruno, ayer fuiste al cine, ¿verdad?
Bruno   No, ayer estuve en un concierto de 'El canto del loco'.
Miranda   ¿Y te gustó?
Bruno   El cantante es increíble y el ambiente era excelente. Estuvimos cantando toda la noche porque todo el mundo estaba animado. Normalmente es un grupo que no me gusta mucho, porque sus canciones tienen todas el mismo ritmo, pero en directo es completamente diferente y el público cantaba con ellos todas las canciones. Ahora me encanta este grupo.
Miranda   Me lo imagino. A mí me pasa un poco como a ti, no suelo ir a conciertos, pero el sábado pasado fui a ver 'La quinta estación' y me fascinó. La cantante tiene una voz increíble y sabe cómo animar al público. ¡Yo estaba en primera fila y bailé durante todo el concierto. ¡Fue increíble!

Answers: **a** Bruno, **b** Bruno, **c** Miranda, **d** Bruno, **e** Bruno, **f** Miranda, **g** Miranda, **h** Bruno

3 **Habla con tu compañero/a. Después haced preguntas por turnos.**

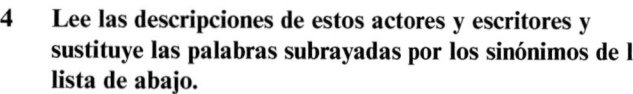

- Students talk to their partner about music and actors. They should make brief notes so they can either feed back to the class, or write a brief paragraph in the 3rd person explaining their partner's likes and dislikes. Give them some examples of how to do this.

4 **Lee las descripciones de estos actores y escritores y sustituye las palabras subrayadas por los sinónimos de la lista de abajo.**

- Students read the descriptions and substitute the synonyms. Make sure they keep the pairs of words for reference. If they time themselves, they can refer back to it when doing the Habilidades section later in the unit.

Answers: **famoso** – célebre, **afable** – amistoso, **parlanchín** – hablador, **simpático** – agradable, **perezoso** – vago, **dinámico** – activo, **altivo** – orgulloso, **callado** – reservado, **contento** – feliz

5 **Utiliza las palabras necesarias de la actividad 4 para describir a una persona famosa de tu elección. Tu compañero/a tiene que adivinar quién es.**

- Students describe someone famous for their partner to identify. Model an example to the whole class first. Students can play this as a game in small groups, taking turns to describe someone. More confident students can describe someone for the whole class to identify.

6 **Lee los artículos del periódico. ¿Quién ...**

- Students read the newspaper articles and answer the questions.

Answers: **a** Bardem, **b** Juanes, **c** Bardem, **d** Bardem, **e** Juanes, **f** Juanes

7 **Lee la discusión de estos jóvenes sobre un actor y decide cuál es la opción correcta.**

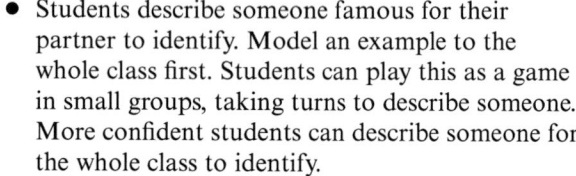

- Students read the discussion and choose the correct option.

Answers: **1** egoísta, **2** camaleónico, **3** cariñoso, **4** agresivo, **5** gracioso, **6** insoportable

8 **Mira los artículos de la actividad 6 y busca todas las estructuras seguidas de infinitivo. ¿Sabes qué significan?**

- Students look for all the expressions followed by an infinitive in activity 6 and write down what they mean. Split the class in half, and each do a different text, then combine their results; or spend a set time on each text and swap. Draw attention to the different ways of saying "to play a role".

Answers: **Juanes** *para ayudar* – to help, *acaba de fundar* – has just founded, *después de inaugurar* – after opening **Bardem** *al empezar* – in the beginning, *iba a hacer* – was going to do (play), *para representar* – to play, *antes de ser* – before being (playing)

9 **Habla con tu compañero/a y practica las estructuras:**

- This could be started off as teacher-to-class questions then turn it into a survey or question chain – person A asks person B, who asks person C and so on round the room, choosing different questions from the list to keep people on their toes.

Remate

10 **Write a web page for the fan club of your favourite actor.**

- Discuss in class or look up similar web pages to find out what kind of details to include – history, biography, acheivements, current projects, blogs from fans etc. If the school has an intranet it might be possible to post these "for real".

Success criteria activity 10:
- *students give information accurately and in the appropriate style*
- *students express personal opinions and justify points of view*
- *students use a variety of vocabulary and structures*
- *students use different tenses or time frames*

11 **Work with a partner and record an interview. You're at a concert of your favourite band. Talk to the singer or the group.**

- Students may need some help setting up this very open-ended activity. For less able groups, the teacher can provide or work out with them a list of questions. More advanced groups can brainstorm vocabulary in Spanish, then build up questions e.g. *tour – la gira – ¿La gira va bien?* – *¿Está usted contento con la gira?* One partner plays the star, the other the interviewer. Make notes first as to what questions you want to ask – How is the tour going? Are they happy with the success of the last album? What are their future projects? Are the rumours of a split true?

Success criteria activity 11:
- *students communicate effectively and accurately*
- *students express personal opinions and justify points of view*
- *students use a variety of vocabulary and structures*
- *students deal with unpredictable elements*
- *students use different tenses or time frames*

Cómo hablar sobre las carreras artísticas

Planner

➤ Objectives
- Talking about an actor's or a musician's career

➤ Resources
Students' Book, pages 96–97
CD 2, tracks 42–43
Grammar Workbook, pages 43–46
Activity sheet 36–39

➤ Key language
al fin, desde entonces, desde hace …, hace ya …, más adelante
estudioso/a, rico/a, soñador(a), tímido/a

➤ Skills
- Using expressions of time to improve your written and spoken work

➤ Grammar
- The imperfect and the preterite tenses

➤ PLTS
Students' Book, page 97, activity 10,
Self-Managers
Students' Book, page 97, activity 11,
Independent Enquirers

➤ Starters
- Give students a form to fill in headed Actor / Cantante / Director Famoso (they choose the option). It shows information such as Nombre, Fecha de nacimiento, País, Más famoso por, En el pasado, Proyectos futuros. They fill it in for themselves, but inventing whatever details they want. Discuss some options – do they have a stage name? Are they most famous for a hit record or a band bust-up? They can use this information later on in the spread.
- Students' Book, page 96, activity 2. Before listening, brainstorm some vocabulary the students might expect to hear e.g. if they think one of the photos shows a singer they may hear *cantante, grupo, música, canciones*, etc. Leave the words displayed while they listen, and tick off any they hear,
- Students' Book, page 96, activity 4. Before matching the texts to the statements, ask students to pick out information from the texts by giving them categories to classify under (*name, famous for, current project, future aims*) or sentences in English to complete (e.g. *The actress is called … She is famous for the series …*)
- Students' Book, page 97, activity 6. Check students understand all the adjectives they have to choose from. Write a list of words in English on the board and get them to choose the correct meaning in Spanish. They should be familiar with or able to guess at most, but *internado* will probably be new.

➤ Plenaries
- Run a quiz on the famous people described in this spread and the previous one. Either students can make up a list of questions and give it to another group to answer, or the teacher can read out / display questions for groups to compete pub-quiz style. Advanced students can do the quiz from memory, with the books closed.
- Students' Book, page 97, activity 8. Students write their own rose-tinted view of childhood, using the imperfect tense, and the paragraph at activity 8 as a model. They do it for themselves, but it does not have to be strictly true, and a partner can play the role of a sibling or parent who corrects their memory e.g. *No es cierto, no llorabas al final de las vacaciones, siempre estabas muy contento volver a casa etc.*
- Students make up statements using expressions of time, and their partner or other students in the class decide if they are true or lies. The statements can be spoken or written e.g. *Hace un año me compré un elefante* could actually be true if they've taken up sponsorship of an animal in the local zoo.
- Students' Book, page 97, activity 10. This is another activity which has great potential to be adapted for dramatic purposes, and lends itself perfectly to a charity fundraising event with "simultaneous translation" so the rest of the school or year group can follow what is going on. It also provides a real audience for the students' work.

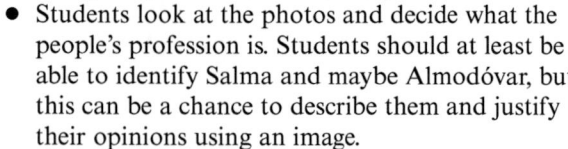

1 Mira las fotografías de los famosos. ¿Cuál crees que es su profesión? ¿Por qué? Habla con tu compañero/a.

4–9

- Students look at the photos and decide what the people's profession is. Students should at least be able to identify Salma and maybe Almodóvar, but this can be a chance to describe them and justify their opinions using an image.

Answers: **1 singer** – Raquel del Rosario of 'El sueño de Morfeo', **2 actor** – the Mexican Gael García Bernal, **3 actress** – the Mexican Salma Hayek, **4 film director** – Spaniard Pedro Almodóvar

2 Ahora escucha y rellena los espacios.

- Students listen and complete the table to check their answers to activity 1.

5–9

> **CD 2, track 42**   **página 96, actividad 2**
>
> Raquel del Rosario es la cantante del grupo *El sueño de Morfeo*. Nació en Gran Canaria el 3 de noviembre de 1982. Desde el año 2000 ha formado parte del grupo cantando y componiendo canciones junto con sus otros dos compañeros. Los tres son muy famosos, pero ninguno tanto como Raquel, no sólo por su talento sino también porque está casada con el piloto de Fórmula 1 Fernando Alonso. Raquel es muy discreta y nunca habla de su vida privada.
>
> Gael García Bernal nació en México el 30 de noviembre de 1978. Ha trabajado desde muy pequeño en series y en muchas películas, una de las últimas Babel. Gael habla cuatro idiomas perfectamente y ha sido el primer mexicano admitido en la escuela de Arte Dramático de Londres, donde estudió durante 3 años.
>
> Salma Hayek es también mexicana y nació en el estado de Veracruz el 2 de septiembre de 1966. Comenzó participando en series pero ahora es una de las artistas más codiciadas de Hollywood. Salma también es una buena cantante y ha cantado temas en algunas de sus películas, como, por ejemplo, en Frida. Salma es también una famosa activista, en la lucha por los derechaos de las mujeres.
>
> Pedro Almodóvar nació cerca de Ciudad Real el 24 de septiembre de 1949, y es ahora uno de los directores españoles más famosos. En los años 60 se muda a Madrid y allí comienza a hacer cine después del trabajo. Pedro ha colaborado en teatro y ha sido también cantante, pero ahora es famoso internacionalmente tras haber conseguido un Oscar por su película *Todo sobre mi madre*.

3 Trabaja con tu compañero/a y escribe las preguntas de la actividad 2.

4–7

- Students work with a partner to write questions to accompany activity 2.

Answers (example): Raquel, ¿cuál es tu profesión? ¿Cuándo es tu cumpleaños?

4 Lee estos artículos sobre dos actores famosos en España y decide a qué texto se refiere cada frase.

5–8

- Students read about two famous Spanish actors and match the texts to the statements.

Answers: **a** A, **b** B, **c** A, **d** A, **e** B, **f** B, **g** A, **h** A, **i** A

5 Haz una presentación sobre la carrera artística de tus actores favoritos y enséñala a toda la clase. ¡Cuatro personas son los jueces!

4–9

- Students work in small groups and make a presentation to the class about their favourite actor. As in The X-factor, the teacher chooses four or five people to judge the presentations according to the best language used from the spread and originality. If they can use visuals / music clips / power point etc. it adds to the realism of the activity, but the judges should focus on quality of language.

6 Lee las descripciones de estos famosos cuando eran jóvenes y elige el adjetivo adecuado.

5–8

- Students read the texts and choose the correct adjectives to complete the sentences.

Answers: **a** deportista, **b** interna, **c** rica, **d** joven, **e** reservado, **f** abierta, **g** mayor

Answers:

	Profesión	Fecha de nacimiento	País	Otra información
Raquel del Rosario	cantante	3 noviembre 1982	España (Gran Canaria)	componista de canciones, marido – Alonso, piloto de Fórmula 1
Gael García Bernal	actor	30 noviembre 1978	México	series y películas desde pequeño, habla 4 idiomas, primer mexicano a la Escuela de Arte Dramático en Londres
Salma Hayek	actriz	2 septiembre 1966	México	nació en Veracruz, comenzó con series, cantante, activista por los derechos de mujeres
Pedro Almodóvar	director	24 septiembre 1949	España	uno de los directores españoles más famosos, comenzó hacer cine después del trabajo, colaborado en teatro, un Oscar por *Todo sobre mi madre*

7 **Escucha la entrevista con el cantante Juanes y escoge verdadero, falso o no mencionado.**

- Students listen to the interview with Juanes and decide if the statements are True, False or Not Mentioned.

5–9

 **CD 2, track 43**   **página 97, actividad 7**

Entrevistador	Buenas tarde, Juanes, y gracias por estar aquí con nosotros en Los 40 principales. Antes de nada, ¿por qué Juanes? Es un nombre un poco inusual …
Juanes	Sí, bueno, en realidad me llamo Juan Esteban pero todos me llaman desde chiquitito Juanes y por eso es también mi nombre artístico.
Entrevistador	Cuéntanos un poco de tu infancia y tu carrera musical.
Juanes	Pues yo aprendí a tocar la guitarra acústica de mi padre, y siempre me había gustado componer mis canciones y tocar para mis amigos.
Entrevistador	Eres una persona positiva, pero has tenido momentos duros en tu vida …
Juanes	Sí, claro, soy colombiano y creo que lo más importante es la paz y tenemos que luchar por ella con todas nuestras fuerzas.
Entrevistador	¿Qué influencias tiene tu música?
Juanes	Pues la música tradicional colombiana y el folklore de mi país, ya que fueron las primeras melodías que aprendí a tocar, y también el Heavy Metal, porque Metallica siempre ha sido uno de mis grupos preferidos. De hecho, mi primer grupo era un grupo heavy.
Entrevistador	¿Y cuándo decidiste empezar tu carrera en solitario?
Juanes	En 1998, ¡y desde entonces no he parado!
Entrevistador	Has ganado Grammys latinos y mucha fama, conciertos en todo el mundo …
Juanes	Sí, claro que me gusta que aprecien mi música, pero en el fondo lo que me gusta es estar en casa con mi mujer y con mis hijas.

Answers: **a** F, **b** NM, **c** V, **d** V, **e** V, **f** F, **g** F, **h** NM, **i** V, **j** F

8 **Lee el texto y escribe los verbos en el imperfecto.**
Grammar reference page 205

- Students read the text and write out all the verbs in the imperfect.

Answers: era, salíamos, volvíamos, dormían, jugaba, tenía, encantaba, lloraba, venían

5–8

9 **Lee los articulos de la actividad 4 otra vez y escribe todas las expresiones temporales que puedas encontrar. ¿Cuáles son más sofisticadas?**

- Students re-read activity 4, looking for expressions of time, and decide which are the more sophisticated (*).

*Answers (*suggested):* Hace ya un año y medio*, desde entonces*, que nunca*, más adelante*, Al fin, lleva años*, desde hace dos o tres años

5–8

Remate

10 *Big Brother* **is looking for contestants. Create a perfect contestant for the programme.**

 PLTS

- Students use the questions to create the contestant's profile. Use the characteristics adjectives on the previous spread as well. This can be a class competition in which the funniest candidate wins – students need to get into character to convince the series producers, who can be students from a parrallel or older class if possible.

4–9

Success criteria activity 10:
- *students communicate effectively and accurately*
- *students express personal opinions and justify points of view*
- *students use a variety of vocabulary and structures*
- *students deal with unpredictable elements*
- *students use different tenses or time frames*

11 **Choose two famous people and find out about their childhood, from the Internet. Write some phrases using the imperfect tense. Your classmates have to discover who they are.**

 PLTS

- The completed profiles could be displayed around the class for comment, and guesses as to the identity of the person described posted on them.

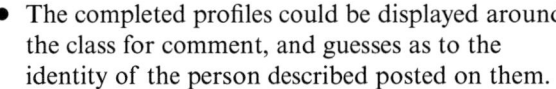

Success criteria activity 11:
- *students give information accurately and in the appropriate style*
- *students use a variety of vocabulary and structures*
- *students use different tenses or time frames*

4–9

Cómo hablar sobre diferentes actividades

páginas 98 y 99

Planner

> ### Objectives
> - Describing the pros and cons of free time activities

> ### Resources
> Students' Book, pages 98–99
> CD 2, tracks 44–46
> Grammar Workbook, pages 57
> Activity sheets 36–39

> ### Key language
> *el ajedrez, la escalada, el footing, el forofo, la pesca submarina, el senderismo*
> *bucear, comenzar a, dar comienzo, depender de, estar a favor, estar de buen humor, estar en contra, estar loco por, estar obsesionado con, ser frustrante*
> *nada, nadie, ni ... ni, ningunola, nuncaljamás, raramente, también, tampoco,*
> *casi siempre, de vez en cuando, no me pierdo ..., no soporto ..., siempre que puedo*

> ### Skills
> - Adapting a model conversation for personal use and defending your point of view

> ### Grammar
> - Negatives

> ### PLTS
> Students' Book, page 99, activity 9,
> *Effective Participators*
> Students' Book, page 99, activity 13,
> *Creative Thinkers*

> ### Starters
> - Students' Book, page 98, activity 1. Students look at the picture and make predictions as to what is going on, where the boy is going to, what he might do there, how he feels about the prospect etc. They then do the listening activity and see how cloes their predictions were.
> - Students' Book, page 98, activity 5. Before doing the matching activity, tell students to read the four statements and note down which sports the people like and which they don't. Different groups can read different statements and combine their answers.
> - Students' Book, page 98, activity 7. Ask students what sports and activities their families do. They can play the True / False game in pairs or groups.
> - Students' Book, page 99, activity 13. In class, discuss any holiday camps (for young people or for families) that the students have been to. Collect opinions, vocabulary and phrases.

> ### Plenaries
> - Students' Book, page 98, activities 1–3. Display the activities (at camp and at home) discussed by Paco and his friend. Which ones have the students done? Which did they enjoy? What do they prefer – outdoor activities or stay-at-home ones? You can turn it into a class vote or survey.
> - Students' Book, page 98, activities 1-3. Give students a copy of the transcript, and a list of collquial expressions to find. They can use these expressions in activities 4 and 10.
> - Students' Book, page 99, activity 13. Students read or listen to the different holiday adverts prepared in this activity. They vote which camp they would take the group to for a class holiday. There can be eliminating rounds, and students can speak in defence of "their" holiday.

---

1 **Escucha a Paco y a su amigo hablando del campamento de verano. ¿Qué actividades mencionan?**

- Students listen and note down the activities mentioned that can be done at the camp.

5–8

> **CD 2, track 44** **página 98, actividades 1 y 2**
>
> **Paco** ¡Mira a lo que me quieren mandar mis padres!
> **Amigo** ¡El campamento de verano! ¿Y por qué?
> **Paco** Pues porque mi padre tiene una conferencia en París y mi madre va a ir con él y así no me quedo solo en casa. Mira – ¡como si yo fuera a practicar la equitación! ¡No he montado a caballo en mi vida!
> **Amigo** ¡Y hay clases de ballet!

> **Paco** Menudo aburrimiento ... Si hace buen tiempo, a lo mejor sí me gustaría practicar el remo, dicen que el río donde está el campamento no está mal.
> **Amigo** Pero si hace mal tiempo, que es lo normal, acabaréis cantando canciones en la tienda ...
> **Paco** Bueno, a mí no me disgusta el ping pong ...
> **Amigo** ¡O hacer montañismo!
> **Paco** Qué quieres que te diga, no entiendo por qué no me dejan quedarme en casa solo. Así podría levantarme tarde, ver la tele hasta cansarme y salir hasta tarde, ir a todos los conciertos, y jugar con el ordenador sin que me controlen lo que hago ...
> **Amigo** Ya, ¡y hacer fiestas en casa! ... pero ya han decidido que te toca ir al campamento, así que ¡prepárate para la diversión!

Answers: (at camp) la equitación, el ballet, el remo, cantar, el ping-pong, el tenis de mesa, el montañismo

2 Escucha otra vez y escribe cuáles son las actividades ideales del chico que no quiere ir al campamento.

- Students listen for the stay-at-home activities.

Answers: (at home) ver la tele, salir, ir a conciertos, jugar con el ordenador, hacer fiestas

5–8

3 Une las preguntas y las respuestas.

- Students match up the questions and the answers. Tell them to look out for clues in vocabulary and tenses.

Answers: **a** 3, **b** 4, **c** 2, **d** 5, **e** 1

4–6

4 Practica con tu compañero/a. Responde a las preguntas de la actividad 3 y utiliza expresiones de frecuencia.

- Students take it in turns to answer the questions with a partner. Compile a list of sports activities before they start. They should take notes, and then feed back about their partner to a third party, the class, or write a brief paragraph in the 3rd person.

4–7

5 Lee las siguientes opiniones sobre las actividades de tiempo libre y los anuncios del periódico. Une los anuncios con la persona adecuada. ¡Cuidado! hay una persona de más.

- Students read the opinions about leisure activities and match them to an advert.

Answers: Anuncio **1** b, Anuncio **2** c, Anuncio **3** a, (Opinión d is deliberately superfluous.)

5–8

6 Lee otra vez los textos la actividad 5 y habla con tu compañero/a. ¿Qué persona sería la más apropiada para ti y por qué?

- Students read again and with a partner decide who would be the best companion for themselves. If there is no one suitable they have to say why *No hay nadie a quien le gusta bailar.* They can also pair off other class members, tell them of their decision and receive their reaction.

4–9

7 Escucha a Eva hablar de los pasatiempos de su familia. ¿Verdadero, falso o no mencionado?

- Students listen to Eva and decide if the statements are True, False or Not Mentioned.

5–8

> **CD 2, track 45   página 99, actividad 7**
>
> En mi familia todos practicamos deportes menos mi madre. Nos gusta estar al aire libre y jugar al fútbol, al baloncesto … Mi padre es profesor de gimnasia y siempre se levanta temprano para ir a correr, y mi madre prefiere quedarse en casa leyendo el periódico. De vez en cuando, si vamos a la piscina, viene con nosotros, pero normalmente prefiere quedar con sus amigas a tomar café o ir al cine. ¡A nosotros no nos importa ni nos parece mal porque cada persona tiene gustos diferentes!

Answers: **a** V, **b** F, **c** F, **d** NM, **e** V, **f** NM

8 Lee las frases y escoge la opción apropiada.

- Students read the sentences and choose the correct word to complete them. Ask them to make up some more sentences using the negative words. These can be prompted e.g. *Nadie – clase – equitación, Nadie en la clase hace la equitación.*

4–9

Answers: **a** nunca, **b** Nadie, **c** nada, **d** tampoco, **e** Ninguna

9 Habla con tu compañero/a. Elegid un deporte y uno tiene que estar a favor y el otro en contra.

PLTS

- Students debate the merits of a sport with a partner, or prepare a point of view with a partner to be debated in class. They should offer convincing arguments for or against. Tell them to look back through the spread for vocabulary, and do an example with the whole class to start them off.

4–9

10 Escucha la crónica sobre la Semana Negra de Gijón y elige la opción adecuada.

- Students listen to the description of Semana Negra and complete the statements. Get students to read the statements first, and say what type of event they think *Semana Negra* is. This will give them a basis to do the listening activity.

5–8

> **CD 2, track 46   página 99, actividad 10**
>
> Finalmente da comienzo la Semana Negra de Gijón en Julio, diez días llenos de creatividad y de escritores célebres que vienen a hablar de sus libros. Todo comenzó hace ya dos décadas, cuando se hacía un pequeño festival de literatura policíaca; hoy en día, visitan la semana negra autores de cómic, de novela histórica y de ciencia-ficción y hay de todo para todos los gustos: desde poesía a medianoche hasta un festival internacional de fotoperiodismo para todos aquellos que estén interesados en las imágenes más famosas del año.

Answers: **a** en el verano, **b** más de una semana, **c** veinte años, **d** escuchar poemas, **e** fotográficas

11 Lee las siguientes opiniones de la encuesta sobre la Semana Negra y responde a las preguntas.

- Students read the opinions and answer the questions.

Answers: **a** No soporta el ruido **b** Para el ambiente y la cultura **c** Pasarlo bien tirando basura y bebiendo demasiado **d** Más policía en las calles **e** Hacer propaganda para Gijón

5–8

12 Une las preguntas con las respuestas.

- Students match up the questions and the answers.

Answers:

4–6

¿Qué tienes en la mano?	Nada
¿Quién te ayuda con los deberes?	Nadie
¿Tienes alguna amiga en clase?	No, ninguna
¿Has fumado alguna vez?	Nunca/jamás
¿Has visto a tu hermana?	No, ni a ella ni a mi madre
¿Tienes un bolígrafo? Yo no.	Yo tampoco

Remate

13 Write a leaflet advertising a summer camp and try to convince your friends to spend their holidays there.

4–9

- Students can choose a real holiday camp, or invent one if they prefer. They can be serious in their attempt ot advertise something they enjoyed, or take a tongue-in-cheek approach – *¡Ven a Butlins! ¿Te apetece estar con miles de personas quemadas del sol? ¿Te gusta hacer cola en el restaurante y participar en juegos idióticos? ¡Entonces, Butlins es para tí!*

Success criteria activity 13:
- *students give information accurately and in the appropriate style*
- *students express personal opinions and justify points of view*
- *students use a variety of vocabulary and structures*
- *students use different tenses or time frames*

Cómo hablar sobre tus gustos

páginas 100 y 101

Planner

➤ **Objectives**
- Discussing former and present tastes

➤ **Resources**
Students' Book, pages 100–101
CD 2, tracks 47–48
Grammar Workbook, page 68
Activity sheets 36–39

➤ **Key language**
acabar de, aprender a, dejar de, empezar a, estar enganchado/a, hablar de, hartarse de, no parar de, volver a
ahora, antes, en cuanto a …
cuenta la historia de …, me obligaban a, me relaja, no me pierdo, suelo leer …

➤ **Skills**
- Finding out and discussing other people's opinions

➤ **Grammar**
- Verbs followed by prepositions

➤ **PLTS**
Students' Book, page 101, activity 10, *Reflective Learners*
Students' Book, page 101, activity 12, *Team Workers*

➤ **Starters**
- Which magazines do students read? Write the names on the board, and score how many read each one. Elicit reasons.
- Students' Book, page 100, activity 3. Give students a transcript of the listening from activity 2, and get them to underline or highlight words and phrases to do with opinions that they can use in their discussion with their partner.
- Students' Book, page 100, activity 4. Give students a list of English words to find the Spanish for in the texts before they do the activity.
- Students' Book, page 101, activity 8. Before doing the matching activity, students read through the texts and pick out key phrases which help them understand them. Encourage them to look for phrases rather than single words. Ask them what they understand of the texts and make notes on the board. Ask them some questions in English and how they know it is *used to*.

➤ **Plenaries**
- Students' Book, page 100, activity 4. The teacher says a statement either directly from the texts e.g. *la biografía del bailarín cubano* or adapted *es la historia de un bailarín que viene de Cuba*. Students have to say which text it comes from.
- Give students key words to make up comparison sentences e.g. *antes – Los Simpsons – ahora – South Park; Antes veía siempre los Simpons, pero ahora prefiero South Park*. This can be done individually and orally, or groups see who can produce the sentence first.
- Students' Book, page 101, activity 12. Discuss the results of the survey in class. The teacher can then ask if other people had similar results. Figures can be collated and commented upon.
- Students' Book, page 101, activity 13. The guessing of who is described can be done by a student reading out a description and everyone having a guess. Alternatively, the descriptions (numbered for identification) can be passed around the class, and students can write a list of who they think the people are. The teacher asks for answers, (*Número 2, ¿quién es?*) and see how many people were right.

1 Mira las revistas españolas. ¿Cuál te interesa y por qué? ¿Cuál no y por qué?

- Students look at the pictures of the Spanish magazines and say which ones they like the look of and why.

4–9

2 Escucha y rellena el cuadro con las preferencias de estos jóvenes. ¿Qué tipo de revistas les gustan? ¿Por qué?

- Students listen and fill in the table.

5–9

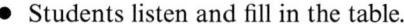 CD 2, track 47	página 100, actividad 2

Chico Mari, ¿ya te has comprado el *Quo*?
Chica Sí, al fin me lo han traído al quiosco.
Chico ¿Y de qué va? Yo nunca me la he comprado y no tengo ni idea del contenido.
Chica Pues es una revista científica pero muy entretenida. Me gusta porque aprendo mucho pero de una manera divertida. No es la típica revista del corazón con famosos y cosas así.
Chico Pues a mí me encanta ¡*Hola*!. No estoy obsesionada con las estrellas y los famosos pero me gusta ver las fotografías y saber qué pasa en sus vidas. Está bien para pasar el rato.
Chica Pues si te gustan las fotografías, *Geo* es la mejor – ¡qué fotos tiene de países! Y los reportajes de viajes son impresionantes. Te dan ganas de coger la maleta y marcharte.
Chico ¿Y qué opinas de *Diez minutos*?
Chica Creo que es para chicas más jóvenes y a mí se me hace un poco aburrida.
Chico La que me encanta es *Fotogramas* – siempre estoy al corriente de los estrenos y también de los nuevos actores. No me la pierdo nunca.
Chica ¿Y +*quefútbol*?
Chico No está nada mal. Es la primera revista multimedia de deportes y además habla de vídeos, animaciones … un poco diferente de las típicas revistas de deportes que son siempre iguales.

Answers:

	Quo	**¡Hola!**	**Geo**
opinión	me gusta	me encanta	impresionante
razón	aprende cosas de una manera divertida	le gusta ver las fotos de los famosos y leer lo que pasa en sus vidas	tiene los mejores fotos y reportajes de viajes
	Patrones	**Fotogramas**	**+quefutbol**
opinión	aburrida	me encanta	no está mal
razón	es para chicas más jóvenes	está al corriente de los estrenos y nuevos actores	es la primera revista multimedia de deportes, habla de vídeos y animaciones, es un poco diferente

3 Habla con tu compañero/a. Preparad una respuesta en español a esta pregunta:

- Students answer the question with their partner. They can draw on material used in the first two Starter activities to help them. They can feed back this information in the 3rd person to the class or another student, and find a "magazine buddy" for their partner who has the same tastes.

4–9

4 Lee las sugerencias de los lectores de la revista *Qué leer*. ¿A qué libro se refiere?

- Students match the questions to the book reviews.

5–8

Answers: **a** World Press Photo y Carlos Acosta, **b** Cuentos de Eva Luna y El amor en los tiempos del cólera, **c** El amor en los tiempos del cólera, **d** Carlos Acosta y Cuentos de Eva Luna, **e** World Press Photo

5 Describe un libro. La clase tiene que adivinar qué libro es.

- Students describe a book to the class. They can work with a partner to prepare their description.

5–8

6 Escucha a los jóvenes hablando de sus gustos antes y ahora y elige la opción adecuada. ¿Verdadero o falso?

- Students listen and decide if the statements are true or false. Tell them to pay attention to tenses.

5–8

CD 2, track 48	página 100, actividad 6

Chica ¡Rocío, mira esta caja de vídeos!
Rocío Sí, es la caja con los vídeos que tenía de pequeña. Ahora no tengo mucho espacio y por eso tengo que guardarlos ahí.
Chica ¡Series policíacas! No sabía que te gustaban esas cosas.
Rocío Antes sí, me encantaban las historias de Hitchcock, las series de misterio … nada me gustaba más que una historia de terror.
Chica ¿Y ahora?
Rocío Ahora prefiero las series históricas o biográficas. De vez en cuando veo una película de miedo, algo tipo Stephen King, pero no como antes. ¿Y tú?
Chica Pues yo no veía mucho la tele ni tampoco películas. No tenía mucha paciencia, me gustaban los deportes y estar activa.
Rocío Yo no iba al cine a menudo, pero veía vídeos que mi madre alquilaba. ¿Y tú?
Chica A mí solamente me gustaban los programas para niños tipo Barrio Sésamo, y luego los deportes. Odiaba estar sentada en el sofá, me gustaba la acción.
Rocío ¿Y ahora?
Chica Ahora sí, ahora me encanta una buena película.

Answers: **a** V, **b** F, **c** V, **d** V, **e** V, **f** F

7 **Haz una encuesta en clase. ¿Qué tipo de programas de televisión prefieren tus compañeros/as y por qué?**

* Students carry out a survey in class about people's viewing preferences. More advanced groups can include "before" and "now" questions. Make the questions up in class, or each student can make up their own. Give them a copy of the transcript of the previous activity for more vocabulary.

4–9

8 **Lee las opiniones 1–4 sobre los programas de televisión y emparéjalos con las siguientes frases.**

* Students match the sentences to the paragraphs.

Answers: **a** 4, **b** 4, **c** 3, **d** 2, **e** 1

4–9

9 **Practica con tu compañero/a. ¿Qué leías antes y ahora? ¿Han cambiado mucho tus gustos?**

* Students discuss reading habits with their partner. Pick out some useful phrases from the texts above to start with that they can use e.g. *antes, no paraba de, ahora, cuando era* etc. Encourage them to include their opinions.

4–9

10 **¿Qué verbos conoces que no necesitan de preposición?**
Grammar reference page 206

PLTS

* Students look through the unit for examples. They should make up some memorable sentences possibly in a short story using them.

Answers: Verbs which are not followed by a preposition include: me gusta+infinitive, preferir, querer, desear, dudar, necesitar, etc.

4–6

11 **Mira de la actividad 8 y escribe la preposición.**
Students find the preposition for each verb in activity 8. If they find this concept difficult, point out verbs in English that use prepositions.

Answers:

verbo	preposición	significado
Hartarse	**de**	To be fed up with
Dejar	**de**	To stop doing something, quit
Volver	**a**	To do something again
Empezar	**a**	To start to
Acabar	**de**	To finish doing something

Remate

12 **Do a survey in class.**

PLTS

* Students can use the questions provided, or make up more. They note down the replies and write short paragraphs.

Success criteria activity 12:

4–9
* *students communicate effectively and accurately*
* *students express personal opinions and justify points of view*
* *students use a variety of vocabulary and structures*
* *students deal with unpredictable elements*
* *students use different tenses or time frames*

13 **Talk to several classmates and write about what they used to like watching on TV and what they watch now. The rest of the class then have to guess which person it is.**

* Students make detailed notes about a few people's past and present viewing habits, and write a short paragraph about them. They should refer to *esta persona* rather than *el chico* or *la chica* to make it a bit harder.

4–9

Success criteria activity 13:
* *students give information accurately and in the appropriate style*
* *students express personal opinions and justify points of view*
* *students use a variety of vocabulary and structures*
* *students use different tenses or time frames*

Gramática en acción

páginas 102 y 103

Planner

➤ Objectives
* Practising the correct use of the imperfect and preterite tenses.

➤ Resources
Students' Book, pages 102–103
Exam Skills Workbook, page 46
Grammar Workbook, pages 43–46, 57, 68
Activity sheet 40
Resources and Planning OxBox CD-ROM

➤ Grammar
* Using the preterite and imperfect
* Using negatives
* Using verbs with prepositions

➤ PLTS
Students' Book, page 102, activity 1,
Reflective Learners
Students' Book, page 102, activity 3,
Self-Managers

➤ Imperfect and preterite

1 **Fill in the grid with the correct endings for each tense.**
Grammar reference page 211

PLTS *Answers:*

Preterite tense		Imperfect tense	
-ar	**-er, -ir**	**-ar**	**-er, -ir**
-é	-í	-aba	-ía
-aste	-iste	-abas	-ías
-ó	-ió	-aba	-ía
-amos	-imos	-ábamos	-íamos
-ásteis	-isteis	-abais	-íais
-aron	-ieron	-aban	-ían

2 **Which of these verbs are irregular in the preterite? Can you think of more?**
Grammar reference page 211
● Students can look for examples in the Students' Book, or refer to the Grammar section.

Answers: hacer, poder, estar, dar, ver

3 **Make yourself a set of numbered cards, writing a verb infinitive on each card. Use different coloured cards for irregular and regular verbs. Then throw dice to choose the cards and practise the verb endings.**
Grammar reference page 211

PLTS ● Start with a few cards, and increase the number as students get more confident. To begin with, students should recite the whole verb in the preterite or imperfect. As they become more proficient, the partner picks a pronoun – *yo, tu, nosotros* – and the first person has to give the correct part of the verb.

4 **Complete the sentences with the right verb.**
● Students complete the sentences choosing from the verbs in the box below.

Answers: **a** 3, **b** 6, **c** 4, **d** 1, **e** 5, **f** 2

5 **Choose the right ending for the sentence.**

Answers: **a** iba, **b** era, **c** tenían, **d** vivíamos, teníamos

➤ Negatives

6 **Fill the gaps in these sentences with the right negative.**

Answers: **a** 4, **b** 1, **c** 6, **d** 2, **e** 3, **f** 5,

➤ Verbs with prepositions

7 **Some verbs need certain prepositions to work properly. Check the following sentences and add the right prepositions.**
Grammar reference page 201

Answers: **a** a, **b** a, **c** de, **d** a, **e** de, **f** de, **g** de

8 **Read this letter and write down all the imperfect and preterite verbs in two columns. Then write a reply using all the grammar of this Unit.**
● Discuss some ideas in class to start them off. Remind them it does not have to be remotely true. They get points for each correct use of a past tense, a negative or a verb with a preposition.

Habilidades
página 104

Planner

➤ Objectives
● Improving learning skills and working out meaning from context

➤ Resources
Students' Book, page 104
Exam Skills Workbook, page 46 (F), page 47 (H)
Activity sheet 41
Resources and Planning OxBox CD-ROM

➤ Skills
● Learning and remembering vocabulary
● Learning positive and negative adjectives
● Learning synonyms
● Expanding your answers about likes and dislikes

➤ PLTS
Students' Book, page 104, activity 4,
Reflective Learners
Students' Book, page 104, activity 6,
Creative Thinkers

➤ Aprender

1 Learn and remember vocabulary.
- At the beginning of the lesson give students five minutes with their cue cards, and at the end give them a quick test.

2 Learn positive and negative adjectives.
- On the back of each card they can write an example to help them remember e.g. *El autobús es lento*. Alliteration can be helpful e.g. *Adriano es aburrido* (but be careful of gender and agreement).

3 Learn synonyms.
- Students can play synonym Snap or Pairs with the cards.

4 Check your learning.
 PLTS
- Students can time themselves and see how quickly they can match up the synonyms.

➤ Leer

5 Recognise words in a text.
- Students look back through the unit for examples, and make a note of them in categories.

➤ Escribir

6 Expand your answers about likes and dislikes.
PLTS
- Students make up examples. They should be things that are real to them e.g. *Me apasiona ir al cine*.
- Students should try and remember what these mean before checking back in the unit and writing out an example – *Coronation Street – ¡Menuda pérdida de tiempo!*

Escenario

página 105

Planner

➤ Objectives
- Writing a film review and researching a Spanish festival

➤ Resources
Students' Book, page 105
Exam Skills WorkBook, page 43–44 (F), pages 44–45 (H)
Assessment sheets 17–24
Resources and Planning OxBox CD-ROM

➤ Skills
- Writing practice
- Speaking practice

➤ PLTS
Students' Book, page 105, Escenario Oral, *Team Workers*
Students' Book, page 105, Escenario Escrito, *Independent Enquirers*

➤ Oral

PLTS   **4–9**

Prepare a film review to be spoken aloud in Spanish.
- Students can choose any film they have seen. They should look at reviews in magazines or on websites for format ideas.
- The actor and director biographies should not be too long. They can focus on that person's achievements in relation to the film under discussion.
- The plot summary should contain a brief overview and particular highlights.
- The critics' comments should be in the 3rd person.
- Students divide the presentation between them, prepare it (with accompanying visuals / Powerpoint etc.) and rehearse it for confidence and fluency.

- Students should have a pre-prepared score sheet to write marks and comments on. Everyone can comment, or the class can elect judges. There is a lot of information to include, but a time guide should be set.
- *GCSE Grades A*-C*
- *Grade C Students use past, present and future tenses. They express opinions, and deal with some unpredictability.*
- *Grade A Students express and justify opinions. They use a variety of vocabulary and structure in longer speech sequences.*

➤ **Escrito**

PLTS **El Festival de Benicàssim.**

4–9

- www.fiberfib.com is the official website. Students will be aware from earlier work of the vast quantity of festivals in Spain. Travel guides are a good starting point for research; the internet is invaluable once you have a festival name.
- Students can consider the points of view of the locals, the festival goers, and unsuspecting tourists.

- *GCSE Grades A*-C*
- *Grade C Students use opinions and past, present and future tenses, both factually and imaginatively. Register is appropriate and style is basic.*
- *Grade A Students write factually and imaginatively using longer sequences and a range of vocabulary and structure. They express and justify opinions in an appropriate style.*

Vocabulario   página 74

This is a summary of key language from the unit, organised by spread and theme. Students can use it for reference while working on the unit, and as an aid to learning vocabulary.

Lectura   páginas 181 y 182

Planner

➤ **Objectives**
- Reading about the world of cinema.
- To encourage independent reading and develop reading strategies.

➤ **Resources**
Students' Book, page 181-182

➤ **PLTS**
Students' Book, page 181, activity 2,
Effective Participators
Students' Book, page 182, activity 4,
Creative Thinkers

➤ **Lectura A – ¿Eres un loco del cine? ¡Descúbrelo en este test!**

1 **Lee y busca el equivalente en español de las siguientes palabras.**

5–9

- Students read the quiz and look for the words in Spanish.

Answers: **a** elegir, **b** no te importa, **c** la portada, **d** el argumento, **e** ahorras, **f** esperas, **g** saber de memoria

2 **¿Es verdad tu resultado del test? Discute con tu compañero/a en inglés.**

PLTS

- Students take the test and discuss with a partner if it is an accurate reflection of their attitude to cinema.

4–9

3 **Escribe tu opinión en español sobre el cine y las películas.**

4–9

- Students write a brief paragraph about how they like the cinema using the prompts and drawing on the vocabulary of the quiz to help them.

➤ **Lectura B – Alejandro Amenábar**

1 **Lee y busca el equivalente español de las siguientes palabras.**

5–9

- Students read the text and look for the words in Spanish.

Answers: **a** se mudó, **b** descubre, **c** éxitos – TB false friends, **d** premios, **e** controvertido, **f** rodada, **g** protagonistas, **h** bandas sonoras

2 **Con tu compañero/a, utiliza la información del texto para hacer una entrevista a Alejandro Amenábar.**

- Students use the information to carry out an interview with Amenábar. They look for key words in the text to write their questions e.g. *nació – ¿Cuando nació usted?*

4–9

3 **Responde a las preguntas en inglés.**

5–9

- Students answer the questions in English. Some students may find it easier to do this activity before the interview above.

Answers: **a** when he was one year old, **b** it was the background for the story, **c** a student who discovers a crime which took place at the university a few years before, **d** because it deals with the topic of euthanasia, **e** that it was filmed completely in English, **f** soundtracks

4 **Imagínate que eres un director de cine famoso en tu país. Escribe tu propia biografía haciéndola lo más interesante posible.**

PLTS

4–9

- Students use the text about Amenábar as a basis to write their directorial autobiography. What was their family background? When did they direct their first film? What successes have they had? Which famous actors have acted for them?

Unit 4A Mis vacaciones			Overview grid	
Spread	**Contexts**	**Skills**	**Grammar**	**Vocabulary**
Spread title	• Topic areas covered within the unit	• Key skills focus	• Grammar covered in the unit	Key vocabulary
pages 108–109 **Cómo describir tus destinos de vacaciones**	• Describing your favourite holiday destination	• Giving opinions	• The conditional	las aduanas, los atascos, la belleza, las carreteras, el equipaje, un fastidio, los países menos desarrollados, los regalos, los vuelos agotado/a, fiable conocer la cultura, descansar, ir de fiesta, te da libertad
pages 110–111 **Cómo reservar alojamiento**	• Reserving accommodation	• Reading strategies – using context • Hearing the difference between questions and statements	• Correct use of *tú* and *usted*	agua caliente, el albergue, el alojamiento, alquiler de bicicletas, los alrededores, una caja fuerte, los demás gastos, un dormitorio común, efectivo, un folleto, forma de pago, una habitación de matrimonio, instalaciones, la lavandería, media pensión, una parcela, pensión completa, la primera quincena, un señor mayor, sólo alojamiento, la ubicación, vistas al mar, le recuerdo, me pidió, atentamente
pages 112–113 **Cómo relatar tus vacaciones pasadas**	• Talking about past holidays, problems and their solutions	• Anticipating what vocabulary to expect	• Ordinal numbers	el jabón, la llave equivocada, las maletas, el piragüismo, el ruido, las sábanas, el submarinismo, la temporada alta, las toallas, el wáter acogedor(a), sencillo/a, poco seguro/a bajar, dormir, subir cuéntanos tu historia, daba asco, el grifo estaba roto, la luz no funcionaba, me alojé, no estaba lista, no tuvo nada de gracia, nos dimos cuenta, el retrete se atascó
pages 114–115 **Cómo describir tus vacaciones ideales**	• Talking about leisure activities on holiday	• Asking questions	• The future tense	la entrevista, el mismo sitio, el/la periodista, las tonterías estar harto/a, estar molesto/a, ir solo, malgastar, pasear, tener muchas ganas de moda, sin duda
pages 116–117 **Cómo hablar de las vacaciones en el extranjero**	• Making comparisons between different types of holidays	• Reading long texts	• Expressions of time	un abrazo, los/las bañistas, la colonia, los extranjeros, la fábrica, la madrugada, las mascotas, el país, la piscina cubierta empollar, hacer el vago, ligar, bajarse música fuerte, al aire libre, habitualmente, por desgracia ¿Cuánto duran?,¡Qué agobio!
pages 118–119 **Gramática en acción**	• Using regular verbs	• Using ordinal numbers • Using the formal and informal forms • Choosing between *ser* and *estar* correctly • Using reflexive and non-reflexive verbs in different tenses • Using expresions of time		
page 120 **Habilidades**	• Using accent and intonation to sound more authentic when speaking, and recognising different tenses	• Recognising questions from statements • Using context to help you • Anticipating the likely answers • Avoiding getting hung up on what you don't know • Working out the meaning of unfamliar words • Using grammar to help you answer questions		
page 121 **Escenario**	• Plan and organise an end–of–year class trip.			
page 122 **Vocabulario**	• Summary of key vocabulary for the unit. • Write a letter to parents with an overview of the trip you have planned.			
pages 183–184 **Reading pages**	Travelling in South America: • to encourage independent reading and to develop reading strategies. • to provide alternative class and homework material for students who finish other activities quickly.			

4A Mis vacaciones

Unit Objectives

Contexts: reserving and talking about holidays past and future

Skills focus: recognising questions, using context to understand, anticipating answers; dealing with the unknown, working out unfamiliar meanings, using grammar to answer questions

Grammar: ordinal numbers, formal and informal forms, using *ser* and *estar* correctly, using reflexive and non-reflexive verbs in different tenses, expressions of time

Controlled assessment opportunities

Writing: Students' Book, page 109, activity 7
Speaking: Students' Book, page 111, activity 5d
Writing: Students' Book, page 113, activity 8
Speaking: Students' Book, page 115, activity 7
Writing: Students' Book, page 117, activity 6

See also *GCSE Spanish for OCR Assessment OxBox CD-ROM.*

An introduction to the unit página 107

- *Aim*: To introduce the themes of the unit and encourage students to think about the reasons for learning Spanish.
- The opening page is designed with captions, pictures and page cross-references to provide a preview of what is to come:

	Students' Book
Cómo describir tus destinos de vacaciones	page 108
Cómo reservar alojamiento	page 110
Cómo relatar tus vacaciones pasadas	page 112
Cómo describir tus vacaciones ideales	page 114
Cómo hablar de las vacaciones extranjeras	page 116
Gramática – improving your use and understanding of Spanish	page 118
Habilidades – increasing your language skills for fluency	page 120
Escenario – ¡Planifica el viaje de fin de curso! Escenario – Escribe una carta a los padres con la información.	page 121

- Allow time for students to read the questions and cross-refer to the relevant pages of the Students' Book. They could do this individually or in pairs / small groups, followed by whole-class discussion.
- This spread also provides an opportunity for students to recap on familiar language. Ask them to think about language they already know that might be useful when working on the themes of the unit.
- Mindmap any language they produce, and if possible, keep it on display as reference as you progress through the unit. It can be added to at intervals as new language becomes familiar.

- At the end of work on the unit, allow time for students to return to this spread and repeat the mind-mapping process, this time including what they have learned over the course of the unit. Get them to answer the questions in their own words, and encourage them to use the results for revision purposes.
- Ask them what they found difficult, interesting etc. What do they think are the important things they have learned in this unit? What do they still need to improve on?
- If time permits, get the students to redesign the page. How would they set it out so it reflects the unit? How would they make it attractive to other learners of their age? How would they make it easy to follow? What would they include in terms of text, pictures, captions, page references? Ask them to imagine they are producing material for next year's class who will be learning the same thing – what would they have found it useful to know?

¿Por qué aprender el español? Para organizar y hablar de vacaciones.
- Students share any experiences they have had going on holiday in Spain, including finding out information about accommodation either before or during their stay.
- Ask them to consider what sort of language they would need to talk about their holiday to a Spanish person, or to plan one for themselves.

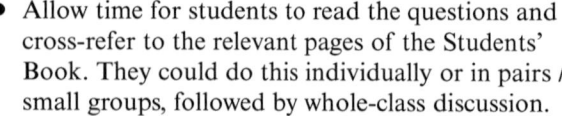

Cómo describir tus destinos de vacaciones

páginas 108 and 109

Planner

➤ Objectives
- Describing your favourite holiday destination

➤ Resources
Students' Book, pages 108–109
CD 3, tracks 2–3
Grammar Workbook, pages 53–54
Activity sheets 43–46

➤ Key language
las aduanas, los atascos, la belleza, las carreteras, el equipaje, un fastidio, los países menos desarrollados, los regalos, los vuelos agotado/a, fiable
conocer la cultura, descansar, ir de fiesta, te da libertad

➤ Skills
- Giving opinions

➤ Grammar
- The conditional

➤ PLTS
Students' Book, page 109, activity 3,
Effective Participators
Students' Book, page 109, activity 7,
Self-Managers

➤ Starters
- Make a spidergram for holidays with the word vacaciones in the middle. Include countries, destinations, accommodation, companions, activities etc.
- Students' Book, page 109, activity 1. Students look at the pictures and make lists of vocabulary or make up sentences about them in Spanish.

- Students' Book, page 109, activity 2. Before listening, students see how many different type of weather they can remember from previous work. Note the words down on the board for students to look at as they listen.
- Students' Book, page 109 activity 7. Before starting to write their description, students should compile a list of words and phrases from the spread that they can use or adapt for their particular description.

➤ Plenaries
- Students' Book, page 109, activity 1. Ask students which picture they would pick as a holiday destination and why. Encourage them to use phrases from the texts on page 108 in their reasons.
- Students' Book, page 109, activity 3. Use the grid on page 108 as a whole class or in groups to make up chain sentences. Students take it in turns to say an element from the grid – the next student has to continue the sentence and so on. The aim is to continue making sentences without repeating any phrases, and while making sense. Each complete correct sentence wins a point, each repeated phrase and incorrect sentence loses one.
- Students' Book, page 109, activity 6. Students give their spoken replies to a small group or the class. Other students can award points for a clear explanation, correct language, interesting vocabulary, and a good reason.
- The teacher gives statements, and the students have to decide to which picture at activity 1 they refer e.g. *Prefiero vacaciones tranquilas.* They can call out the answers, or note them down like a quiz, and check the answers at the end.

1a   Mira la página anterior. Empareja cada frase con la foto más adecuada.

- Students look at the previous page and match the pictures and the statements. Ask them on what they based their decisions.

Answers: **1** b, **2** e, **3** d, **4** a, **5** c

1b   Encuentra la traducción de estas palabras en la página anterior.

- Students look for the Spanish of the phrases in the texts on page 108.

Answers: **1** los países menos desarrollados, **2** llego **a** las vacaciones agotada, **3** sólo me apetece relajarme, **4** lo que me encanta es ir de fiesta, **5** Me fascina

2a Escucha y decide quién menciona estos aspectos del clima – ¿Mikel, Arantxa, Betty o Salva?

- Students listen and decide who mentions which type of weather.

CD 3, track 2   página 109, actividad 2

1 Me llamo Mikel y a mí me gusta ir a Marruecos porque siempre hace calor y buen tiempo. Me gusta pasar las mañanas en la playa y por la tarde visitar los mercadillos. Además, allí todo es muy barato y siempre me compro algo.

2 Soy Arantxa: yo lo paso mal con el calor y prefiero las vacaciones de invierno. Me gusta mucho esquiar y mi destino ideal es Andorra porque allí cuando hace frío siempre nieva. Si hace mal tiempo o hay niebla no importa porque hay muchísimos centros comerciales así que voy de tiendas o a veces vamos a la pista de hielo a patinar.

3 Mi nombre es Betty y lo mío es arena, sol y mar así que Canarias es perfecto para mí y aunque a menudo hace viento; siempre hace buen tiempo para pasar el día en la playa leyendo un buen libro o jugando a voleibol con los amigos.

4 Yo soy Salva y a mí me fascina Bolivia por sus costumbres y su variedad. Allí se puede hacer de todo: visitar los mercados, bajar en bici por la carretera de la muerte, pescar en el lago Titicaca, esquiar en Chacaltaya o incluso alojarte en un hotel de sal en el Salar de Uyuni. Lo único es que tienes que ir cuando no llueve porque si vas en la temporada de las lluvias, siempre está nublado o lloviendo.

Answers: **a** Betty, **b** Salva, **c** Salva, **d** Arantxa, **e** Mikel y Betty, **f** Arantxa, **g** Mikel y Arantxa **h** Arantxa, **i** Arantxa

2b Escucha otra vez y rellena la tabla.

- Listen again and complete the grid.

Answers:

Mikel – Marruecos
Razones: siempre hace calor y buen tiempo
Actividades: la playa, visitar los mercadillos

Arantxa – Andorra
Razones: cuando hace frío siempre nieva
Actividades: esquiar, centros comerciales, patinar

3 Utiliza la tabla en la página 108 para escribir una frase secreta con un elemento de cada columna. Túrnate con un compañero/a para adivinar las frases secretas. Debéis dar ✓ o ✗ para cada elemento.

PLTS

- Students take it in turns with a partner to write secret sentences using the table, and guess what their partner has written. Students need a copy of the table each that they can write on while guessing. They take it in turns to guess their partner's sentence, and the first one to complete the sentence wins.

4a Copia las frases y completa con la palabra que falta.

- Students copy down the sentences, completing them with the correct form of transport.

Answers: **a** avión. **b** tren, **c** autocar, **d** coche, **e** moto

4b Escribe las ventajas y desventajas de los medios de transporte que se mencionan en la actividad 4a. Utiliza un diccionario si es necesario.

- Students write about the advantages and disadvantages of the methods of transport in 4a. This is an objective view, not a personal one. Before they do so, get them to pick out useful and transferable phrases from 4a such as *para largas distancias, es más rápido, se viaja bien* etc.

5a Rellena los huecos con el verbo adecuado.

- Students complete the gaps in the text with the correct verb. Ask them how they made their decisions especially for 2, 11 and 12.

5b Escucha y corrige tus respuestas.

- Students listen and check their own answers.

CD 3, track 3   página 109, actividad 5b

Para mis vacaciones ideales iría al Caribe para seis semanas con mis amigos porque me gusta la playa y el buen tiempo. Volaría en primera clase ya que es más cómodo y me alojaría en un hotel de cinco estrellas con piscina, jacuzzi y pistas de tenis. Todas las mañanas dormiría hasta muy tarde, después tomaría el sol en la playa, nadaría en el mar o en la piscina y jugaría a voleibol con mis amigos. Por las tardes pasearía por la ciudad y compraría regalos caros para mi familia. También me gustaría comprar un yate en el que mis amigos y yo pasaríamos una semana.

Answers: **1** iría, **2** me gusta, **3** volaría, **4** me alojaría, **5** dormiría, **6** tomaría, **7** nadaría, **8** jugaría, **9** pasearía, **10** compraría, **11** me gustaría, **12** pasaríamos

Remate

6 What type of holiday do you prefer and why? Prepare some notes for a spoken reply lasting at least 30 seconds.

- Encourage students to draw on the vocabulary and structures from the spread, and look up any more that they need. They should not write it out in full, and they should speak in full sentences.

7 Write a description of your ideal holiday in 60–120 words. You can use ideas from page 108 if you want.

PLTS

- Counting words encourages students to realise they do not need to write pages to complete a task. The teacher can provide a check list of items to include – destination, accomodation etc. They can draw on the Plenary discussion they had after activity 1 for material also.

Success criteria activities 6 & 7:
- *students give information accurately and in the appropriate style*
- *students express personal opinions and justify points of view*
- *students use a variety of vocabulary and structures*

Cómo reservar alojamiento

Planner

➤ Objectives
- Reserving accommodation

➤ Resources
Students' Book, pages 110–111
CD 3, tracks 4–5
Grammar Workbook, page 22
Activity sheets 43–46

➤ Key language
agua caliente, el albergue, el alojamiento, alquiler de bicicletas, los alrededores, una caja fuerte, los demás gastos, un dormitorio común, efectivo, un folleto, forma de pago, una habitación de matrimonio, instalaciones, la lavandería, media pensión, una parcela, pensión completa, la primera quincena, un señor mayor, sólo alojamiento, la ubicación, vistas al mar, le recuerdo, me pidió, atentamente

➤ Skills
- Reading strategies – using context
- Difference between questions and statements

➤ Grammar
- Correct use of *tú* and *usted*

➤ PLTS
Students' Book, page 110, activity 1,
Independent Enquirers
Students' Book, page 111, activity 5,
Team Workers

➤ Starters
- Before doing activity 1, students look at the photos and describe what they see, what type of holiday it is, and what type of accommodation the people are likely to want. They can check their predictions after doing the activity.
- Students' Book, page 111, activity 2. Before doing the listening activity draw up a grid to use for the answers. Ask the students questions to elicit the names for the different boxes in the grid e.g. *¿Cómo se dice* accomodation *en español?*

- Students' Book, page 111, activity 4. Ask students what *tú* and *usted* mean and when they would use them. Ask how they would ask the question *Do you want a coffee?* in each case. Practise with more verbs if necessary.
- Students' Book, page 111, activity 6. Give the students a list of useful phrases in English which they might need in their emails. The phrases exist in the emails at the beginning of the page, but in another form, and the students have to adapt them e.g. *We would like to reserve* has to be adapted from *quisiera reservar* to *quisieramos reservar*.

➤ Plenaries
- Students' Book, page 110, activity 1. The teacher says a statement about one of the emails and students have to say if it is true or false. They can work in teams, pub quiz style, to see how many they get right. More advanced groups can prepare statements and be quiz masters for each other.
- Students' Book, page 111, activity 2. Give students a copy of the transcript, and ask them to find "phrases that mean…" This could be played as a team game, where the first group to find the phrase wins a point.
- Students' Book, page 111, activity 5d. Students can elaborate and be more inventive with their conversations, including new situations. Advanced students should play this "blind" – without knowing the preconditions set by their partner – for realistic and hopefully humorous effect. The conversations can be performed for the class.
- Students' Book, page 111, activity 6. Students can exchange their reservation emails with another student, who writes a reply and answers any questions. They may also pose problems: it depends how long you want to keep the correspondance going. If the school has an intranet, this could actually be done by email for realism.

1a **Empareja estos emails con la familia o grupo a quien pertenecen.**

- Students match the emails to the photos of the people going on holiday. Ask them to explain which bits of vocabulary helped them decide.

Answers: **1** B, **2** D, **3** A, **4** C

1b **¿Qué significan en inglés las palabras subrayadas?**

- Students write out what the underlined phrases mean. Tell them to look for the words they do understand and try to work it out.

Answers: a leaflet of tourist attractions, a map of the city, the bus timetable, the map of the area

1c **Lee otra vez y encuentra la palabra o palabras más adecuadas para estos símbolos.**

- Students identify the Spanish words for the symbols. Before they look through the texts, ask if they know or can remember any.

Answers: **1** aire acondicionado, **2** caja fuerte, **3** aparcamiento, **4** calefacción, **5** ascensor, **6** alquiler de bicicletas, **7** efectivo o tarjetas de crédito, **8** duchas con agua caliente, **9** lavandería, **10** terraza y vistas al mar

2a **Escucha estas conversaciones (1–4) y escribe la información.**

- Students listen to the four conversations and note down the information.

 CD 3, track 4   **página 111, actividad 2**

1
- Hotel Palmeral, buenas tardes.
- Quiero reservar una habitación del 8 al 13 de agosto.
- Muy bien señora, déjeme ver ¿Qué tipo de habitación desea?
- Una habitación de matrimonio con ducha.
- Todas nuestras habitaciones tienen terraza. ¿Prefiere vistas al mar o la piscina?
- Vistas al mar por favor. ¿Está incluido el desayuno?
- Sí, está incluido. Además tenemos una oferta para esas fechas: régimen de pensión completa en nuestro buffet libre por 15€ por persona por noche. ¿Le interesa?
- No, no. Vamos a hacer muchas excursiones y sería un poco difícil volver al hotel para comer pero para cenar sí estaremos de vuelta. ¿Ofrecen media pensión?
- Sí, por supuesto.
- Media pensión entonces.
- ¿Hay aparcamiento en el hotel?
- No, pero se puede aparcar gratuitamente en la plaza que está sólo a dos minutos. Bueno, a ver... Una habitación de matrimonio con vistas al mar para dos personas a media pensión del 8 al 13 de agosto. Son... 450€ las cinco noches.
- ¿Aceptan tarjetas de crédito?..

2
- Buenos días, Camping los Cuatro Vientos. ¿Sí? ¿Dígame?
- Hola buenos días. ¿Tiene parcelas disponibles para este fin de semana?
- ¿Es para una tienda o una caravana?
- Para una tienda. Somos dos adultos y tres niños.
- Sí, señor para una tienda sí. ¿Prefiere estar cerca de las duchas o de la pista de tenis?
- Cerca de la pista de tenis gracias.
- Está bien. Son 15 euros por noche. ¿Cómo desea pagar?
- ¿Aceptan cheques?
- No, lo siento señor. Sólo tarjetas de crédito o efectivo.
- Bueno ... Le pago con una Mastercard; el número es ...

3
- Buenos días. Hotel Carlos V, Rosalina al aparato.
- Hola, ¿tiene habitaciones disponibles para San Juan?
- ¿Para cuántas noches?
- Del viernes 23 al domingo 25 de junio, dos noches.
- ¿Para cuántas personas?
- Somos 3 adultos y un bebé.
- ¿Una habitación doble con una cuna y una individual les va bien?
- ¿Cuánto cuesta?
- Son 58€ por persona por noche, desayuno incluido.
- Huy., un poquitín caro. Bueno, ¿qué comodidades hay en el hotel?
- Todas nuestras habitaciones tienen baño, mini bar y aire acondicionado . Ah, y también secador de pelo. Hay aparcamiento, jardín e incluso tienda de recuerdos y piscina y sauna. Y servicio de habitaciones, claro.
- Bueno, estoy segura que disfrutaremos. ¿Puedo pagar en efectivo a la llegada?
- Sí por supuesto señora, como prefiera.

4
- Hola, bienvenido al Barcelona Dream. ¿Tienes una reserva?
- Sí, a nombre de Elisa Coca.
- ¿Cómo vas a pagar?
- En efectivo. Son 69€ las tres noches ¿no?
- Sí, 23€ por noche. Toma, aquí tienes la llave, estás en el tercer piso en el dormitorio a la derecha. Tu cama es la 8. El aseo y las duchas están en el pasillo y tienes una taquilla grande al lado de la cama para que metas tu maleta.
- ¿A qué hora abre la cocina?
- La cocina abre de 8 de la mañana a las diez de la noche. Hay armarios y neveras para tu comida pero asegúrate que pones tu nombre en todas tus cosas.
- Muy bien, muchas gracias. Tercer piso, a la derecha, cama 8.

Answers:

	1	2	3	4
Alojamiento	una habitación matrimonial	una parcela para una tienda	una habitación doble con una cuna y una individual	una cama en un dormitorio
Personas	dos	dos adultos y tres niños	tres adultos y un bebé	un adulto
Fecha/Noches	8-18 agosto	fin de semana	23-25 junio	tres noches
Régimen*	media pensión			
Precio	450€	15€ por noche	58€ por persona por noche	69€
Instalaciones	con ducha, restaurante	duchas, pista de tenís	baño, minibar, aire acondicionado, secador de pelo, aparcamiento, jardín, tienda de recuerdos, piscina y sauna, servicio de habitaciones	aseo, duchas, taquilla de maleta, armarios y nevera en la cocina para la comida
Modo de pago	tarjeta de crédito	tarjeta de crédito	efectivo	efectivo
Información adicional	vistas al mar, desayuno incluido	cerca de la pista de tenís	desayuno incluido	tercer piso, cama 8, la cocina abre de las 8 a las 10 de la noche

2b Escucha otra vez. Encuentra las palabras o expresiones que significan: room with a double bed, sea view, 'eat as much as you can' buffet, the tennis court, a double room with a cot, a souvenirs shop, a big locker next to the bed.

- Students listen again for the Spanish for the phrases.

Answers: **1** room with a double bed – una habitación de matrimonio, **2** sea view – vistas al mar, **3** 'eat as much as you can' buffet, **4** the tennis courts, **5** a double room with a cot, **6** a souvenir shop, **7** a big locker next to the bed

3 Ordena las conversaciones.

PLTS

- Students put the conversations in order. You can split the class into two groups, and each does one, and combine results. Alternatively, split the students into pairs.

Answers: b, e, d, f, g, i, a, c, h

c, h, d, j, i, f, a, g, b, k

4 Escoge la respuesta correcta.

- Students choose the correct word to complete the question.

Answers: **a** Tiene, **b** Necesita, **c** tu, **d** desea, **e** Quieres, **f** tu

Remate

5a You're a client and you call to make the following reservations. Prepare the questions and answers suggested by the information below for each of the conversations A, B and C.

PLTS

- Students play the part of the customer. The markers should award points for correct language, intonation in the questions, and re-use of language from the spread.

5b Listen and complete the dialogues with your notes from 5a.

- Students use the listening activity to fill in any gaps they have in their dialogues of language they did not know. There is a pause built into the recording which should be sufficient for higher ability pupils but it is best to pause the recording for groups or individuals that may find it a little more challenging.

 CD 3, track 5 página 111, actividades 5b y 5c

Reserva A

- Hotel Salamar ¿dígame?
- Muy bien, vamos a ver .. ¿Para cuántas noches?
- Cinco noches, vale. ¿Cuántas personas son?
- Muy bien, ¿Qué tipo de habitación prefiere?
- Una habitación de matrimonio con ducha el cuatro de agosto para cinco noches.
- Son 78€ por noche desayuno incluido.
- Sí, hay piscina y jardín. ¿Cómo desea pagar?
- Bien, ¿a qué nombre hago la reserva?
- Muy bien, muchas gracias. Le veremos el cuatro de agosto. Adiós.

Reserva B

- Hostal Maspalomas. ¿Dígame?
- Para Noche Buena, vamos a ver .. Sí, hay habitaciones libres ¿Para cuántas noches?
- Una semana, vale. ¿Para cuántas personas?
- Una persona sola. ¿Quieres una habitación individual o doble?
- De acuerdo; una habitación individual con ducha.
- Sí, el desayuno está incluido. Son 36€ por noche.
- La estación está cerca. A diez minutos a pie. ¿Cómo quieres pagar?
- Bien, puedes pagar cuando llegues. ¿Cómo te llamas?
- Gracias. Te vemos en diciembre. Adiós.

Reserva C

- Camping Don Quijote. ¿Dígame?
- Déjeme ver ... una parcela para una tienda el quince de marzo .. ¿Para cuántas noches?
- Tres noches sí, sí hay parcelas libres. ¿Para cuántas personas?
- Sí, nuestras duchas tienen agua caliente.
- Son 20€ por noche. ¿Cómo quiere pagar?
- Sí, por supuesto.
- ¿A qué nombre hago la reserva?
- Perfecto. Le esperamos en el Don Quijote en marzo. Adiós, buenas tardes.

5c Practise again. Pay attention! Which receptionist doesn't use formal language?

Answers: Reserva B, Hostal Maspalomas

5–9

5d Take turns with a partner to play the role of the receptionist. Invent and practise other similar conversations.

- The caller can make brief notes beforehand as to what they require (double room, sea views etc), and the receptionist can decide in advance what facilities and rooms they have available.

4–9

6 Make a reservation by email for your family's summer holidays. Mention: when, how many nights, type of room, meals, method of payment, and ask for information about the facilities available.

- Remind them to look back at the emails at the start of the unit for formal language.

4–9

Success criteria activities 5 & 6:
- *students give information accurately and in the appropriate style*
- *students use a variety of vocabulary and structures*
- *students use different tenses or time frames*

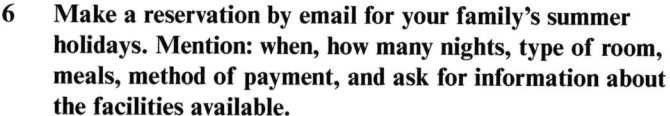

Cómo relatar tus vacaciones pasadas

páginas 112 y 113

Planner

➤ Objectives
- Talking about past holidays, problems and their solutions

➤ Resources
Students' Book, pages 112–113
CD 3, tracks 6–7
Grammar Workbook, page 72
Activity sheets 43–46

➤ Key language
el jabón, la llave equivocada, las maletas, el piragüismo, el ruido, las sábanas, el submarinismo, la temporada alta, las toallas, el wáter
acogedor(a), sencillo/a, poco seguro/a
bajar, dormir, subir
cuéntanos tu historia, daba asco, el grifo estaba roto, la luz no funcionaba, me alojé, no estaba lista, no tuvo nada de gracia, nos dimos cuenta, el retrete se atascó

➤ Skills
- Anticipating what vocabulary to expect

➤ Grammar
- Ordinal numbers

➤ PLTS
Students' Book, page 113, activity 6,
Team Workers
Students' Book, page 113, activity 8,
Creative Thinkers

➤ Starters
- Ask students if they have encountered any problems on holiday, and get them to explain

them in simple language. Classify them under headings such as *problemas de viaje, problemas de alojamiento* etc.
- Students' Book, page 113, activity 5c. Before questioning their partner about a holiday, go through the text highlighting any useful words or verbs in the past tense they can re-use.
- Students' Book, page 113, activity 7. Students predict the kind of vocabulary they would expect to hear for each category. They keep this vocabulary and make a note of any correct predictions.
- Students' Book, page 113, activity 8. Before writing the account, get students to brainstorm some descriptions. Say or write up *playa*, and ask for as many words or phrases that describe it as possible, then do the same with *hotel, tiempo* etc.

➤ Plenaries
- Students' Book, page 112, activity 1. Students re-write the web page comments as *vacaciones perfectas*, changing all the negatives to positives, and correcting all the problems.
- Students' Book, page 113, activity 5c. The notes made during this activity can also be used to write up a third person account of someone else's holiday.
- Students' Book, page 113, activity 5. After doing all the activities, close the Students' Books and display a copy of Ariel's letter with all the verbs removed.
- Play *vacaciones perfectas, vacaciones catastróficas*. The teacher says a phrase and the students have to say if it was a perfect or catastrophic holiday.

1a **Mira estas ilustraciones. Para cada una anota el vocabulario relacionado que se te ocurra.**

- Students look at the pictures and note down any related vocabulary. This can be done from memory or as a finding-out exercise, individually, or in groups.

4–7

1b **Lee lo que han escrito estos jóvenes. ¿Quién menciona cada uno de estos problemas?**

- Students read the web page comments, and decide which person mentions which problem.

Answers: **Malagueña** 9, 10, 13, 14; **Cyber** 4, 5; **Enamorada** 1, 2, 3, 7, 8, 11, 12

5–8

1c **Encuentra palabras o frases con el mismo significado.**

- Students look for the synonyms in the texts.

Answers: **a** la octava planta, **b** el equipaje, **c** no conocíamos, **d** el retrete, **e** desagradable

5–8

2 **Escucha estas conversaciones. Identifica en cada caso problema, solución, número de habitación:**

- Students listen to the conversations and identify problems, solutions and the room number.

4–8

 CD 3, track 6   **página 112, actividad 2**

1

Recepcionista	Buenos días, ¿Qué puedo hacer por usted?
Cliente	En mi habitación no hay toallas.
Recepcionista	Disculpe señora, ahora le pido al botones que se las suba. ¿En qué habitación está?
Cliente	La 304, gracias.

2

Recepcionista	¿Todo bien?
Cliente	No, tengo que subir a la habitación 509 en el quinto piso y el ascensor no funciona. Mi equipaje pesa mucho.
Recepcionista	No se preocupe, deje aquí las maletas y ahora le pido al conserje que se las suba.

3

Recepcionista	Buenas tardes, ¿Qué le pasa?
Cliente	En mi habitación hay mucho ruido y no puedo dormir.
Recepcionista	Lo siento, ¿qué quiere que haga?
Cliente	Quiero cambiar de habitación.
Recepcionista	¿En qué habitación está usted ahora?
Cliente	En la 713.
Recepcionista	Está bien, un momento por favor, vamos a ver qué hay disponible.

4

Recepcionista	Buenas tardes ¿Qué puedo hacer por usted?
Cliente	El wáter está atascado.
Recepcionista	¡Ay! Lo siento mucho, no puedo cambiarle de habitación porque el hotel está completo pero puedo llamar al fontanero. ¿En qué habitación se aloja usted?
Cliente	En la 415.

5

Recepcionista	Hola, ¿Qué le ocurre?
Cliente	Esta mañana no han cambiado las sábanas de mi habitación.
Recepcionista	Vaya, lo siento. No suele ocurrir. ¿En qué habitación está usted?
Cliente	En la habitación 76.
Recepcionista	Ahora le pido al servicio de limpieza que suba a cambiárselas.

Answers:

¿Problema?	¿Solución?	¿Número de habitación?
1 no hay toallas	le pido al botones que se las suba	304
2 el ascensor no funciona	deje aquí las maletas y ahora le pido al conserje que se las suba	509
3 hay mucho ruido	cambiar de habitación	713
4 El wáter está atascado	llamar al fontanero	415
5 no han cambiado las sábanas	le pido al servicio de limpieza que suba a cambiárselas	76

3a **¿Qué significan las palabras subrayadas de la actividad 1b?**

- Students decide what the underlined words in activity 1b mean.

Answers: first, fourth, eighth, second

5–8

3b **Ordena estos números ordinales de menor a mayor.**

- Students put the ordinal numbers in order. They should have a complete list written out in order for future reference.

Answers: h, a, j, e, b, f, g, i, c, d

3–6

3c **Traduce al inglés.**

- Students translate the phrases into English. They can then make up other humorous examples for a partner to translate e.g. *the fith elephant.*

Answers: **a** el cuarto día, **b** el tercer año, **c** la segunda puerta, **d** el primer tren

4–7

4 **Lea el texto y encuentra un antónimo de: agradable, simpático, cómodo, aceptable, estable.**

- Students read the text and look for the antonyms. Remind them they do not need to understand all the text to find the words they need.

Answers: incómodas, antipático, desagradable, inaceptable, inestable

5–9

5a **Lee estas preguntas. ¿Qué significan? ¿Qué tipo de respuesta es más adecuada?**

- Students read the questions and decide what they mean and what category of answer they would give to each.

Answers: **a** lugar, **b** lugar, **c** opinión, **d** tipo de acomodación, **e** opinión, **f** actividades, **g** tiempo, **h** opinión

4–7

5b Imagina que eres Ariel. Contesta a las preguntas de 5a según el texto.

- Students answer the questions as Ariel. This can be done as a role play with one student asking the questions and the other answering as Ariel.

5–8

Answers: **a** Normalmente voy de vacaciones a Francia. **b** El añ pasado fui a Puerto Rico. **c** El viaje fue muy largo pero cómodo. **d** Me alojé en un hotel en el capital. (Y en un albergue en el pueblo de Rincón.) **e** Me gustó el alojamiento porque tenía una piscina muy grande, pero el recepcionista era bastabte desagradable. (El albergue era sencillo y acogedor, pero las camas eran un poco incómodas.) **f** En el hotel nadé en la piscina y tomé el sol. Alquilé un coche con mi amiga y visitamos un pueblo pequeño. Hicimos surf, nos relajamos en la playa, hicimos submarinismo y piragüismo. **g** Hizo sol excepto el lunes cuando el tiempo era inestable. **h** Lo mejor era la música reggaetón.

5c Ahora piensa en tus vacaciones pasadas o unas vacaciones imaginarias. Túrnate con un compañero/a para preguntar y responder las preguntas de la actividad 5a.

- Students use the questions to ask their partner about a real holiday. Their partner should make notes in a grid about what the person answering the questions did. Alternatively they can play the conversation to other students.

4–9

6 En equipos completad estas frases. Tenéis un minuto para cada categoría para anotar todas las posibilidades que podáis.

PLTS

- Students work in groups to brainstorm as many answers to the questions as possible in one minute. This can also be arranged with each question written out on a very large piece of paper, and each group swaps papers or moves to the next one after one minute.

4–8

Remate

7 Listen and take notes on the following.

- Students make notes under the category headings given. These notes can be written up as full sentences to provide more material for activity 8.

5–9

Success criteria activity 7:

- *students use a variety of vocabulary and structures*
- *students deal with unpredictable elements*
- *students use different tenses or time frames*

 CD 3, track 7   **página 113, actividad 7**

Generalmente no me gusta ir de vacaciones muy lejos porque odio viajar en avión así que normalmente me quedo en Buenos Aires. Sin embargo, el año pasado fui a Barcelona todo el mes de julio y me alojé en casa de mi prima que vive allí. El vuelo fue larguísimo y muy aburrido.

La casa de mi prima es acogedora pero estaba un poco sucia. En mi habitación la ventana estaba rota y la luz no funcionaba.

La mayoría de los días hizo buen tiempo así que pasé muchas horas en la playa donde tomé el sol, jugué a voleibol con mi prima y sus amigas y nadé en el mar. Me encantó la comida y mi lugar preferido para cenar fue un restaurante en la Plaza de la Catedral.

Durante mi estancia visité el museo Picasso y fui a ver las obras del arquitecto Gaudí porque me fascina su estilo, particularmente el Parque Güell que es magnifico aunque la Sagrada Familia me decepcionó un poco porque no está terminada.

El último día fui de compras y llovió toda [de] la tarde. ¡Qué desastre!

Barcelona me encantó porque es una ciudad fascinante y con mucha variedad. Lo que más me gustó fue su arquitectura y el paseo de Las Ramblas porque es muy entretenido.

Answers:

1. Usual/recent destination – Buenos Aires / Barcelona
2. Length of stay – whole of July
3. Journey – aeroplane, long and boring
4. Accommodation – cousin's house, bit dirty, broken window and light
5. Weather – good except last day when it rained
6. Activities – beach, sunbathing, volleyball, swimming, eating out, visiting Picasso museum and Gaudí architecture, shopping
7. Opinion – fascinating city, very varied, Las Ramblas is very exciting

8 Write an account of a previous holiday.

PLTS

- Students use the support to write their account. Another student can award points for having followed the instructions correctly – are there 10 phrases, do they include description, is there use of connectors etc. Groups of four can collaborate in the marking of four different people's work.

4–9

Success criteria activity 8:

- *students give information accurately and in the appropriate style*
- *students express personal opinions and justify points of view*
- *students use a variety of vocabulary and structures*
- *students use different tenses or time frames*

Cómo describir tus vacaciones ideales

Planner

➤ **Objectives**
- Talking about leisure activities on holiday

➤ **Resources**
Students' Book, pages 114–115
CD 3, track 8
Grammar Workbook, pages 49–50
Activity sheets 43–46

➤ **Key language**
la entrevista, el mismo sitio, el/la periodista, las tonterías
estar harto/a, estar molesto/a, ir solo, malgastar, pasear, tener muchas ganas
de moda, sin duda

➤ **Skills**
- Asking questions

➤ **Grammar**
- The future tense

➤ **PLTS**
Students' Book, page 115, activity 4,
Reflective Learners
Students' Book, page 115, activity 8,
Creative Thinkers

➤ **Starters**
- Students' Book, page 114, activity 1. Students look at the two pictures, and say what they think the problem is. Ask them what problems they have with familiy holidays, and if any of the boy's complaints apply to them.
- Students' Book, page 114, activity 2. Students read through the incomplete text. Ask them in English what they understand. Correct any misapprehensions, but do not reveal any additional content yet. This gives them a little background to do the activities.

- Students' Book, page 115, activity 5. Students brainstorm as many different answers as possible before listening to the text. The *¿Adónde?* section can contain country or resort names, or things like *mountains, my grandmother's, my friend's canal boat*, for example. The idea is to predict vocabulary, and explore wider possibilities.
- Students' Book, page 115, activity 7. Split students into small groups and give each a large sheet of paper. At the head of each write a word such as *país, lugar, alojamiento, tiempo, actividades* etc. Students create a mindmap of related words on each sheet e.g. under *lugar* could be *playa, campaña, montaña*.

➤ **Plenaries**
- Students' Book, page 115, activity 4. Students can use the results from their groups surveys as the basis for some revision of comparatives and superlatives, by writing some concluding sentences to their survey material.
- Students' Book, page 115, activity 8. Students read out or pass round their fantasy future holiday descriptions. They give each one a mark out of 5 for how much they would like to go on that holiday (it is best if the descriptions are anonymous if written). The one with the most points wins.
- Quick fire quiz. The teacher calls out a verb in the future and the students have to complete the sentence. With the class split into groups, each group has to come up with a different answer to gain a point. They have to come up with an answer within a time limit or lose a point.
- Reverse quiz. The teacher calls out e.g. *en un hotel*, and students have to provide the verb *me alojaré* or *voy a alojarme*. This is better done written down pub-quiz style so the accuracy of the verbs can be checked.

---

1 **Empareja lo que dice el joven con lo que dicen sus padres.**

- Students match the boy's words to what his parents are saying.

Answers: **1** e, **2** c, **3** a, **4** d, **5** b, **6** f (**Note:** The answers to 1 and 6 are interchangeable.)

4–7

2a **Lee este email y rellena los espacios con el verbo adecuado en futuro inmediato.**
Grammar reference page 210

- Students read the email and complete it with the correct verb in the immediate future.

Answers:
1 voy a volar, **2** voy a coger, **3** voy a pasear, **4** voy a ir, **5** vamos a pasar, **6** va a hacer, **7** vamos a pasarlo

5–8

2b Lee el texto completo y contesta a las preguntas.

- Students read the completed text and answer the questions.

Answers: **1** Susana va a ir a Ronda. **2** Va a ir en avión y en tren. **3** Va a ir en abril. **4** Hay el muse de arte, el Puente Nuevo, el barrio de San Francisco y el Palacio Mondragón. **5** Va a hacer viento. **6** Solamente aprendió a esquiar hace seis meses. **7** Van a pasar un fin de semana allí. **8** Alicia es su amiga. Está harta de escuchar los planes de Susana.

2c Encuentra en el email las expresiones que significan: I am looking forward to, fashionable, three years ago, six months ago, (she) is fed up.

- Students find the phrases in Susana's email.

Answers: **1** tengo muchas ganas de, **2** de moda, **3** hace tres años, **4** hace seis meses, **5** está harta

3a Copia y rellena la tabla.
Grammar reference page 210

- Students copy and complete the table. If necessary, complete the first one or two lines in class to start with. Students can work with a partner.

Futuro inmediato		Futuro simple	
Voy a pasear	I am going to take a walk	Pasearé	I will take a walk
Voy a volar	**I am going to fly**	Volaré	**I will fly**
Voy a coger	**I am going to catch**	**Cogeré**	**I will catch**
Voy a jugar	I am going to play	**Jugaré**	**I will play**
Voy a viajar	**I am going to travel**	**Viajaré**	I will travel
Voy a alojarme	**I am going to stay**	Me alojaré	**I will stay**
Voy a nadar	**I am going to swim**	**Nadaré**	**I will swim**
Voy a tomar el sol	I am going to sunbathe	**Tomaré el sol**	**I will sunbathe**
Voy a visitar	**I am going to visit**	**Visitaré**	I will visit
Voy a ir	**I am going to go**	**Iré**	**I will go**

3b ¿A qué verbos muy comunes pertenecen estos futuros irregulares?

- Students identify the verbs that belong to the future tenses given. They should write them out for reference.

Answers: tener, hacer, salir, poder, venir

4a Empareja estas preguntas con sus respuestas.

PLTS

- Students match the questions and the answers.

Answers: **1** e, **2** b, **3** d, **4** c, **5** a

4b Utiliza las preguntas de la actividad anterior para entrevistar a diez de tus compañeros. Contesta a las preguntas cuando seas entrevistado.

- To avoid students waiting to ask particular peers it is suggested that you run the activity as a "speed dating" event. You could ask students to invent their holiday plans to make answers more original.

4c Presenta tus descubrimientos de una forma gráfica.

- Students use the results to draw up a results graph.

5 Este joven periodista entrevista a los ciudadanos sobre sus planes para las vacaciones para un programa de verano. Escucha y rellena la tabla.

- Students listen to the interviews and complete the table.

 CD 3, track 8   **página 115, actividad 5**

1
— Buenos días. ¿Cómo se llama usted?
— Me llamo Sara.
— Dígame Sara ¿adónde va a ir este año de vacaciones?
— La próxima semana voy a ir a Veracruz en México a visitar las ruinas del Tajin y la reserva del Cofre de Perote. También haré rafting en el río y espero divertirme mucho.
— ¿Va a ir sola?
— No, voy a viajar con mi amiga Lucía.

2
— Y usted caballero ¿cómo se llama? Y. ¿Qué planes tiene para sus vacaciones?
— Me llamo Javier y voy a ir a Vinarós en la provincia de Valencia del 3 al 30 de Agosto.
— ¿Qué va a hacer allí?
— Nada, lo menos posible … voy a relajarme en la playa tomando el sol y voy a comer gambas todos los días.

3
— Señora, permítame que tome unos minutos de su tiempo. ¿Cómo se llama usted?
— Me llamo Nuria.
— Nuria, ¿qué va a hacer usted para sus vacaciones este año?
— No tengo vacaciones en agosto y tendré que esperar a la Navidad. En diciembre voy a ir dos semanas a Colombia, a Barranquilla. Voy a visitar a mi familia y voy a ver los carnavales que son muy espectaculares.

4
— Caballero y .. ¿usted? Díganos su nombre y sus planes para las vacaciones que se avecinan.
— A partir del 3 de julio voy a ir 10 días a Santiago de Cuba con mi hermano a participar en la Fiesta del Fuego. También espero hacer algo de submarinismo y practicar deporte en la playa.
— ¡Santiago de Cuba! ¡Qué envidia! Y … ¿Su nombre caballero?
— Enrique, soy Enrique.

5
— Y finalmente usted señor. ¿Cómo se llama?
— Carlos.
— Carlos, cuéntenos. ¿Qué va a hacer para las vacaciones?
— Pues voy a ir a Florida la segunda quincena de agosto.
— ¿Qué va a hacer allí? ¿Va a visitar Disney?
— No, no .. haré lo que más me gusta – pescar y bucear en el mar: estar en contacto con la naturaleza que me falta al vivir en esta ciudad tan contaminada..

6   Lee estas respuestas. Escribe una pregunta adecuada.

- Students read the answers and make up a question to go with each one.

Answers: **a** ¿Adónde vas el año que viene? **b** ¿Cómo vas a viajar? **c** ¿Dónde vas a alojarte? **d** ¿Qué tiempo va a hacer? **e** ¿Qué vas a hacer?

5–8

Remate

7   The reporter from activity 5 needs your help for his programme this evening. Prepare an interview of about 10 questions (or more) about the future holidays of a friend. Take turns to play the interviewer and the interviewee.

- Students can use the questions from activity 6, and should look back through the unit for any other information they can use. This does not have to be the same conversation as the students had on page 113. Encourage the students to make up the details of a fantasy holiday.

4–9

Answers:

1 Sara
¿Cuándo?: la próxima semana **¿Adónde?:** Veracruz en México **Actividades:** visitar las ruinas del Tajin, la reserva del Cofre de Perote, hacer rafting **Información adicional:**

2 Javier
¿Cuándo?: del 3 al 30 de Agosto **¿Adónde?:** Vinarós en la provincia de Valencia **Actividades:** Nada, lo menos posible, relajar en la playa tomando el sol **Información adicional:** comer gambas cada día

3 Nuria
¿Cuándo?: Navidad, en diciembre **¿Adónde?:** Barranquilla en Colombia **Actividades:** visitar a la familia ver los carnavales **Información adicional:**

4 Enrique
¿Cuándo?: 10 días a partir del 3 de julio **¿Adónde?:** Santiago de Cuba **Actividades:** participar en la Fiesta del Fuego, hacer algo de submarinismo y practicar deporte en la playa **Información adicional:** con mi hermano

5 Carlos
¿Cuándo?: la segunda quincena de agosto **¿Adónde?:** Florida **Actividades:** pescar en el mar y bucear en el mar **Información adicional:** le falta estar en contacto con la naturaleza como vive en una ciudad llena de contaminación

8   Use your imagination to plan your intergalactic holiday to Venus or another planet in the solar system. How will you get there? With whom? Where will you stay? What will the accommodation be like? What are you going to do there? Write a summary.

PLTS

- Students can also choose to plan a holiday under the sea, in another time, in the fantasy world of a favourite film etc. if they prefer.

4–9

Success criteria activities 7 & 8:
- *students communicate effectively and accurately*
- *students express personal opinions and justify points of view*
- *students use a variety of vocabulary and structures*
- *students deal with unpredictable elements*
- *students use different tenses or time frames*

Cómo hablar de las vacaciones en el extranjero

Planner

➤ **Objectives**
  • Making comparisons between different types of holidays

➤ **Resources**
  Students' Book, pages 116–117
  CD 3, track 9
  Grammar Workbook, page 72
  Activity sheets 43–46

➤ **Key language**
  un abrazo, los/las bañistas, la colonia, los extranjeros, la fábrica, la madrugada, las mascotas, el país, la piscina cubierta
  empollar, hacer el vago, ligar, bajarse música fuerte, al aire libre, habitualmente, por desgracia
  ¿Cuánto duran?,¡Qué agobio!

➤ **Skills**
  • Reading long texts

➤ **Grammar**
  • Expressions of time

➤ **PLTS**
  Students' Book, page 116, activity 3,
  Effective Participators
  Students' Book, page 117, activity 6,
  Self-Managers

➤ **Starters**
  • Students look at the pictures on page 116 and read the sentences about Mazarrón to themselves. Ask them to identify words or phrases that they do not understand. Give them a limited amount of time to look up or otherwise work out some of these, then in class check their current understanding of the sentences. Ask them what techniques they used.
  • Students' Book, page 116, activity 2. Check students understand the words in the box. If they don't, give them a simple example in Spanish unrelated to the sentences in the activity.
  • Students' Book, page 116, activity 3. Ask students if they prefer holidaying abroad or in this country and ask for one or two opinions and reasons.
  • Students' Book, page 117, activity 7. Before students answer the questions in Spanish, play *Verdad o Mentira* with the email text. Give statements (in Spanish or English, depending on the ability of the group) which students have to answer true or false to. Play in groups against the clock.

➤ **Plenaries**
  • Students' Book, page 116, activity 2. Students make up their own examples using the comparison phrases. They should be as silly or as unlikely as possible to be more memorable.
  • Students' Book, page 116, activity 3. Give students a copy of the transcript. Ask them if they agree that the reasons given for holidaying in different places are good or not. Why?
  • Students' Book, page 117, activity 7. In small groups, students make a list of any remaining vocabulary or phrases they still do not understand from the email. They give their list to another group who have to find out the meanings. They get one point for each item correctly looked up, and two points if they know it already. Then they give the list back to the original group.
  • Play "Consequences" with the questions from the postscript to the email. Each student writes the answer to one question, folds the paper over and passes it on. The idea is to come up with a highly unlikely holiday scenario.

1a **Escribe frases pertinentes para la foto de Bournemouth.**

4–8

- Following the model of the sentences about Mazarrón, students write similar ones about Bournemouth.

1b **Identifica las formas de los verbos ser y estar en el texto en las frases de la actividad 1a. ¿Por qué se usa ser o estar en cada ocasión?**

5–8

- Students identify the forms of *ser* and *estar* and say why they are used.

Answers: **1** están – situation, **2** está – temporary condition, **3** están – temporary condition, **5** es – permanent fact, **8** son – permanent fact

2 **Completa estas frases con las palabras que faltan.**

4–7

- Students complete the sentences with the words from the box.

Answers: **1** mientras que, **2** más tarde que, **3** más sana que, **4** menos turistas que

3a **Escucha la grabación. ¿Prefieren las vacaciones en su país o en el extranjero? ¿Por qué?**

4–8

- Students listen and decide if the speakers prefer holidays at home or abroad and why.

 CD 3, track 9   **página 116, actividad 3a**

1
Depende de qué tipo de vacaciones busques. Aquí el buen tiempo no está garantizado. Aunque hay muchos lugares bonitos para visitar y relajarte, si te gusta el calor y el sol deberías ir al extranjero.

2
Quedarse uno en su país no son vacaciones. Lo bueno de las vacaciones es descubrir las diferencias culturales de otros países.

3
Ir al extranjero es mejor por el buen tiempo aunque el Reino Unido tiene algunos de los paisajes más bonitos si no te importa el tiempo inestable.

4
Yo prefiero no ir al extranjero así me ahorro problemas de moneda y con el idioma.

Answers: **1** extranjero – el tiempo, en mi país – lugares bonitos a visitar, **2** extranjero – diferencias culturales, **3** extranjero – el tiempo, Reino Unido – el paisaje, **4** en mi país – no hay problemas de dinero o idiomas

3b **Trabaja con un compañero/a. Haced una lista de las ventajas y desventajas de las vacaciones en Inglaterra.**

PLTS

4–8

- Students work with a partner and write a list of the advantages and disadvantages of holidaying in England.

4a Observa brevemente el texto de la página opuesta. En no más de un minuto decide de qué se trata.

- Students look briefly at the long text on page 117 and decide what it is about using the pointers. Discuss their thoughts in class.

4b Lee estas afirmaciones y decide qué tipo de información deberías buscar en el texto para saber si son correctas.

- Students read the sentences and decide what kind of information they will need to look for in order to decide if the statements are true or false. Get them to highlight key words.

4c Ahora decide si las frases de la actividad 4b son correctas o falsas según el texto.

- Students now decide if the statements are True or False.

Answers: **a** V, **b** V, **c** F, **d** F, **e** V, **f** F

5a Busca en el email las expresiones que significan: *I've been going for eight years, a week ago.*

- Students look in the email for the Spanish equivalent of the phrases.

Answers: **a** Voy desde hace 8 años. **b** hace una semana

5b Traduce las frases: I've been going to Devon for five years, I went to Port Aventura two years ago, I've been surfing for two years, I had exams a week ago.

- Students translate the sentences. Get them to first identify sentences in the text that can be adapted.

Answers: **a** Voy a Devon desde hace cinco años. **b** Fui a Port Aventura hace dos años. **c** Practico el surf desde hace dos años. **d** Tuve examenes hace una semana.

Remate

6 Read the postscript of Juanma's email and write an email answering his questions.

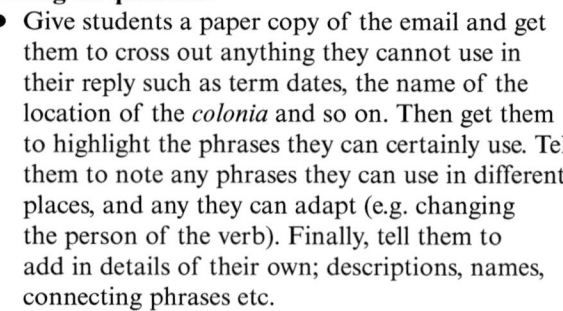

- Give students a paper copy of the email and get them to cross out anything they cannot use in their reply such as term dates, the name of the location of the *colonia* and so on. Then get them to highlight the phrases they can certainly use. Tell them to note any phrases they can use in different places, and any they can adapt (e.g. changing the person of the verb). Finally, tell them to add in details of their own; descriptions, names, connecting phrases etc.

7 Read Juanma's email again and answer the following questions.

- They can work on the questions individually or in pairs.

Answers: **a** Terminan el 15 de septiembre. **b** Las colonias son vacaciones de grupo para los jovenes donde se aprende inglés y juega mucho deporte. **c** Tiene que ir a clases de repaso porque suspendió a tres asignaturas. **d** Va a la plaza o da vueltas por la ciudad en moto. **e** Sí, tiene ordenador. **f** Va a la playa en agosto porque muchas fábricas y comercios cieeran en agosto así que todo el mundo va de vacaciones. **g** Los españoles no tienen tanto dinero. **h** Monta a caballo, va al karting, alquila motos aquáticos y juega al fútbol. **i** Sale a pasear por la tarde después de cenar. **j** En septiembre tiene que empollar para los examenes y hacer los deberes.

Success criteria activities 6 & 7:
- *students give information accurately and in the appropriate style*
- *students express personal opinions and justify points of view*
- *students use a variety of vocabulary and structures*
- *students use different tenses or time frames*

Gramática en acción

Planner

➤ **Objectives**
- Using regular verbs

➤ **Resources**
Students' Book, pages 118–119
Exam Skills Workbook, page 49 (F), page 50 (H)
Grammar Workbook, pages 43–46, 48–54
Activity sheet 47
Resources and Planning OxBox CD-ROM

Grammar
- Choosing the correct past tense
- Deciding between immediate future, future simple and conditional

➤ **PLTS**
Students' Book, page 118, activity 1, *Independent Enquirers*
Students' Book, page 119, activity 9, *Reflective Learners*

➤ Regular verbs

1 Choose the correct tense for each sentence.

PLTS • Students choose between the preterite and the imperfect.

Answers: **a** pasaba, **b** pasamos, **c** viví, salía, **d** tomaba el sol, saqué, **e** estuve, **f** durmieron, estaba, **g** fui, suspendí, **h** pasaron (**Note:** in **h** The imperfect can be used to say that the grandparents used to spend their holidays with us.)

2 Translate these sentences into Spanish.
- Remind students to focus on choosing the correct tenses. They look back at activity 1 for help.

Answers: **a** Cuando era pequeño, me encantaba ir a la playa con mi abuela. **b** El año pasado fui a Puerto Rico con mi hermana. **c** Viajábamos a Andalucía en coche pero el año pasado volamos con easyJet. **d** Hice una reserva para dos habitaciones con ducha. **e** Tomaba el sol cuando empezó a llover.

3 Write the following in Spanish.
- Students use the immediate future to translate the sentences.

Answers: **a** Voy a ir de vacaciones. **b** Vamos a viajar en avión. **c** Van a tomar el sol en la playa. **d** Va a hacer surf. **e** Va a sacar un montón de fotos. **f** Vamos a visitar a nuestros abuelos.

4 Write out the future tense of: nadar, leer, dormir.
Grammar reference page 210

5 Complete the sentences using the correct form of the future tense of the verbs in activity 4.

Answers: **a** nadaremos **b** leeráan **c** dormiré **d** leeráa **e** nadará

6 Translate these sentences into Spanish.

Answers:

Leer – leeré, leerás, leerá, leeremos, leeréis, leerán
Dormir – dormiré, dormirás, dormirá, dormiremos, dormiréis, dormirán
Nadar – nadaré, nadarás, nadará, nadaremos, nadaréis, nadarán

7 Immediate future, future simple or conditional?
Grammar reference page 210
- Students identify the tense.

Answers: **a** conditional, **b** immediate future, **c** conditional, **d** future simple, **e** conditional, **f** immediate future, **g** immediate future, **h** future simple

➤ Reflexive verbs

8 Write the following.

Answers: **a** me levantaba, **b** se alojará, **c** nos aburrimos, **d** se bañarían

➤ Ser and estar

9 Work out the correct tense of the verbs in parenthesis.

PLTS • Students should be able to explain their choices.

Answers: **a** conditional – compraría, **b** immediate future – voy a ir, **c** present – paso, **d** future simple – viviré, **e** preterite – visité

10 Es or está?
- Students should be able to explain their choices.

Answers: **a** es, **b** es, **c** es, **d** está, **e** está

Habilidades

Planner

> **Objectives**
> - Using accent and intonation to sound more authentic when speaking, and recognising different tenses

> **Resources**
> Students' Book, page 120
> CD 3, tracks 10–12
> Exam Skills Workbook, page 50 (F), page 51 (H)
> Activity sheet 48
> Resources and Planning OxBox CD-ROM

> **Skills**
> - Identifying the strongest syllable in a word
> - Getting your intonation right in questions
> - Answering questions about recordings and readings
> - Looking for adjectives and link words
> - Recognising verb tenses

> **PLTS**
> Students' Book, page 120, activity 2, *Reflective Learners*
> Students' Book, page 120, activity 4, *Self-Managers*

> **Hablar**

1 Identifying the strongest syllable in a word.

Answers: **e**sta mal**e**ta, est**á** cans**a**do, un l**a**rgo vi**a**je, se larg**ó** a las tres, viaj**é** en tren

2 Get your intontation right in questions.

❏ Remember that all question words have an accent in Spanish.

PLTS • Students listen and note the difference between the statement and the question.

 CD 3, track 10   página 120, actividad 2a

Viajarás en tren. ¿Viajarás en tren?
Viajarás en tren. ¿Viajarás en tren?

• Students then listen to the recording and decide which are questions and which are not.

 CD 3, track 11   página 120, actividad 2b

1 Iremos de paseo.
2 ¿Haremos surf?
3 ¿Vendrás a la playa?
4 Voy a ir a pescar con mi padre.
5 ¿Voy a venir con vosotros?
6 ¿Te gustó el hotel?
7 Te encantó el viaje a Canarias.
8 Viajarías en primera clase.
9 ¿Viajarías en tren?
10 ¿Pasarías el verano con tus padres?

Answers: questions – 2, 3, 5, 6, 9, 10, statements – 1, 4, 7, 8

❏ Practise saying these sentences aloud. Can your partner tell if you are saying the statement or the question.

 • Students work with a partner, or volunteers could read out questions / statements to the whole class. The listener can mark their partner on how good their intonation is – 2 for instantly recogniseable, 1 for some doubt, 0 for no idea.

> **Escuchar y leer**

3 Answer questions about recordings and readings.

❏ Question words help you get marks even if you are not entirely sure of what the question mean.
• Students can also make up examples using the question words to act as memory prompts.

Answers: **¿Quién...?** people's names, relationships (*su padre*), and professions (*la secretaria*), **¿Cuándo...?** days, months, times, and time phrases (*ayer*), **¿Cuánto...?** numbers and quantities, **¿Dónde...?** / **¿Adónde...?** places (*la piscina* or *Madrid*)

4 Look for adjectives and link words.

❏ When a question refers to opinion, adjectives and linking words become crucial.

PLTS • After reading the advice, students pick a reading text from the unit, and search it for adjectives and linking words. They make a note of them and what information can be gained from them. This can be done individually or in groups and fed back to the class.

5 Recognise verb tenses.
• Students listen and answer the questions. Get them to feedback how they decided on their answers to emphasise the importance of listening for detail and the accents on words.

 CD 3, track 12   página 120, actividad 5

Este año voy a ir a Holanda de vacaciones en junio con mi padre, mi hermano pequeño y su novia que es muy agradable y habladora, pero hasta recientemente viajaba a Bilbao todos los años para pasar el verano con mis tíos. Con mis tíos alquilábamos un apartamento y aunque las camas eran un poco incómodas y muy viejas, el piso era cómodo y perfecto para nosotros.

Answers: **1** Bilbao, **2** junio, **3** la novia de su hermano, **4** cómodo y perfecto para ellos

Escenario
página 121

> ### Oral

You have been appointed to draw up a proposal for an end-of-year school trip for your Spanish class.

PLTS

4–9

• Students work with a partner to prepare their presentation, making sure they include all the information on the check list.
• The other students should take notes, checking they have covered all the information required, and ask for additional details. Students can pre-prepare the type of question they might want to ask.
• It is far more important here that students respond to the questions: the aim is to be as fluent as possible.
• Students have to justify their choice. There can be a class vote. To try and mitigate the effects of people voting for their friends, students can adopt an alternative (Spanish) identity for this activity.
• *GCSE Grades A*-C*
• *Grade C Students use past, present and future tenses. They express opinions, and deal with some unpredictability.*

• *Grade A Students express and justify opinions. They use a variety of vocabulary and structure in longer speech sequences.*

> ### Escrito

1 **You have to comply with the school's regulations, so make a copy of the school trip proposal form shown at the top of this page, and fill in the details. Then, write a letter to parents with an overview of the trip you have planned.**

PLTS

4–9

• The language should be brief but precise.
• Students use the information from their presentation to write a formal letter. They must aim to be descriptive and persuasive – why should the parents spend money on this trip?
• *GCSE Grades A*-C*
• *Grade C Students use opinions and past, present and future tenses, both factually and imaginatively. Register is appropriate and style is basic.*
• *Grade A Students write factually and imaginatively using longer sequences and a range of vocabulary and structure. They express and justify opinions in an appropriate style.*

Vocabulario
página 122

This is a summary of key language from the unit, organised by spread and theme. Students can use it for reference while working on the unit, and as an aid to learning vocabulary.

Lectura

> *Planner*
>
> ➤ **Objectives**
> - Travelling in South America.
> - To encourage independent reading and develop reading strategies.
> - These pages also provide alternative class and homework material for students who work quickly and require extension work.
>
> ➤ **Resources**
> Students' Book, page 183–184
>
> ➤ **PLTS**
> Students' Book, page 183, activity 2, *Independent Enquirers*
> Students' Book, page 184, activity 2, *Self-Managers*

➤ **Lectura A – Un viaje al fin del mundo**

1 Lee el artículo. ¿Verdadero o falso?

- Students read the letter and decide if the statements are true (V) or false (F).

Answers: **a** V, **b** F, **c** V, **d** V, **e** F, **f** F, **g** F, **h** F, **i** F, **j** F

2 Corrige las frases incorrectas de la actividad anterior.

 PLTS

- Students correct the false statements.

Answers: **b** La Patagonia está al sur de Argentina. **e** Van a viajar durante un mes. **f** El hotel donde se alojan en Ushuaia no es muy caro. **g** Le encantó la arquitectura de las casa de El Calafate. **h** Juan Carlos no podría vivir sin su ordenador. **i** Hace tres años que Juan Carlos no esquía. **j** Le gusta mucho su país.

3 Termina estas frases según lo que pone en la carta de Juan Carlos.

- Students use the information from the letter to complete the sentences.

Answers: **a** en Argentina cerca del Polo Sur. **b** avión. **c** pingüinos. **d** muy caro vivir en hoteles durante un mes. **e** tiene casas muy pintorescas. **f** no hay internet. **g** es invierno y no hace mucho calor. **h** las montañas.

➤ **Lectura B – Sueños sudamericanos**

1 Busca estas frases en el texto.

- Students look for the Spanish for the phrases in the text.

Answers: **a** por encima del nivel del mar, **b** tres horas más, **c** la falta de oxígeno, **d** nada que ver con, **e** en hamacas al aire libre, **f** es todavía más impresionante, **g** era increíble, **h** largo pero agradable, **i** se parecía al conejo, **j** todo es muy barato, **k** eran casi insoportables, **l** seis semanas de mi vida, **m** En cuanto llegamos

2 Contesta a las preguntas en inglés.

 PLTS

- Students answer the questions in English.

Answers: **a** the lack of oxygen at the high altitude **b** guinea-pig, **c** on a boat in the nature reserve in the rain forest, **d** they will live for five days with no electricity or running water, they will sleep in hammocks in the open air, fish for piranhas and go on long walks **e** hot and incredibly humid, **f** there were huge spiders and other strange insects everywhere, **g** her suitcase is already very heavy and she doesn't want problems with Customs, **h** they are majestic and ten times bigger than the Pyrenees **i** it was made entirely of salt

3 Traduce al inglés las frases subrayadas en el texto.

- Students translate the underlined phrases into English. Discuss with them how we might say some things in a slightly different way in English to highlight the different nuances of meaning between the two languages.

Answers: The city is very pretty with magnificent squares and a combination of impressive Inca architecture and colonial Spanish architecture.
The flight from Cuxco to Puerto Maldonado is very short and the view from the aeroplane was incredible.
We found an internet café here, so we took the opportunity to read our emails and write home.
These are the best six weeks of my life! I don't want to return home.

Unit 4B Nuestro mundo			Overview grid	
Spread	**Contexts**	**Skills**	**Grammar**	**Vocabulary**
Spread title	• Topic areas covered within the unit	• Key skills focus	• Grammar covered in the unit	Key vocabulary
pages 124–125 **Cómo describir la contaminación**	• Talking about environmental problems	• Listening for gist	• Revision of the future and the conditional	el cambio climático, una campaña, la caza, la central nuclear, la contaminación, los desechos, el efecto invernadero, el humedal, los incendios, las inundaciones, el lema,. un paraíso, el peligro, los pescadores, los residuos, el ruido, la sequía, la subida, los vertidos indígena
pages 126–127 **Cómo conservar el planeta**	• Discussing conservation and recycling	• Understanding instructions	• Positive and negative commands • The subjunctive	los bosques, las botellas, la calefacción, el camino, el grifo, las latas, la luz, el medio ambiente, los panales solares, la selva encendido, eólica apagar, caminar, cuidar, cultivar, fumar, matar, proteger, tirar
pages 128–129 **Cómo hablar del ecoturismo**	• Talking about the pros and cons of ecoturism	• Reading strategies	• Impersonal verbs	el comportamiento, los consejos, el corazón, el desarrollo, la despoblación, la mezcla, un mirador, el mundo, la rabia, la riqueza, la travesía extraño/a, inquieto/a, salvaje adentrarse, aportar, deteriorarse, inscribirse, salvaguardar
pages 130–131 **Cómo comparar tu vida con las de otros**	• Talking about our lives in relation to others	• Listening for detail	• Correct choice of *ser* and *estar*	los aplausos, las costumbres, los gritos, los lagos, la madera, la merienda aislado/a, amable, bromista, cortés, helado/a, humilde, lindo/a, seco/a acostumbrarse, hacer cola, limitar con, sorprender, tener prisa mientras que, sin embargo
pages 132–133 **Cómo apreciar la cultura ajena**	• Talking about music, dance and culture	• Exam techniques for reading passages	• Questions and indirect exclamations	el bailarín, la cantautor(a), el mensaje, el orgullo, el recuerdo, el sonido, el torero afortunado/a, gitano/a apoyar, decir, enseñar, estar de acuerdo, tardar en se crió, nació, siendo (ser) bajo, cien por cien, no cabe duda
pages 134–135 **Gramática en acción**	• Commands and the subjunctive		• Giving positive and negative instructions • Using the subjunctive • Using time clauses like *desde hace* • Using ser and estar correctly • Writing indirect questions	
page 136 **Habilidades**	• Understanding the questions • Working out the meaning of a text	• Reading a text with questions in mind • Reading a text for specific details • Analyse a text • Listening for gist and detail • Taking notes effectively • Checking your answers		
page 137 **Escenario**	• Give a presentation on a typical element of Spanish culture. • Research an environmental group.			
page 138 **Vocabulario**	• Summary of key vocabulary for the unit.			
pages 185–186 **Reading pages**	Being 'green', life on Lake Titicaca: • to encourage independent reading and develop reading strategies. • these pages also provide alternative class and homework material for students who work quickly and require extension work.			

4B Nuestro mundo

Unit Objectives

Contexts: talking about environmental issues and comparing our lives to other people's

Skills focus: listening for gist and detail, taking effective notes, checking answers; reading a text for specific details, and analysing it

Grammar: positive and negative instructions, the subjunctive, desde hacía, using *ser* and *estar* correctly, writing indirect questions

Controlled assessment opportunities

Writing: Students' Book, page 125, activity 7
Writing: Students' Book, page 127, activity 8
Speaking: Students' Book, page 129, activity 7
Speaking: Students' Book, page 131, activity 7
Writing: Students' Book, page 133, activity 4

See also *GCSE Spanish for OCR Assessment OxBox CD-ROM*.

An introduction to the unit página 123

- *Aim*: To introduce the themes of the unit and encourage students to think about the reasons for learning Spanish.
- The opening page is designed with captions, pictures and page cross-references to provide a preview of what is to come:

	Students' Book
Cómo describir la contaminación	page 124
Cómo conservar el planeta	page 126
Cómo hablar del ecoturismo	page 128
Cómo comparar tu vida con las de otros	page 130
Cómo apreciar la cultura ajena	page 132
Gramática an acción – improving your use and understanding of Spanish	page 134
Habilidades – increasing your language skills for fluency	page 136
Escenario – presentar un símbolo de la cultura hispanica Escenario – investigar un grupo ecológico	page 137

- Allow time for students to read the questions and cross-refer to the relevant pages of the Students' Book. They could do this individually or in pairs / small groups, followed by whole-class discussion.
- This spread also provides an opportunity for students to recap on familiar language. Ask them to think about language they already know that might be useful when working on the themes of the unit.
- Mindmap any language they produce, and if possible, keep it on display as reference as you progress through the unit. It can be added to at intervals as new language becomes familiar.

- At the end of work on the unit, allow time for students to return to this spread and repeat the mind-mapping process, this time including what they have learned over the course of the unit. Get them to answer the questions in their own words, and encourage them to use the results for revision purposes.
- Ask them what they found difficult, interesting etc. What do they think are the important things they have learned in this unit? What do they still need to improve on?
- If time permits, get the students to redesign the page. How would they set it out so it reflects the unit? How would they make it attractive to other learners of their age? How would they make it easy to follow? What would they include in terms of text, pictures, captions, page references? Ask them to imagine they are producing material for next year's class who will be learning the same thing – what would they have found it useful to know?

¿Por qué aprender el español? Para hablar con otras personas de la cultura, y de problemas ecologicos.

- Students share any experiences they have had of environmental problems either here or abroad, and any groups working to solve them.
- Ask them to consider what sort of language they would need to discuss music and other types of culture with a Spanish person their age e.g. What type of music do they like, who is their favourite artist?

Cómo describir la contaminación

Planner

➤ Objectives
- Talking about environmental problems

➤ Resources
Students' Book, pages 124–125
CD 3, track 17
Grammar Workbook, pages 48–50, 53–54
Activity sheets 50–53

➤ Key language
*el cambio climático, una campaña, la caza,
la central nuclear, la contaminación, los desechos,
el efecto invernadero, el humedal, los incendios,
las inundaciones, el lema,. un paraíso, el peligro,
los pescadores, los residuos, el ruido, la sequía,
la subida, los vertidos
indígena*

➤ Skills
- Listening for gist

➤ Grammar
- Revision of the future and the conditional

➤ PLTS
Students' Book, page 125, activity 6,
Creative Thinkers
Students' Book, page 125, activity 7,
Effective Participators

➤ Starters
- In class, look at the photos of the environmental problems on page 124. Brainstorm any language that students know or can quickly look up. The idea is to think of other ways of describing these things.
- Students' Book, page 124, activity 1. Students read the texts about the Galápagos and Doñana. Ask them some questions in English. They then choose the specific problem from the list to match to the pictures.

- Students' Book, page 125, activity 2. In pairs, students predict which problem is going to appear for each section of the listening activity. At the end, you can see how many each pair guessed correctly.
- Students' Book, page 125 activity 7. Spend some time reminding students how to set out a formal letter. Discuss how to organise the content sensibly. Encourage them to re-use as much language from the spread as possible, while adding in the local factors. Tell them to use and adapt the language available as much as possible rather than attempting to translate complicated sentences into Spanish.

➤ Plenaries
- Students' Book, page 125, activity 2. Give students a copy of the transcript. Discuss the style of language. Where would this type of language be used? (News bulletins, reports to government etc). The texts can also be further exploited for language.
- In class, groups or pairs, one student reads out a definition from the list at activity 3, and another has to give the name of the problem described without looking at their books. Teams can compete to get the most right, or it can be played against the clock with students attempting to recognise and name all the problems in the shortest length of time.
- Extend the discussion in activities 5 and 6 by surveying other people outside the Spanish class on their opinions and bringing the results back to class. These can be dealt with orally or written and can form the basis for an extended piece of work on environmental problems.
- Students' Book, page 125, activity 7. Students form a "Town Council" and vote on which problem raised in the letter of complaint will be dealt with.

1a Lee los dos textos de la página 124 e identifica los problemas.
- Students read the text and identify the environmental problems described.

Answers: E, F

5–8

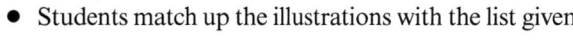

1b Empareja las ilustraciones A–F con un problema de la lista de abajo.
- Students match up the illustrations with the list given.

Answers: **1** D, **2** A, **3** F, **4** B, **5** C, **6** E

4–7

2a **Escucha e identifica el problema y emparéjalo con un dibujo de la página 124.**

- Students listen and match the problem to the picture on page 124.

5–9

 CD 3, track 17   **página 125, actividad 2**

1
Cada día perdemos más y más árboles en el mundo. Hoy presentamos una campaña para reducir el número de incendios forestales en España. En Guadalajara el incendio de Los Pinares del Ducado acabó con la vida de once personas y 13.000 hectáreas de pinos.

2
Cochabamba, Bolivia – a la zona Sur llegan todas las basuras y las aguas negras de la ciudad. Hay alto riesgo de contaminación y enfermemdades.

3
Hoy 24 de agosto de 2008 – esta mañana la Central nuclear de Vandellós II cerca de Tarragona ha sufrido un incendio en la sala de turbinas. Es hora de decir basta a las centrales y sus desechos. Envie su petición hoy mismo.

4
Los pájaros exóticos de las selvas peruanas y colombianas están en peligro de extincción porque se cazan para venderlos como mascotas o por sus plumas coloradas.

5
¡Ríos y cultivos azules! Las fábricas de vaqueros americanos en México han contaminado las tierras locales. Vierten sus desechos a los ríos y ahora hasta los cultivos ya se han puesto azules.

6
La temperatura media sigue subiendo y el nivel del mar también. ¿Cuántos años tardarán las islas Baleares o las Canarias en desaparecer? ¿Preguntas serias o fantásticas?

Answers: **1** la deforestación, **2** la basura doméstica, **3** los desechos radioactivos, **4** la destrucción de especies, **5** la polución industrial, **6** el cambio climático

2b **Escucha otra vez y relaciona el problema con un lugar en el mapa.**

- Listen again, and match the problems to a place on one of the maps.

 Answers: **1** Guadalajara, **2** Bolivia, **3** Tarragona, **4** Perú y Colombia, **5** México, **6** Islas Baleares y Canarias

5–9

3a **Empareja cada problema con una definición o causa.**

- Students read the statements and match problems and causes.

 Answers: **1** e, **2** j, **3** g, **4** f, **5** d, **6** k, **7** c, **8** i, **9** a, **10** h, **11** b

4–8

3b **Escribe la definición o causa de estos fenómenos.**

- Students write their own definitions for the two problems. Encourage them to look back through the previous statements and the texts on page 124 for any vocabulary they can recycle.

5–7

Remate

4 **Use the phrases below and discuss what you think the most serious problems are.**

- Students should attempt to justify their reasons. They can make notes, and they will use their opinions in the class discussion.

4–9

5 **Then the whole class should discuss the problems. Which do you think will be the most serious problems in the future?**

- Ask students for their opinons and reasons. Take a vote on it. Display the problems, and note down how many people think they are the most serious. Encourage them to agree and / or disagree.

5–9

6 **Now discuss what you think are the most serious problems in your local area. How do you propose to resolve them?**

PLTS

- Remind students how to talk about the future and conditional – look back at relevant sections in Units 3A and 4A.
- Refer back to the initial discussion about the pictures on page 124. Students can rate the problems out of 5 for how much they affect their local environment, and also for how easy it is for them as individuals to have an effect or take action about these things.

5–9

Success criteria activities 4, 5 & 6:
- *students communicate effectively and accurately*
- *students express personal opinions and justify points of view*
- *students use a variety of vocabulary and structures*
- *students deal with unpredictable elements*
- *students use different tenses or time frames*

7 **Write a letter to your local council and tell them about the problem you think is most serious in your area and what you propose to do about it.**

PLTS

- It is easier to deal with local problems as the students are familiar with them, but for the sake of realism they can also research a Spanish location and write, in Spanish, as if to the Spanish local council with their complaints and suggestions.

6–9

Success criteria activity 7:
- *students give information accurately and in the appropriate style*
- *students express personal opinions and justify points of view*
- *students use a variety of vocabulary and structures*
- *students use different tenses or time frames*

Cómo conservar el planeta

páginas 126 y 127

Planner

➤ Objectives
- Discussing conservation and recycling

➤ Resources
Students' Book, pages 126–127
CD 3, track 18
Grammar Workbook, page 57, 62, 64–65
Activity sheets 50–53

➤ Key language
los bosques, las botellas, la calefacción, el camino, el grifo, las latas, la luz, el medio ambiente, los panales solares, la selva
encendido, eólica
apagar, caminar, cuidar, cultivar, fumar, matar, proteger, tirar

➤ Skills
- Understanding instructions

➤ Grammar
- Positive and negative commands
- The subjunctive

➤ PLTS
Students' Book, page 127, activity 7,
Team Workers
Students' Book, page 127, activity 8,
Effective Participators

➤ Starters
- Revise imperatives by asking students for any commands they can think of. Ask if they can remember how to issue a command to more than one person. Then turn to the grammar box on page 126.
- Students' Book, page 127 activity 5a. Look at the poster and discuss what it is about. Without looking up any vocabulary, ask students to explain as much of it as they can in English, and make a note of what they say, to be checked on completing the relevant activities.
- Students' Book, page 127, activity 8. Ask students what the environmental problems are in their school, and see if they can come up with some unusual and interesting ones.
- Students' Book, page 127, activity 5b. In class, ask students if they can think of other ways of giving the instructions on the poster. It may be helpful to give a few examples on English as well e.g. *Take care of the environment, Look after the environment, Don't damage the environment* etc.

➤ Plenaries
- Students' Book, page 126 activities 2, 3 & 4. When students have matched up the commands, get them to think of scenarios when they could be used, the more memorable the better. They can be illustrated cartoon style, or even acted out e.g. group of kids messing around in the lavatories at break time, enter a teacher saying *¡Salid de allá en seguida!*
- Run a caption competition with magazine pictures or (suitable) material from the internet. Students suggest command captions for the pictures (e.g. zookeeper shouting at lion *¡No comas mis bocadillos!*). Non-Spanish classes could guess what the caption means.
- Students' Book, page 127, activity 5b. Get the students to put the commands from the transcript into the *ustedes* form, and possibly the *tú* and *vosotros* ones also. This can be an extra activity, or a game against the clock.
- Students' Book, page 127, activity 7. The results of the survey can be discussed in class and / or written up e.g. *20% de personas dejan el grifo abierto mientras que limpian los dientes. ¡Hay que cerrarlo!*

---

1 **Traduce las últimas dos frases de arriba al inglés.**

- Students translate the two sentences. Explain that the subjunctive usually refers to potential and uncertain future events rather than definite ones.

4–8

Answers: When I am 80 years old, I hope the planet will still exist! (With the implication that I may not reach 80, and the planet may no longer be there.) It can also be expressed as: Should I reach the age of 80 …

Once you begin recycling you will be helping to preserve the planet. (But it is uncertain if you will recycle or not.) It can also be expressed in English: Should you recycle, you will…

2 **Empareja los imperativos formales (irregulares) con los imperativos informales de abajo.**

- Students match the formal and informal commands.

Answers: **a** pon, **b** ten, **c** ve, **d** di, **e** ven, **f** haz, **g** ve(te), **h** oye, **i** sal

4–7

3 **¿Qué significa cada verbo de la actividad 2? Utiliza tu diccionario y escribe el infinitivo.**

- Students work out the meaning of each verb and write down the infinitive and the command forms with it for reference.

Answers: **put** – poner, **have** – tener, **see** – ver, **say** – decir, **come** – venir, **do/make** – hacer, **go** – ir, **hear** – oir, go **out** – salir

4 **Escribe las frases con la forma correcta del verbo.**

- Students write out the sentences using the correct form of the verb. Do the first one or two together if necessary, reminding students how to choose the correct imperative form.

Answers: **a** escribid, **b** hables, **c** tiren, **d** pongan, **e** reciclad, **f** uséis, **g** monten, **h** apaga, **i** reduzcan, **j** consumid

5a **Lee el póster.**

- Students read the poster. See starter activities.

5b **Escucha y relaciona lo que oyes con una instrucción de arriba.**

- Students listen and match to the instructions on the poster.

CD 3, track 18	página 126, actividad 5b

1 No mate a los animales
2 No camine por las rocas
3 No coja las flores
4 No descuide el entorno
5 No tire papeles
6 No fume aquí

Answers: **1** Respete los animales, **2** Vaya por los caminos indicados, **3** Proteja la flora y fauna, **4** Cuide la naturaleza, **5** Ponga su basura en una bolsa. **6** Apague su cigarrillo con mucho cuidado

6a **Lee y empareja cada dibujo con una frase.**

- Students match the pictures and the instructions.

Answers: **a** 5, **b** 9, **c** 8, **d** 10, **e** 6, **f** 1, **g** 4, **h** 3, **i** 2, **j** 7

6b **Para cada frase escoge una instrucción adecuada.**

- Students match the instructions to the command.

Answers: **1** c, **2** g, **3** j, **4** a, **5** h, **6** i, **7** d, **8** f, **9** e, **10**, b

6c **¡Busca otra manera de decir lo mismo! Utiliza las palabras de la caja.**

- Students use the words from the box to find another way of giving the same instructions.

Answers: **1** economizar. **2** cuidar, **3** proteger, **4** reciclar, **5** bajar, **6** cambiar

Remate

7 **Prepare questions with a friend to find out what the rest of the class do in the home to help the situation. Then carry out a survey.**

PLTS

- Discuss some ideas in class first. Which of these ideas apply to the home situation? What kind of environmentally friendly options are there in the home? How to phrase the question? Set a limit on the number of questions to be asked. Groups / partners can carry out their own survey, or the whole class can use the same questions, with each person asking some of them to a few people.

Success criteria activity 7:
- *students communicate effectively and accurately*
- *students express personal opinions and justify points of view*
- *students use a variety of vocabulary and structures*
- *students deal with unpredictable elements*
- *students use different tenses or time frames*

8 **Design a poster campaign for school: use the *tú* form to give instructions.**

PLTS

- Students use the ideas given as a starting point, and adapt them for their local circumstances.

Success criteria activity 8:
- *students give information accurately and in the appropriate style*
- *students use a variety of vocabulary and structures*

Cómo hablar del ecoturismo

Planner

> ### Objectives
> - Talking about the pros and cons of ecotourism

> ### Resources
> Students' Book, pages 128–129
> Grammar Workbook, page 66
> Activity sheets 50–53

> ### Key language
> *el comportamiento, los consejos, el corazón, el desarrollo, la despoblación, la mezcla, un mirador, el mundo, la rabia, la riqueza, la travesía extraña/o, inquieto/a, salvaje adentrarse, aportar, deteriorarse, inscribirse, salvaguardar*

> ### Skills
> - Reading strategies

> ### Grammar
> - Impersonal verbs

> ### PLTS
> Students' Book, page 128, activity 2,
> *Reflective Learners*
> Students' Book, page 129, activity 8,
> *Self-Managers*

> ### Starters
> - Focus on the Reading skills section at the beginning of page 128 and with the class apply them to activities 1 and 2. When the students tackle the longer text on the next page, refer them to the skills, but give them the responsibility of applying them.
> - Students read the long text on page 128 and pick out any words they recognise. Make a list of these words and their meanings, and discuss what they can deduce about the text from them. Then continue with the activities.
> - Students' Book, page 129, activity 6. Before students discuss the issues with their partner, deal with one in depth with the whole class. Show students how to build up longer replies

– *Es un problema – Es un problema muy grave*
– *Es un problema muy grave para las personas que viven allí* etc. Look at possible solutions, at who might be responsible for dealing with the problem. Encourage different opinions – *En mi opinión el cambio climático es un problema más grave que la sobrepoblación porque...*
> - Students' Book, page 129, activity 8. Ask students (probably in English) if they know what a National Park is and what it is for. Have they visited one? Do they live in or near one? What kind of activities go on there?

> ### Plenaries
> - Give students a copy of the *Ecotursimo o ecodesastre* text with the verbs blanked out. Depending on the level of the students, ask them to complete the text with no support, with a list of verbs in the infinitive, or with a list of verbs in the correct form.
> - Students' Book, page 129, activity 4. Ask students to summarise in their own words the long text about Bierzo. Discuss in English first what it is about – where, what is the project, who runs it, what are the aims etc. Then ask them to write five or six sentences summarising the issue.
> - Students' Book, page 129, activities 6 & 7. Students use the material from the discussions as the basis for a piece of written work. They should set it out as an article for publication in a magazine. Several or all of the issues should be covered, along with an opinion as to their severity, and suggestions for dealing with the problem. They should write as though addressing other people their age, and attempting to raise awareness and concern for these issues.
> - Students' Book, page 129, activity 8. Students write about a National Park in this country as though to a Spanish penfriend or a student in a Spanish school, explaining where it is, what it is like, what kind of lanscape and wildlife there is, what activities can be done there etc. If the school has a partner school in Spain, these could actually be sent to the Spanish students to be read and commented upon.

---

1 **Usa los consejos para analizar el texto, y contesta a las preguntas en inglés.**

- Students read and follow the advice, then answer the questions in English. See also page 136 of this unit for more on reading strategies.

5–9

Answers: **a** There weren't many ecotourists. **b** Far more people want to take part in ecotourism. **c** They are losing weight, having heart problems and catching our diseases. **d** They are having too much contact with humans. **e** Humans and wild animals are not a good mix, and the attempt to educate people by showing them animals in the wild is having the opposite effect to that intended.

2 Lee la primera frase otra vez, y analízala.

- Students read and follow the advice, then answer the questions in English.

  Answers: **a** animales, **b** naturaleza, ecosaludable, **c** adentrase – infinitve, observar – infinitive, es – present, **d** *eco* is the same as in English, *salud* means healthy, and *able* is the suffix indicating an adjective

5–9

3 Contesta a las preguntas en inglés.

- Students answer the questions in English. This last section refers to higher reading tests more than basic ones.

5–9

  Answers: **1** five (including "birds"), **2** biologists, **3** they have been infected with human diseases, **4** the opposite effect to that originally intended – it was supposed to help the animals, and it is harming them

4 Usa los consejos de la página 128 para leer los dos textos de abajo.

- Students use the same advice to read the next two texts.

5–9

5 Contesta a las preguntas en inglés.

- Students answer the questions in English.

  Answers: **a** B, **b** A, **c** A, **d** B, **e** A

5–9

Remate

6 Discuss any of the issues in the box with a partner. Start with simple questions and use the help box below to help with your answers.

- See the Starters section for ideas on how to set up the discussion. Different pairs can discuss different issues and then bring their ideas together as a whole class.

5–9

7 Then go on to discuss these questions.

- Students should say why or why not they agree or disagree with these questions, and elaborate as much as possible. They can use the vocabulary supplied to help their arguments. If they present their arguments to the class, they can be awarded points by the other students on how many of the helpful phrases they manage to use correctly.

5–9

Success criteria activities 6 & 7:
- *students communicate effectively and accurately*
- *students express personal opinions and justify points of view*
- *students use a variety of vocabulary and structures*
- *students deal with unpredictable elements*
- *students use different tenses or time frames*

8 Research into the National Parks of Spain. Choose one and write a brief description of it using the headings below.

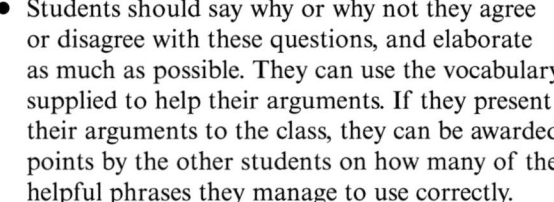

- http://www.spain.info/TourSpain/Destinos/mapas/sus+Parques+Nacionales/?language=EN
- http://en.wikipedia.org/wiki/List_of_National_Parks_in_Spain
- The above internet links are quite good places to start the research. There are 11 main national parks, so they could be divided up between the class to end up with a comprehensive account.

4–9

Success criteria activity 8:
- *students give information accurately and in the appropriate style*
- *students use a variety of vocabulary and structures*
- *students use different tenses or time frames*

Cómo comparar tu vida con las de otros

páginas 130 y 131

Planner

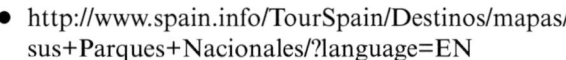

➤ **Objectives**
- Talking about our lives in relation to others

➤ **Resources**
Students' Book, pages 130–131
CD 3, tracks 19–21
Grammar Workbook, pages 38–40
Activity sheets 50–53

➤ **Key language**
los aplausos, las costumbres, los gritos, los lagos, la madera, la merienda
aisladola, amable, bromista, cortés, heladola, humilde, lindola, secola
acostumbrarse, hacer cola, limitar con, sorprender, tener prisa
mientras que, sin embargo

➤ **Skills**
- Listening for detail

➤ **Grammar**
  ● Correct choice of *ser* and *estar*

➤ **PLTS**
Students' Book, page 131, activity 3,
Reflective Learners
Students' Book, page 131, activity 6b,
Team Workers

➤ **Starters**
  ● Display some photos, possibly taken from magazines, of a few very different looking people – old, young, celebrities, poor refugees, business people, students etc. Ask students how they think their lives differ – what do they do, how much money do they have, what are their interests, activities and concerns? Keep a record of their ideas for reference later on in the unit.
  ● Students' Book, page 130, activity 1. Before doing the activities in the Students' Book, the class read through the letter in pairs or small groups and note down, in English, anything they understand about what Isidoro is talking about. They pool these notes in class – the teacher can write them on the board. The teacher says if they have understood something wrongly, but does not at this stage give the correct version; that is for the students to find out as they do the activities.
  ● Students' Book, page 131, activity 2. Possibly as a research homework ask students to find out some differences between Argentina and Spain e.g. their winter is our summer, and the implications for this i.e. the school year is the other way round and they can go skiing in August. This gives them some preparation

for the listening. Or you may prefer to do the listening activity "cold" and ask them to research more differences later.
  ● Students' Book, page 131, activity 6. Before beginning the conversation with their partners, as a class look back at Unit 1, and pick out some points of information about the different places the characters live, their families and lifestyles. Leave this information displayed while students make further notes and discuss with their partner.

➤ **Plenaries**
  ● Students' Book, page 131, activity 3c. After listening to the letter read by Jorge, students read it again, trying to improve their pronunciation. This can be done in pairs, with each partner reading a paragraph in turn, or around the class, with each person reading a sentence.
  ● Students' Book, page 131, activity 5. After doing all the activities related to Jorge's letter, the teacher calls out some statements such as *Es muy tranquilo, Todo el mundo está de prisa* etc. and the students have to say if these describe Urubicha or Madrid.
  ● Students' Book, page 131, activity 7. If students are familiar with other contrasting places e.g. they live in the city but their aunt lives by the sea, they could use this as a basis for a conversation instead.
  ● Students' Book, page 131, activity 8. If students research a number of different unusual places they could be combined into a display / guide to *lugares diferentes del mundo*

1a Lee la carta de Isidoro y contesta a las preguntas.

  ● Students read Isidoro's letter and answer the questions in Spanish.

Answers: **1** Isidoro está en Inglaterra. **2** Se queda con la familia Roberts y va al colegio de idiomas. **3** Le sorprende que no se come el pan con la comida. **4** Le gusta la familia inglesa – dice que son amables. **5** Indica cuatro diferencias, por ejemplo se come pan en sándwiches para la merienda / todos hacen cola para el autobús o para entrar en el cine / el clima no es muy bueno aunque es agosto / el campo es muy verde con muchos flores. **6** Le gusta la manera de hacer cola pero no le gusta la clima. **7** Compara Inglaterra con Andalucía donde el paisaje es mucho más seco. **8** El concierto fue fenomenal.

1b Busca estas palabras o frases en español.

  ● Students look through the letter to find the equivalent words in Spanish.

Answers: hace quince días, me he acostumbrado, la merienda, hacen cola, aunque, sin embargo, comparado con, seco, anteayer, al principio

1c Busca las frases que contienen los verbos *ser* y *estar*. Indica por qué se usa cada uno.

  ● Students find all the sentences using the verbs *ser* and *estar*, and say why each is used.

Answers:
Hace quince días que **1 estoy** con la familia Roberts y todos **2 son** muy amables. **1** location, **2** personality

En el colegio de idiomas **3 estoy** aprendiendo bastante. **3** temporary state

Lo que no me gusta **4 es** el clima porque hay días tan grises cuando no sale el sol aunque **5 estamos** en agosto. **4** physical description, **5** location

Sin embargo aquí en el campo donde **6 estoy** todo parece muy verde y las flores **7 son** lindas comparado con Andalucía donde todo **8 es** tan seco y marrón en esta época del año. **6** location, **7** physical description, **8** physical description

Anteayer Matthew y yo fuimos a Londres a un concierto donde tocaba la orquesta juvenil de Venezuela – **9 fue** algo fenomenal. **9** physical description/personality (permanent characteristic)

2a Lorena le pregunta a Mari Ángeles sobre su vida en Argentina. Lee la lista de preguntas. ¿Qué tipo de información vas a buscar?

● Students read through the strategies for listening, then match up the questions and information.

Answers: **1** c, **2** f, **3** e, **4** b, **5** a, **6** d

4–6

2b Escucha la conversación y concéntrate en cada pregunta. No escribas nada.

● Students listen carefully to the questions, but don't write anything down. The teacher can ask them after the first listening how much they understood and can remember, but orally only, and don't give them any more information than they have remembered for themselves.

5–8

CD 3, track 19   página 130, actividades 2b y 2c

Lorena	Oye Mari Ángeles cuéntame un poco más de tu vida en Argentina – por ejemplo ahora en agosto ¿Qué tiempo hace allí en tu pueblo?
Mari Ángeles	¡Fácil! En Bariloche como es tan alto en las montañas, en agosto hace un frío terrible; hay nieve en los picos de las montañas y corre un viento helado que viene del Antártida.
Lorena	¡No me lo puedo creer! –¿Y entonces, qué hacías durante el día cuándo vivías allí?
Mari Ángeles	Normalmente como es el invierno tenemos unas vacaciones cortas en agosto. Yo siempre iba a esquiar por las mañanas y por las tardes iba con mis amigos a tomar chocolate caliente en una cafetería.
Lorena	Y ¿Cómo son las casas?
Mari Ángeles	Todas las casas son de madera, similares a los chalets de Austria o Francia en los Alpes.
Lorena	¡Qué bonito! Y cuándo son las vacaciones de verano?¿Y dónde las pasabas?
Mari Ángeles	Iba siempre con mis padres por los lagos en diciembre. Son unos lagos espectaculares y en el verano hacíamos camping o nos alojábamos en un hotel aislado que limita con la frontera de Chile.
Lorena	Me parece una vida fenomenal! ¿Por qué viniste a España?
Mari Ángeles	Pues porque quería estudiar música europea, sobre todo la movida moderna aquí en España y no quería ir a Miami aunque me han dicho que allí habría más oportunidad para triunfar que aquí.
Lorena	¡Ojalá, pero quién sabe – vamos a ver!

2c Escucha otra vez y anota los detalles para cada pregunta.

● Students listen again for the details about each question. When they have finished listening, go through the activity with the class building up the questions.

5–8

Answers: **1** hace en agosto? **2** durante el día? **3** las casas? **4** tienen las vacaciones largas? **5** las pasabas? **6** viniste a España?

2d Ahora contesta a las preguntas en inglés.

● Students answer questions about the conversation in English.

Answers: **1** It is very cold. **2** In December. **3** They are wooden, like chalets in Austria and France. **4** By the lakes, or in an isolated hotel near the Chilean frontier. **5** She wanted to study European music. **6** There are more opportunities for success there.

3a Lee la carta y busca: nombres de lugares, palabras o frases que contrastan, opiniones y palabras descriptivas; los diferentes usos de ser y estar.

● Students read the letter looking for the information. The class can be split into groups and each one looks for a different type of information, combining it all at the end. If they have a paper copy, they can underline the relevant bits in different colours.

5–9

Answers:
1

lugares: Urubicha, Madrid, Bolivia, España, el pueblo, la ciudad, la casa, la capital

palabras o frases que contrastan: comparado con, no tiene nada que ver con, mientras que, pero

opiniones y palabras descriptivas: diferente, parece que estamos en otro mundo, distinta, sensacional, grande, humilde, gentil, ocupados, teníamos tanta prisa, lento, amablemente, indígena, me parecen tan bonitos, los encontraríais curiosos, natural, Me encanta, tranquila, fuerte

2

los usos diferentes de ser y estar: la vida en Urubicha **es** tan diferente, parece que **estamos** en otro mundo, la geografía **es** distinta, Lo único que sigue igual **es** el amor a la música, la gente **es** muy humilde, todos **estábamos** tan ocupados

3b Túrnate col un(a) compañero/a para leer la carta.

PLTS

● Students take it in turns with a partner to read the letter out loud for pronunciation practice. This can be done sentence by sentence, or in sections as appropriate for the ability level of the group.

4–6

3c Escucha. ¿Quién pronuncia mejor y tiene mejor entonación?

● Students listen and decide who has the best pronunciation.

CD 3, track 20   página 131, actividad 3c

Hola amigos míos.

Os cuento que la vida en Urubichá es muy diferente anuestra vida en Madrid. Aquí en el noreste de Bolivia parece que estamos en otro mundo porque no sólo la geografía es distinta, las costumbres, la gente y hasta el idioma no tiene nada que ver con España. Lo único que sigue igual es el amor por la música, y la orquesta del pueblo me parece sensacional sobre todo si tenemos en cuenta que no tiene las facilidades de una ciudad grande. Me levanto temprano para ayudar a mi madre con las faenas de la casa – éstas no varían nunca. Aquí en el pueblo la gente es muy humilde y amable mientras que en la capital todos estábamos muy ocupados y siempre teníamos mucha prisa. Aquí todo va mucho más lento y la gente se habla y conversa amablemente.

La gente indígena se viste con sus trajes regionales que a mí me parecen tan bonitos pero creo que vosotros los encontraríais curiosos. Además hablan guarayo, su idioma nativo y hasta algunos no hablan español. Me encanta esta vida tan tranquila pero como quiero seguir con mis estudios volveré a Madrid muy pronto.
Hasta entonces un abrazo fuerte de Jorge.

4   Busca frases o palabras equivalentes en el texto.

● Students look for the equivalent Spanish phrases in the text.

Answers: **a** en otro mundo, **b** hasta el idioma, **c** Lo único, **d** sobre todo cuando, **e** éstas no cambian nunca, **f** mientras que, **g** tener tanta prisa, **h** además

5–8

5   Contesta a las preguntas en inglés.

● Students answer the questions in English.

Answers: **a** It is so completely different to life in Madrid. **b** Household chores and the love of music are still the same. **c** The local people are quieter and more gentle and have more time for each other than in Madrid where everyone is so busy all the time. **d** He likes his home town very much – he says he loves the peaceful lifestyle.

5–8

6a   Escucha y anota las diferencias entre España e Inglaterra. Escribe una palabra para cada diferencia. Tienes que acordarte del resto.

● Students listen to the differences between Spain and England. They may only make a one word note for each difference, and must try to remember the rest of the information.

5–8

> 🎧 **CD 3, track 21   página 131, actividad 6a**
>
> **Madre**   Isidoro, hace ya varias semanas que estás en Inglaterra ¿Cómo te parece la vida allí hijo mío?
> **Isidoro**   Pues todavía no puedo acostumbrarme a que conducen por la izquierda – siempre que salimos en coche me parece que vamos a tener un accidente.
> **Madre**   No seas tan bromista –¿Qué tal la familia?
> **Isidoro**   Bueno es más pequeña que la nuestra porque los abuelos viven lejos y solamente son Matthew y su hermana menor – no es tan grande como la nuestra. Lo bueno es que Matthew no tiene que compartir su habitación como yo.
> **Madre**   ¿Y las comidas?
> **Isidoro**   Muy diferentes: por ejemplo a veces desayunan mucho – huevos con tocineta, pan tostado y habas blancas con salsa de tomate – me parece delicioso pero demasiado.
> **Madre**   ¿Y la cena?
> **Isidoro**   Bueno no comen tan tarde como nosotros y no suelen comer tanto tampoco. Comen muchas comidas rápidas lo cual es una lástima y tampoco comen juntos durante la semana.
> **Madre**   ¿Qué más me cuentas? ¿Me imagino que las tiendas son grandes y bonitas?
> **Isidoro**   A ver ... sí y no ... me parecen iguales que las de España – hay tiendas pequeñas del pueblo pero también almacenes enormes como los hipermercados allí.

> **Madre**   ¿Y del colegio qué?
> **Isidoro**   Pues yo voy a uno escuela de idiomas y ¡menos mal que no tengo que llevar uniforme! Matthew me mostró el que tiene que ponerse para ir a su colegio y me pareció que es de un color horrible. Además la camisa con corabata sería insoportable con el calor de Andalucía. También me contó que las clases son igual de aburridas, que los profes son igual de estrictos, que los exámenes son igual de difíciles …
> **Madre**   Ya, ya – no tomas nada en serio ... bueno hijo hasta la próxima – un besote
> **Isidoro**   Gracias mamá – hasta pronto.

Answers (suggested): Students will pick their own key words, and can discuss their answers in English or Spanish as appropriate to their ability
conducir (in England they drive on the left), **familia** (smaller than his, grandparents live further away), **habitación** (Matthew doesn't have to share his bedroom), **comidas** (big breakfasts, don't eat late in the evening or as much as in Spain, lots of fast food, don't eat together often), **tiendas** (similar to Spain), **colegio** (they have to wear uniform)

6b   Con tus notas discute las diferencias con un(a) compañero/a. Usa las frases clave.

PLTS

● Students use their notes to discuss the differences with a partner – they can compare what they understood and see if it is the same. If they can't agree on what they heard, they should ask a further student for corroboration.

5–9

6c   ¿Hay algunos aspectos similares entre los dos países? ¿Cuáles son?

● Students decide what the similarities are between the two countries. They may need to listen again here, still applying the techniques. After discussing in pairs, they should feed back to the whole class to check their answers.

5–9

6d   Ahora escribe cinco frases comparando la vida de España e Inglaterra según Isidoro. Usa las frases clave de arriba. Acuérdate de la primera carta en la actividad 1a también.

● Students write five sentences comparing the two countries using their notes and the key words suggested. They should also look back at Isidoro's letter in activity 1a. If they disagree with any of the comparisons they should explain why.

4–9

Remate

7   Imagine another conversation between Lorena and Mari Ángeles or Isidoro and their family. Speak about the differences between their lives. Use the questions from activity 2a.

● Students may need to look back at Unit 1 for information about the various characters. Discuss some information in class first to get them started. Students may make notes, but should not write out a whole conversation. Other students can give them points for factual and grammatical accuracy.

4–9

Success criteria activity 7:
- *students communicate effectively and accurately*
- *students express personal opinions and justify points of view*
- *students use a variety of vocabulary and structures*
- *students deal with unpredictable elements*
- *students use different tenses or time frames*

Success criteria activity 8:
- *students give information accurately and in the appropriate style*
- *students express personal opinions and justify points of view*
- *students use a variety of vocabulary and structures*
- *students use different tenses or time frames*

8   **Research information about Bariloche or Urubicha. Imagine you are Mari Ángeles or Jorge and write about life in your village. Comment on the different aspects and the similarities between life at home and in Madrid. Explain which you prefer and say why.**

4–9

- Both are fascinating places and worth the research, but other places of contrast can be used if wished. This can be done as an oral presentation or as a written piece of work. Who can find out the most unusual piece of information?

Cómo apreciar la cultura ajena   páginas 132 y 133

Planner

➤ **Objectives**
- Talking about music, dance and culture

➤ **Resources**
Students' Book, pages 132–133
Grammar Workbook, page 19
Activity sheet 50–53

➤ **Key language**
el bailarín, la cantautor(a), el mensaje, el orgullo, el recuerdo, el sonido, el torero
afortunado/a, gitano/a
apoyar, decir, enseñar, estar de acuerdo, tardar en
se crió, nació, siendo (ser)
bajo, cien por cien, no cabe duda

➤ **Skills**
- Exam techniques for reading passages

➤ **Grammar**
- Questions and indirect exclamations

➤ **PLTS**
Students' Book, page 133, Exam Strategies 2
Reflective Learners
Students' Book, page 133, activity 4,
Self-Managers

➤ **Starters**
- Brainstorm in class what students think *cultura* means. What types of activities does it include? What types do they like and take part in? Why / Why not? Is it important? Why?
- Students' Book, page 132, activity 1. Read the texts first with the class and ask for any information they understand. Their combined knowledge will give them the confidence to tackle the subsequent activities.
- Ask the students (in English) what strategies they apply when reading a long passage in an exam situation. Ask them how helpful these are. Ask them what is important when doing such an exercise. There are no necessarily right or wrong answer – it is to get them thinking before looking at the Habilidades boxes.
- Students' Book, page 133, activity 2. Ask the students, in English or Spanish, what they can remember about Jorge's life in Urubicha so far. Then do the activities.

➤ **Plenaries**
- Students' Book, page 132, activity 1. Who are the students' *ídolos*? Using some of the ideas from the reading passages, get them to write a brief paragraph (no more than 3 – 4 sentences) describing someone they admire and saying why. They read these out or pass them round the class for others to agree or disagree with – also saying why. Not all will be musiscians – the primary aim of this spread – so keep the descriptions brief.

- Students' Book, page 133, activity 2. By now, students should have built up a picture of Urubicha. Get them to describe in their own words the town and the orchestra and why the place is special. This can be done orally in class with each student proving a sentence or part of one, or written as a collaboration in a pair or a small group.
- Students' Book, page 133, activity 3. Having talked to their partner, students ask other people in the class at random what type of music they like, if they like music X, if they play an instrument. The person who answers has to ask the next question, creating a chain of questions and answers until everyone has answered.
- Students' Book, page 133, activity 4. Students read what the others have written, preferably choosing a type of music they know something about, and comment on whether the research is accurate or not.

1a Lee lo que ha dicho Lorena, Isidoro y Mari Ángeles sobre sus ídolos y su amor por la música y el baile. ¿Quién menciona …

- Students read the texts and decide who mentions the items on the list.

Answers: **1** Lorena, **2** Isidoro, **3** Mari Ángeles, **4** Isidoro, **5** Lorena, **6** Isidoro, Mari Ángeles

1b Anota las diferentes clases de música mencionadas. ¿Cómo se dicen en inglés?

- Students make a note of the different types of music mentioned and translate them into English.

1c Contesta a las preguntas en inglés.

- Students answer the questions in English. They should give as much detail as is necessary to fully answer the question.

Answers: **1** They admire their talent and what they do to help other people. **2** They have the same name. **3** The message. **4** a mixture of flamenco with elements of classical music, arabic, jewish, afrocuban and jazz influences.

1d Busca estas palabras en español.

- Students look for the equivalent words in Spanish. Discuss how students found the words they were looking for and what clue they used.

Answers: **1** se crió, **2** no tardó mucho en, **3** Mi primer recuerdo, **4** su padre siendo de, **5** no le han ganado amigos, **6** persona comprometida, **7** Siempre apoya a los menos afortunados, **8** Estoy de acuerdo cien por cien, **9** una mezcla, **10** quisiera cantar

Habilidades – Exam strategies 1

- Students go through these strategies, applying them to the reading passages. Make sure they understand and use them correctly.

Answers: **cuando** *tenga* oportunidad, **Cuando** *pueda*, No *olvidemos* **que** al final del día **cuando** todos se *vayan* a casa

2a Lee el texto.

PLTS

- Students read the text.

Habilidades – Exam strategies 2
Did you remember to apply all the reading strategies systematically?

- Refer students back to these strategies on page 128 before they start reading.

Take it in turns with a partner to read the text aloud.

- Students can read one or two sentences in turn, and comment on each other's pronunciation.

Now read the questions and then discuss the details you think you need to include in your answers. It's obvious you don't need to know what every word means. Are there any you think are essential which you still can't work out? Write them down and look at the way they work in the sentence.

- The amount of words students look up should be strictly limited.

Find two examples of the subjunctive used with reference to the future.

Answers: cuando tengamos, cuando veas, Ojalá siga

Write down examples of the different tenses you can find.

Answers: es diferente – present, fue creado – preterite (passive), fundaron – preterite, hemos aprendido – perfect, cuando tengamos – subjunctive, no te cabrá duda – future simple

2b Contesta a las preguntas en inglés.

- Students answer the questions in English.

Answers: **1** a group of Franciscan monks founded Urubicha and taught Baroque music to the local inhabitants, beginning the musical tradition. **2** When they are good enough, they become teachers to the younger pupils. **3** They are a very humble people from an isolated place in Bolivia, and they have learnt to work wood to make violins. **4** Three of his friends have been selected to play in the Latinamerican Youth Orchestra, which draws players from 22 different countries.

2c Traduce el texto en negrita al inglés.

- Students translate the text in bold into English.

Answer (approximate): "Play and struggle" which means it doesn't matter how much money you have, how old you are or what colour your skin is, the important thing is to play music.

Remate

3 Think of all the different types of music you know and discuss them with a partner. Invent some questions for a class survey on music and dance. Use the prompts below to help you get started.

4–9

- Students can name groups, but should not use that as an excuse for not giving the Spanish for the type of music. Encourage them to talk about and describe their favourite artists and why they admire them.

4 Research any one of the styles of music or dance mentioned in the texts and make notes. Then write a brief paragraph and explain why you have chosen this particular style.

4–9

- Encourage students to choose a style of music that is not necessarily their favourite. It would be good to get someone who prefers heavy metal to research classical music and vice versa.

Success criteria activities 3 & 4:
- *students communicate effectively and accurately*
- *students express personal opinions and justify points of view*
- *students use a variety of vocabulary and structures*
- *students deal with unpredictable elements*
- *students use different tenses or time frames*

Gramática en acción

páginas 134 y 135

➤ **Review of commands and instructions**

1 Remember there are several irregular commands in the *tú* form. Here are the first letters. Write them down from memory and add what they mean in English.

PLTS *Answers:* haz, oye, pon, sal, ten, ve, ven, ve(te)

2 Write out a table as above for the following verbs:
Grammar reference page 211

Answers:

	tú	vosotros	usted	ustedes
preferir	prefiere	preferid	prefiera	prefieran
poder	puede	poded	pueda	puedan
empezar	empieza	empezad	empiece	empiecen
cerrar	cierra	cerrad	cierre	cierren
querer	quiere	quered	quiera	quieran
volver	vuelve	volved	vuelva	vuelvan
elegir	elige	elegid	elija	elijan

3 Write out a table of negative commands for the verbs in activity 2.

Answers:

	tú	vosotros	usted	ustedes
preferir	no prefieras	no preferáis	no prefiera	no prefieran
poder	no puedas	no podáis	no pueda	no puedan
empezar	no empieces	no empecéis	no empiece	no empiecen
cerrar	no cierres	no cerréis	no cierre	no cierren
querer	no quieras	no queráis	no quiera	no quieran
volver	no vuelvas	no volváis	no vuelva	no vuelvan
elegir	no elijas	no elejáis	no elija	no elijan

➤ The subjunctive

4a For the following words, write down the Spanish verb in the *tú* form of the subjunctive mood.
Grammar reference page 211

Answers: leas, escribas, hables, busques, respondas, elijas, des, preguntes, notes, averigües

4b Now write down the *nosotros* form of the subjunctive for the verbs in activity 4a.

Answers: leamos, escribamos, hablemos, busquemos, respondamos, elijamos, demos, preguntemos, notemos, averigüemos

5 Translate the last two sentences in the box above into English.

Answers: When I (should) finish my studies, I'm going to travel round the world. As soon as (whenever) we have the results we will be happy.

6 Change these positive instructions into negative ones.

Answers: **a** No escribes una frase entera. **b** No te acuestes en seguida. **c** No contestes ahora mismo. **d** No corréis por el pasillo. **e** To te vayas todo recto. **f** No te calles inmediatamente. **g** No penséis un poco. **h** No vengan a mi casa.

➤ Review of (*desde*) *hace / hacia*

7 Say how long you have been doing the following.
- Students should write down and retain their answers.

➤ Review of *ser* and *estar*

8 Translate these sentences into Spanish and, for each underlined verb, explain why you have used *ser* or *estar*.

PLTS

Answers: **a** Madrid está (location) en el centro de España y es (fact) la capital. **b** ¿Dónde están (location) los billetes para el concierto? Ya son (time) las seis. **c** Joaquín Cortés es (profession) bailarín muy famoso. **d** ¿Está (changeable state) casado?

Habilidades

página 136

Planner

➤ Objectives
- Increasing your language skills for fluency.

➤ Resources
Students' Book, page 136
Exam Skills Workbook, page 54 (F), page 55 (H)
Activity sheet 55
Resources and Planning OxBox CD-ROM

➤ Skills
- Understanding the questions.

Working out the meaning of a text.
Concentrating on the spoken text.
Developing effective note-taking.
Thinking about how to manage the examinations.
Learning to check your answers systematically.

➤ PLTS
Students' Book, page 136, activity 2, *Self-Managers*
Students' Book, page 136, activity 6, *Reflective Learners*

➤ Leer

1 Understand the questions.
- ❑ Write down as many question words as you can remember in Spanish then write the meaning of each one.
  - Think of more question words in English and look them up in a dictionary if you can't remember what they are in Spanish.

2 Work out the meaning of a text.
PLTS Students can use a Lectura or Worksheet text for this purpose.

➤ Escuchar

3 Concentrate on the spoken text.
- Emphasise the final point very strongly!

4 Develop effective note-taking.
- Remind students that it is not a good idea to try to write down full answers while listening, and therefore abbreviations are very helpful.

➤ Aprender

5 Think about how to manage the examinations.
- Students can use these techniques on a practise paper.

6 Check your answers systematically.
PLTS
- You can make your own checklist – for example: TAPAS = Tense/Agreements (masc/fem/plural), Person/pronouns, Accents, Spelling
- Try out your checklist on any piece of written work.

Escenario

Planner

➤ **Objectives**
- Giving a presentation on a typical element of Spanish culture and researching an environmental group.

➤ **Resources**
Students' Book, page 137
Exam Skills Workbook, pages 51–52 (F),
pages 52–53 (H)
Assessment sheets 27–32
Resources and Planning OxBox CD-ROM

➤ **Skills**
- Writing practice
- Speaking practice

➤ **PLTS**
Students' Book, page 137, Escenario Oral,
Effective Participators
Students' Book, page 137, Escenario Escrito,
Independent Enquirers

➤ **Oral**

Spanish and Latin american life.

4–9
- Students give a presentation to the class on their chosen topic, explaining why they chose that one. The class judges it on how interesting it is, and how well and fluently delivered. A more advanced group can be given the grade descriptors to judge the presentations by.
- *GCSE Grades A*-C*
- *Grade C Students use past, present and future tenses. They express opinions, and deal with some unpredictability.*
- *Grade A Students express and justify opinions. They use a variety of vocabulary and structure in longer speech sequences.*

➤ **Escrito**

Local environmental group.

4–9
- Students record a 3 minute report as if for radio, so their information must be precise and concise.
- It helps if students imagine they are directing their report at an audience who broadly understands what such groups do, but has never heard of this particular one and its work.
- *GCSE Grades A*-C*
- *Grade C Students use opinions and past, present and future tenses, both factually and imaginatively. Register is appropriate and style is basic.*
- *Grade A Students write factually and imaginatively using longer sequences and a range of vocabulary and structure. They express and justify opinions in an appropriate style.*

Vocabulario

This is a summary of key language from the unit, organised by spread and theme. Students can use it for reference while working on the unit, and as an aid to learning vocabulary.

Lectura

Planner

> ### Objectives
> - Being "green", life on Lake Titicaca
> - To encourage independent reading and develop reading strategies.
> - These pages also provide alternative class and homework material for students who work quickly and require extension work.

> ### Resources
> Students' Book, page 185-186

> ### PLTS
> Students' Book, page 185, activity 2,
> *Team Workers*
> Students' Book, page 186, activity 5,
> *Creative Thinkers*

> ### Lectura A – ¿Eres verde, amarillo ó o rojo?

1 **Busca y anota las palabras que significan:** *reuse, the leftovers, too, to clean, write, shred, switch off, on the way to, the tap, magazines.*

- Students read the quiz and find the words in Spanish.

2a **¿Cuántos puntos tienes?**

- Students do the quiz and add up their score.

2b **Compara tus respuestas con las de un(a) compañero/a ¿Quién es más verde?**

PLTS
- Students compare their results. Who is the greenest person in the class?

3 **Inventa un póster 'verde'. Para cada letra escribe una norma.**
- Students can write a word or a sentence beginning with the correct letter.

> ### Lectura B – ¡Hola, me llamo Rosa!

1 **Lee el texto y usa todas las estrategias que has aprendido para leer.**

- Students read the text, applying all the reading strategies they have learnt up until now.
- Note: Amantaní is not to be confused with the floating reed islands described earlier in the book.

2 **Haz tres listas.**

- Students write three lists as required.

Answers: **a** isla, maíz, aislada, existimos, turistas, visitar, caramelos, eléctrica, gobierno, panales solares, habitantes, típico, único, problema, botella, colegio, aire, puro, contaminación industrial, causar, grave, continuar

Note: Answers to **b** and **c** depend on students' level of understanding.

3 **Contesta a las preguntas en inglés.**

- Students answers the questions in English.

Answers: **a** At the weekend, because they work in the city of Puno at the side of the lake. **b** The grow maize and keep chickens, and tourists stay in their house. **c** She likes hearing about their lives in far away countries. **d** They now have electric light from solar panels. **e** She likes them because now it's not so dark and they can take turns hosting the tourists. **f** It is always very cool because it is always windy, but the air is very pure and clean.

4 **Imagina que vas a visitar la isla. Escribe unas preguntas que le gustaría poner a Rosa para saber más acerca de su vida. Cambia de papel con un(a) compañero/a.**

- Students write questions about island life they would like to put to Rosa.

5 **Por turnos pregunta y contesta a las preguntas con mucha imaginación.**

PLTS

- Students answer their partner's questions. If there is time, there are many internet sites with travelblogs describing people's experiences visiting Amantaní which can be used to discuss this further.

Unit 5A Mis estudios y mi trabajo — Overview grid

Spread	Contexts	Skills	Grammar	Vocabulary
Spread title	• Topic areas covered within the unit	• Key skills focus	• Grammar covered in the unit	Key vocabulary
pages 140–141 **Cómo cotillear sobre asignaturas y profesores**	• Chatting about lessons and teachers	• Using a varied vocabulary	• Negatives	las asignaturas, el comportamiento, el horario estupendo/a, insoportable aburrirse, aprobar, comportarse mal, divertirse, suspender me agobia …, (no) me agrada …, (no) me desagrada …, no aguanto/ no soporto …, (no) se me dan bien …, voy bien en …
pages 142–143 **Cómo conversar sobre tu instituto**	• Talking about the facilities in school	• Focussed listening	• Revision of articles	el ambiente, el aula, el edificio, las instalaciones, el patio cubierto, la sala de actos acogedor(a), bien equipado/a, débil, minusválido/a construir, romper abajo, al aire libre
pages 144–145 **Cómo describir tu vida escolar**	• Talking about life at school	• Giving grammatically correct replies	• Numbers	la carpeta, el descanso, el equipo, el inconveniente, la Navidad, (tu propia) ropa, la Semana Santa, el trimestre cansado/a, igual, incómodo/a acabar de …, pertenecer a …, quejarse aún no, cada día
pages 146–147 **Cómo hablar sobre tu paga**	• Talking about pocket money and jobs at home	• Writing and speaking longer sentences	• Revision of inperatives	el aumento, la colada, (algo de) dinero, la paga, las tareas conseguir, estar de acuerdo, estar harto/a, portarse, sacar buenas notas, ser justo/a al mismo tiempo, mientras me dejan, se lo da, (no) se pueden permitir
pages 148–149 **Cómo hablar sobre los trabajos a tiempo parcial**	• Talking about part time jobs	• Improving pronunciation	• Reflexive verbs	el/la aprendiz(a) de peluquería, el camarero, el canguro, las chucherías, la cita, el folleto, el/la dependiente, el/la jefe/a, la obra, el/la repartidor(a), el/la vecino/a ahorrar, arreglarse, cuidar, intentar, maquillarse, repartir en cuanto llego, le hace falta, paga bien, me sienta bien
pages 150–151 **Gramática en acción**	• Reflexive verbs		• Imperative • Articles • Preterite • Adjectives, quantifiers and intensifiers • Reflexive pronouns	
page 152 **Habilidades**	• Developing strategies for timed conversations	• Evaluating your guesses • Reducing the possibilities in multiple choices • Getting marks for answers you don't know • Pronouncing words that look English. • Keeping speaking to avoid more questions • Adding variety to your vocabulary		
page 153 **Escenario**	• Plan a virtual school and discuss working while studying. • Design a game screen about a new virtual school.			
page 154 **Vocabulario**	• Summary of key vocabulary for the unit.			
pages 187–188 **Reading pages**	Students talk about different aspects of school life: • To encourage independent reading and to develop reading strategies. • To provide alternative class and homework material for students who finish other activities quickly.			

5A Mis estudios y mi trabajo

Unit Objectives

Contexts: school, education, pocket money and part-time work

Skills focus: evaluating your guesses, reducing the possibilities in multiple choices, getting marks for answers you don't know, pronouncing words that look English, keeping speaking to avoid more questions, adding variety to your vocabulary

Grammar: using the imperative, articles, the preterite, adjectives, quantifiers and intensifiers, and reflexive pronouns

Controlled assessment opportunities

Writing: Students' Book, page 141, activity 7
Speaking: Students' Book, page 143, activity 8
Writing: Students' Book, page 145, activity 7
Writing: Students' Book, page 147, activity 9
Speaking: Students' Book, page 149, activity 7a

See also *GCSE Spanish for OCR Assessment OxBox CD-ROM*.

An introduction to the unit   página 139

- *Aim*: To introduce the themes of the unit and encourage students to think about the reasons for learning Spanish.
- The opening page is designed with captions, pictures and page cross-references to provide a preview of what is to come:

	Students' Book
Cómo cotillear sobre asignaturas y profesores	page 140
Cómo conversar sobre tu instituto	page 142
Cómo describir tu vida escolar	page 144
Cómo hablar sobre tu paga	page 146
Cómo hablar sobre los trabajos a tiempo parcial	page 148
Gramática en acción – improving your use and understanding of Spanish	page 150
Habilidades – increasing your language skills for fluency	page 152
Escenario – trabajar a tiempo parcial: ¿es bueno o malo? Escenario – ¡promocionar tu nuevo instituto virtual!	page 153

- Allow time for students to read the questions and cross-refer to the relevant pages of the Students' Book. They could do this individually or in pairs / small groups, followed by whole-class discussion.
- This spread also provides an opportunity for students to recap on familiar language. Ask them to think about language they already know that might be useful when working on the themes of the unit.

- Mindmap any language they produce, and if possible, keep it on display as reference as you progress through the unit. It can be added to at intervals as new language becomes familiar.
- At the end of work on the unit, allow time for students to return to this spread and repeat the mind-mapping process, this time including what they have learned over the course of the unit. Get them to answer the questions in their own words, and encourage them to use the results for revision purposes.
- Ask them what they found difficult, interesting etc. What do they think are the important things they have learned in this unit? What do they still need to improve on?
- If time permits, get the students to redesign the page. How would they set it out so it reflects the unit? How would they make it attractive to other learners of their age? How would they make it easy to follow? What would they include in terms of text, pictures, captions, page references? Ask them to imagine they are producing material for next year's class who will be learning the same thing – what would they have found it useful to know?

¿Por qué aprender el español? Para hablar de la vida escolar.

- Students share any experiences they have had of education in another country e.g. on an exchange, visiting a relative.
- Ask them to consider what sort of language they would need to describe their school and its daily life to a young person in a Spanish speaking country.

Cómo cotillear sobre asignaturas y profesores

páginas 140 y 141

Planner

> ### Objectives
> - Chatting about lessons and teachers

> ### Resources
> Students' Book, pages 140–141
> CD 3, track 25
> Grammar Workbook, page 57
> Activity sheets 57–60

> ### Key language
> *las asignaturas, el comportamiento, el horario*
> *estupendo/a, insoportable*
> *aburrirse, aprobar, comportarse mal, divertirse,*
> *suspender*
> *me agobia..., (no) me agrada..., (no) me*
> *desagrada..., no aguanto/no soporto..., (no) se me*
> *dan bien..., voy bien en...*

> ### Skills
> - Using a varied vocabulary

> ### Grammar
> - Negatives

> ### PLTS
> Students' Book, page 141, activity 6,
> *Team Workers*
> Students' Book, page 141, activity 7,
> *Creative Thinkers*

> ### Starters
> - Brainstorm school vocabulary in small groups.
>   Students write down anything they can
>   remember from previous learning and group
>   the words appropriately – subjects, uniform,
>   opinions, buildings and facilities etc.

- Students look at the pictures on page 140 and
  decide which subjects the teachers deliver.
  They write down a brief prediction about each
  teacher, and see if they were right after reading
  Miguel's comments later in the spread.
- Explain what *3° Educación Secundaria
  Obligatoria (ESO)* means, and how the Spanish
  system works. Draw up two tables side by side
  to show how the British and Spanish systems.
- Students' Book, page 141, activity 3. Run
  a prediction "sweepstake" before doing the
  listening activity.

> ### Plenaries
> - What makes a good teacher? In pairs or small
>   groups students draw up a definition of a good
>   and bad teacher. Tell them they must describe
>   the teacher's qualities, not name them! They
>   read out or pass round their definitions, and
>   must be prepared to defend them if others
>   disagree.
> - Students' Book, page 141, activity 6. Class
>   challenge. Ask any students the questions and
>   they have to reply against the clock.
> - Play opinions Pairs. On one set of cards
>   students write down all the subjects, on another
>   the opinons words from activities 4 & 5. When
>   they turn over a subject and an opinion they
>   have of that subject, they keep the cards. This
>   can be made more difficult for more able
>   students by having half a sentence written out
>   on each card, and they have to match them by
>   checking the adjectival agreements.
> - Students' Book, page 141, activity 7. Students
>   correct the false statements made in the
>   paragraphs written by others in the class.

---

1 **¿Qué asignatura es? Lee *¿Quién habla?* en la página 140
y encuentra las parejas. ¡Atención! Dos asignaturas tienen
más de una repuesta.**

- Students match the subjects to the *¿Quién habla?*
  statements. Some subjects have more than one
  answer.

Answers: **a** 3, **b** 6, **c** 2, **d** 1, **e** 7, 10, **f** 4, 9, **g** 8, **h** 5

4–8

2a **Lee lo que dice Miguel. ¿Qué asignaturas enseñan los
profesores de la página anterior?**

- Students read Miguel's comments and decide what
  the teachers pictured on the previous page teach.

Answers: **Ardiel Ventura** Matemáticas **Clara Suarez** Inglés,
Ignacio Velazquez Ciencias sociales

5–8

2b **Lee las frases. ¿Verdaderas, falsas o no se menciona?**

- Students decide if the sentences are True (V),
  False (F) or Not Mentioned (NM).

Answers: **1** F, **2** NM, **3** V, **4** V, **5** F

4–8

2c **Corrige las frases falsas.**

- Students correct the incorrect sentences.

Answers: **1** Las clases del profesor de ciencias sociales son
aburridas. **5** Las matemáticas se le dan bien.

4–7

3a Escucha. ¿Qué dicen sobre sus asignaturas? Rellena la tabla.

- Students listen to what the different people say about their school subjects and complete the table.

5–8

CD 3, track 25   **página 141, actividad 3**

Sara	Soy muy deportista así que mi asignatura favorita es la educación física, además me llevo muy bien con Merche, la profesora. La asignatura que menos me gusta es la literatura porque no me gusta nada leer y además la profe nos pone muchos deberes.
Josema	Soy bastante bueno con los números así que me gustan las mates sin embargo, aunque me gusta mucho escuchar reggaeton, en el colegio no me gusta nada la música porque los instrumentos que hay son muy aburridos y me llevo fatal con el profesor que además es mi tutor. ¡Qué mala suerte!
Silvi	Me encantan los idiomas porque mi padre es francés y mi madre es italiana pero no soy para nada artística y todo lo que tenga que ver con crear arte se me da fatal y en el instituto odio el arte.
Moisés	Me gustan todas mis asignaturas, particularmente las ciencias naturales porque la profesora es muy guapa y simpática. Quizás la que me gusta menos es la tecnología porque el profesor es demasiado estricto.

Answers:

nombre	asignaturas	opinión	información adicional
Sara	Educación física Literatura	Asignatura favorita No le gusta	Se lleva bien con la profe No le gusta leer, muchos deberes
Josema	Mates Música	Le gustan No le gusta nada	Bueno con números Instrumentos aburridos, se lleva mal con el profesor, el profesor es su tutor
Silvi	Idiomas Arte	Le encantan Odia	Padre francés, madre italiana Se le da fatal, no es artística
Moisés	Ciencias naturales Tecnología	Asignatura favorita Le gusta menos	Profesora guapa y simpática El profesor es muy estricto

3b Compara tus respuestas de la actividad 3a con el horario de la página anterior. Escribe una frase para cada estudiante: explica cuál es su día preferido y por qué. Escucha otra vez si es necesario.

4–8

- Students compare their answers to 3a to the timetable on page 140. They write a sentence for each student saying what their favourite day is and why. They listen again if necessary.

Answers:

Sara: martes (not *viernes* because she doesn't like *literatura*)

Josema: lunes y miercoles (not *viernes* because he doesn't like *música*)

Silvi: lunes y viernes (not *jueves* because she doesn't like *arte*)

Moisés: miércoles y viernes (not *lunes* or *martes* because he doesn't like *tecnología*)

4 ¿Qué significan en inglés estas opiniones?

4–7

- What do these opinions mean in English?

Answers:

Me interesa *I am interested by … or X interest(s) me*

Me fascina *I am fascinated by … or X fascinate(s) me*

Me apasiona *I am passionate about …*

Me agrada *I am pleased by … or X please(s) me*

Me atrae(n) *I am attracted by … or X attract(s) me*

No aguanto/No soporto *I can't stand …*

Me desagrada(n) *I dislike …*

Me aburre(n) *I am bored by … or X bore(s) me*

Me agobia(n) *I am annoyed by … or X annoy(s) me*

No me importa(n) *I don't care about …*

5a Empareja los contrarios. Utiliza un diccionario si es necesario.

4–7

- Students match up the opposite opinions.

Answers: inútil – útil, agradable – desagradable, antipático – simpático, insoportable – soportable, monótono – entretenido, tolerante – estricto

5b Expresa la misma idea utilizando la forma negatira y el adjetivo contrario.

4–7

- Students use negatives to write sentences that mean the same thing.

Answers: **1** Las matemáticas no son inútiles. **2** La profesora de inglés no es agradable. **3** Las clases de historia no son monótonas. **4** Los deberes de ciencias no son soportables.

Remate

6 In two minutes, try to memorise the vocabulary from activities 4 and 5a. With a partner, take turns to ask these questions, in any order.

PLTS
● Students can compete using a scoring system.

Success criteria activity 6:
● *students communicate effectively and accurately*
● *students express personal opinions and justify points of view*
● *students use a variety of vocabulary and structures*
● *students deal with unpredictable elements*

4–9

7 Write a paragraph about your teachers and subjects. Use your new vocabulary and link your sentences.

PLTS
● Students can do this anonymously for others to guess who the author is, or they can play the True / False game, and the others have to decide if what they have written is the truth.

4–9

Success criteria activity 7:
● *students give information accurately and in the appropriate style*
● *students express personal opinions and justify points of view*
● *students use a variety of vocabulary and structures*

Cómo conversar sobre tu instituto
páginas 142 y 143

Planner

➤ **Objectives**
● Talking about the facilities in school

➤ **Resources**
Students' Book, pages 142–143
CD 3, tracks 26–27
Grammar Workbook, pages 5–6
Activity sheets 57–60

➤ **Key language**
el ambiente, el aula, el edificio, las instalaciones, el patio cubierto, la sala de actos
acogedor(a), bien equipado/a, débil, minusválido/a
construir, romper
abajo, al aire libre

➤ **Skills**
● Focussed listening

➤ **Grammar**
● Revision of articles

➤ **PLTS**
Students' Book, page 143, activity 7,
Effective Participators
Students' Book, page 143, activity 8,
Creative Thinkers

➤ **Starters**
● Look at the photos of the school on page 142, and compare it with the students' own. If possible have a couple of photos of their school available too. In class build up a list of words that describe both schools. Keep these for reference later on in the spread.

● Students' Book, page 143, activity 4a. Before listening to what Alex says, ask students to complete the sentences for their school. Point out adjectival agreement endings in preparation for the listening activity.
● Students' Book, page 143, activity 7. Predict Soraya's answers; in class compile a list (in Spanish) of what students guess her school will be like. Check your predictions against the fact after listening to activity 7.
● Students' Book, page 143, activity 8. Brainstorm in class or small groups ideas for your ideal secondary school.

➤ **Plenaries**
● Students' Book, page 142, activity 3. Tell students to find all the phrases expressing an opinion in the email, and to make them negative e.g. *tiene buenas instalaciones – no tiene buenas instalaciones / tiene malas instalaciones*.
● Students' Book, page 143, activity 7. Give students a copy of the transcript and ask them to pick out phrases they can use, perhaps with adaptation, to describe their own school (e.g. they might need to make a positive sentence negative, or change *grande* to *pequeño* etc.)
● Students' Book, page 143, activity 8. Students vote on the presentations. The class or a panel of judges drawn from it can mark their presentation on length, content, fluency, accuracy and justification of ideas.
● Research a secondary school in another part of the world. Students can pick a country at random and see what they can find out e.g. on the internet, or if they have any experience such as via an exchange programme, they can draw on that. The research can be presented in oral or written form.

1   Copia y completa el email con los artículos que faltan.

*   Students copy out and complete the email with the missing articles. Do the first one or two gaps as a class so they understand what is being looked for.

5–8

Answers:
¡Hola Alex!

Te envío **[unas]** fotos de mi nuevo instituto que se llama Ben Arabi. Es **[un]** instituto mixto con quinientos alumnos de ESO y otros doscientos de Bachillerato. **[El]** edificio es grande y moderno porque se construyó hace sólo cuatro años así que tiene buenas instalaciones particularmente si te gusta **[el]** deporte.

Hay canchas de tenis y de baloncesto y además tenemos dos campos de fútbol. **[El]** gimnasio también es muy grande y está bien equipado. No tenemos piscina pero **[la]** piscina pública del pueblo está a cinco minutos así que no importa.

En Ben Arabi hay veinte aulas normales, **[un]** laboratorio para los experimentos de ciencias, **[una]** sala de ordenadores, **[una]** biblioteca bastante espaciosa con **[la]** sala de profesores al lado y **[la]**sala de actos que es enorme. Por desgracia **[la]** sala de ordenadores siempre está llena y aunque tiene treinta ordenadores, es muy difícil encontrar uno libre durante **[el]** recreo o **[el]** almuerzo.

[La] cantina es acogedora y **[la]** comida no está mal pero es un poco cara. También tenemos **[un]** patio cubierto y otro al aire libre con mesas y bancos para relajarnos durante **[el]** recreo. En Ben Arabi hay dos ascensores y aseos especiales porque está acondicionado para estudiantes minusválidos.

[La] verdad es que me encanta **[el]** instituto porque **[el]** ambiente es muy distinto al mi colegio de antes. ¡Creo que a ti también te gustaría!

Rosa

2   Haz una lista con las instalaciones que se mencionan en el email de Rosa. ¿Qué significan?

*   Students list and translate all the facilities mentioned.

5–8

Answers: **canchas de baloncesto** – basketball courts, **dos campos de fútbol** – two football pitches, **un gimnasio** – a gym, **una piscina pública** – public swimming pool, **aulas normales** – normal classrooms, **un laboratorio** – a laboratory, **una sala de ordenadores** – ICT room, **una biblioteca** – a library, **una sala de profesores** – a staffroom, **una sala de actos** – an (assembly) hall, **una cantina** – a dinner hall / canteen, **un patio cubierto** –

indoors playground (chill out area), **un patio al aire libre** – outdoors playground (chill out area), **ascensores** – lifts, **aseos especiales** – disabled toilets

3   Lee el email y contesta a las preguntas en inglés.

*   Students read the completed email and answer the questions in English. Students can make notes and give the answers orally in class.

5–9

Answers: **a** 700, **b** big and modern, built 4 years ago, **c** very good – there are tennis and basket ball courts, football pitches and a well-equipped gym **d** there is a public pool a few minutes away **e** it is always very busy, there are no free computers at break or lunch, **f** if it rains they can use the covered playground, if the weather is good they can go outside **g** disabled students **h** very much; the atmosphere is very different to her previous school

4a   Escucha lo que dice Alex sobre su instituto. Completa las frases con las palabras en el recuadro de abajo.
Grammar reference page 150

*   Listen to Alex talking about his school and complete the sentences.

5–8

 CD 3, track 26   página 143, actividad 4

1 Voy a un instituto público situado en el norte de Londres. Está bastante lejos de mi casa así que voy en metro o a veces me lleva mi padre en coche. El instituto no es pequeño pero es sólo para chicos …

2 Hay tres edificios donde están las aulas, la biblioteca, los laboratorios. ¡Vaya! Ya sabes … lo normal. En el edificio principal hay la recepción, la oficina del director, y los de cuarto de ESO pero es un bloque pequeño.

3 Las instalaciones de deporte no son muy buenas y solamente tenemos una cancha asfaltada que sirve para todo: baloncesto, fútbol, voleibol, footing … o sea, todo. También tenemos un gimnasio pero es igual de triste.

4 Por suerte las instalaciones de informática no están nada mal porque tenemos dos aulas con treinta ordenadores cada una y hay diez ordenadores más en la biblioteca. Todos están disponibles media hora antes del colegio, durante el almuerzo y por la tarde hasta las seis pero no durante el recreo porque están reservados para los de cuarto de ESO.

Answers: **1** bastante grande, mixto **2** no es grande **3** pobres **4** muy buenas

4b **Escucha otra vez y contesta a las preguntas en inglés.**

- Students listen again and answer the questions in English. Point out the Exam tip box, and tell students to pay particular attention to how much each question is worth.

4–9

Answers: **1** (2) By tube/sometimes by car with dad, **2** (3) Reception/head's office/year 4 of ESO, **3** (1) Tarmac pitch used for everything, **4** (3) Half hour before school/during lunch/after school until 6pm.

5 **Jugad a 'El rival más débil' y contestad a las preguntas.**

- Explain the rules to the class:
  - Work in small groups to answer the questions.
  - Each group member takes it in turns to add an element to the sentence.

4–9

  - Five coherent elements per question mean a completed chain.
  - If an element is not coherent, is repeated or the group member takes more than ten seconds in responding, the chain is broken. And the team must move on to the next question.
  - At the end of the round the team members must vote for the weakest link, and begin again until there is a winner.

This could be done as a whole class activity or in smaller groups where an able child acts as arbitrator and asks the questions and rejects answers. This could be done as a whole class activity or in smaller groups where an able child acts as arbitrator and asks the questions and rejects answers. Another child can be given the task of timing the group if appropriate. If done in teams, the winners could compete against each other. The activity is based in the game show "The Weakest link" and aims at students practising and extending their sentences and improvising Accept any answers that would make reasonable sense, expecting able groups to come up with full sentences with a verb (1 Hay un gimnasio, 2 es grande, 3 está bien equipado ... etc.) and less able groups to extend the original sentence (1 Hay un gimnasio, 2 una cantina grande, 3 una sala de profesores verde ... etc)

6 **Escribe una descripción de tu instituto.**

- Students write a description of their own school.

4–9

Remate

7 **Listen and answer the questions in English.**

- Again, tell students to be careful of how many points each question is worth.

PLTS

 CD 3, track 27   **página 143, actividad 7**

¡Hola! Me llamo Soraya y os voy a hablar de mi instituto. Mi instituto se llama San Juan Baptista de la Salle y está situado a las afueras de la ciudad de Cancún, en Méjico. Hay 1.200 chicos y chicas de 12 a 16 años.

Hay 4 edificios muy viejos y en las aulas a veces se oye mucho ruido del tráfico porque hay algunas ventanas rotas. Las aulas son cómodas y espaciosas y las instalaciones deportivas son estupendas porque tenemos mucho espacio, no como los institutos del centro de la ciudad. Por desgracia no puedo decir lo mismo de las instalaciones de informática ... No son muy buenas y solo tenemos dos aulas con unos 50 ordenadores muy viejos para 1.200 estudiantes y además solo una de las aulas tiene conexión a internet. La biblioteca no está mal y a menudo me quedo después del instituto y hago los deberes allí. En cuanto a la cantina... bueno, sólo hay comida fría y dulces pero la mayoría de estudiantes traen un bocadillo de casa porque las familias de mi vecindario son más bien pobres. En fin, lo importante no son las instalaciones, los ordenadores, la comida de la cantina y esas cosas... lo importante es tener una educación. Muchos de mis amigos no asisten a clase porque tienen que trabajar o ayudar en la casa.

Answers: **1** In the outskirts of Cancún in Mexico. **2** It is mixed. **3** 1.200 **4** They are old/broken windows **5** Comfortable/spacious **6** Great/they have a lot of space **7** In only one **8** She does her homework **9** There is cold food/sweets **10** To have an education

Success criteria activity 7:

- *students communicate effectively and accurately*
- *students express personal opinions and justify points of view*
- *students use a variety of vocabulary and structures*
- *students deal with unpredictable elements*
- *students use different tenses or time frames*

8 **Imagine your ideal secondary school or college.**

PLTS

- Students must give reasons for their decisions where possible. If they prefer, they can set the school in an alternate reality – science fiction, costume drama, the far future, a submarine world etc. Decide if they need to use the present tense: *está / es / hay / tiene* or the conditional tense: *estaría / sería / habría / tendría*

4–9

Success criteria activity 8:

- *students give information accurately and in the appropriate style*
- *students express personal opinions and justify points of view*
- *students use a variety of vocabulary and structures*
- *students use different tenses or time frames*

Cómo describir tu vida escolar

páginas 144 y 145

Planner

➤ Objectives
- Talking about life at school

➤ Resources
Students' Book, pages 144–145
CD 3, track 28
Grammar Workbook, page 72
Activity sheets 57–60

➤ Key language
la carpeta, el descanso, el equipo, el inconveniente, la Navidad, (tu propia) ropa, la Semana Santa, el trimestre
cansado/a, igual, incómodo/a
acabar de ..., pertenecer a ..., quejarse
aún no, cada día

➤ Skills
- Giving grammatically correct replies

➤ Grammar
- Numbers

➤ PLTS
Students' Book, page 144, activity 1,
Effective Participators
Students' Book, page 145, activity 7,
Independent Enquirers

➤ Starters
- Students' Book, page 144, activity 1. Do the comparison activity as a whole class to introduce the idea of differences in school life. Elicit phrases or sentences in Spanish from the students, and make a note of them for use further on in the spread.

- Students look at the photos on page 144 and describe in Spanish what they can see there. Say if these are likely to be in this country or Spain.
- Students' Book, page 144, activity 4. Students predict what they think Alicia's answers are likely to be. Remind them to check the adjectival agreements. When they have done the listening, they can check to see how accurate they were.
- Students' Book, page 145, activities 6 & 7. Brainstorm in class arguments for and against long summer holidays versus half term breaks. They can use these in the Remate activities.

➤ Plenaries
- Students' Book, page 144, activity 2. Can the students think of any other arguments for and against uniform? Can they spot the flaws in any of the arguments? Hold a class debate; two teams prepare arguments for and against (not necessarily what they believe personally), and then vote on whether to abolish uniform or not.
- Students' Book, page 144, activity 3. Students adapt the phrases and describe their own school.
- Students' Book, page 145, activity 5. Students find all the quantifiers and intensifiers in the chatlines, and use them in their own examples about school. As ever, the more absurd the example, the more likely they are to remember it.
- Students' Book, page 145, activities 6 & 7. If the school has a partner school in Spain, students can debate the merits of uniform and long school holidays directly with their Spanish counterparts.

---

1 El horario escolar de la página 140 pertenece a un estudiante español de 15 años. Míralo. ¿Qué diferencias hay con tu horario? Compara.

- Students compare the timetable on page 140 with their own. This can be done in pairs or as a whole class.

4–9

2 Lee las frases y clasifica las ideas como 'Lleva uniforme' o 'No lleva uniforme'.

- Students read the sentences and classify them.

Answers: **Lleva uniforme** – 1, 3, 5, 6
No lleva uniforme – 2, 4, 7

4–7

3 Empareja estas frases con los dibujos.

4–6

- Students match the sentences to the pictures. Draw the students' attention to the Habilidades box below the activities before they begin, reminding them about adjectival agreements.

Answers: **1** b, **2** g, **3** f, **4** a, **5** e, **6** c, **7** i, **8** j

4 Alicia visitó un colegio en el norte de Londres recientemente. Escucha lo que dice y completa las frases con un adjetivo de la caja (sobran dos).

- Listen to Alicia describing her visit to a London school and complete the sentences.

5-9

🔊 **CD 3, track 28**   **página 144, actividad 4**

¡Hola! Soy Alicia y estoy en cuarto de ESO aquí en Cartagena en el Sur de España. En marzo estuve en Londres con el colegio y allí visitamos un instituto de secundaria donde fuimos emparejados con estudiantes ingleses y fuimos a sus clases con ellos. Fue una experiencia fantástica y al mismo tiempo sorprendente porque hay muchas diferencias. Me sorprendió que los estudiantes tengan que llevar uniforme que no parece muy cómodo y protestan llevando las corbatas muy cortas, las camisas fuera de los pantalones y calcetines por encima de las rodillas. Aquí en España sólo se lleva uniforme en los colegios privados.

También me asombró que los alumnos cambien de aula para cada asignatura mientras que aquí son los profesores los que van de aula en aula y nosotros no nos movemos. La segunda clase que tuve cocina. ¡Sí, cocina! Para nosotros la cocina no existe como asignatura ni tampoco la informática que aprendemos en clubs extraescolares no como allí que está integrada en el horario.

El instituto que visitamos es muy antiguo y las aulas están muy viejas, además hay mucho chicle en los suelos y pintadas en las paredes. Eso sí, las instalaciones deportivas dan envidia porque tienen mucho espacio y es todo muy verde.

Answers: **a** fenomenal, **b** incómodo, **c** públicos, **d** sorprendente, **e** viejo, **f** buenas

5a Busca los números que se mencionan en el chat. Escríbelos en español, en inglés y explica a qué hacen referencia.

- Students look for the numbers mentioned in the chatlines.

Answers: **ocho y media** – half past eight – when his after school club ends, **dieciocho euros** – 18€ – how much the club costs, **ciento treinta y seis euros** – 136€ – how much his school books have cost this year, **siete de enero** – 7th January – when the new term starts after Christmas holiday, **una semana** – one week – the length of the Easter holiday, **tres meses** – three months – the length of the summer holiday, **las cinco** – five o'clock – the time his primary school finished every day, **sobre las tres** – three o'clock – approximate time he eats lunch at home, **quince minutos** – fifteen minutes – how long the bus journey from school to home takes

5-8

5b Busca en el chat: *a little tired, costs a lot, she is very pretty, quite good reputation, it's better, too far.*

- Students find the phrases in the chatlines.

Answers: **1** un poco cansado, **2** cuesta mucho, **3** Es guapísima, **4** bastante buena reputación, **5** es mucho mejor, **6** demasiado lejos

5-8

5c Ahora busca: *I have just arrived, in addition to, besides Christmas, about three o'clock.*

Answers: **1** acabo de llegar, **2** además de, **3** aparte de la Navidad, **4** sobre las tres

Remate

6 Jorge is online and wants to have a conversation with you. Answer his questions.

- Students should write in correct Spanish, but not necessarily in formal complete sentences.

4-9

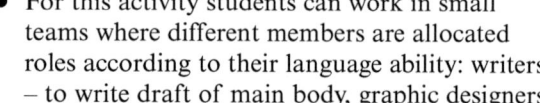

7 Choose one of the titles below and write an article for the school magazine. You should aim to write more than 100 words in any format you like, and include at least one illustration.

PLTS

- For this activity students can work in small teams where different members are allocated roles according to their language ability: writers – to write draft of main body, graphic designers – to design a title and provide illustrations, proofreaders – to work with writers to correct language (but following the lead of less able writers) and editors – to set final look of article and assist with ideas. Where possible, this activity would work better in an ICT classroom. Possible formats: interview with contrasting parts, results of a research study, a parent's account, a student's account, a promotional campaign ... etc.

4-9

Success criteria activities 6 & 7:
- *students give information accurately and in the appropriate style*
- *students express personal opinions and justify points of view*
- *students use a variety of vocabulary and structures*
- *students use different tenses or time frames*

Cómo hablar sobre tu paga

Planner

➤ **Objectives**
- Talking about pocket money and jobs at home

➤ **Resources**
Students' Book, pages 146–147
CD 3, tracks 29–30
Grammar Workbook, page 62
Activity sheets 57–60

➤ **Key language**
el aumento, la colada, (algo de) dinero, la paga,
las tareas
conseguir, estar de acuerdo, estar harto/a, portarse,
sacar buenas notas, ser justo/a
al mismo tiempo, mientras
me dejan, se lo da, (no) se pueden permitir

➤ **Skills**
- Writing and speaking longer sentences

➤ **Grammar**
- Revision of imperatives

➤ **PLTS**
Students' Book, page 146, activity 3,
Reflective Learners
Students' Book, page 147, activity 9,
Creative Thinkers

➤ **Starters**
- After doing activity 1a, ask students how much money they get and if they have to do any jobs to earn it. If this is likely to be a sensitive issue, turn it into a True / False activity where others have to decide if the speaker's claims of being overworked and underpaid are real or not.

- Play "I Went To The Market" with chores. The first student says *Para conseguir dinero, tengo que arreglar mi dormitorio*, and the second says *Para conseguir dinero, tengo que arreglar mi dormitorio y pasear el perro*, and so on round the class. How long can you make the chain?
- Students' Book, page 146, activity 1b. Play prediction Bingo. Students fill in the grid for questions 2, 3, 4 & 5 with a prediction of their choice for each person. They listen, and each time they guess correctly, they get a point. Then they do activity 1b, listening for the actual information.
- Students' Book, page 147, activity 8. In class, discuss the type of answers they will need to listen out for e.g. **a** an amount of money.

➤ **Plenaries**
- Students' Book, page 146, activity 1b. Give students a copy of the transcript. They swap books with a partner and mark each other's work.
- Students' Book, page 146, activity 1. *¿Es justo?* Ask the students if they think the pocket money / jobs exchange described by the people in 1a and 1b is fair or not, and why. They can work in pairs or small groups to make their decisions.
- Students' Book, page 146, activity 2. Tell the students to put themselves in their parents' shoes, and write a series of post-it notes like the ones to Joaquín. What would their parents tell them to do?
- Students' Book, page 147, activity 4. Give the students various words and phrases in English and tell them to find these in Luz's email e.g. *I'm fed up, it's not fair, every afternoon* etc. They can use these later in the spread.

1a Lee lo que dicen estos jóvenes y contesta a las preguntas sobre cada persona. Mira el ejemplo de Elisa.

- Students read about the four people and answer the questions for each one.

Answers:

4–9

1	Elisa	Alberto	Celia	Juanjo
2	30€	20€		15€
3	sus padres	su abuela		sus padres
4	pasear el perro / sacar la basura	ayudar a su madre con sus hermanos / preparar el desayuno	lavar los platos todos los días / pasar la aspiradora los sábados	arreglar su dormitorio / lavar la coche de su padre / ayudar a su madre con la colada / pasar el polvo / vaciar el lavaplatos
5	cine / ropa	salir con amigos	ropa / música y salir con sus amigos	gasolina para su moto
6		son seis hermanos / sus padres no se lo pueden permitir darle dinero	los padres pagan todo	piensa que no es justo lo que tiene que hacer

1b Ahora escucha a cuatro jóvenes más. Contesta a las preguntas de la actividad 1a.

- Students answer the questions for four more people. A grid may be the easiest way to collect the answers.

4–9

 CD 3, track 29   **página 146, actividad 1b**

Susana	Vivo con mis tíos porque está más cerca del instituto. Tengo que cuidar a mi primo de tres años dos tardes por semana mientras mi tía va al gimnasio y recibo 25€ que luego gasto en ir de comprar con mis amigas.
Florentina	Mi madre trabaja así que tengo que ayudar con las tareas de la casa y luego ella me da 35€ por semana. Los gasto en CDs, DVDs y libros.
David	Mis padres están divorciados y mi padre ahora vive en Sudamérica así que casi no le veo nunca, pero mi madre me da 20€ los viernes. No tengo que hacer nada en casa, mi trabajo es estudiar y sacar buenas notas. Gasto mi dinero en juegos de ordenador.
Simón	Soy un poco rebelde y he tenido algunos problemillas en el instituto. Ahora mi madre me da 5€ cada día pero sólo si ni mi tutor ni ningún profesor le llama con historias de que me porté mal, no hice los deberes o suspendí algún examen. Cuando tengo dinero lo gasto en ropa o música.

Answers:

1	Susana	Florentina	David	Simón
2	25€	35€	20€	5€ (cada día)
3	su tía	su madre	su madre	su madre
4	cuidar a su primo	ayudar con las tareas de la casa	estudiar/sacar buenas notas	no tener problemas en el instituto
5	ir de compras con sus amigas	CDs/DVDs/ libros	juegos de ordenador	ropa o música
6	vive con tíos	su madre trabaja	padres divorciados/ padre vive en Sudamérica	

2 Lee esta nota. Copia las frases y complétalas con los imperativos del recuadro.

- Students complete the imperatives. Tell them to look back at Unit 4B to remind them how they are formed.

4–6

Answers: **2** pasea, **3** saca, **4** lava, **5** cuida, **6** plancha, **7** haz, **8** no suspendas

3a ¿Qué debe hacer Joaquín para conseguir su paga? Utiliza tus respuestas de la actividad anterior.

- Students re-write what Joaquín has to do in the third person. *Tiene que* and *debe* can be used interchangeably.

4–7

Answers: **2** Joaquín tiene que pasear el perro. **3** Tiene que sacar la basura. **4** Tiene que lavar los platos. **5** Debe cuidar a su hermano. **6** Tiene que planchar la ropa. **7** Debe hacer sus deberes. No tiene que suspender sus exámenes / tiene que aprobar sus exámenes.

3b Ahora convierte tus respuestas de la actividad anterior en un párrafo. Utiliza conectores y añade adverbios de tiempo.

PLTS

- Students use the connectors to turn the answers to 3a into a paragraph. There are various ways of doing this.

5–8

4a Lee el email de Luz y las afirmaciones de abajo. ¿Son verdaderas o falsas?

- Students read Luz's email and decide if the statements are True (V) or False (F).

5–8

Answers: **1** F, **2** V, **3** F, **4** F, **5** F, **6** F, **7** V, **8** V

4b Corrige las afirmaciones falsas.

- Students correct the false statements.

5–8

Answers: **1** Luz cree que sus padres son injustos. **3** Esta semana Luz preparó el desayuno todos los días. **4** Luz paseó al perro todas las tardes. **5** Luz cocinó dos noches. **6** Luz cree que 20€ a la semana no es suficiente dinero.

5 Busca los verbos en el pretérito del email de Luz. ¿Qué significan?

- Students look for the preterite verbs used by Luz and write down what they mean.

Answers: **fui** a buscar – I went to meet (ir), **hice** – I made (hacer), **puse** la mesa – I set the table (poner), **lavé** – I washed (lavar)

5–8

6 Responde el email de Luz. Contesta a todas sus preguntas.

- Students reply to Luz, answering her questions with their thoughts and experiences.

5–8

7 Túrnate con un(a) compañero/a para preguntar y contestar. Sigue los consejos del recuadro de Habilidades y alarga tus respuestas.

- Go through some examples in class first as to how to give longer responses, then do the activity in pairs. Volunteers can perform their conversation, and be awarded points for how well they extend their answers.

4–9

Remate

8 Listen to Iván and answer the questions.

- Remind students of the listening techniques they have covered previously such as predicting type of answers, writing abbreviated notes, listening for detail etc.

5–9

 CD 3, track 30   **página 147, actividad 8**

Hola, me llamo Iván y voy hablaros de mi paga. Mis padres normalmente me dan 20€ a la semana aunque algunas veces me dan un poquito más si hago alguna tarea extra. Tengo que arreglar mi dormitorio y también debo poner la mesa y lavar los platos después de cenar pero no me importa hacer tareas a cambio de mi paga porque mis padres trabajan y no tienen mucho tiempo. Generalmente con mis 20€ voy al cine el viernes por la tarde y el sábado voy a cenar un bocadillo o una pizza en alguna cafetería con mis amigos, aunque esta semana no puedo salir porque gasté mi dinero en una camiseta bastante cara.

Answers: **a** 20€ a la semana, **b** sus padres, **c** arreglar su dormitorio, poner la mesa, lavar los platos, **d** sí, sus padres trabajan, **e** va al cine, el sábado cena un bocadillo o una pizza en alguna cafetería con sus amigos **f** gastó su dinero en una camiseta bastante cara

9 Look at the comic strip and write a passage about the character's pocket money situation. Refer back to activities 1a and 4a for help with ideas and sentence structures you can use.

PLTS

- Students can write as if adding caption explanations to the cartoon frames, including appropriate speech bubbles.

Success criteria activities 8 & 9:

4–9

- *students give information accurately and in the appropriate style*
- *students express personal opinions and justify points of view*
- *students use a variety of vocabulary and structures*
- *students use different tenses or time frames*

Cómo hablar sobre los trabajos a tiempo parcial
páginas 148 y 149

Planner

➤ **Objectives**
- Talking about part time jobs

➤ **Resources**
Students' Book, pages 148–149
CD 3, tracks 31–33
Grammar Workbook, page 37
Activity sheets 57–60

➤ **Key language**
el/la aprendiz(a) de peluquería, el camarero, el canguro, las chucherías, la cita, el folleto, el/la dependiente, el/la jefe/a, la obra, el/la repartidor(a), el/la vecino/a
ahorrar, arreglarse, cuidar, intentar, maquillarse, repartir
en cuanto llego, le hace falta, paga bien, me sienta bien

➤ **Skills**
- Improving pronunciation

➤ **Grammar**
- Reflexive verbs

➤ **PLTS**
Students' Book, page 149, activity 5,
Independent Enquirers
Students' Book, page 149, activity 7,
Team Workers

➤ **Starters**
- Students' Book, page 148, activity 1. Can students think of any jobs other than the ones listed here? Set a time limit, and brainstorm in small groups. Which of these can people of their age do part time?

- Students' Book, page 148, activity 1b. How would students describe, in Spanish, the jobs pictured? Listen, and see how close they were to the text.
- Students' Book, page 148, activity 2a. Divide the class into three, and each section take one person. They write down anything they understand about the text before looking at the questions. Then they do activity 2. After, decide if those who pre-discussed Sofía's text, for example, found it easier to answer her questions than those for the others. The aim is to emphasise the value of reading through a text before beginning to answer any related questions.
- Students' Book, page 149, activity 7a. Give a profile (in English) of a young person e.g. They work in a shop on Saturday from 8:30 – 16:00, earning £3:00 an hour etc. With the class work through how they would answer the questions at 6a, and how they could make them longer and more interesting. Then students work on 7a with a partner.

➤ **Plenaries**

- Students' Book, page 149, activity 3. Reflexive verbs quiz. The teacher asks questions based on the reflexive verbs in the activity 2a reading passages such as *What is the infinitive of me acuesto? How do you say "he wakes up"?* Students compete in pairs or small groups like a pub quiz. They can be givena few minutes to look back at the Grammar section for reflexive verbs first.
- Students' Book, page 149, activity 4. Students read out the paragraph they wrote from the prompts, firstly to a partner who listens to their pronunciation and corrects it. Students can then take part in a class "Strictly Speaking Spanish Competition", where the aim is to sound as authentic as possible. A panel of judges can award marks for pronunciation, fluency, accent etc. a bit like "Strictly Come Dancing".
- Students' Book, page 149, activity 5. Students can share their comments as described by picking a name or number out of a hat, and "passing the discussion on" to that person.
- Students' Book, page 149, activity 6b. Students mark each others answers in English, paying particular attention to if all the details have been given e.g. **two** things she does at work in question 2.

1a   Empareja los trabajos con los dibujos.

- Students match the pictures to the jobs.

Answers: **1** h, **2** d, **3** g, **4** c, **5** e, **6** b, **7** f, **8** a

4–6

1b   Escucha. ¿Cuál es su trabajo? Escribe la letra adecuada.

- Students listen and note down the correct letter of the picture for the job mentioned.

4–7

🎧 **CD 3, track 31**	**página 148, actividad 1b**

1   Trabajo por las tardes después de clases. Ayudo a mi tío en el garaje donde trabaja.

2   Trabajo los sábados en la cafetería de la plaza del mercado. Sirvo a los clientes y limpio las mesas.

3   Cuido a los niños de una señora dos noches por semana cuando ella sale con sus amigas.

4   Mi vecina ha suspendido dos asignaturas. Le doy clases de repaso dos veces a la semana.

5   Trabajo los sábados por la mañana en una panadería.

6   Reparto folletos publicitarios para un restaurante de comida rápida.

7   Trabajo tres tardes por semana en el consultorio de un pediatra donde contesto el teléfono y hago pasar a los clientes según sus citas.

8   Los sábados por la mañana ayudo a mi hermana en su salón. Lavo el pelo de los clientes y barro el suelo.

Answers: **1** b, **2** c, **3** d, **4** e, **5** g, **6** h, **7** a, **8** f

2a   Lee lo que dicen estos jóvenes. ¿Cuál de los jóvenes …?

- Students read the descriptions and match the people to the questions.

Answers: 1 Oscar, **2** Sofía, **3** Oscar, **4** Rubén, **5** Sofía

5–8

2b   Lee de nuevo lo que dicen los jóvenes y contesta a las preguntas para Rubén y Oscar. Mira el ejemplo de Sofía.

- Students re-read the descriptions and answer the questions for Rubén and Oscar.

5–8   *Answers:*

	Rubén	**Oscar**
1	Repartidor	Obrero
2	afuera	afuera
3	06:00 a 08:00 durante semana, 08:00 a 10:00 sábado	07:00 a 13:00 y 15:30 a 19:00 sábado
4	reparte periódicos	trabaja en una obra
5	48€ la semana	70€ la semana
6	no le gusta	no le gusta mucho
7	es muy duro y paga mal	es muy duro y el día es largo
8	ahorra para comprar un moto	ahorra para ir a la universidad, gasta 30€ en chuchearías, música y salir

3 **Busca los ejemplos de verbos reflexivos en primera persona en los textos de la actividad 2a.**

- Students find examples of first person reflexive verbs in activity 2a.

Answers: me gasto, me levanto, me sienta, me despierto, me ducho

5–7

4a **Escribe un párrafo. Debes escoger un elemento de cada sección.**

- Students write a paragraph using an element from each section. Students must do this independently and "win" if their version is either exactly the same as someone else's, or a completely different combination to anyone else in the class.

5–7

4b **Juego: ¡Empieza de nuevo! En que equipos turnaos para adivinar el párrafo de un(a) compañero/a. Si cometéis un error el escritor dirá ¡NO! ¡Empieza de nuevo! Otro compañero tiene que intentarlo empezando desde el principio.**

- The aim of the exercise is to have students repeat the structures of this extended passage over and over. It is a good idea to model the activity with the whole class where the teacher chooses the paragraph and gets volunteers to try to guess. If a student chooses an option not in the original paragraph the teacher says NO and asks someone else to try again. Every time a mistake is made the paragraph must be started from the beginning and every student can go on until they make a mistake. After the model, the class should be divided in groups of 3 or 4. Larger groups mean that students get less opportunity to repeat the passage out loud. This can be turned into a competition to see which group gets a paragraph right with the least number of attempts. And in the case of more able groups, the teacher may want to encourage the writer of the paragraph to extend the NO answer to a negative sentence i.e. *No, no trabajo de canguro.*

5 **Completa alarga las frases. Utiliza los conectores y tus propias ideas.**

PLTS
- Students use the phrases to express their own opinion. They share these in turn with the class, who reply by agreeing or disagreeing and giving their opinion.

5–8

Remate

6a **Listen to Elena's answers. Choose the correct question for each of her answers (a–f).**

- Remind the students to think about what kind of information they need to be listening for.

5–8

 CD 3, track 32   **página 149, actividad 6a**

a Creo que es importante ahorrar así que ingreso la mitad de mi salario en mi cuenta en el banco y con el resto voy al cine el viernes por la tarde y salgo con mis amigos los sábados.

b Es bastante duro porque son muchas horas después del instituto pero no me desagrada porque soy una persona muy sociable y tengo oportunidad de estar con gente y charlar.

c Trabajo de aprendiz de peluquera en un salón en mi barrio. Lavo el pelo de las clientas, barro el suelo y me ocupo de servir refrescos o café a mis compañeras y a las señoras que vienen a cortarse el pelo.

d Trabajo todos los días después del instituto menos el lunes porque en España muchas peluquerías cierran ese día. También trabajo los sábados todo el día.

e Creo que es buena idea tener un trabajo a tiempo parcial aunque esté estudiando, pues evita discusiones con mis padres porque ahora tengo mi propio dinero. Además no gasto tanto porque sé lo duro que es ganar un sueldo.

f Gano 3,50€ la hora así que está mal pagado pero la ventaja es que son muchas horas y a final de semana sale bien: a 84€. Mis amigas ganan bastante menos haciendo de canguro.

Answers: **1** c, **2** d, **3** f, **4** b, **5** a, **6** e

6b **Now listen and answer the questions in English.**

- Remind students to answer fully – if the question asks for three details, they must supply all three to get full marks.

5–8

 CD 3, track 33   **página 149, actividad 6b**

Trabajo de aprendiz de peluquera en un salón en mi barrio. Lavo el pelo de las clientas, barro el suelo y me ocupo de servir refrescos o café a mis compañeras y a las señoras que vienen a cortarse el pelo. Trabajo todos los días después del instituto menos el lunes porque en España muchas peluquerías cierran ese día. También trabajo los sábados todo el día.
Gano 3,50€ la hora así que está mal pagado pero la ventaja es que son muchas horas y a final de semana sale bien: a 84€. Mis amigas ganan bastante menos haciendo de canguro. Es bastante duro porque son muchas horas después del instituto pero no me desagrada porque soy una persona muy sociable y tengo oportunidad de estar con gente y charlar.
Creo que es importante ahorrar así que ingreso la mitad de mi salario en mi cuenta en el banco y con el resto voy al cine el viernes por la tarde y salgo con mis amigos los sábados. Creo que es buena idea tener un trabajo a tiempo parcial aunque esté estudiando, pues evita discusiones con mis padres porque ahora tengo mi propio dinero. Además no gasto tanto porque sé lo duro que es ganar un sueldo.

Answers: **1** She is a trainee hairdresser **2** Wash hair/sweep floor/serve refreshments **3** Some salons close on that day in Spain **4** 84€ **5** They earn a lot less babysitting **6** It's hard but doesn't dislike it because she is outgoing and can chat to people **7** She saves half in the bank/goes to the cinema on Friday/goes out with friends on Saturday **8** She argues less with her parents/spends less because she knows how hard it is to earn

Success criteria activity 6:
- *students give information accurately and in the appropriate style*
- *students express personal opinions and justify points of view*
- *students use a variety of vocabulary and structures*
- *students use different tenses or time frames*

7a **Now it is your turn to answer the questions to activity 6a for yourself. Take turns with a partner to ask and answer the questions. Remember to extend your answers by including as much detail as possible.**

- Students can invent the details; it does not have to be the strict truth. Partners can decide if it is true, or simply note down the information given and check if they understood correctly.

4–9

7b **Report to the rest of the class the information you found out about your partner. Remember to change verbs to the third person!**

PLTS

- This could be another opportunity for the class to decide if the original speaker is telling the truth or not.

4–9

Success criteria activity 7:
- *students communicate effectively and accurately*
- *students express personal opinions and justify points of view*
- *students use a variety of vocabulary and structures*
- *students deal with unpredictable elements*
- *students use different tenses or time frames*

Gramática en acción

páginas 150 y 151

Planner

> **Objectives**
- Reflexive verbs

> **Resources**

Students' Book, pages 150–151
Exam Skills Workbook, page 56 (F), page 58 (H)
Grammar Workbook, pages 21, 62, 43–45, 37
Activity sheet 61
Resources and Planning OxBox CD-ROM

> **Grammar**
- Definite and indefinite articles

> **Adjectives**
- Quantifiers and intensifiers
- Imperative (revision)
- Preterite
- Reflexive verbs

> **PLTS**

Students' Book, page 151, activity 7,
Reflective Learners
Students' Book, page 151, activity 13,
Creative Thinkers

> ## Definite and indefinite articles

1 **Definite or indefinite? Copy and complete with the correct article.**

Answers: **a** la, **b** un, **c** el, **d** un, **e** las, **f** unos, **g** las, **h** la

> ## Adjectives

2 **Translate these phrases.**

Answers: **a** un profesor bueno, **b** un buen profesor, **c** el primer piso, **d** buena suerte, **e** el mejor día, **f** la peor asignatura, **g** la tercera clase, **h** el pobre profesor

3 **Chose the correct quantifier or intensifier for each sentence.**

Answers: **a** muy, **b** un poco, **c** poco, **d** bastante, **e** muy, **f** demasiado

4 **Write the absolute superlative of these adjectives. Careful with spelling!**

Answers: **b** grandísimo, **c** pequeñísimo, **d** modernísimo, **e** guapísima, **f** tristísimo, **g** buenísima, **h** malísimo

5 **Write two possible translations of these sentences.**

Answers: **a** La clase de matemáticas es muy grande / grandísima. **b** Señorita Solano es muy buena / buenísima. **c** Trabajar y estudiar es muy duro / durísimo. **d** Es muy importante / importantísimo sacar buenas notas. **e** Nuestro patio es muy pequeño / pequeñísimo. **f** Tengo amigos muy buenos / buenísimos. **g** El laboratorio es muy pequeño / pequeñísimo. **h** El profesor de inglés es muy guapo I guapísimo.

➤ Imperative (Revision)

6 **Now translate this advice using the *tú* form.**

Answers: **a** ¡Trabaja bien! **b** ¡No suspendas tus examenes! **c** ¡Llega a tiempo! **d** ¡Ahorra dinero! **e** ¡No compres tantos CDs!

7 **Now change your answers to the *Ud.* and *vosotros* forms.**

PLTS *Answers* – **Ud**: **a** ¡Trabaje bien! **b** ¡No suspenda sus examenes! **c** ¡Llegue a tiempo! **d** ¡Ahorre dinero! **e** ¡Gaste menos! **f** ¡No compre tantos CDs!
Answers – **vosotros**: **a** ¡Trabajad bien! **b** ¡No suspendáis vuestros examenes! **c** ¡Llegad a tiempo! **d** ¡Ahorrad dinero! **e** ¡Gastad menos! **f** ¡No compréis tantos CDs!

➤ Preterite

8 **Translate these preterites into Spanish.**

Answers: **a** estudié, **b** ganó, **c** prefirieron, **d** aprendí, **f** trabajamos, **g** caminaste, **h** os lavasteis, **i** comió, **j** bebimos

9 **These are some very common irregular preterites. What do they mean?**

Answers:

a I did/made	**e** he/she did/made	**i** we did/made	**m** they did/made
b I had	**f** he/she had	**j** we had	**n** they had
c I went/was	**g** he/she went/was	**k** we went/were	**o** they went/were
d Iwas	**h** he/she was	**l** we were	**p** they were

10 **Complete the sentences using the preterite form of the verb in parentheses.**

Answers: **a** estudiaron, **b** hice, **c** estuvo, **d** fui, **e** hicieron, **f** trabajó, **g** tuvimos, **h** estuvo, **i** fui, **j** fue

➤ Reflexive verbs

11 **Look these verbs up in the dictionary.**

Answers:

maquillarse	lavarse
despertarse	bañarse
mirarse	ponerse
quitarse	acercarse
negarse	volverse

12 **What do these mean.**

Answers: **a** I'm putting on my make-up. **b** Have you washed your hands? **c** Wake up! **d** They are going to have a bath tonight. **e** He looked at himself in the window. **f** I put my uniform on. **g** We take our shoes off. **h** Don't come any closer! **i** He refused to work. **j** He's becoming very responsible.

➤ Stem-changing verbs

13 **Compare the infinitives you found in activity 11 with their conjugated form in activity 12 and identify the two stem-changing verbs.**

Encourage students to make up their own examples using these verbs to help them remember the stem changes.

Answers: despertarse, volver

14 **Now write ten sentences about yourself, using the ten reflexive verbs of activity 11.**

PLTS ● Students should try to make the sentences interesting so they will remember them as examples more easily.

Habilidades
página 152

Planner

➤ Objectives
● Developing strategies for timed conversations.

➤ Resources
Students' Book, pages 152
CD 3, track 27
Exam Skills Workbook, page 58 (F), page 59 (H)
Activity sheet 62
Resources and Planning OxBox CD-ROM

➤ Skills
● Sounding Spanish even when pronouncing words that look English.
● Developing strategies for timed conversations.

● Building your answer by a series of steps.
● Using different tenses.
● Asking questions yourself.
● Practising your answering skills.
● Making accurate guesses for multiple choice questions.

➤ PLTS
Students' Book, page 152, activity 2, *Reflective Learners*
Students' Book, page 152, activity 6, *Self-Managers*

➤ Hablar

1 Sound Spanish even when pronouncing words that look English.
- Students practice pronouncing the words aloud; tell them to concentrate on vowels but also pay attention to *r* and *v* sounds.

2 Develop strategies for timed conversations.

PLTS
- Students decide which strategy is being used in the examples and then try using the strategies themselves.

3 Build your answer by a series of steps.
- Remind students to be very careful to drop the question word and change the person of the verb when recycling material from the question. They follow the steps to build a full answer.

4 Use different tenses.
- Or they can talk about something they are planning on buying in the future, or something they *would* buy *if they had* more money.

5 Ask questions yourself.
- Or they can ask what they normally / would like to spend their money on.

6 Practise your answering skills.

PLTS
- Students combine all the skills on this page to give extended answers. They can write them down for reference, but should "speak" them first using only notes.

➤ Escuchar

7 Make accurate guesses for multiple choice questions.
- Ask for some examples of verb tense and adjectival endings.
- Tell the students not to worry if they did not understand much as they are unlikely to get something that fast in the exam. As a class, ask for anything they did understand; together they may be able to build up quite a lot of information.

 CD 3, track 34   **página 152, Escuchar**

Me llamo María y se me dan fatal las matemáticas porque soy muy perezosa y no me gusta nada estudiar. Mi hermano es un aburrido, muy antipático y soso. Además, es un empollón responsable que siempre aprueba todo. Yo soy todo lo contrario, por eso nos llevamos fatal.

- Ask students why they made their choice.
- Emphasise again the importance of making a sensible guess rather than leaving a blank.

Answers: **María** – perezosa simpática alegre responsable, **her brother** – aburrido antipático soso alegre responsable

Escenario   página 153

Planner

➤ Objectives
- Planning a virtual school and discussing working while studying.

➤ Resources
Students' Book, page 153
Exam Skills Workbook, pages 55–56 (F), pages 56–57 (H)
Resources and Planning OxBox CD-ROM

➤ Skills
- Writing practice
- Speaking practice

➤ PLTS
Students' Book, page 153, Escenario Oral, *Team Workers*
Students' Book, page 153, Escenario Escrito, *Effective Participators*

➤ Oral

Work in groups of four. Discuss types of paid part-time jobs the new school could offer older students: tasks, hours of work and pay. Make some notes. Decide what the tasks would be, the hours of work and the pay. Brainstorm your ideas and write them down.

PLTS

- Students can discuss in Spanish or English as appropriate to their ability.

4–9

Now divide the group into two teams to represent the students and the school's leadership team.
- Students prepare their presentation for and against part-time jobs as detailed in the Students' Book.

Present your case to the governors.

After each presentation, there will be up to three minutes to debate and answer questions from the other team and the school governors.

- At the end, a vote can be taken to allow or not allow part-time jobs in the new school.
- *GCSE Grades A*-C*
- *Grade C Students use past, present and future tenses. They express opinions, and deal with some unpredictability.*
- *Grade A Students express and justify opinions. They use a variety of vocabulary and structure in longer speech sequences.*

➤ **Escrito**

Design a game screen providing a snapshot of the key information about the new virtual school. It must include one sentence about each of these points.

4–9

- Remind students to make their sentences full, grammatically correct and interesting – they are trying to attract people to play the game.

Imagine you are a virtual student who attends the virtual school. The headteacher wants to send 10,000 emails to prospective students and parents promoting the school and canvassing for new pupils. He/she has entrusted you with the task of writing the email.

- As this is promotional material, it must be attractive in content but appropriate in tone.
- *GCSE Grades A*-C*
- *Grade C Students use opinions and past, present and future tenses, both factually and imaginatively. Register is appropriate and style is basic.*
- *Grade A Students write factually and imaginatively using longer sequences and a range of vocabulary and structure. They express and justify opinions in an appropriate style.*

Vocabulario
página 154

This is a summary of key language from the unit, organised by spread and theme. Students can use it for reference while working on the unit, and as an aid to learning vocabulary.

Lectura
páginas 187 y 188

Planner

➤ **Objectives**
- Students talk about different aspects of school life
- To encourage independent reading and develop reading strategies.
- These pages also provide alternative class and homework material for students who work quickly and require extension work.

➤ **Resources**
Students' Book, page 187–188

➤ **PLTS**
Students' Book, page 187, activity 3, *Effective Participators*
Students' Book, page 188, activity 1, *Self-Managers*

➤ Lectura A – Una letra de Gustavo

1 **Lee la carta y encuentra las palabras o expresiones equivalentes a las de abajo. Todas las palabras y expresiones necesarias están en el texto en negrita.**

- Students identify the matching Spanish expressions in bold in the letter.

4–8

Answers: **a** por desgracia, **b** al amanecer, **c** hay una pizarra, **d** es un poco incierto, **e** la gente, **f** para esos lujos, **g** la dirección, **h** barco a motor, **i** barcas a remo, **j** de todas las edades

2 **Contesta a las preguntas en inglés.**

- Students answer the questions in English.

5–9

Answers: **a** They come from the city of Puno – the islanders are mainly fishermen. **b** They travel by motor boat. **c** He travels by rowing boat – 15km each way. **d** a long time! **e** There are 38. **f** There is only one teacher. **g** Their parents can't afford to buy them the books and other things they need. **h** There is one room, 30 desks (so the little ones have to sit on the floor) and a blackboard. **i** He would like to continue studying, but would have to go to Puno, and it is too far to go and come back every day. **j** There is no postal service on the islands.

3 **Escribe diez frases comparando la experiencia escolar de Gustavo con tu experiencia escolar.**

- Students compare their school to Gustavo's.

5–9

4 **¿Te gustaría ir al colegio de Gustavo? ¿Por qué?**

PLTS

- Students write or discuss what they think about Gustavo's school. Why does he value his education so highly? How does that compare with how the students view their own education?

5–9

➤ Lectura B – La voz del estudiante

1 **Lee lo que dicen los jóvenes y contesta a las preguntas.**

PLTS

- Read what the young people say and answer the questions.

5–9

Answers: **a** Abdullah, **b** Pablo, **c** Felipe, **d** Mireia, **e** Marta

2 **¿Cómo se describen en el texto estos aspectos de la educación?**

- How are these things described in the texts?

5–9

Answers:

deberes	numerosos
las clases de ciencias	originales
los profesores	injustos
los castigos	prohibidos
las reglas	prácticas

3 **Lee otra vez y contesta a las preguntas.**

- Students answer the questions in note or full sentence form, or as a discussion in class as appropriate.

Answers: **a** la dificultad de combinar los deberes y su equipo, **b** los profesores no tratan los chicos con el mismo respecto que las chicas, **c** es muy interesante y innovador, **d** a causa de la desaparición de la familia tradicional y porque respetan demasiado los derechos de los alumnos y no bastante la autoridad de los profesores, **e** sí, respeta las normas útiles que hay en su colegio

Unit 5B Mi futuro			Overview grid	
Spread	**Contexts**	**Skills**	**Grammar**	**Vocabulary**
Spread title	• Topic areas covered within the unit	• Key skills focus	• Grammar covered in the unit	Key vocabulary
pages 156–157 **Cómo empezar a pensar en tu futuro**	• Beginning to think about the future	• Using accents correctly	• *Esto/eso*, tenses	aprovechar, conseguir, correr riesgos, discutir, experimentar, hacerse, solicitar, satisfacer el contable, la muerte, la receta, el reportaje, el sueño, el tema emocionante, enriquecedor(a), gratificante, inquisitivo/a, maravilloso/a, satisfecho/a me chifla, horas intensivas, horas reducidas
pages 158–159 **Cómo aprovechar las prácticas laborales**	• Getting the most out of work experience	• Writing informal letters and using capital letters correctly	• *Sin, para, al +* infinitive	apreciar, cometer errores, crecer, ganarse la vida, merecer la pena, subestimar el beneficio, la chavala, la fábrica, un montón, el negocio, las prácticas laborales desastroso/a, inolvidable, maduro/a de hecho, dentro de, quizás, sin embargo
pages 160–161 **Cómo investigar todas las oportunidades**	• Finding out about different opportunities in the world of work	• Translating fluently	• Infinitives and gerunds	asegurarse de, consistir en, diseñar, esforzarse, hacer falta, independizarse, marcharse de casa, meter la pata, tener confianza el albañil, el aprendizaje, la carrera universitaria, el cirujano, el diseñador, la empresa, el fontanero, el jinete, la niñera, el periodismo, el puesto, los requísitos, los títulos
pages 162–163 **Cómo solicitar un trabajo**	• Applying for a job	• Writing formal letters, reading without problems	• *lo que*	caerse, contar mentiras, enfrentarse con entrevistar, juntarse con, volverse loco la ansiedad, el aparato, la calidad, la carta de solicitud, el empleado, el empleo, la entrevista, la fluidez, la tarea, la temporada, los turnos noctivos, el varón fiable, imprescindible
pages 164–165 **Cómo trabajar en el extranjero**	• Working abroad	• Recognising and dealing with "false friends"	• Revision of the subjunctive	acostumbrarse a, aguantar, darse cuenta de, desaparecer, echar de menos, hacer un esfuerzo, mejorar, perder, respetar, sorprender, valer el corazón, la mayoría de, el pulpo, el reto insoportable, lleno/a, valiente al principio, me costó mucho
pages 166–167 **Gramática en acción**	• Using the subjunctive, practising verbs with prepositions		• Using all the tenses confidently • Using the present participles *–ando* and *–iendo* in other contexts • Using the infinitive and verbs which take prepositions correctly • Recognising a simple subjunctive	
page 168 **Habilidades**	• Accents, stress and memory aids	• Reading for gist • Deciphering Spanish words suing clues from the English • Recognising a "false friend" • Writing in a formal and informal way • Using capital letters and accents correctly • Translating in a proper and natural fashion		
page 169 **Escenario**	• Take part in a balloon debate. • Describe the life and career of a famous person/celebrity.			
page 170 **Vocabulario**	• Summary of key vocabulary for the unit.			
pages 189–190 **Reading pages**	Describing people, their professions and characters: • to encourage independent reading and to develop reading strategies. • to provide alternative class and homework material for students who finish other activities quickly.			

5B Mi futuro

Unit Objectives

Contexts: work and the future
Skills focus: reading for gist, deciphering Spanish words using clues from the English, recognising a 'false friend', writing in a formal and informal way, using capital letters and accents correctly, translating in a proper and natural fashion
Grammar: using all the tenses confidently, using the present participles *-ando* and *-iendo* in other contexts, using the infinitive and verbs which take prepositions, and the phrase *lo que* correctly, recognising a simple subjunctive

Controlled assessment opportunities

Writing: Students' Book, page 157, activity 9
Speaking: Students' Book, page 159, activity 5
Writing: Students' Book, page 161, activity 9
Writing: Students' Book, page 163, activity 8
Speaking: Students' Book, page 165, activity 5

See also *GCSE Spanish for OCR Assessment OxBox CD-ROM.*

An introduction to the unit página 155

- *Aim*: To introduce the themes of the unit and encourage students to think about the reasons for learning Spanish.
- The opening page is designed with captions, pictures and page cross-references to provide a preview of what is to come:

- Allow time for students to read the questions and cross-refer to the relevant pages of the Students' Book. They could do this individually or in pairs / small groups, followed by whole-class discussion.
- This spread also provides an opportunity for students to recap on familiar language. Ask them to think about language they already know that might be useful when working on the themes of the unit.

- Mindmap any language they produce, and if possible, keep it on display as reference as you progress through the unit. It can be added to at intervals as new language becomes familiar.
- At the end of work on the unit, allow time for students to return to this spread and repeat the mind-mapping process, this time including what they have learned over the course of the unit. Get them to answer the questions in their own words, and encourage them to use the results for revision purposes.
- Ask them what they found difficult, interesting etc. What do they think are the important things they have learned in this unit? What do they still need to improve on?
- If time permits, get the students to redesign the page. How would they set it out so it reflects the unit? How would they make it attractive to other learners of their age? How would they make it easy to follow? What would they include in terms of text, pictures, captions, page references? Ask them to imagine they are producing material for next year's class who will be learning the same thing – what would they have found it useful to know?

¿Por qué aprender el español? Para hablar del futuro y el mundo del trabajo.

- Students share any experiences they have had of the world of work including any work experience they have undertaken. Would they consider working abroad in the future?
- Ask them to consider what sort of language they would need to talk about their hopes and plans for the future to a Spanish person of their age.

Cómo empezar a pensar en tu futuro

páginas 156 y 157

Planner

➤ Objectives
- Beginning to think about the future

➤ Resources
Students' Book, pages 156–157
CD 3, track 39
Grammar Workbook, pages 12–13
Activity sheets 64–67

➤ Key language
aprovechar, conseguir, correr riesgos, discutir, experimentar, hacerse, solicitar, satisfacer
el contable, la muerte, la receta, el reportaje, el sueño, el tema
emocionante, enriquecedor(a), gratificante, inquisitivo/a, maravilloso/a, satisfecho/a
me chifla, horas intensivas, horas reducidas

➤ Skills
- Using accents correctly

➤ Grammar
- *Esto/eso*

➤ PLTS
Students' Book, page 157, activity 7,
Reflective Learners
Students' Book, page 157, activity 9,
Creative Thinkers

➤ Starters
- Choose a tense with your partner. Choose a regular verb. Roll a dice. 1 to 6 represent the six parts of the verb. Say the part of the verb out loud. Keep score. e.g. They may choose *trabajar*. If the pupil rolls a 3, they say *trabaja*, if they roll a 6 – *trabajan*. To extend the activity, if they roll a 2 they might say e.g. *¿Trabajas en un banco? ¿Dónde trabajas? ¿Trabajas los sábados?*
- Students' Book, page 157, activity 3. In class or small groups, brainstorm jobs and what they are like and how they are seen e.g. working in an office is often seen as dull. Is this necessarily true? What kind of qualities would the students ideally like in a job?
- Students' Book, page 157, activity 9. The teacher calls out a sentence in English such as *I wouldn't want to work in a bank*, or *I've always wanted to work in a hospital*, and the students have to say which of the four sentences at activity 8 they could adapt to say that in Spanish.
- Play word association. The teacher, or a pupil, calls out a job, and someone else has to provide an appropriate adjective e.g. *soldado – peligroso, cocinero – enfadado, cantante – orgulloso* etc. The person giving the adjective nominates the next person to give a profession.

➤ Plenaries
- Students' Book, page 157, activity 5. Students make up their own memorable sentences containing these phrases, or come up with ways to remember them e.g. *sí – yes, there's an accent!*
- Who's plan is it? Students write out a sentence or two (it can be a shortened version of their work for activity 9) and either someone else reads it out, or it is passed round, and the others have to decide who the author was. They can work in pairs or teams and gain points for guessing correctly.
- The best job for you is... Working in groups, students decide what the best job for other people in the class (not necessarily in their groups) would be, and give reasons e.g. *Alan debe ser piloto de Formula 1 porque siempre corre muy rápido a casa despúes de las clases.* They can, and preferably should be, humorous; but be aware of local sensitivities and steer clear of hurtful comments.
- Quick quiz. Write a pair of words on the board, e.g. *estudio – estudió*. The first group to explain the difference correctly wins a point.

1a Empareja las caricaturas con las opiniones en la página 156.

- Students match the pictures to the opinions.

Answers: **Ana** f, **Pablo** d, **Juan** c, **Beatriz** e, **Alberto** b, **María** a, **Mario** h, **Verónica** g

5–8

1b Completa las frases con una posible profesión de las personas de la actividad 1a.

- Students complete the sentences appropriately with the words given.

Answers: **a** banquero, **b** futbolista, **c** mecánica, **d** soldado, **e** cocinero, **f** profesora, **g** política

4–8

2 **Escucha y decide quién habla.**

- Students listen and decide which person from the pictures on the previous page is talking.

> **CD 3, track 39**   **página 157, actividad 2**
>
> **a** Cuando tenga mi propio restaurante, será fantástico.
> **b** De mayor, me gustaría trabajar en un garaje porque me gusta hacer cosas prácticas.
> **c** Necesito aventura en mi vida. Mi futuro trabajo tendría ser arriesgado y peligroso.
> **d** Para mí, aprender es una parte esencial de la vida. Querría compartir esta pasión con otra gente.
> **e** Escribiré mis propias canciones y conseguiré un contrato con una compañía discográfica.
> **f** Tendré que mantenerme en forma y marcar muchos goles para mi equipo.
> **g** Tengo talento para expresarme bien. La gente suele escuchar lo que digo.
> **h** Cuando sea mayor, quiero trabajar en un banco internacional.

Answers: **a** Mario, **b** María, **c** Juan, **d** Beatriz, **e** Ana, **f** Pablo, **g** Verónica, **h** Alberto

3 **¿A ti qué tipo de trabajo te gustaría tener? Practica con tu compañero/a usando los adjetivos de abajo.**

4–9

- Students discuss with their partner what type of job they would like and why. Perhaps start by choosing an adjective e.g. *interesante* and seeing how many people would want a job that was *interesante*. Then pupils see how many adjectives they can put in sentence which would makes sense. Give a point for each adjective used. Encourage pupils to look up more sophisticated adjectives e.g. *Busco un trabajo divertido, variado y peligroso. No quiero un trabajo muy exhaustivo.* Encourage students to start their sentences in different ways e.g:
- *Quiero/no quiero un trabajo …*
- *Quisiera/no quisiera un trabajo …*
- *Busco/no busco un trabajo …*
- *Deseo/no deseo un trabajo …*
- *Me gustaría tener un trabajo / no me gustaría tener un trabajo …*
- *Me encantaría tener un trabajo / Odiaría tener un trabajo …*

4 **Escribe estas palabras en el singular o en masculino.**
Grammar reference page 201

- Students write the singular of the words given.

Answers: intención, profesión, marrón, jamón, inglés, alemán

5 **Completa las frases.**

- Students complete the phrases.

Answers: **a** mí, **b** mi, **c** solo, **d** sólo, **e** si, **f** sí

4–6

6 **Completa las frases.**

- Students complete the sentences.

Answers: **a** este, **b** esto, **c** eso, **d** esa

4–6

Remate

7 **Choose any page of your text book, and look at the accents on the words. Read a paragraph out loud and ask yourself why the accents are where they are.**

 **PLTS**

- Remind them of the possibilities – stress, meaning and tense.

4–7

Success criteria activity 7:
- *students communicate effectively and accurately*
- *students use a variety of vocabulary and structures*
- *students use different tenses or time frames*

8 **Translate these sentences into English.**

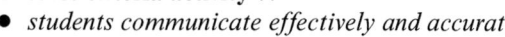

- Highlight that *querría* can mean *would want* or *would like.*

5–8

Answers: **a** I wouldn't want such a difficult job because I would like to have time for other things. **b** When I was five years old I wanted to be an actor but I'm not interested in that anymore. **c** I've always wanted to work with animals even though I know it will be difficult. **d** As I'm quite patient and friendly, there are lots of jobs I can do.

9 **Write ten sentences about your possible plans using different tenses. Look at the sentences above and try to use the same tenses.**

PLTS

- Do some examples in class first, showing the students how to adapt the language for their purposes.

4–9

Success criteria activities 8 & 9:
- *students give information accurately and in the appropriate style*
- *students express personal opinions and justify points of view*
- *students use a variety of vocabulary and structures*
- *students use different tenses or time frames*

Cómo aprovechar las prácticas laborales

Planner

➤ **Objectives**
- Getting the most out of work experience

➤ **Resources**
Students' Book, pages 158–159
CD 3, tracks 40–41
Grammar Workbook, page 70
Activity sheets 64–67

➤ **Key language**
apreciar, cometer errores, crecer, ganarse la vida,
merecer la pena, subestimar
el beneficio, la chavala, la fábrica, un montón,
el negocio, las prácticas laborales
desastroso/a, inolvidable, maduro/a
de hecho, dentro de, quizás, sin embargo

➤ **Skills**
- Writing informal letters and using capital letters correctly

➤ **Grammar**
- *Sin, para, al* + infinitive

➤ **PLTS**
Students' Book, page 159, activity 5,
Effective Participators
Students' Book, page 159, activity 8,
Creative Thinkers

➤ **Starters**
- Brainstorm students' experiences of work experience if they have done this already. Where did they go? What as it like? Were the people friendly? What did they do that was new? Was it useful? Why? Why not?

- Students' Book, page 159, activity 5. Do a couple of examples in class first to show students how to present an argument for or against before they discuss it with their partners.
- Students' Book, page 159 activity 6. In pairs, set a time limit for students to write down or look up all the professions shown in the pictures. Then do the listening activity.
- Students' Book, page 159 activity 7. Quickly review different verb endings for different tenses before doing the listening activity – elicit examples from the students.

➤ **Plenaries**
- Students' Book, page 159, activity 5. Hold a class debate on the worth of work experience. Encourage students to hold firm views on one side or the other (whatever their true feelings are), and hold a vote at the end. Everyone can contribute a comment, or there can be a few main speakers but everybody else has to ask a question.
- Write to order. The teacher can supply words to include e.g. *desastroso / pero / fenomenal – situación: en un garaje* etc and students have to write a sentence or short paragraph containing all the ideas. Other students work out if the story is basically positive or negative. They can also award points for humour.
- Students' Book, page 159, activity 8. Students can also write about their actual experiences, if relevant, and their actual thoughts before they went on their placements, and how the two matched up. However, it is worth pointing out that it is often easier to write about something invented because they can make the story fit the language they know rather than the other way round.

---

1 **Carta 1 – ¿verdadero o falso?**

- Students decide if the statements are true (V) or false (F) about the first letter.

Answers: **a** F, **b** F, **c** V, **d** F, **e** F, **f** V, **g** F, **h** V, **i** F, **j** V

5–8

2 **Busca estas palabras (subrayadas abajo) en la carta 2, y escribe estas frases en español.**

- Students look for the Spanish of the underlined words in the second letter and use them to write the sentences in Spanish.

Answers: **a** De hecho, podría escribir una carta. **b** Tengo un par de buenas ideas. **c** Nunca se sabe si la experiencia va a ser positiva. **d** ¿ Siempre has querido ser abogado? **e** Quizás me darán un empleo. **f** Hay una ventajas. **g** Me gustaría el ambiente de una oficina. **h** Gracias por ayudarme.

5–8

3 Rellena los huecos con 'sin', 'al' o 'para'.

- Students complete the gaps with the correct word.

Answers: **a** sin, **b** para, **c** al, **d** para, **e** sin

4–8

4 Mira las ventajas y desventajas de la experiencia laboral. Escríbelas en dos listas. ¿Puedes pensar en más?

- Students decide if the phrases are advantages or disadvantages to doing work experience.

Answers:

5–8

ventajas	desventajas
usar la imaginación	cometer errores
sentirse maduro/a	aburrirse
trabajar en equipo	no ver a los amigos
divertirse	sentirse nervioso/a
ser estimulante	no comprender
aprender cosas nuevas	tener/pasar miedo
crecer personalmente	trabajar más horas
no tener deberes	

5 ¿Las prácticas laborales te parecen una experiencia positiva o una pérdida del tiempo? Usa las listas para discutir el tema con tu pareja. Intenta usar diferentes tiempos.

PLTS

- Students discuss what they feel about work experience with a partner. Encourage them to go through the phrases in activity 4, commenting on these ideas. Pupils' opinions on this may vary quite a lot depending on the character of the student. It would make for a livelier debate if pupils could come up with individual responses. Encourage them to go beyond the obvious.

4–9

6 Escucha. ¿A qué trabajo se refiere?

PLTS

- Students listen and decide which job is being talked about.

4–8

🎧 **CD 3, track 40   página 159, actividad 6**

Woman 1	¡Qué lata! Todo ese ruido de niños llorando y gritando. ¡Eso no es para mí!
Man 1	Yo no tendría la paciencia para pasar dos semanas con gente mayor.
Man 2	Me encantaría poder reservar las vacaciones de otra gente en países exóticos.
Woman 2	Preparar el escenario para obras teatrales sería de lo más divertido.
Woman 3	Me imagino que tendrías que ser inteligente, formal y organizado para hacer esto.
Man 3	Charlar con el público, limpiar, sí. Pero lavar el pelo a otros. No, señor. Ni hablar.
Woman 4	Estar al aire libre y en contacto con la naturaleza. Eso sí que me encantaría hacer.
Man 4	Si pudiera aprender a escribir artículos para un periódico, sería genial.

Answers: **1** e, **2** d, **3** h, **4** g, **5** f, **6** a, **7** b, **8** c

7 Escucha. ¿Han hecho sus prácticas laborales ya? Escribe sí o no. ¿Qué tiempo usan?

- Students listen and decide if the speakers have done their work experience yet or not. Write *sí* or *no*. What tense do they use?

4–8

🎧 **CD 3, track 41   página 159, actividad 7**

a Pues yo pasé dos semanas trabajando en un teatro. Lo pasé fenomenal. Lo único que no me gustó fue el horario.

b Yo no lo he hecho todavía pero mi colegio lo organizará el año que viene. Será divertidísimo.

c Desafortunadamente no hemos tenido esa oportunidad todavía pero lo haremos dentro de un año.

d Hice mis prácticas hace dos años. No lo pasé muy bien porque creo que era demasiado joven para apreciarlo.

e Yo pasé una semana en una panadería. Me aburrí como una ostra pero aprendí a hacer pan!

f La gente era muy simpática en la oficina donde yo trabajé pero lo que hice no era muy estimulante.

g Empezaré mis prácticas laborales al final de este curso cuando haya terminado mis exámenes.

h Como mis padres tienen un negocio, podré trabajar con ellos este verano. ¡Y me pagarán!

i Nuestro colegio organiza las plazas. No quiero que me manden a un puesto aburrido. Quiero hacerlo en un sitio interesante.

j En mi instituto es obligatorio hacer las prácticas laborales pero no me interesa nada la idea.

k He cambiado mucho desde que terminé mis prácticas. Ahora soy más madura y organizada.

l Creo que fue una experiencia que nunca olvidaré.

Answers: **b** no, perfecto y futuro, **c** no, perfecto y futuro, **d** sí, preterito y imperfecto, **e** sí, preterito, **f** sí, preterito y imperfecto, **g** no, futuro y subjunctivo, **h** no, futuro, **i** no, presente y subjunctive, **j** no, presente, **k** sí, perfecto y preterito, **l** sí, preterito

Remate

8a Choose one of these places where you would like to work. Write a short account of what a typical day would be like.

PLTS

- Emphasise that they are speculating here, not recounting an experience and will need to use future and conditional tenses, and possibly the subjunctive. They can include if this is a good place for them to work or not and why (character? interests?) They can make the scenarios amusing e.g. someone scared of flying working in a travel agency specialising in long haul flights. Remind students they can be very generous with the truth when writing this kind of piece.

4–8

8b Imagine that you have just finished working in one of the above places. Write a paragraph about the experience.

- They can either choose a completely different place, or use the same one and say if the experience lived up to the anticipation or not.

4–9

Success criteria activity 8:

- *students give information accurately and in the appropriate style*
- *students express personal opinions and justify points of view*
- *students use a variety of vocabulary and structures*
- *students use different tenses or time frames*

Cómo investigar todas las oportunidades

Planner

➤ Objectives
- Finding out about different opportunities in the world of work

➤ Resources
Students' Book, pages 160–161
CD 3, track 42
Grammar Workbook, page 59
Activity sheets 64–67

➤ Key language
asegurarse de, consistir en, diseñar, esforzarse, hacer falta, independizarse, marcharse de casa, meter la pata, tener confianza
el albañil, el aprendizaje, la carrera universitaria, el cirujano, el diseñador, la empresa, el fontanero, el jinete, la niñera, el periodismo, el puesto, los requisitos, los títulos

➤ Skills
- Translating fluently

➤ Grammar
- Infinitives and gerunds

➤ PLTS
Students' Book, page 160, activity 1,
Team Workers
Students' Book, page 161, activity 9,
Independent Enquirers

➤ Starters
- Have all the professions written out on individual cards, Spanish and English. In pairs or small groups, play Pairs, Snap, or simply Beat-the-Clock matching to familiarise students with the vocabulary before continuing with the activities on the spread.
- Students' Book, page 160, activity 1. Get the class to pick a profession, and go through one conversation with them, showing them how to use and adapt the questions and answers given. It helps to have the statements on Powerpoint or OHP transparencies rather than laboriously writing everything out as you go through it.
- Students' Book, page 161, activity 9. Pick a profession and model with the class how to write about it in the way described in the activity. Give the students a check list of things to include. Students then write their own paragraphs.
- Play a chain game. One student says e.g. *Quiero ser abogado porque paga bien*, and the next student says *quiero ser médico porque me interesa ayudar a la gente*, and so on. It can be made more complicated by insisting professions follow alphabetical order. Do not allow *es interesante* as a reason.

➤ Plenaries
- Students' Book, page 160, activity 1. Students perform their conversation for others, either a group or the whole class, who have to guess which profession they are describing.
- Students' Book, page 160, activity 2. Which of the jobs described would the students like and why? What is it about the job, the qualities required, the reponsibilities that attract them?
- Students' Book, page 161, activity 6. Students make up their own (preferably amusing) examples and illustrate them as memory aids e.g *Tengo la intención de hacer mis deberes* illustrated by person sat in front of TV, feet up, school bag dropped down the back of the sofa. Pairs could each do one or two, and they could all be displayed.
- Students' Book, page 161, activity 8. Students can write two paragraphs, one of which is an honest account of their peresonality, and an "airbrushed" version for a job application, where *soy un poco tímido* becomes *soy una persona tranquila*. Discuss with students how to present their qualities in the best light.

---

1   **Elige una profesión de arriba. Con un(a) compañero/a haz una conversación usando las preguntas y las respuestas de abajo.**

PLTS
- Students pick a profession, and talk about it with their partner, using and adapting the questions and answers shown.

5–8

2a   **Escucha. Empareja los dibujos con las personas que hablan.**

- Students listen and match the pictures to the person speaking.

5–8

CD 3, track 42   **página 160, actividad 2**

1 Lo que hago es traducir documentos y hacer de intérprete en comisarías y juicios. Hay que ser metódico y organizado. Tienes que mantener el control constantemente.

2 Mi trabajo consiste en ofrecer tratamientos de belleza y vender cosméticos. Necesito ser paciente y servicial. La gente está cómoda en mi compañía.

3 Enseño a la gente a conducir. Son muchas horas pero no me aburro nunca. No puedes ser nervioso si quieres prepararte para este trabajo.

4 Diseño edificios y hago los planes para las compañías de construcción. El salario es atractivo pero son muchos años de estudiar.

5 Preparo y sirvo el almuerzo a los alumnos a la hora de comer. No hay que estudiar, simplemente llevarse bien con la gente y no tener miedo de trabajar duro.

6 Mi responsabilidad es asegurarme de que mis pasajeros lleguen sanos y salvos a su destino. Hay que tener la vista perfecta y saber reaccionar con calma en una emergencia.

7 Soy jefe de una empresa de electrodomésticos. Comunicarse bien con el público es imprescindible. Si estás dispuesto a trabajar, se puede ganar mucho.

8 A mí me toca proteger y ofrecer ayuda al público. Mi responsabilidad es mantener el órden público. Hay que pasar un año haciendo un curso de formación.

Answers: **1** e, **2** d, **3** b, **4** f, **5** h, **6** g, **7** a, **8** c

2b Vuelve a escuchar. Escribe en inglés las cualidades y responsabilidades.

- Students listen again and write down the personal qualities and responsibilities involved in English. A copy of the transcript can be given to the pupils at this point. They listen to again to build up confidence with more difficult vocabulary.

5–8

Answers:

	cualidades	responsabilidades
1	metódico, organizado, en control	traducir documentos, interpretar en comisarías y juicios
2	paciente, servicial	ofrecer tratamientos de belleza, vender cosméticos
3	no ser nervioso	enseñar a la gente a conducir
4	estudiar muchos años	diseñar edificios, hacer los planes para las compañías de construcción
5	llevarse bien con la gente, no tener miedo de trabajar duro	preparar y servir el almuerzo a los alumnos a la hora de comer
6	tener la vista perfecta, saber reaccionar tranquilamente en una crisis	asegurarse de que los pasajeros lleguen sanos y salvos a su destino
7	comunicarse bien con el público, estar dispuesto a trabajar	jefe de una empresa de productos electrodomésticos
8	pasar un año haciendo un curso de formación	proteger y ofrecer ayuda al público, mantener el órden público.

3 **¿Qué profesión es?**

- What job is it? Students unscramble the anagrams.

4–6

Answers: **a** médico **b** periodista **c** niñera **d** peluquera, **e** cocinero, **f** actor, **g** profesor

4 **Rellena los huecos con un infinitivo de abajo.**

- Students look at the examples in the grammar box, then fill in the blanks using the infinitives provided.

4–7

Answers: **a** conducir / ir, **b** conseguir / terminar, **c** ser / estudiar, **d** trabajar / ganar, **e** salir / buscar

5 **Rellena los huecos con un gerundio de arriba.**

- Students refer back to the Grammar box, then fill in the blanks with the correct gerund forms of the verbs.

4–7

Answers: **a** haciendo, **b** fotocopiando, **c** entrevistando, **d** buscando, **e** practicando

6 **Traduce al inglés.**

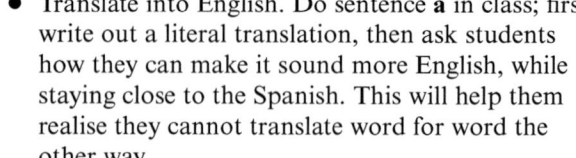

- Translate into English. Do sentence **a** in class; first write out a literal translation, then ask students how they can make it sound more English, while staying close to the Spanish. This will help them realise they cannot translate word for word the other way.

5–9

Answers:

a I think I will carry on studying (stay on at school) in order to get a place on a University course (at University)

b I hope to get a degree despite what it costs.

c I want to leave home because I dream of being independent.

d I intend to stop studying and begin to earn my own money as soon as possible.

e Leaving school means starting again from zero. This is very exciting for me.

7 **Traduce al español.**

- Students translate into Spanish. Encourage them to look for parts of sentences they can "lift" from elsewhere on these pages, and remind them not to translate word for word.

5–9

Answers:

a Pretendo seguir estudiando en vez de dejar el colegio.

b Intento pasar tiempo aprendiendo mi vocabulario.

c Sueño con vivir al extranjero despúes de terminar el colegio.

d Pienso ir a la universidad para estudiar medicina.

e No puedes aprender una lengua sin pasar tiempo estudiando.

Remate

8 **Use this vocabulary to write a paragraph about your personality.**

- Explain that most job applications will require people to describe their personality, and how that fits with the job they are applying for.

4–9

9 Write a paragraph about a profession which interests you. Use a variety of tenses, vocabulary and structures.

- Talk about it from the point of view of what they will have to do to get there (more studies, work experience, university?), what they will have to in the job (work hard, talk to people?) and the personal qualities necessary (responsibility etc). What interests them about this profession?

4–9

Success criteria activities 9 & 10:
- *students give information accurately and in the appropriate style*
- *students express personal opinions and justify points of view*
- *students use a variety of vocabulary and structures*
- *students use different tenses or time frames*

Cómo solicitar un trabajo

páginas 162 y 163

Planner

➤ Objectives
- Applying for a job

➤ Resources
Students' Book, pages 162–163
CD 3, track 43
Grammar Workbook, page 13
Activity sheets 64–67

➤ Key language
caerse, contar mentiras, enfrentarse con, entrevistar, juntarse con, volverse loco
la ansiedad, el aparato, la calidad, la carta de solicitud, el empleado, el empleo, la entrevista, la fluidez, la tarea, la temporada, los turnos noctivos, el varón
fiable, imprescindible

➤ Skills
- Writing formal letters, reading without problems

➤ Grammar
- *lo que*

➤ PLTS
Students' Book, page 162, activity 4,
Team Workers
Students' Book, page 163, activity 8,
Self-Managers

➤ Starters
- Write the English version of the CV headings at random on the board (surname, date of birth, educational establishment etc) and ask students to identify the Spanish on the CV.
- Students' Book, page 162, activity 4. One of the students asks the questions (or several can act as an interview panel) and the teacher models how to respond. Ask the students to note down any instances of talking more formally, extending an answer, or presenting oneself in the best light. Then they interview their partners.
- Students' Book, page 163, activity 5. Brainstorm reasons in class for failing at interview. Reasons should be realistic but may be humorous.
- Students' Book, page 163, activity 8. Ask students what information Mary includes in her letter and discuss how they can adapt this for their own use. Do some examples with the class.

➤ Plenaries
- Students complete the CV proforma with their information (it does not have to be strictly true!)
- Students' Book, page 162, activity 4. Students perform their interview for others to decide if the interviewee would get the job. They can write up their conversation as reference for examples of formal speech for role plays.
- Students' Book, page 163, activity 5. Which of these reasons for not getting a job are good ones, and why? Can students think of circumstances where for example, turning up late might not be a valid reason for failing an interview?

1 ¿Verdadero o falso?

- Students read the CV and decide which of the statements are true (V) or false (F).

Answers: **a** F, **b** V, **c** F, **d** V, **e** F, **f** V, **g** F, **h** V

5–8

2 Reemplaza las palabras cursiva en la carta con uno de los sinónimos de abajo.

- Students replace the words in italics in the letter with the correct synonym provided.

5–7

Answers: terminar – completar, empezar – comenzar, temporada – estancia, compañía – empresa, serviría – valdría, trabajo – puesto, realmente – verdaderamente, considero – creo, llevo – entiendo, bastante – algo, ver – observar, sitios diferentes – lugares, equipo – grupo,

3 Mira la carta de Mary otra vez. ¿Qué significan estas frases en inglés?

- Students re-read the letter and decide how to say the phrases in English.

Answers: **a** at the moment, **b** I have just finished, **c** before starting, **d** abroad, **e** an enriching experience, **f** I have been studying for five years, **g** there is nothing better, **h** because, **i** as you can see, **j** it has helped me

5–8

4 Imagina que te están entrevistando para un trabajo. Haz un diálogo formal con tu compañero/a, usando las preguntas de abajo.

 PLTS

- Students carry out an interview dialogue with their partner. How many replies can they use *lo que* in?

4–9

5 Escucha. ¿Por qué no han conseguido trabajo? Contesta en inglés.

- Students listen and decide why the speakers did not get the job.

4–8

CD 3, track 43   **página 163, actividad 5**

1 Pues, no pude encontrar la oficina donde se hacía la entrevista.
2 Llegué dos horas tarde a la entrevista.
3 Se me olvidó llevar una copia de mi curriculum.
4 Me dijeron que no había tenido bastante experiencia en ese campo.
5 El hombre que me entrevistó dijo que era demasiado inmaduro.
6 Tenía que haberme puesto unos zapatos más cómodos porque me caí nada más entrar en la oficina.
7 Había cenado una comida muy picante la noche anterior y olía a ajo que apestaba.
8 Estaba tan nervioso durante la entrevista que no pude decir una palabra.
9 Me equivoqué de día y llegué a la oficina el martes en lugar del lunes.
10 El entrevistador era el ex novio de mi hermana y no me llevé bien con él.

Answers: **2** Arrived 2 hours late; **3** Forgot a copy of their CV; **4** Not enough experience; **5** Interviewer said the interviewee was too immature; **6** Should have worn more practical shoes – she fell over as she walked in the office;

7 Ate spicy food the night before and smelt of garlic; **8** Was so nervous that couldn't say a word; **9** Got the day wrong – arrived on Tuesday not Monday; **10** The interviewer was the ex-boyfriend of the interviewee's sister – they never got on with him.

Remate

6 Look at the pictures on the right. Which job should they apply for?

- Students read the adverts and match them to the people.

Answers: Marta **C**, Estéban **D**, Felipe **E**, Manolita **A**

5–8

Success criteria activity 6:
- *students give information accurately and in the appropriate style*
- *students use a variety of vocabulary and structures*
- *students use different tenses or time frames*

7 Write sentences explaining why they should or should not choose these jobs.

- Justifying opinions is an advanced skill which will gain students extra marks.

4–9

8 Write a letter of application to one of the following businesses. Look at the structure of Mary Jackson's letter on page 162.

 PLTS
- Students must include what they are doing now, what they want to do, why they want that job specifically and why they would be good at it. Get students to prepare their vocabulary carefully, e.g. for *Restaurante 'Platástrofe'*:

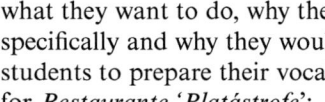 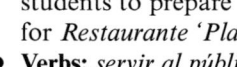
4–9
- **Verbs:** *servir al público, cocinar bien, cooperarse con los compañeros, mantener la calma, no perder el genio*
- **Adjectives:** *imaginativo/a, flexible, enérgico/a*
- **Nouns:** *energía, adaptabilidad, talento, experiencia*

Success criteria activities 7 & 8:
- *students give information accurately and in the appropriate style*
- *students express personal opinions and justify points of view*
- *students use a variety of vocabulary and structures*
- *students use different tenses or time frames*

Cómo trabajar en el extranjero

Planner

➤ Objectives
- Working abroad

➤ Resources
Students' Book, pages 164–165
CD 3, track 44
Grammar Workbook, pages 64–65
Activity sheets 64–67

➤ Key language
acostumbrarse a, aguantar, darse cuenta de, desaparecer, echar de menos, hacer un esfuerzo, mejorar, perder, respetar, sorprender, valer el corazón, la mayoría de, el pulpo, el reto insoportable, llenola, valiente al principio, me costó mucho

➤ Skills
- Recognising and dealing with "false friends"

➤ Grammar
- Revision of the subjunctive

➤ PLTS
Students' Book, page 165, activity 11,
Independent Enquirers
Students' Book, page 165, activity 12,
Self-Managers

➤ Starters
- Students look at the pictures on page 164 and describe what jobs the four people are doing abroad. Is anyone in the class interested in working abroad? Why / why not? Ask the question again at the end of the spread and see if anyone has changed their opinion.
- Students' Book, page 164, activity 2. Ask students (preferably in Spanish, but it is valid to do this in English) why they think the items on the list are potential problems (accommodation – having to understand adverts and make telephone calls to arrange to view flats etc). How could they begin to deal with these?
- Students' Book, page 165, activity 6. There are three different ways of saying *to get used to*. Ask students for English synonyms that look like the Spanish. This also increases their awareness of a wider English vocabulary.
- Students' Book, page 165, activity 7. Before they match up the sentences, ask students to go through and pick out any words or phrases they really do not understand. Ask for their best guess, or ask if another person in the class has any ideas. Ask them to apply their reading skills regarding context and synonyms, and help them pick apart the vocabulary.

➤ Plenaries
- Students' Book, page 164, activity 1. Give students a list of expressions in English such as make an effort, show respect, it's a bit arrogant. Don't necessarily give them in the order they appear in the texts. Students work in groups or pairs to find the expressions. The teacher can set a time limit, or the first group to finish with a correct list wins.
- Students' Book, page 164, activity 2. After listening, give students a copy of the transcript. Ask for ideas as to how these problems could be overcome or pre-empted. This is useful material for the subsequent activities and the debate.
- Students' Book, page 164, activity 3. Using the grammar section and looking back through the book for examples, draw up a list with the students of a few useful expressions in the subjunctive that they can learn, use and adapt in their work such as *cuando sea mayor, ¡no seas tonto!, no quiero que hagas eso* etc.
- Students' Book, page 165, activity 7. Which statements do students agree with and why?

1 Contesta a las preguntas en inglés.

- Students answer the questions in English.

Answers:

a Making an effort to speak the language shows respect.

b His team mates respect him more for speaking their language.

c Tourists who don't try to speak the language miss out on a lot of the country – people, culture and food.

d It will be a valuable experience when she returns home.

e You can improve with patience and determination.

f He can express himself much more fluently now.

g She practises with her friends when she goes out with them.

h She is much more confident now.

2 Escucha. ¿Qué aspecto de vivir y trabajar en el extranjero les resultó problemático?

- Students listen and decide which problems the speakers had.

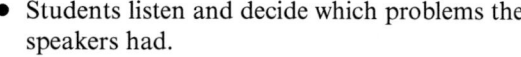

> **CD 3, track 44   página 164, actividad 2**
>
> **1** Para mí, cenar a las diez de la noche me resultó un poco incómodo.
> **2** Ganaba bastante para pagarme las necesidades básicas pero no mucho más.
> **3** No me di cuenta de lo caro que era alquilar un piso en el centro de la ciudad.
> **4** Al principio me costó mucho entender lo que me decían.
> **5** A mediodía hacía un calor insoportable y no se podía estar por la calle.
> **6** Me sorprendió lo caro que era todo, desde la fruta hasta los billetes de tren.
> **7** No estaba acostumbrado a comer platos tan raros. Comí pulpo por primera vez.
> **8** Encontré bastante difícil hacer amigos durante los primeros seis meses.

Answers: **1** g, **2** c, **3** a, **4** h, **5** f, **6** e, **7** b, **8** d

3 Traduce las frases al inglés.

- Students translate the sentences into English. Point out that the subjunctive rarely translates obviously into English. It may help if students think of it as drawing attention to uncertainty.

Answers: **a** When I am older, I want to live in another country. **b** My parents don't want me to live abroad. **c** Many companies expect their employees to travel abroad. **d** When I arrive, I will write to everyone. **e** I hope you don't miss me. **f** I want you to come and visit me.

4 Prepara una lista de la ventajas y desventajas de vivir y trabajar en el extranjero.

- Students prepare a list of advantages and disadvantages of living abroad. They should look back through this page for ideas from both sides.

Half the class can prepare advantages, the other half disadvantages.

It would be worth spending time setting up this activity in class in order to build students' confidence, e.g. by brain storming. Once pairwork has been practised, they can perform their debate to the class, or divide the class into two for a proper debate. This is good practice for scenarios. Pupils should receive feedback from other students as to how convincing they were.

5 Debate con tu compañero/a sobre los aspectos positivos y negativos de pasar tiempo viviendo y trabajando en el extranjero. Una persona está a favor, la otra en contra.

- Students debate with a partner the merits of living and working abroad. Their partner should come from the side of the class who compiled the list for the opposite viewpoint.

6 Traduce las frases al inglés.

- Students translate the sentences into English.

Answers: **a** It's not easy to get used to the changes in another country. **b** Some people can't get used to the climate. **c** It's difficult, but I'm getting used to the different mealtimes. **d** You won't take long to understand the language. **e** The first week I spent in Spain I got fed up with not understanding anything.

7 Empareja las frases 1–10 y a–j. Recuerda mirar bien cómo termina la primera frase.

- Students match up the beginning and the ends of the sentences. How the first half ends is very important; remind them to look for verb endings and agreements.

Answers: **1** f, **2** i, **3** e, **4** g, **5** c, **6** a, **7** d, **8** j, **9** b, **10** h

8 Lee el texto y apunta los falsos amigos (las palabras en negrita). Escribe lo que significan en inglés.

- Students note down the highlighted "false friends" and say what they actually mean in English.

Answers: **emocionante** – exciting, **sana** – wholesome, **recordarás** – you will remember, **larga** – long, **molestarán** – they will bother, **sensible** – sensitive, **actualmente** – currently, **en absoluto** – at all, **suceso** – event, **realizar** – fulfill, **asistir** – attend, **atender** – look after, **embarazada** – pregnant, **sopa** – soup, **droguería** – chemist's, **pretendo** – I intend

9 Traduce las frases al inglés.

- Students translate the sentences into English.

Answers: **a** An exciting day, **b** I don't like it at all, **c** My sister is very sensitive, **d** I have long hair, **e** My current boss is called Pedro, **f** I hate chicken soup, **g** My colleague really bothers me, **h** You have to attend the meeting.

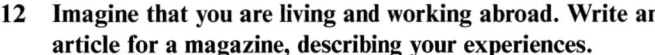

10 Traduce las frases al español.

- Students translate the sentences into Spanish.

Answers: **a** Un trabajo emocionante, **b** No les gusta en absoluto, **c** Era muy sensible cuando era menor, **d** Este artículo es demasiado largo, **e** No tengo trabajo actualmente, **f** No hay sopa en el menú, **g** Mi hermano mo me molesta mucho, **h** Asistí a la reunión el martes.

4–8

Remate

11 Write ten questions you would ask a person who is living and working abroad.

PLTS

- They can imagine they need the information to write up the magazine article below. What information would someone considering going abroad be interested in reading?

4–8

12 Imagine that you are living and working abroad. Write an article for a magazine, describing your experiences.

PLTS

4–9

- Write as if for people considering making the move themselves. Students can research websites and blogs of people living abroad to get a flavour of what it is like. If they know any people from abroad living in this country, they can ask them about their experiences too.

Success criteria activities 11 & 12:

- *students give information accurately and in the appropriate style*
- *students express personal opinions and justify points of view*
- *students use a variety of vocabulary and structures*

Gramática en acción

páginas 166 y 167

> ## *Planner*

> ### Objectives
> - Using the subjunctive, practising verbs with prepositions

> ### Resources
> Students' Book, pages 166–167
> Exam Skills Workbook, page 61 (F and H)
> Grammar Workbook, page 38–40, 59, 64–65, 68
> Activity sheet 68
> Resources and Planning OxBox CD-ROM

> ### Grammar
> - Gerunds
> - Verb followed by a preposition
> - *Ser* or *estar*
> - The subjunctive
> - More verbs which take a preposition

> ### PLTS
> Students' Book, page 167, activity 9,
> *Reflective Learners*
> Students' Book, page 167, activity 10,
> *Self-Managers*

> ## Gerunds

1 Look up the correct form of the gerund for these verbs.
- Students should write out the gerunds with their verb infinitives for reference.

Answers: pidiendo, leyendo, construyendo, repitiendo, durmiendo, siguiendo, muriendo, cayendo, sintiendo, reyendo, oyendo, trayendo

2 Fill in the blanks with the gerund of one of the verbs from the box below.

Answers: **a** estudiando, **b** trabajando, **c** leyendo, **d** construyendo, **e** repitiendo

Verbs followed by a preposition

3 Fill in the blanks with a preposition from the box.
- Tell students to look back to pages 161 and 165 to revise the verbs which take a preposition first.

Answers: **a** de, **b** sin, **c** para, **d** al, **e** a, **f** de, **g** con, **h** a, **i** de, **j** a

4 Write in the correct form of the verb. Remember to use clues such as tenses of the other verbs in the sentence/time references etc.
- Students follow the revision instructions in the box first. This can be done from memory or it can be a class collaborative effort. Finally students do the activity.

Answers: **a** quería, **b** fui, hablé, **c** terminaban, **d** podría, **e** seguiré, **f** han prometido / prometen

Ser or *estar*

5 Fill in the blanks with a part of *ser* or *estar* from the box below. Look carefully at the tense required.
- Ask students when to use ser and when estar before they start this activity.

Answers: **1** estoy, **2** están, **3** Son, **4** sea, **5** seré, **6** es, **7** sido, **8** Será, **9** estar, **10** fuera, **11** sería, **13** son

The subjunctive

6 Now translate these sentences.

- Students should read the section on the subunctive thoroughly, and look back at the examples on previous spreads before doing this activity.

Answers: **a** Many companies expect you to have a lot of qualifications. **b** I don't want my parents to decide my future. **c** When I am twenty, I'll go and live in another country.

7 Now form the subjunctive in these sentences and then translate them.

Answers: **a** ayuden − Many young people expect their parents to help them with their studies. **b** trabajen − The bank wants its employees to work hard. **c** viva − When I live in Spain in the future, it will be marvellous for me.

8 Match the question with the answer. Look carefully at the tense.

- Students can go through the questions identifying the verb and saying what tense it is in before doing the matching activity.

Answers: **1** d, **2** b, **3** e, **4** h, **5** c, **6** f, **7** a, **8** g

9 Find the errors in these passages. There are five mistakes in each passage.

PLTS *Answers:*

- **a** Si yo fuera rico, **irías** (iría) a vivir **a** (en) **una** (un) país muy exótico cerca **de el** (del) mar. Pasaría **la** (el) día tomando el sol y por la noche **saliría** (saldría) con mis amigos.
- **b** No **se** (sé) **(lo) qué** (que) quiero hacer en el futuro. Es **mucho** (muy) **dificil** (difícil) decidir el trabajo que me gustaría hacer por qué hay muchas profesiónes que me **gusta** (gustan).
- **c** Cuando sea mayor, **haceré** (haré) un trabajo muy **divertida** (divertido) y ganaré **mucha** (mucho) dinero. Las horas no **será** (serán) largas y no tendré que **trabajo** (trabajar) mucho.

More verbs which take a preposition

10 Translate the following sentences.

PLTS *Answers:* **a** Me acostumbré a vivir al extranjero. **b** Se negaron a darme el puesto. **c** No me acordé de escribir la carta. **d** La paga tende a ser buena. **e** Hay que estudiar mucho si quieres tener excito. **f** Cuidaba de todos los problemas.

Habilidades

página 168

Planner

Objectives
- Accents, stress and memory aids

Resources
Students' Book, pages 168
Exam Skills Workbook, page 62 (F), page 63 (H)
Activity sheet 69
Resources and Planning OxBox CD-ROM

Skills
- Recognising how accents can change the meaning
- Putting the stress in the right place
- Knowing when to use capital letters
- Avoiding some common mistranslations
- Opening and closing a letter
- Using *lo que* correctly
- Knowing which double letters are used in Spanish

PLTS
Students' Book, page 168, activity 2, *Reflective Learners*
Students' Book, page 168, activity 6, *Creative Thinkers*

Leer

1 Recognise how accents can change the meaning.

❑ Explain the different meanings of the words in italics.

Answers: you / your, How? / as, the / him, this / is, this / east, this person / is (subjunctive)

❑ What do the following words mean?

Answers: practica − he / she practises, práctica − practice (noun), hacia − towards, hacía − he / she did / made

Hablar

2 Put the stress in the right place.

❑ Try saying these words.

PLTS
- Students can say them slowly for accuracy, then when they are more confident they can try saying them very quickly all in a row like a tongue twister
- Remind students of the pronunciation rules − stress does not fall on the second to last syllable when the word ends in l and z.

- Students can write them out and use a highlighter on the stressed syllables, then they can say them like a tongue twister as before. Who can say it most quickly?
- If possible, display a map with the places marked. Students have to say the names while pointing to them. How quickly can they do it?

➤ Escribir

3 Know when to use capital letters.

❏ Write out the days of the week, the months of the year and as many nationalities and countries as you can remember.
  - Students can brainstorm in groups or pairs. Which group has the most unusual nationalities?

❏ Now write out the following in Spanish.

Answer: Los franceses viven en Francia y hablan francés pero los españoles viven en España y hablan español.

4 Avoid some common mistranslations.

❏ How would you write these in Spanish? They are often mistranslated.

Answers: Estoy en casa – Voy a casa, Estoy en el colegio – Voy al colegio, Estoy en la universidad – Voy a la universidad

5 Open and close a letter.

❏ For an informal letter, use *querido*.
  - Draw attention to the agreements on the end of *querido*.

❏ For a formal letter, use one of these forms.
  - Ask students what equivalent forms are used in English.

6 Use *lo que* correctly.

❏ Write five sentences beginning with *lo que* meaning 'what'.
  - Ask students for five opinion words to act as triggers for their sentences e.g *me gusta, me encanta, no aguanto*

❏ Now write five sentences which have *lo que* in the middle, still meaning 'what'.

PLTS • Ask students for verbs to begin their sentences e.g. *no sé, no entiendo, veo*

❏ Now write five sentences with *lo que* joining two ideas together, meaning 'which'.
  - Divide the class into five groups and ask each to come up with one example.

7 Know which double letters are used in Spanish.

❏ Learn this simple memory aid: CaRoLiNa.
  - Tell students to write out the examples.

Escenario

página 169

Planner

➤ Objectives
- Writing a report about your ideal profesion and taking part in a balloon debate.

➤ Resources
Students' Book, pages 169
Exam Skills Workbook, pages 59–60 (F), pages 60–61 (H)
Assessment sheets 33–40
Resources and Planning OxBox CD-ROM

➤ Skills
- Writing practice
- Speaking practice

➤ PLTS
Students' Book, page 169, Escenario Oral, *Effective Participators*
Students' Book, page 169, Escenario Escrito, *Independent Enquirers*

➤ Oral

You are going to take part in a hot air balloon debate. You are in a balloon with a group of other people (see main cartoon on page 155). The balloon is sinking. One of you must be thrown out to save the lives of the others.

PLTS
4–9
- Students read the instructions on the Escenario page. They can choose to debate in small groups, or prepare their characters in groups and present their debate to the rest of the class who decide who should be thrown out of the balloon.

- Famous people could be:
- *Martin Luther King, Emily Pankhurst, John Lennon, Florence Nightingale, Mother Theresa, Elizabeth 1, David Beckham, Winston Churchill, Alexander Graham Bell, Nelson Mandela, Marie Curie, Leonardo da Vinci*
- Professions could be:
- *teacher, scientist, dustman, surgeon, soldier, doctor, musician, engineer, train driver, farmer, pilot, artist, inventor, solicitor*
- *GCSE Grades A*-C*

- *Grade C Students use past, present and future tenses. They express opinions, and deal with some unpredictability.*
- *Grade A Students express and justify opinions. They use a variety of vocabulary and structure in longer speech sequences.*

➤ Escrito

Research a chosen career or describe the life and career of a famous person / celebrity. Talk about childhood / family background / studies / experiences / personality / qualities etc.

 PLTS
- Brainstorm a selection of famous people. Try for a wide range of professions, characters and eras of history. Suggest students research someone

similar to their usual idol e.g. if they admire a film star like Nicole Kidman, they could look at the life of an earlier star like Ingrid Bergman, or even an actress from history like Sarah Bernhardt. What particular qualities did that person need to be a success in that time?
- *GCSE Grades A*-C*
- *Grade C Students use opinions and past, present and future tenses, both factually and imaginatively. Register is appropriate and style is basic.*
- *Grade A Students write factually and imaginatively using longer sequences and a range of vocabulary and structure. They express and justify opinions in an appropriate style.*

Vocabulario
página 170

This is a summary of key language from the unit, organised by spread and theme. Students can use it for reference while working on the unit, and as an aid to learning vocabulary.

Lectura
páginas 189 y 190

Planner

➤ Objectives
- Describing people, their professions and characters
- To encourage independent reading and develop reading strategies.
- These pages also provide alternative class and homework material for students who work quickly and require extension work.

➤ Resources
Students' Book, page 189–190

➤ PLTS
Students' Book, page 189, activity 5, *Independent Enquirers*
Students' Book, page 190, activity 1, *Self-Managers*

➤ Lectura A – ¿Quién soy?

1 ¿Quién soy?

- Students decide who the person described is.

Answer: doctor

2 ¿Quién soy?

- Students decide who the person described is.

Answer: physiotherapist

3 ¿Quién soy?

- Students decide who the person described is.

Answer: supermarket shelf-stacker

4 ¿Quién soy?

- Students decide who the person described is.

Answer: Mum / housewife

5 ¿Quién soy?
PLTS
- Students decide who the person described is.

Answer: Father Christmas

➤ Lectura B – Gloria Fuertes

1 Lee el artículo y rellena los huecos con las palabras de la caja.
PLTS
- Students read the article and fill in the blanks with the words provided.

Answers: **1** nació, **2** era, **3** murieron, **4** pasó, **5** aprendió, **6** quiso, **7** recibió, **8** consistía, **9** murió, **10** marcaron, **11** entró, **13** publicó, 13 fue, **14** empezó, **15** perdió

2   Traduce las siguientes citas.

6–9

- Translate the following famous sayings. Get the students to research the originals to see how their translation compares.

Answers:

Education is the key to the future, the key to man's destiny and his opportunity to have an effect on the world. *Robert F Kennedy*

Only through education can a man become a man. Man is no more than what education makes him. *Immanuel Kant*

It is necessary to learn what we need and not just what we want. *Paulo Coelho*

Success is learning to go from disaster to disaster without losing hope. *Winston Churchill*

The important thing is how much love we put into the work we carry out. *Mother Theresa of Calcutta*

Learning without thinking is useless. Thinking without learning is dangerous. *Confucius*

Educating a child is not teaching him something that he did not know, but to make of him someone that did not exist before. *John Ruskin*

Exam Practice

Listening
pages 191-193

Foundation level

1 Listen to these short statements in Spanish about planned activities for holiday makers. You will hear each statement twice. Read the questions below and choose the correct answer, one per question.

CD 4, track 2   page 192, exercise 1

Example: El domingo vamos a visitar una iglesia muy antigua. The correct answer is A.

Question 1: El miércoles por la mañana visitaremos el museo.

Question 2: Por la tarde hay tiempo para las compras y los mercados.

Question 3: El jueves vamos a pasar el día en la playa tomando el sol.

Question 4: Y por la noche, una fiesta con música.

Question 5: El viernes nos dan un día libre en la ciudad.

Question 6: El sábado por la mañana hay una excursión en autobús.

Question 7: Y por la tarde, vamos a ir a una fábrica de chocolate.

Question 8: El último día hay una cena deliciosa en el comedor del hotel.

Answers: **1** C, **2** A, **3** C, **4** C, **5** C, **6** A, **7** C, **8** C

2 Listen to the tour guide, Manolo, telling you about himself and his job, then answer the questions.

CD 4, track 3   page 192, exercise 2

Question 9
Manolo: Me levanto sobre las seis menos cuarto.

Question 10
Manolo: Suelo desayunar con mis padres.

Question 11
Manolo: Salgo de casa a las seis y media y voy a mi trabajo en coche.

Qxestion 12
Manolo: Al llegar a la oficina, trabajo con mi ordenador.

Question 13
Manolo: A veces tengo que ir al aeropuerto a esperar la llegada de un vuelo y a ayudar a los pasajeros con su equipaje.

Question 14
Manolo: Trabajo muchas horas, y a veces por la noche, pero no me importa.

Question 15
Manolo: El único problema es el dinero. No gano bastante para pagar mis gastos.

Question 16
Manolo: Mi ambición es viajar e ir a trabajar a otros países.

Answers: **9** C, **10** B, **11** C, **12** C, **13** B, **14** B, **15** A, **16** B

3 What have the following people lost? Choose one answer for each question.

CD 4, track 4   page 192, exercise 3

Question 17
Woman 1: Era un bolso negro y tenía mis llaves y mi monedero dentro.

Question 18
Man 1: Es una cartera con sesenta y cinco euros y unas fotos de mi madre.

Question 19
Man 2: Es una bolsa de deporte con mis playeros blancos y una camiseta gris.

Question 20
Woman 2: No recuerdo donde aparqué mi coche. La matrícula es B256 ADZ.

Question 21
Man 3: Dejé mi mochila en el autobús número 17. Tenía cuatro libros y mis gafas de sol.

Question 22
Woman 3: No encuentro a mi hija. Es baja, rubia y lleva pantalones cortos y un jersey de rayas.

Question 23
Man 4: Ha desaparecido mi gato. Su collar lleva el número de teléfono de nuestra casa. El número es 9,05,34,16.

Question 24
Woman 4: He dejado en la tienda mi bolsa de la compra, con los huevos, la sopa, y una barra de pan.

Answers: **17** C, **18** B, **19** A, **20** B, **21** C, **22** C, **23** B, **24** A

4 Listen to Pablo's account of his weekend, the answer the questions.

CD 4, track 5 — page 193, exercise 4 4

Question 25
Pablo: El sábado pasado fue el cumpleaños de mi primo, Arturo.

Question 26
Pablo: Organizamos una fiesta en un restaurante chino en el centro de la ciudad.

Question 27
Pablo: La comida fue riquísima pero hubo un problema cuando llegó la cuenta.

Question 28
Pablo: Y yo tuve que pagar el doble porque mi amiga Julia se había olvidado su dinero.

Question 29
Pablo: Después de cenar, nos acercamos a una discoteca pero no había nadie. La gente no empezó a llegar hasta las doce y media

Questions 30-32
Pablo: Al día siguiente estaba exhausto. Tuve un partido de baloncesto y no jugué muy bien porque no había dormido suficiente la noche anterior. Perdimos 35–26.

Answers: **25** Pablo's cousin, **26** in a Chinese restaurant in the city centre, **27** there was a problem, **28** she had forgotten her money, **29** half past midnight, **30** a basketball match, **31** he hadn't slept enough the night before, **32** Pablo's team lost **35-26**

5 Listen to the weather forecast and fill in the blanks.

CD 4, track 6 — page 192, exercise 5

Example: En Gijón habrá bastante lluvia y temperaturas bajas.

Questions 33 and 34: Valencia
Forecaster: Se esperan fuertes vientos en la costa valenciana pero las temperaturas serán moderadas con 27 grados. Un día perfecto para hacer vela.

Questions 35 and 36: Granada
Forecaster: Un día maravilloso para los aficionados al esquí. Por la noche caerá una nevada que alcanzará los tres metros de altura en la estación invernal de Sierra Nevada. ¡Qué suerte para los granadinos! Y temperaturas muy altas.

Questions 37 and 38: Málaga
Forecaster: Si le gusta el windsurf es un día perfecto para pasarlo en las costas del sur. Las olas alcanzarán un metro y medio hoy, y toda la tarde será soleada.

Questions 39 and 40: Madrid
Forecaster: En la capital hoy cielos despejados por la mañana pero con posibilidades de chubascos por la tarde. Así que hay que llevar paraguas.

Answers: **33** coast, **34** sailing, **35** skiers, **36** snow, **37** windsurfing, **38** 1.5m, **39** clear, **40** an umbrella

Higher level

3 Listen to these people talking about their environmental concerns. Match the person with the problem that concerns them.

CD 4, track 7 — page 193, exercise 3

Example:
Javier: La destrucción de las selvas tropicales es un problema que me preocupa mucho.

Question 17
Pablo: A mí lo que más me preocupa es la cantidad de emisiones nocivas que echan las fábricas.

Question 18
Rosa: Los embotellamientos en las carreteras son un problema tremendo también.

Question 19
Sara: Los semáforos también son un problema, por eso hay tantas colas por la mañana.

Question 20
Juan: No es por eso. Es que la gente no respeta el medio ambiente. ¿Por qué no pueden usar otra forma de transporte que no sea el coche?

Question 21
Inma: En mi casa reciclamos todo pero los vecinos no hacen nada en absoluto.

Question 22
Nacho: Para mí lo más problemático es el empaquetado de los productos. Tanto cartón y papel para luego tirarlo a la basura. Es imperdonable.

Question 23
Lidia: Pues yo he decidido que no voy a volver a comprar libros nunca más. Iré a la biblioteca y los sacaré de allí.

Question 24
Estéban: Mira. El mayor problema es el tráfico aéreo. El número de vuelos se ha triplicado en los últimos diez años.

Answers: **17** D, **18** F, **19** B, **20** H, **21** G, **22** A, **23** E, **24** C

4 Listen to thses oung people talking about their future. Then, complete the positive (P) and negative (N) comments in English.

> **CD 4, track 8**   page 193, exercise 4
>
> **Example:**
> **Sonia:** No tendré que compartir una habitación con mi hermana pero echaré de menos a mi gato.
>
> **Questions 25 and 26**
> **Ana:** Creo que será maravilloso independizarme de mis padres pero ahora es difícil porque dependo de ellos económicamente.
>
> **Questions 27 and 28**
> **José:** Pues lo bueno es que hay muchas oportunidades si estás dispuesto a trabajar duro pero hay a la vez mucha gente compitiendo por los mismos puestos.
>
> **Questions 29 and 30**
> **Teresa:** La idea de no tener que volver a casa a cierta hora me chifla pero estoy algo preocupada por tener que prepararme todas las comidas.
>
> **Questions 31 and 32**
> **Jorge:** Aprender a conducir me apetece mucho porque podré ir adonde quiera en cualquier momento aunque la responsabilidad de mantener el vehículo no me atrae mucho.

Answers: **25** be independent of her parents, **26** her parents financially, **27** there are a lot of opportunities, **28** competing for the same jobs, **29** be home by a certain time, **30** having to prepare all her own meals, **31** learning to drive, **32** maintain his car

5 Listen to the interview with María Gómez Pando, Minister for Health and Safety in a Latin American county. Then, complete these notes, in English.

> **CD 4, track 9**   page 193, exercise 5
>
> **Interviewer:** ¿Cuándo le empezó a interesar la política?
> **María:** Pues siempre he tenido talento para expresarme bien y he mantenido opiniones muy firmes. Mis padres me dicen que desde pequeñita, yo reaccionaba mucho contra cualquier injusticia o desastre en la tele por ejemplo, una guerra, un terremoto … Supongo que fue entonces cuando me comenzó a fascinar.
> **Interviewer:** ¿Ha trabajado en cualquier otro campo que no sea la política?
> **María:** Pues sí. De estudiante universitaria me fui a un pueblecito de Nicaragua durante un verano a ayudar a construir una escuela primaria pero eso fue un trabajo voluntario.
> **Interviewer:** Y ¿qué aprendió de esa experiencia?
> **María:** Bueno, lo que aprendí allí es algo que llevaré conmigo durante el resto de mi vida. Me enseñaron que la riqueza no se trata de cuántas posesiones o dinero tengas.
> **Interviewer:** Y ¿a qué edad se metió en la política?

> **María:** Pues al volver de Nicaragua me di cuenta de que tenía que hacer algo en mi propio país para aliviar el sufrimiento por ejemplo de los niños abandonados, los ancianos sin familia, las madres solteras, así que me hice socia de un grupo activista 'Jóvenes por la Justicia'. Estuve con ellos unos cuatro años.
> **Interviewer:** ¿Qué tal esa experiencia?
> **María:** Hombre, hubo momentos difíciles pero creo que las dificultades nos enseñan a ser más fuertes, ¿no?
> **Interviewer:** ¿Y su puesto actual, le satisface?
> **María:** Sí totalmente, aunque ha habido momentos en los que me hubiera gustado no tener que trabajar hasta tan tarde. Eso ha sido difícil. Sí. No lo niego. No poder darle un beso de buenas noches a mi hija por ejemplo, pero sí, sí me satisface.
> **Interviewer:** ¿Y su mayor éxito desde que ocupa el puesto, cuál es?
> **María:** Pues tendría que decir que … la introducción de comidas gratuitas para todos los niños de edad primaria. Hay un sentido de satisfacción enorme en saber que cada niño esté bien alimentado por lo menos una vez al día. Para mí, es importante eso.

Answers: **33** (she reacted strongly to any injustice on the TV such as) war and earthquake, **34** construct a primary school, **35** that being rich is not about how much money or how many possesions you have, **36** single mothers, **37** a group called *Youth for Justice*, **38** teach you to be stronger, **39** she can't always kiss her daughter goodnight, **40** introducing free school meals for all primary school children

Reading   pages 196–199

Foundation level

1 Look at the categories of books (A–I) on offer in the school library at your exchange school. Match the content to the correct book.

Answers: **1** E, **2** G, **3** H, **4** B, **5** D, **6** F, **7** A, **8** C

2 Read this email from your Mexican pen-friend. Then choose the correct answer.

Answers: **9** C, **10** C, **11** A, **12** B, **13** A, **14** C, **15** B, **16** A

3 Read the complaints about home life sent in to a magazine problem page. Write the name of the correct person.

Answers: **17** Paco, **18** Juan, **19** Ana, **20** Carlos, **21** Susi, **22** Marta, **23** Paula, **24** Bea

4 Read the following statements about eating and cooking arrangements. Then write the name of the correct person.

Answers: **25** Nacho, **26** Rafa, **27** Pili, **28** Javi, **29** Pedro, **30** Claudia, **31** Inés, **32** Sara

5 Read this letter from Isabel and answer the questions in English.

Answers: **33** she's had too much homework, **34** dancing, **35** do exercises / learn vocabulary, **36** she didn't finish working until 20 past 10, **37** they don't understand her point of view, **38** they have never argued, **39** they are still very much in love, **40** Do you see your grandparents often?

Higher level

3 Read the following article about Santa Teresa School. Then complete each sentence, using a word or phrase from the box as in the example.

Answers: **17** near, **18** outside, **19** attend lessons, **20** relaxed, **21** sit exams, **22** learning, **23** understand, **24** cooperation

4 Read the following article about immigration in USA. Answer the questions in English.

Answers: **25** nearly half a million, **26** to find a way to earn their living, **27** to escape the poverty of their own country, **28** they are detained and deported, **29** it is a very dangerous journey, **30** one in four Americans will be hispanic, **31** it is the proportion of the workforce that are Latin Americans, **32** without them many companies would have difficulty finding enough workers

5 Read the article about Pilar's first trip abroad. Then choose the correct answer.

Answers: **33** C, **34** A, **35** B, **36** C, **37** C, **38** B, **39** B, **40** B

203

Grammar Bank

➤ **Objectives**
Practising grammar

➤ **Resources**
Students' Book, page 201-212

Unit 1A

1.1   Form the plural of these:

Answers: **2** los ojos, **3** las orejas, **4** los pelos, **5** los relojes, **6** unas cantantes, **7** unos paises, **8** las ventanas

1.2   Translate:

Answers: **1** a la casa, **2** del parque, **3** al coche, **4** al dormitorio, **5** de la cama, **6** de la ciudad, **7** del pueblo, **8** al aeropuerto, **9** al instituto, **10** a la piscina, **11** de la estación, **12** a la iglesia

1.3   Find these verbs in a dictionary and group them according to their infinitive:

Answers: **-ar verbs** estudiar, fumar, ayudar, odiar, jugar, hablar, **-er verbs** aprender, beber, **-ir verbs** compartir, dormir

1.4   Translate the following:

Answers: **1** estudiamos, **2** aprendes, **3** fumo, **4** compartís, **5** ayudan, **6** usted odia, **7** jugamos, **8** habla

1.5   Complete the sentences with the correct form of the present tense of the verb in brackets.

Answers: **1** compra, **2** vive, **3** escribo, **4** fuman, **5** hablan, **6** celebramos, **7** aprende, **8** ayudan

1.6a   Choose the correct verb.

Answers: **1** Soy, **2** es, **3** es, **4** Estoy, **5** estamos, **6** está, **7** está, **8** es

1.6b   Use the correct form of the present tense of the irregular verbs *ser, estar, tener, hacer* and *ir* to fill in the gaps in this paragraph.

Answers: voy, hace, voy, tiene, es, tiene, Es, hace

1.7a   What do these reflexive verbs mean?

Answers: **1** to get up, **2** to have a shave, **3** to take off (an item of clothing), **4** to comb one's hair, **5** to take a shower, **6** to wake up, **7** to get dry, **8** to look at oneself, **9** to take a bath, **10** to put on (an item of clothing), **11** to put on make up, **12** to get washed

1.7b   Use the verbs of exercise 1.7a to complete each sentence using the '*yo*' form.

Answers: **1** me levanto, **2** me lavo, me miro, **3** me quito, **4** me seco, me pongo

1.7c   Rewrite the sentences of exercise 1.7b in the third person singular (he/she).

Answers: **1** se levanta, **2** se lava, se mira, **3** se quita, **4** se seca, se pone

1.8   Answer these questions using the negative form.

Answers: **1** No, no tengo **18** años. **2** No, no vivo en Madrid. **3** No, no soy un(a) buen(a) estudiante. **4** No, no hay seis personas en mi familia. **5** No, no me gusta ver la tele. **6** No, no paso la aspiradora en casa. **7** No, no me llevo mal con mis padres. **8** No, no llevamos uniforme en nuestro instituto.

1.9a   Translate the following:

Answers: **1** Voy a visitar mi abuela. **2** Vamos a estudiar matemáticas. **3** Van a jugar a tenis en el polideportivo. **4** Vamos a hacer las compras después del desayuno. **5** Voy a mirar la tele en el salón. **6** Mamá va a bailar con sus amigos.

1.9b   Say what your plans are for tomorrow.

Answers: **1** Si mañana llueve, primero voy a desayunar en la cocina y después voy a leer mi emails. **2** Por la tarder voy a ir a casa de mi amigo/a. **3** Por la noche voy a alquilar un DVD y voy a ller veinte minutos.

1.10a Complete the table.

Answers:

English	Masculine singular	Feminine singular	Masculine plural	Feminine plural
crazy	**loco**	loca	locos	locas
tall / high	**alto**	alta	altos	altas
blue	**azul**	azul	azules	azules
weak	**débil**	débil	débiles	débiles
handsome / pretty	**guapo**	guapa	guapos	guapas
demanding	**exigente**	exigente	exigentes	exigentes
kind	**amable**	amable	amables	amables

1.10b Translate the following:

Answers: **1** un(a) amigo/a amable, **2** una novia guapa, **3** unos/as profesores locos/as, **4** la mujer inteligente, **5** los pantalones azules, **6** un gran día, **7** las chicas altas, **8** un(a) gran cantante, **9** el/la director(a) artístico(a), **10** los/las estudiantes débiles, **11** los pobres padres, **12** el tercer día

1.11a Compare the following.

Answers: **1** Mi abuelo es mayor que mi padre. **2** Mi dormitorio es más pequeño que la cocina. **3** El colegio está más cerca que la piscina. **4** Los pantalones vaqueros son más caros que el vestido.

1.11b Now compare the following hobbies adding your own adjective.

Encourage students to use a variety of adjectives in their answers.

1.12 Look at the line-up and make sentences using the adjectives in the box.

Answers: (suggested − some answers could be up for debate.) Javier es el más alto. Juan es el más bajo. Josema es el más gordo. Javier es el más delgado. Javier es el más guapo. Juan es el más feo. Javier es el más serio.

1.13 Now rephrase your sentences emphasising the adjectives.

Answers: Javier es altísimo. Juan es bajísimo. Josema es gordísimo. Javier es delgadísimo. Javier es guapísimo. Juan es feísimo. Javier es serísimo.

1.14 Complete the sentences with the correct possessive adjectives.

Answers: **1** Mis, **2** su, sus, **3** tu, **4** sus, **5** mis, mis, mi, **6** su

1.15 Translate the following:

Answers: **1** muy simpático, **2** muchos deberes, **3** demasiado frío, **4** un poco cansado, **5** demasiado grande, **6** muy pequeño, **7** muchas personas, **8** muy estrícto

1.16 Write the correct question word to complete the sentence so that it makes sense.

Answers: **1** A qué hora, **2** Cuándo, **3** Quién, **4** Adónde, **5** Dónde, **6** Cuántos, **7** Cuál, **8** Cómo

1.17 Rewrite the following sentences filling in the blanks with the personal 'a' where necessary.

Answers: **1** a, **2** a, **3** N/A, **4** a, **5** N/A, **6** N/A

Unit 1B

1.18 Form adverbs from these adjectives.

Answers: **1** claramente, **2** rápidamente, **3** ciertamente, **4** nuevamente, **5** tristemente, **6** verdaderamente, **7** felizmente, **8** agradablemente, **9** afortunadamente, **10** normalmente

1.19 Use your imagination and answer these questions.

Encourage students to extend their Answers where they are able.

1.20a Think back to when you were in primary school and use the verbs in the box to make sentences using the imperfect tense.

Encourage students to draw on their own experience; these are the verbs in the first person singular.

Answers: me levantaba, estudiaba, me gustaba(n), tenía, llamaba, leía, hacía

1.20b Preterite or imperfect? Circle the correct verb.

Answers: **1** dormía, llegó, **2** Había, fui, fueron, **3** Entré, empezaba, **4** Me bañaba, sonó, **5** escuchaba, interrumpió, **6** Estaba, telefoneó

1.21 Fill in the gaps with 'por' or 'para' as appropriate.

Answers: **1** por, **2** para, **3** para, **4** para, **5** por, **6** por, **7** para, **8** para

1.22a Who are these gifts for? Follow the example.

Answers: **1** Estos pantalones son para Jesús, pero esos son para Jorge y aquellos para Gema. **2** Estes zapatos son para papá, pero esos son para mamá y aquellos para la abuela. **3** Esta pelota es para el perro pero esa es para el gato y aquella para el hamster. **4** Esta camiseta es para mi hermano pero esa es para mi primo y aquella es para mi amigo. **5** Estes flores son para mamá pero esos son para mi novia y aquellos para mi profesora. **6** Estes CDs son para mi amiga pero esos son para mi hermana y aquellos para mi padre.

1.22b **Replace the words in brackets by the correct form of the demonstrative adjective or pronoun.**

Answers: **1** estas, esas, **2** este, aquel, **3** aquella, esta, **4** esta, aquella, **5** Esta, esa, **6** Ese, este, **7** Estos, esos, **8** Estas, aquellas.

1.23a **Practice saying these phone numbers out loud.**
These are the numbers the students should say; they can test each other.

Answers: **1** noventa y cuatro, ocho cero tres, tres cuatro, tres cero, **2** noventa y dos, siete cero seis, cuatro nueve, nueve cuatro, **3** noventa y tres, ocho seis nueve, nueve tres, nueve tres, **4** noventa y siete, ocho siete siete, tres nueve, seis cinco, **5** noventa y tres, tres ocho cuatro, nueve cuatro, dos cero, **6** noventa y tres, cuatro cuatro cinco, tres cinco, dos cinco, **7** noventa y siete, dos tres cuatro, nueve tres, uno nueve, **8** noventa y uno, ocho ocho dos, ocho tres, uno cinco

1.23b **Write these numbers out.**

Answers: **1** un millón ocho mil novecientos y siete, **2** ocenta y siete mil setecientos noventa y ocho, **3** catorce mil seiscientos setenta y nueve, **4** ciento setenta y seis mil setenta y siete, **5** setecientos sesenta y ocho mil novecientos y nueve, **6** tres millones cuatrocientos sesenta y siete mil ochocientos noventa y dos, **7** siete millones novecientos cuarenta y cinco mil, novecientos treinta y dos, **8** setenta y ocho mil, seiscientos cincuenta y siete

1.24 **Translate the following**

Answers: **1** el tercer piso, **2** el quinto año, **3** la décima calle, **4** la tercera mesa, **5** el nueve de enero, **6** los primerso libros, **7** el tercer estudiante, **8** la sexta puerta

Unit 2A

2.1a **Classify these verbs in three groups according to their stem change:**

Answers: **o or u − ue:** dormir, jugar, contar, volver, volar, **e − ie:** empezar, entender, preferir, cerrar, **e − i:** conseguir, pedir, elgir

2.1b **Complete these sentences with the correct form of the verb in brackets.**

Answers: **1** prefiero, **2** recomienda, **3** entienden, **4** piensa, **5** jugamos, **6** llueve, **7** soléis, **8** almuerzan

2.2 **Say in Spanish that…**
This can also be done orally in class.

Answers: **1** Me encanta hacer el puenting, **2** Le fascina hacer canoë, **3** Nos interesa la escalada, **4** Les encanta el fútbol, **5** No me gusta el tenís, **6** No le interesan las ciencias, **7** Les fascina la medicina, **8** Me interesa perder peso, **9** Me duelen los pies, **10** Le duele el estómago

2.3 **Answer the questions.**
Students will have their own responses; encourage them to use a variety of time clauses in their answers.

2.4 **Use the verbs in the box with their correct present perfect forms to complete these sentences.**

Answers: **1** he dormido, **2** han vuelto, **3** has jugado, **4** han desayunado, **5** hemos practicado, **6** han dolido, **7** he visto, **8** ha escrito

2.5 **Translate these sentences.**

Answers: **1** Mi cumpleaños es el veinticinco de febrero. **2** Los miércoles juego a golf con mi hermano. **3** El martes por la noche voy al cine con mi amigo/a. **4** Anteayer me dolía la cabeza. **5** El año que viene compraré un caballo. **6** Los lunes y los martes voy al gimnasio.

2.6a **Answer these questions.**
Students write their own answers.

2.6b **Join the two parts of the sentences so that it makes the most sense.**

Answers: **1** f, **2** h, **3** a, **4** b, **5** c, **6**, g, **7** d, **8** e

Unit 2B

2.7 **Answer these questions. Use direct object pronouns to avoid repetition.**

Answers: **1** Sí, la invité. **2** No, no los compré. **3** Sí, las tengo. **4** No, no los llamé. **5** Sí, la comí. **6** Sí, la ganaron.

2.8a **Rewrite these sentences substituting the underlined words for the correct pronoun.**

Answers: **1** Le pidió dinero. **2** Le devolví los libros. **3** Luis les prepara comida. **4** Te escribí un email. **5** Les repartimos los juguetes. **6** Me envió una postal.

2.8b **Substitute the direct and indirect objects.**

Answers: **1** El agente de viajes se las hace. **2** El hombre del tiempo se lo explica. **3** Jorge nos lo trae. **4** Rosario me lo prepara. **5** Pedro no os la dice. **6** El médico se la da.

2.9 **Complete these sentences with the present or past continuous of the verbs in the box.**

Answers: **1** está / estaba escuchando, **2** están / estaban haciendo, **3** estaba mirando, **4** está / estaba nadando, **5** están / estaban comprando, **6** estaba estudiando, **7** estoy preparando, **8** estamos / estábamos veyendo

Unit 3A and 3B

3.1 **Combine both sentences in one using a relative pronoun to avoid repetition.**

Answers: **1** Las flores cuales están en el parque son más bonitas. **2** Los leones cuales vimos en el zoo son de Kenia. **3** La película que vimos no fue interesante. **4** Esteban vio a las mujeres quienes no pagaron por sus entradas. **5** La cantante quién es muy famoso tiene miedo de engordar. **6** Mario quién toca el piano es un buen amigo.

3.2 Fill in the blanks with the appropriate negative word.

Answers: **1** nada, **2** nadie, **3** nada, **4** nunca, **5** jamás, **6** nunca

3.3 Replace the word in brackets with the appropriate form of the possessive pronoun.

Answers: **1** el suyo, **2** el mío, **3** los tuyos, **4** los vuestros / los suyos, **5** el suyo, **6** la mía, **7** el tuyo, **8** la vuestra / la suya

Unit 4A

4.1 Rewrite these sentences in the future simple.

Answers: **1** Este verano iré a Vietnam de vacaciones. **2** Hará muy buen tiempo. **3** Iremos a una fiesta después del instituto. **4** Soraya irá a Honduras y aprenderá español allí. **5** Viajaré en avión porque es más rápido. **6** Dormiré hasta muy tarde todas las mañanas.

4.2 Imagine what you would do if you won the lottery. Write ten sentences.

Encourage students to use a variety of verbs in their own answers.

4.3a Complete the sentences with the familiar form of the imperative of one of the verbs in the box.

Answers: **1** habla, **2** repite, **3** explica, **4** escucha, **5** cuelga, **6** llama

4.3b Now use the polite form of the imperative in the sentence above, if necessary.

Answers: **1** N/A, **2** N/A, **3** N/A, **4** escuche, **5** cuelgue, **6** llame

4.3c Write the negative of these commands.

Answers: **1** ¡No leas los folletos! **2** ¡No hagas tu reservar! **3** ¡No practiques el golf! **4** ¡No esfuérzete con el idioma!